Native and Spanish New Worlds

I0880268

Amerind Studies in Anthropology

Series Editor **John Ware**

Native and Spanish New Worlds

Sixteenth-Century Entradas in the American Southwest and Southeast

Edited by **Clay Mathers,**
Jeffrey M. Mitchem,
and **Charles M. Haecker**

The University of Arizona Press
Tucson

The University of Arizona Press
www.uapress.arizona.edu

© 2013 The Arizona Board of Regents
All rights reserved. Published 2013
First paperback edition 2014

Printed in the United States of America
19 18 17 16 15 14 6 5 4 3 2

Cover image: "Tabula nouarum insularum," by Sebastian Münster, 1538 [1550]

Publication of this book is made possible in part by the proceeds of a permanent endowment created with the assistance of a Challenge Grant from the National Endowment for the Humanities, a federal agency.

Library of Congress Cataloging-in-Publication Data
Native and Spanish new worlds : sixteenth-century entradas in the American southwest and southeast / edited by Clay Mathers, Jeffrey M. Mitchem, and Charles M. Haecker.
p. cm. — (Amerind studies in anthropology)
Includes bibliographical references and index.
ISBN 978-0-8165-3122-6 (pbk. : alk. paper)
1. Indians of North America—Southwest, New—History—16th century. 2. Indians of North America—Southern States—History—16th century. 3. Indians of North America—First contact with Europeans—Southwest, New. 4. Indians of North America—First contact with Europeans—Southern States. 5. Southwest, New—Discovery and exploration—Spanish. 6. Southern States—Discovery and exploration—Spanish. 7. Spain—Colonies—America. I. Mathers, Clay. II. Mitchem, Jeffrey M. III. Haecker, Charles M.
E78.S7N36 2013
979'.01—dc23

2012028949

∞ This paper meets the requirements of ANSI/NISO Z39.48-1992 (Permanence of Paper).

Contents

Section IV. Disease

Section V. Political Organization

Section VI. Conflict

Section VII. Discussion

Editors' Preface

This volume had its origins in the vanishing twilight of a weekend in the fall of 2007 spent mapping sixteenth-century artifacts in the urban core of Albuquerque, New Mexico. With the light fading, and the only source of illumination for the pin flags at his feet being the dim light of a GPS unit, one of us (CM) felt the gentle tug of a metaphor. Whatever small light our modest findings were going to shed on the Vázquez de Coronado expedition, it seemed clear that we needed to connect our ideas and energies with like-minded colleagues if we were to illuminate anything of broader significance. This volume reflects a considerable effort on the part of many individuals to make meaningful connections between subjects and regions that were, in some cases at least, no more closely connected in the sixteenth century than they are at present.

Inevitably, this formidable endeavor has its historical roots in the pioneering work of scholars such as Henri Ternaux-Compans, Adolf Bandelier, Herbert Bolton, Frederick Hodge, George Hammond, Agapito Rey, and John Swanton. Its more recent scholastic ties lie with a host of other archaeological, anthropological, and historical work, particularly the contributions of Charles Hudson, Kathleen Deagan, David Hurst Thomas, Stanley South, Patricia Galloway, Vernon Knight, Marvin Smith, Chester DePratter, Paul Hoffman, John Hann, Charles Ewen, Russell Skowronek, Jerald Milanich, Robbie Ethridge, Richard and Shirley Cushing Flint, Tom Chávez, Robert Preucel, T. J. Ferguson, Thomas Sheridan, Carroll Riley, John Kessell, Marc Simmons, and David Snow. A more direct line of descent for the book can be traced to two recent conference sessions. The first was organized by Charles Haecker and Clay Mathers for the Society for Historical Archaeology meetings in Albuquerque in 2008, which focused on the activities and impacts of the Vázquez de Coronado entrada in New Mexico. In the following year, a second session with a broader canvas was organized by Clay Mathers, Charles Haecker, and Matthew Schmader at the 2009 meetings of the Society for American Archaeology in Atlanta. The latter was our first attempt to address formally the principal theme of this volume, which is a comparison of sixteenth-century entradas in what is now the Southwestern and Southeastern United States. We owe a profound debt of gratitude to all of the contributors to those sessions including Chris Adams, Nahide Aydin, Robin Beck, Dennis Blanton, Dick Chapman, Jonathan Damp, Robbie Ethridge, Charles Ewen, Richard Flint, Shirley Cushing Flint, Dale Hutchinson, Phil Leckman, Francis Levine, Gene Lyon, David Moore, Ann Ramenofsky, Chris Rodning, Joseph Sánchez, Matt Schmader, Dan Simplicio, David Hurst Thomas, Robert Thrower, Carla Van West, Brad Vierra, Tom Windes, and John Worth. Retracing part of the Soto route through western Tennessee and eastern Arkansas on the drive home to New Mexico from the Atlanta SAAs, we were more fortunate than Don Hernando's entrada nearly 470 years earlier having met and joined forces with Jeffrey Mitchem.

At the University of Arizona Press, we are especially grateful to Editor-in-Chief Allyson Carter and her colleagues for their patience, thoughtful comments, and quintessential professionalism they have extended to us throughout this project. The quality of our final product owes much to their diligent and conscientious work.

A special thanks is owed to our Native American colleagues—Dan Simplicio, Robert Thrower, Tom Kennedy, and Joseph Suina—all of whom helped in a variety of ways to give voice to a very difficult and transformational experience in their communities' pasts. While these perspectives remain sensitive, elusive, and underrepresented for a variety of reasons, they continue to be essential to understanding early entradas and European colonialism in any meaningful way. With their help, and the assistance of others such as Kurt and Cindy Dongoske, we look forward to an ongoing and productive discourse that we feel certain will enrich our understanding of the Early Historic Period in both the Southwest and Southeast.

We also wish to extend our gratitude to the two anonymous reviewers who evaluated an earlier version of this manuscript. Their care, attention, and thoughtful advice were greatly appreciated by all of us.

Finally, our deepest appreciation is to the Amerind Foundation and the Society for American Archaeology for their generosity in granting us their 2009 conference award and for the opportunity to continue and expand our discussions at the Foundation's spectacular facility in

Figure I.1. Amerind Seminar Participants. Front Row (kneeling, left to right), Joseph H. Suina, Ann F. Ramenofsky, Christopher B. Rodning, and Dennis B. Blanton; Rear Row (standing, left to right), Charles R. Ewen, Dale L. Hutchinson, Clay Mathers, Robbie Ethridge, Charles M. Haecker, Jeffrey M. Mitchem, Carla R. Van West, Richard C. Chapman, and David Hurst Thomas. (Not pictured, Richard Flint and Shirley Cushing Flint—who participated in the seminar by telephone from Sevilla—and John E. Worth, who was unable to attend). Photo by John Ware, Courtesy of Amerind Foundation.

Dragoon, Arizona, in October 2009. Dr. John Ware, ably assisted by Dr. Eric Kaldahl and their very capable and friendly staff, were exemplary hosts for an extremely productive and enjoyable seminar replete with the resources, scenery, organization, food, and quality discussions that entrada participants could only have dreamed of in the mythical lands of El Dorado, Quivira, and Bimini. Speaking for all of the seminar participants, that memorable week and the many kindnesses we received from John and the rest of the Amerind staff will remain a very happy and indelible memory for all of us. The friendships we made and solidified there will, we hope, help us to accomplish something that—as Richard Flint reminded us at the seminar—the Vázquez de Coronado and Soto expeditions almost brought about in 1541, but not quite. That achievement was the forging of a lasting link between the two major areas of the Southern Borderlands frontier, Tierra Nueva in the West and La Florida and its continental interior to the east. Our volume represents a modest step toward that goal of a comparative dialogue between these two important regions. Hopefully, it will generate sufficient interest and momentum to encourage additional, similar efforts in the near future.

A Note on Conventions Used in the Text

The terms *Native* and *Indigenous* have been capitalized throughout this volume as a conscious choice by the editors. We have also opted to refer to major expedition leaders by their proper surnames (such as Soto and Vázquez de Coronado) rather than alternative names (like De Soto and Coronado) that are in common usage. In addition, because the term *entrada* is used frequently throughout the book we have chosen not to italicize it. However, other Spanish words that appear less frequently, for example *encomienda* and *repartimiento*, have been italicized.

Native and Spanish New Worlds

1

Entradas in Context

Sixteenth-Century Indigenous and Imperial Trajectories in the American South

Clay Mathers and Jeffrey M. Mitchem

Less than twenty years after the siege of Tenochtitlán and the fall of the Mexica Empire in 1521, a wide range of Spanish-led entradas began probing forward into the unexplored northern frontier of New Spain and La Florida. These events mark some of the most salient historical developments and transformations in the history of the Americas. The repercussions of sixteenth-century entradas were profound, not only for Native communities in what is now the southern United States, but also farther afield for many of the ethnic groups, colonial enterprises, and nation states connected with these expeditions. Whether their role was in the planning, financing, or execution of early Spanish-led entradas, a wide range of actors were affected by these developments and their aftermath. Entradas impacted Indigenous leaders and their communities, Native auxiliaries, African freemen and slaves, the Spanish Crown, other European powers, expedition financiers and participants, fledgling colonial towns and settlements, privateers, *encomenderos*, and a host of others. While the global contest for empire clearly influenced the timing and objectives of sixteenth-century entradas in New Spain and La Florida, the outcome of these entradas also impacted the relationships and geopolitical strategies of Native American communities throughout the northern borderlands, as well as the strategic designs of the Spanish Crown and its European rivals.

Despite their importance, however, the nature and implications of these initial explorations remain something of an enigma. Until recently at least, much of the scholarship devoted to the earliest Spanish-led expeditions in North America has been focused on historical documents, rather than the material record. As a result, our understanding of the conduct and consequences of these important events continues to be patchy and incomplete. For the most part, too, historical and archaeological research focused on the sixteenth century has been characterized by either an emphasis on the generic effects of early expeditions as a whole or, alternatively, entrada-specific studies concentrating on a circumscribed region, period, and set of activities. With a few notable exceptions (Deagan 1998; Fitzhugh 1985; Hudson 1990; McEwan 2000; Thomas 1989–1991), detailed comparisons of Native–European interactions in sixteenth-century North America have been largely absent. In particular, there continues to be a dearth of broadly based temporal and geographic syntheses designed to identify similarities and differences between entradas, the Native communities with which they interacted, and the regions in which these transformational developments took place. Recent studies in both the American Southeast (Ethridge 2010; Ethridge and Shuck-Hall 2009; Knight 2009) and Southwest (Dongoske and Dongoske, this volume; Flint 2008; Kennedy and Simplicio 2009; Mathers and Haecker 2011; Mathers et al. 2011; Skowronek 2009; Wilcox 2009) are beginning to alter this situation as new archaeological and documentary evidence emerges, and as more comparative research orientations are adopted to address and evaluate it.

The primary goal of this volume is a better understanding of the interactions between sixteenth-century Native and European communities in what is now the Southwestern and Southeastern United States. In addressing this broad and complex subject matter, we place special emphasis on the multiplicity of factors involved in this exchange—including social, economic, political, military, environmental, and demographic components. Contributors to this volume focus on how these factors varied geographically, affected one another, and changed through time. Overall, our aim is to better define the motives, relations, reactions, and processes of societal reformation as the first truly global empires engaged the variegated landscape of Native communities across the southern fringe of North America. Evaluating these ongoing transformations, and the reformation of Native and European communities as the pace of interaction intensified, is the central focus of our discussions. These discussions underline the importance of bringing together scholars from both regions to compare and contrast Native–European contacts and their consequences in each area.

The papers offered here highlight important new insights by presenting research results at different scalar levels of analysis: from individual sites to macrolevel evaluations using documentary, paleoclimatic, and regional archaeological data. They also delineate major trends and patterns in more than 170 years of research on early Spanish-led entradas and point the way toward new questions and approaches. Furthermore, these contributions draw on the colonial experience of Native and European communities elsewhere in the Old and New Worlds at the transition between the Medieval and Early Modern eras. In doing so, they seek to link developments in the Southwestern and Southeastern United States with the increasingly connected, international world of the sixteenth century.

A number of recent developments make a volume concerning the nature and impact of sixteenth-century expeditions particularly timely, including the following:

Identification of new entrada-related sites and assemblages. Particularly in the Southwest, such sites and assemblages have expanded the data available for study and the potential scope for interregional analyses and syntheses (Blanton and Snow 2009; Bratten 2009; Cook 2009; Damp 2005; Mathers et al. 2007, 2009, 2010).

Emergence of new documentary and archaeological materials from archival research. Recent investigations concerned with historical collections of documents and artifacts have helped to illuminate aspects of both terrestrial and maritime entradas in the sixteenth-century Southwest and Southeast (Flint 2009; Flint and Flint 2005; Mathers et al. 2009; Worth 2009b). The growing body of data from these sources—not only in the United States but also in Europe, Africa, East Asia, and elsewhere in the Americas—is providing the foundation for more detailed comparative research, from the study of individual objects, sites, and entradas to the modeling of global statecraft and capitalism in the earliest worldwide empires.

Increasing recognition of the importance of linking micro- and macrohistorical analyses. Following pioneering anthropological and historical work in Old World contexts by Eric Wolf (1990), archaeologists, ethnohistorians, and others have begun exploring the linkages between the fine-grained histories of individuals, groups, and localized regions, on the one hand, and the broader perspective of capitalist world systems on the other (e.g., Carmack and Salgado González 2006; Skowronek 1998; Van Buren 2009).

The principal emphases of our volume are directed toward five major variables that affected significantly either the conduct and long-term impacts of early Spanish-led entradas or the subsequent analysis of these expeditions by later generations of scholars—that is, climate, disease, political organization, conflict, and historical/academic traditions. In reviewing the thematic contributions to this volume, our primary aims are to (1) highlight the major points raised in each chapter, and (2) begin comparing the developmental trajectories in the two regions. We conclude our discussion by suggesting future directions for the study of sixteenth-century entradas in borderland areas of the American South.

In undertaking these tasks, we are humbled by the wealth of detail and complexity of the historical and archaeological records in both regions. While being acutely aware of the pitfalls of oversimplified comparisons, we feel it is important to highlight interregional parallels and dichotomies that may prove to be of wider interest in future research. Scholars focused on the study of early entradas in the Southwest and Southeast are, it seems, still in the "Early Contact Period" with respect to developing an active dialogue and broadly based comparative research program. We hope, however, that this volume may offer examples of what such East–West collaboration may have to offer and be a catalyst for those efforts to continue, and to extend North–South.

Sixteenth-Century Entradas in Perspective: An Overview of Thematic Contributions

Native and Historiographic Perspectives. The initial chapters in this volume, by Dongoske and Dongoske, Flint and Flint, as well as Ethridge, trace the historical impact of scholarship on our understanding of early entradas in the American Borderlands South. Focusing on the critically important Zuni area in west-central New Mexico, Dongoske and Dongoske emphasize the importance of Native voices in the dialogue about entradas in general and their significance for the Zuni community in particular. As they point out, while Zuni Pueblos were the focus of some of the earliest, most sustained, and most frequent contacts with sixteenth-century Spanish-led expeditions, the oral traditions and historical perspectives of this community have rarely surfaced in discussions of post-Columbian contacts in the American Southwest (but see Kennedy and Simplicio 2009 and Ladd 1997). This failure of inclusiveness is especially unfortunate since sixteenth-century interactions with Zuni represent the first major contacts between the Pueblo world and the wide range of Mexican, African, and European members of the initial entradas to *Tierra Nueva*. Nevertheless, the increasingly frequent and important contributions of Native scholars to our understanding of early entradas (Kennedy and Simplicio 2009; Simplicio 2009; Thrower 2009), the Pueblo Revolt (Suina 2002; Wilcox 2009), and other major anthropological/archaeological issues (Dongoske and Zimmerman 2010; Echo-Hawk 2000; Smith and Wobst 2005) suggest that a richer and more balanced view of these subjects is beginning to emerge. Further exploration of Native oral traditions at Zuni, combined with ongoing museum-based collections research (Robin Boast, personal communication April 2009) and archaeological fieldwork (Mathers et al. 2009, 2011), further highlight the potential of Zuni contributions and collaborative studies to enhance our collective understanding of post-Columbian contacts in the Southwest. Finally, the paper by Dongoske and Dongoske underlines the significance of Zuni communities as a resource base for entradas throughout the sixteenth century, as well as the active role they played in resisting, negotiating, and deflecting the impact of early expeditions.

The chapters by Flint and Flint on the American Southwest and Ethridge on the Southeastern United States outline the historical roots of early entrada research in these two regions—scholarship that has, to date, been dominated by non-Native scholars. Focusing specifically on the large and impactful Vázquez de Coronado expedition, Flint and Flint remind us of the enduring influence of nineteenth-century perceptions and values on more contemporary research and interpretation. In reviewing the historical literature they take particular issue with earlier notions of the Vázquez de Coronado expedition as a military force whose primary objectives were the conquest of Indigenous communities and the procurement of large quantities of gold. Their decades of archival research suggest the Vázquez de Coronado entrada "was instead a very large, only quasimilitary group comprised, in its European component, primarily of civilian investors, self-organized for the principal purpose of obtaining Indian tribute."[1] Furthermore, they suggest this expedition displayed only a "faintly military complexion" and represented an "ad hoc group, assembled principally for the purpose of taking economic control of a presumably large and prosperous indigenous polity known as Cíbola."[2]

In evaluating sixteenth-century entradas, we clearly need to avoid making judgments about the age, experience, participants in, and conduct of the Vázquez de Coronado entrada, to use the Flints' phrase, based on "assumptions of more modern military stereotypes."[3] Richard Flint suggests that "if a military analog is to be sought for the expedition, it would be a makeshift, untrained civilian militia, which a group of variously experienced combat veterans did their best to field with military effect" (Flint 2008:2).[4]

In her chapter, Ethridge highlights the varied intellectual threads that have enabled scholars in the Southeastern United States to begin bridging what Colin Renfrew (1980) referred to in another context as the "Great Divide"—that is, the problematic gulf between prehistory and history. She traces the origins of a wide range of developments leading to the deep historical approach now being employed in the Southeast to understand the initial contacts between Natives, Europeans, and Africans. As Ethridge has emphasized, these significant advances were founded, in large measure, on the pioneering work and collaboration of Charles Hudson and his colleagues in the 1970s. In addition, she points to the significant influences of *Annales* social history and World Systems Theory in shaping a richer, more multivocal understanding of Native–Colonial interaction in the early historic Southeast. Ethridge goes on to outline some of the major interpretative consequences of these shifts, from a more nuanced, diachronic view of cultural transformations and continuity, to the more fine-grained analyses of the multiple agencies that brought them about. Of particular importance in more recent years is the ability of Southeastern scholars to construct detailed Native social histories and discriminate them successfully on a regional basis. Ethridge concludes with a thoughtful discussion of historicizing the Native Southeast using concepts such as fragmentation and coalescence, together with a greater appreciation of pre-Contact cultural dynamics and their fluidity.

Climatic Fluctuations and Impacts

Recent paleoclimatic work to cross-correlate dendrochronological, sea temperature, volcanic activity, frost ring, and other data sources have produced a very detailed understanding of Historic Period climatic fluctuations in both the Southwest and Southeast. The chapters by Van West, Windes, Levine, Grissino-Mayer, and Salzer on the Southwest, and Blanton on the Southeast, make use of detailed meteorological/archaeological data and comparative regional analyses to assess the impact of climatic fluctuations on Native and European communities during the sixteenth and seventeenth centuries. In systematically evaluating these data, they suggest there are important temporal intersections between major climatic fluctuations and cycles of agricultural/economic productivity, disease, conflict, and residential mobility.

Van West et al. focus on detailed tree-ring sequences from the Middle Rio Grande Valley and surrounding areas in New Mexico. Their research highlights the significance of climatic fluctuations for three key developments in the early historic Southwest:

- the earliest Spanish-led entrada (Vázquez de Coronado, 1539–1542);
- the first Crown-sanctioned colonization effort (Oñate y Salazar, 1598–1610); and
- the first Pueblo Revolt (1680).

The fine detail of these records, and the authors' reconstruction of annual precipitation and temperature patterns, implies that the warm, wet period between 1530 and 1550 would have alleviated some of the pressures on the large reconnaissance parties that preceded the Vázquez de Coronado entrada, as well as the extremely large number of people and animals that accompanied that expedition ultimately in 1540. Van West et al. suggest that deteriorating climatic conditions in the latter half of the sixteenth century ensured that Native communities, as well as Spanish-led entradas and later colonization plans, faced significant obstacles. The megadrought across what is now the American South and northern Mexico during the 1570s to 1590s would not only have impacted long-distance travel within this region (e.g., limiting the availability of water and grazing) but also would have reduced considerably the food resources available to Indigenous communities, expeditionaries, and would-be colonists. Van West et al. hint that the failure of the Oñate y Salazar colony and the reports of epidemic disease and death at various Pueblos by the mid-1700s were influenced to some degree by the dominance of cold-dry, and then cold-wet, conditions in the first half of the seventeenth century. Finally, their results suggest that the extremely cold and dry conditions in the 1660s and 1670s could have fueled the economic decline and distress of Native communities in advance of the region-wide Pueblo Revolt of 1680.

Blanton's discussion of variability in climatic and weather conditions in sixteenth-century La Florida emphasizes the importance of these fluctuations for understanding Native and European cultural dynamics in the Southeastern United States. His summary of historical data from tree rings, radioactive isotopes, documents, and other proxy sources belies the traditional view of Southeastern climates and environments as relatively static. Instead, the sixteenth-century record from La Florida displays evidence of extremes that would have had cultural significance for both Indigenous and European communities. Of particular importance is the series of major droughts that occurred throughout the sixteenth century, as well as the intense dry period in the Southeast between 1555 and 1574 that correlates with similar conditions in Arkansas, the Eastern Plains, and the Chesapeake area during the same period. In addition, Blanton emphasizes the cultural significance of such drought periods for the establishment of the Spanish Jesuit mission of Ajacán, the attempted English colony at Roanoke, and the later settlement efforts at Jamestown. In examining the record of several early entrada shipwrecks and El Niño/La Niña events, as well as proxy rainfall data and documents from the Soto expedition narratives, Blanton finds a reasonably close correspondence between meteorological and archival evidence. He concludes by highlighting the varied Native and Spanish responses to fluctuations in climate and weather, and the value of caution in interpreting the coping strategies employed in each case.

Rethinking Disease

One of the most contentious and emotive subjects relating to sixteenth-century entradas in the southern United States is the impact of disease on Native communities. With the considerable strides made in recent years with respect to forensic anthropology and bioarchaeology, a fresh perspective on this important topic is prudent and timely. The lower figure for early historic Native populations in the Mississippian Southeast suggested in a recent analysis by Milner and Chaplin (2010) also hints that a reevaluation of disease impacts may be appropriate. Both papers in this section emphasize a balanced, contextual, and holistic approach to disease by focusing on the interdependence of documentary, material culture, and bioarchaeological sources.

The contributions by Ramenofsky and Kulisheck on the northern Southwest and Hutchinson on the Southeast reinvigorate the critical debate about the impact of European and African diseases on Indigenous communities in the earliest phases of contact. While both discussions emphasize the serious impact of disease in some spatially limited and temporally specific contexts, they also underline the importance of analytical terms and archaeological evidence in reassessing widely accepted notions about disease and decline among sixteenth-century Native populations in the American South. Their conceptual and methodological approaches, as well as the empirical data they present, challenge the traditional view of disease as a primary destabilizing factor in the early historic Southwest and Southeast. Analyses of archaeological and documentary data from these regions suggest a more complex, subtle interplay of agencies and impacts.

Ramenofsky and Kulisheck use documentary evidence, together with wide-ranging settlement data, to argue for demographic stability in the northern Pueblo world throughout the sixteenth century. The results of their comparative, interregional analyses suggest that while contact with Spanish-led expeditions had significant consequences in localized areas of the Southwest during the 1500s, the overall trend is consistently one of settlement continuity and population stability. Both documentary and archaeological data for the region suggest that disease did not have a significant impact on sixteenth-century Pueblo communities. In concluding their chapter, Ramenofsky and Kulisheck examine three primary agents of mortality in Native populations: warfare, forced labor, and infectious disease. They suggest that none of these factors caused any large-scale demographic decline in the northern Southwest during the sixteenth century, and that disease may have played a less significant role there than in the Southeast. Ramenofsky and Kulisheck point to several factors in the Southwest that may have helped to reduce the spread and impact of disease, including these:

- relative geographic isolation of the region;
- relatively small size of expeditions following the Vázquez de Coronado entrada;
- dispersed nature and low density of Pueblo settlements;
- range of domestic animals introduced by Spaniards (i.e., an absence of pigs and the diseases associated with them); and
- later onset of colonization, missionization, and *reducción*.

The geographic barrier and isolation referred to by Ramenofsky and Kulisheck was not only physiographic, it was the product of other factors as well—among them military, economic, strategic, and climatic ones (see below).

Hutchinson's discussion of the sixteenth-century Southeast confronts our traditional understanding of the speed and magnitude of epidemic disease, as well as the archaeological evidence used in evaluating these phenomena. His focus is on three primary sources of data: (1) direct evidence (in the form of pathological skeletal lesions), (2) indirect evidence (such as ethnohistoric descriptions, demographic estimates, and mortuary patterning), and (3) contextual variables (i.e., factors affecting the maintenance and transmission of epidemic disease). Hutchinson points to the problematic analytical issues associated with each of these data types and the need for clarity in defining, measuring, and interpreting disease in the early historic Southeast. He illustrates a number of these issues using sixteenth-century mortuary data from the Tatham Mound in west-central Florida. Furthermore, in reassessing epidemic disease, Hutchinson points out the importance of distinguishing between population movements and population decline, as well as the need for models that can discriminate between them. Hutchinson highlights the widespread lack of evidence for epidemic disease in the Southeast during the sixteenth century and the need for developing archaeological signatures that could systematically eliminate competing hypotheses. He advocates the use of a multiple-effects, process model—rather than a single-cause, event-based approach—to better understand the complex origins, social context, and cultural impacts of epidemic disease.

Political Organization and Analysis

Another major factor that conditions much of what we understand about early historic interactions in both the Southwest and Southeast is the political organization of Native and European groups. While sixteenth-century Spaniards often failed to understand their Native contemporaries and the structuring principles underlying their communities and behaviors, many latter-day interpretations have often fared little better (Thomas, this volume; Ewen, this volume). As data concerning sixteenth-century political organization have improved in recent years—with respect to both European and Native groups—our understanding of variables such as the nature of status and decision-making hierarchies, polity size and integration, entrada size and composition, and the residential mobility of Native communities have begun to alter significantly our views of these early encounters and their consequences.

Chapman's review of early historic political organization among Pueblo communities in north-central New Mexico offers some insight into the complexities faced by sixteenth-century expeditionaries in navigating the social and political landscape of this region. He suggests the association made by Spaniards between large architectural constructions (Pueblo villages) and permanent, year-round residence patterns was flawed and led to some fundamental misunderstandings about the basic organizing principles of these communities. Chapman indicates that large labor investments in Pueblo architecture helped to mask the dynamic flexibility of Pueblo subsistence and settlement, characterized by "seasonal dispersal and aggregation at village centers each year, coupled with frequent relocation of households among villages over multi-annual time frames." Equally, Chapman points to large-scale phases of abandonment and rebuilding at major Pueblo villages as evidence of population relocations operating on a longer cycle. He suggests these patterns relate to long-term adaptations to dispersed resource zones, an unpredictable climatic regime, and wide temporal and spatial variations in crop yields. Finally, Chapman indicates that the organization of sixteenth-century Pueblo communities may be akin to the Tewa form of household organization (*maatui'in*) described by Ford (2009). These social arrangements are characterized by decision-making structures devolved to family or extended family units and are built on flexible, region-wide social relationships, which allow groups to repeatedly disperse and coalesce. Such elastic and devolved decision-making structures would have proven frustrating to Spanish expeditionaries seeking large aggregated populations, a reliable labor force, and communities accustomed to regular tribute payments.

The discussion of political organization in the Southeastern interior by Ethridge and Mitchem provides an insightful contrast and complement to Worth's chapter on early historic La Florida. Their focus is on the five major Mississippian chiefdoms encountered and described during the 1539–1543 entrada of Hernando de Soto—that is, Cofitachequi, Coosa, Tascalusa, Chicaza, and Casqui. As Ethridge and Mitchem point out, the Soto expedition focused on large, settled agricultural communities capable of supplying badly needed labor and provisions en route and regularly avoided areas where such resources were lacking. Their geopolitical summary of the Southeastern interior toward the middle of the sixteenth century underlines the complexity of internal and external relations as groups negotiated, cooperated, contested, and allied with one another and/or the Soto entrada. In particular, they suggest ways in which the Soto expedition may have tipped the balance in intra- and interregional disputes and rivalries, and thereby may have contributed to the collapse, decline, and expansion of chiefdoms over a wide area of the Southeast. Ethridge and Mitchem also point to the role of other agencies in destabilizing Native political structures such as disease, slave raiding, warfare, reduced fertility, and policies of genocide. Despite the major impact of the Soto entrada and other factors on Mississippian chiefdoms, they suggest that the most transforming effects on Native communities took place not in the sixteenth century with the arrival and activities of Spanish colonialism but in the seventeenth century with the introduction of the Native slave trade. The latter was precipitated by the vigorous engagement of the Mississippian World with the expanding world capitalist system. The result was a fundamental reformation and realignment of Native communities and their geopolitical relations throughout the interior Southeast.

Worth's summary of political organization in La Florida outlines the impact of Native institutions and social geography on Spanish imperial designs throughout the sixteenth century. He highlights the structural contrast between Spanish and other European (notably English) models of colonialism, based on people and land, respectively. Worth describes initial experiments and policies of Native assimilation and how these evolved during the sixteenth century. As a succession of entradas failed to produce evidence of high-value resources, the Southeast was "relegated to a marginal role within the broader Spanish empire, and was eventually colonized primarily for its strategic value in protecting the returning New World treasure fleets." Worth indicates that the marginal position of this territory created a long-term dependency on the labor and resources of Native communities as a buffer against supply shortfalls and that in the late sixteenth century, Spanish colonial policies in the Southeast shifted from military subjugation of Native communities to gift exchange, missionization, and assimilation. The latter strategies were largely successful and led to a complex set of new relationships between Natives and Spaniards. Finally, Worth suggests that this amalgam of Indigenous Mississippian and colonial elements created a form of superpolity, centered on St. Augustine, representing a "unique accommodation between Spanish and Indian political and economic systems."

Conflict and Consequences

Until very recently, the Early Historic Period in the Southwestern and Southeastern United States was full of the sound and fury of contemporary sixteenth-century narratives but had signified nothing very tangible about conflict and violence in that period for twenty-first-century archaeologists. The recent discovery of two early sixteenth-century sites in New Mexico (Hawikku and Piedras Marcadas) with military assemblages and the later sixteenth-century fort of Joara in North Carolina, however, have begun to alter that situation significantly. In addition, the emergence of new documents has begun to reveal important details about the size and composition of early entradas, as well as their associated casualties. The picture that emerges is one of more regular conflict with, and impact on, Native communities. These data offer us new opportunities to not only evaluate the material and documentary record of armed confrontation and resistance but also to assess the lasting impact of these conflicts on Native and European communities.

The chapter by Mathers reviews the history of military conflict in the sixteenth-century Southwest from the perspectives of three major interest groups: Southwestern Native communities, entrada participants, and the Spanish Crown. Their divergent, and sometimes intersecting, objectives led to more than a century of sustained violence and warfare along the frontiers of New Spain. Mathers emphasizes the importance of these conflicts for the parties directly involved in the armed struggle for resources, as well as the geopolitical strategies developed by the Spanish Crown and its rivals. He also highlights the critical role played by Native Mexican auxiliaries, Chichimec and Pueblo resistance, and Crown-sponsored legislation in shaping and transforming the nature of conflict in New Spain throughout the sixteenth century. Major Native uprisings such as the Tiguex, Mixtón, and Chichimec wars in the mid-sixteenth century helped to stall the northern advance of empire, encourage a defensive posture by the Crown, and limit its interest in a territory with marginal returns. Mathers explores the history and wide-ranging consequences of entrada-related conflicts—particularly the changes wrought by early *conquista* campaigns on Native communities (allies and combatants), as well as on the development of Spanish imperial designs in the later sixteenth century. He also reviews archaeological evidence from two recently discovered sixteenth-century sites in New Mexico associated with the Vázquez de Coronado expedition. His chapter concludes with a summary of the long-term consequences of sixteenth-century violence and warfare in Northern New Spain.

Rodning, Beck, and Moore focus on the ideology, origins, and development of Native-European conflict in sixteenth-century La Florida. They point to the deep historical roots of Mississippian warfare in intra- and interpolity status relations. Rodning et al. indicate that many Native groups saw Spanish entradas as an opportunity for advancing their personal and/or community interests. Tributary relationships within and between chiefdoms in La Florida were well developed by the sixteenth century and represented a major advantage to Spain's strategic interests in the region. The authors outline the archaeological and documentary evidence for different forms of conflict during the Early Historic Period in the Southeast, pointing out that Native and Spanish motivations for conflict and warfare were often markedly different. They also indicate that developments such as slave raiding, hostage taking, conversion efforts, and major resource appropriation were some of the flash points for armed conflict. Rodning et al. see the Pardo expeditions of 1566–1568 as the turning point in colonial policy, marking a shift from exploration and *conquista* campaigns to missionization and trade. They also suggest that while sixteenth-century entradas had short-term effects on the fortunes of different Mississippian polities, "they also led to the long-term collapse of chiefdoms as a viable and a sustainable form of social and political organization."

Contrasting, Parallel, and Out-of-Phase Trajectories: Comparing the Sixteenth-Century Southwest and Southeast

No adequate review of sixteenth-century entradas or early Native–European interaction in the American South would be possible without situating this comparison in the broader context in which these developments took place. As the effects of global economics, European military power, and competing imperial designs extended across the Americas, the convergence of powerful local and external forces began to shape the historical development of Spain's northern territories. Throughout the sixteenth century the Crown's economic returns from the Southwest and Southeast proved to be minimal or nonexistent, encouraging the view that these areas were the margins of empire and in many cases likely to remain so. Intermittent European encounters with Mississippian, Pueblo, and other Indian communities in the first half of the century—often with a hiatus of decades in between—may have encouraged Native groups in both regions to believe that the disruptive effects of external contact had passed. Furthermore, and with few exceptions, expeditionaries familiar with these regions via one entrada were disinclined to return. Despite some similarities, however, the strategic value and developmental trajectories of these two areas differed significantly, becoming particularly divergent in the latter half of the sixteenth century. The following section is a modest, initial attempt at understanding the contrasting, parallel, and out-of-phase historical patterns in these two important regions.

Sustaining Empire

The territorial extent and cohesion of Spain's empire in the Americas was more limited and fragile than sixteenth-century cartography or royal propaganda might suggest. Control by agents of the Crown was often achieved in highly localized nodes with broad intervening areas devoid of their management and authority, particularly in regions such as Tierra Nueva, La Florida, and the interior Southeast. As the papers in this volume suggest, the maintenance of empire was particularly problematic, constrained as it was by the Crown's far-flung military-economic commitments; Native political organization, resistance, and mobility patterns; international competition and piracy; climatic fluctuations; local politics and administration; as well as the logistical challenges of travel and communications.

Both the Southwest and Southeast appear to have been on the periphery of more important regions of the Spanish Empire in the sixteenth century—in a political, economic, and strategic sense. Nevertheless, the proximity of the Mississippian Southeast to the island archipelagos of the Caribbean, and to the major shipping lanes plied by Spanish treasure fleets and the privateers/pirates that regularly preyed on them, gave this region a particular significance for the Crown and others. The sixteenth-century Southwest, on the other hand, appears to have been far more marginal with respect to imperial settlement, economic potential, maritime activity, and strategic defense. In essence, it was on the margins of a periphery.

Contrasts

The significant maritime dimension of entradas in the Southeast, as opposed to the overwhelmingly terrestrial nature of expeditions in the Southwest, stands out as a major contrast between the two regions. Entrada logistics in New Spain were not only complicated by the lack of open water, navigable inland waterways, and favorable ocean currents but also by the ubiquity of broken, elevated terrain and arid landscapes populated largely by hostile forager groups. In addition, the scarcity of willing settlers, the costs of far-flung military defenses, the persistence of region-wide droughts, the economic attraction of other regions, and the bureaucratic application of Crown economic and administrative policies all helped to frustrate Spanish colonization efforts in the North Pacific. Although a number of seaborne voyages were initiated along the west coast of Mexico and California from the mid-sixteenth century to the early seventeenth century (Wagner 1966), none were successful in establishing a permanent Spanish port or coastal settlement in the Northern Sea of Cortés, Baja, or along the littoral of California and the Pacific Northwest. Conversely, more favorable conditions in the Southeast—particularly, better maritime/riverine access and the proximity of island clusters—made it possible to bulk transport personnel, animals, and other supplies rapidly by sea without the attrition and insecurity of land-based travel. Nevertheless, colonization efforts in many areas of the Southeast failed to produce lasting settlements or sustained economic activity despite their proximity to major supply bases in neighboring islands, the favorable conditions for agricultural production found in much of the region, and the relative ubiquity of large settled agricultural communities there. As entradas and settlement attempts continued to produce disappointing results, the Southeast assumed a largely strategic role in defending Spanish shipping (Worth, this volume), and later as a key region in the accelerated international slave trade. Again, the logistical dimensions of travel in the Southwest and Southeast, and the relative proximity of these two regions to favorable transoceanic shipping lanes, may help, in part, to explain the relatively low level of European slave raiding in the former area versus its intensity, broad scale, and deep impacts in the latter.

Other significant environmental and political contrasts between the Southwest and Southeast had important consequences for sixteenth-century entradas and the Native communities they encountered. Large tracts of the American Southwest were remote, difficult to access, and lacking in resources—human and otherwise. To make matters worse for entrada participants and would-be *encomenderos*, Native communities in the region were unaccustomed to tribute relations and disinclined to accept them peacefully. Attempts to weld Northern New Spain to the more successful Spanish colonization of the Caribbean, Mexico, and Central America were largely unsuccessful, not only during the

1500s, but in much of the seventeenth and eighteenth centuries as well (Gerhard 1982). From central Texas west to California, large expanses of territory remained outside Spanish control, including the Pacific coastal fringe, lightly populated by hunter-gatherers rather than dense farming communities and settled by Spanish colonists only at the end of the seventeenth century. In the Southeast, however, the political economy of chiefdoms from the Chesapeake and La Florida to the Mississippi Bottomlands was heavily based on hierarchical tribute relations. These intra- and interpolity structures were exploited by early Spanish entradas, settlements, and missions, and were incorporated into a modified pyramidal hierarchy with Spaniards replacing Native chiefs at the top (Worth, this volume; Ethridge and Mitchem, this volume; Rodning et al., this volume). In the Southeast, as in Central and South America (Carroll 2001:61–64), the transition from Indigenous to Spanish colonial hegemony was easier to achieve where a Spanish system of personal and corporate tribute could be grafted onto pre-Contact Native systems that were already well established.

One of the most striking contrasts between the Southwest and Southeast during the sixteenth century is the impact of sustained warfare. While major Native uprisings in the 1540s had halted the northern advance of mining, ranching, and additional entradas in many areas of New Spain, vigorous armed resistance throughout the Gran Chichimeca in the latter half of the sixteenth century made exploration of the northern frontier sporadic and perilous. As emphasized by Mathers (this volume), territorial defense in northern New Spain became especially problematic in the 1580s when Chichimec groups acquired horses and hence more tactical mobility in combat. During the same period in the Southeast, however, entradas continued, forts and settlements were established, and missionization and commerce were expanded.

As Mathers (2013) has suggested, more systematic attempts to explore and settle areas of the Southwest on the far northern frontier came only at the end of the sixteenth century. During the last decades of the 1500s, a related series of developments helped to spur renewed interest in these northern territories, including these:

- successful conclusion of the Chichimec War (Powell 1952:172–178);
- discovery of major new silver mines, such as those at Santa Bárbara (Sánchez-Crispin 1994:159, 164) and San Luis Potosí (Powell 1977:179–182);
- founding of new frontier settlements, which acted as forward bases for exploration further north (Gerhard 1982:201–202, 220; Simmons 1991:48–49);
- recovery of the Crown's finances following a bankruptcy in 1575 (Parker 1998:101, 279);
- intensification of piracy (stimulating the need for improved cartographic knowledge, safe harbors, and more effective maritime defenses; Lane 1998); and
- renewed international competition to locate the elusive Northwest Passage (Wagner 1966).

By the close of the sixteenth century and the beginning of the seventeenth, the Crown's enthusiasm for continuing investments in areas of Tierra Nueva, such as New Mexico, was minimal (Hammond and Rey 1953:1002, 1009, 1057; Simmons 1991:177). Indeed, in describing frontier areas of New Spain over 140 years after the first Spanish-led entrada, Kessell et al. (1998:18) state, "The price of empire was always high, and in the case of New Mexico it kept escalating." By the early seventeenth century, only the renewed efforts of Franciscan missionaries, the glowing reports of their widespread conversions, and a wave of nationalistic pride convinced the Spanish sovereign to maintain a presence in New Mexico.

Parallels

The nodal distribution of resources in the Southwest also frustrated attempts to colonize, missionize, and urbanize areas on New Spain's northern frontier. Sporadic pockets of productive land were often separated by territories largely devoid of people and resources (*despoblados*), making regular communications and resupply a frustrating aspect of colonial life in this region for centuries. While much of the Southeast was characterized by more permissive environments, plentiful supplies of water, and evenly distributed tracts of productive, arable land, the success of colonization efforts there were, as in the Southwest, fairly limited—whether measured in pesos or settled territory. Certainly in the Southeast, the quantity and distribution of resources, together with better maritime and riverine access, ensured that it could sustain large settlement clusters and towns, both Mississippian and European. Nevertheless, only two Spanish colonial towns had been founded successfully in the Southeast by the 1560s (St. Augustine in 1565 and Santa Elena, the capital of La Florida, in 1566), whereas only one had been established tenuously in the Southwest by the end of the sixteenth century (San Gabriel at Ohkay Owingeh Pueblo in 1598). Likewise, while Franciscan missionization was initiated in the Southeast during the later sixteenth century, it only began in earnest in the Southwest during the second quarter of the seventeenth century. Colonization and conversion efforts in both regions were concentrated in localized areas and toward the end of the seventeenth century were vulnerable to attack, contraction, and collapse—due to English colonists and Creek Indians in the Southeast, and major Native revolts in the Southwest.

In the Southeast, the spatial domain of Spanish colonial settlement throughout the sixteenth century was little more than a thin coastal veneer. Settlements, missions, and colonial activity generally developed earlier and more fully in the Southeast than in the Southwest. In the Southeast, the mission system served as the cohesive mechanism to communicate with and extract labor/goods from the interior. Spanish soldiers were garrisoned at some mission villages, but they were no match for the large numbers of English and Creek enemies to the north. Prior to missionization, Spain had little true control in the interior. Nevertheless, the developmental histories of both regions reinforce the notion of limited and tenuous territorial control by the Spanish Crown—something akin to "Swiss cheese," with domains riddled with extensive voids and gaps where control was fleeting or nonexistent.

By the last decades of the 1500s and the first half of the seventeenth century, the Spanish empire found it increasingly difficult to secure critical ports and coastal areas throughout the Americas—from the Atlantic seaboard and the Gulf of Mexico to the Pacific coasts of Chile and Mexico. With broad swaths of territory left unchallenged or inadequately protected, French, English, and Dutch competitors made inroads into domains previously claimed by Spain. The concerns of late sixteenth-century viceroys in New Spain for the security of coastal California and the Pacific Northwest have corollaries with other coastal peripheries of empire from Cape Horn to Cape Hatteras, where Spanish colonization and military defense were inadequate to prevent a variety of incursions by rival European powers, including competitive commerce, raids, and settlements. By the end of the sixteenth century, the crippling military and economic costs of its global empire severely impacted the Crown's ability to maintain its existing territories. As Spain's ability to sustain far-flung colonial enterprises diminished, the spatial extent of their empire began to contract, along with any enthusiasm for investing in marginal provinces like Tierra Nueva and La Florida.

The intense competition between European powers along the Atlantic and Gulf coasts, as well as the sea lanes extending from Mexico south to Tierra del Fuego, contrasts markedly with the more uncontested Spanish domains of Northern New Spain. The wealth of a few lucrative New World provinces, such as Peru, Mexico, and Colombia, appears to have masked the more fragile development of political, social, and economic institutions elsewhere. Even in the richest provinces, such stability (and all that was required to maintain it) was often short-lived, as many regions fell victim to inadequate management, provisioning, defense, and diplomacy at all levels of government and administration.

Other parallels between sixteenth-century entradas in the Southwest and Southeast can be seen in the effects of the New Laws (shifting entradas from *conquista* campaigns to smaller colonization and evangelical efforts), the problems created by demands for Native labor and provisions, as well as the consistent suite of military tactics and gift-giving strategies employed in both regions.

Out-of-Phase Developments

As indicated above, several important trends in late sixteenth-century and early seventeenth-century Spanish colonial activity were manifest in both the Southwest and Southeast, including intensified contacts, settlement, missionization, and colonization. These activities, however, were not only initiated earlier in the Southeast but also more fully developed there. Part of the explanation for these differences is geographic and logistical—that is, the relative proximity of each area to major sea lanes, preexisting colonies, nearby island groupings, the intense military-commercial interaction zone between rival European powers, as well as the ease of access by riverine and marine transportation. Other contributing factors relate more directly to Native social and political organization, specifically the historical development in each region of phenomena such as regional settlement ranking/autonomy, tribute obligations, and slave raiding. It appears that the combination of European territorial rivalries, geographic proximity, logistical access, and Native pre-Contact, historical precedents in the Southeastern United States (e.g., with respect to tributary relations, warfare, and slaving) all played an important role in exposing Native Missississipian groups more rapidly (and comprehensively) to early Spanish and European colonialism than their Native counterparts in the Southwest.

A Connected Web: International and Interregional Linkages

Investments in frontier territories, like Tierra Nueva and La Florida, were always contingent upon the Crown's trade, military, and other fiscal commitments within the New World and beyond. This expanded network of interests and responsibilities often meant that actions taken in one geographic theater of operations had a direct and tangible impact on others. Equally, the decisions of Native leaders in many areas of the Americas could have major implications for Native and Spanish communities elsewhere, particularly with respect to military-political alliances and the provision of Native labor and auxiliaries. Although the organizational coherence, territorial integrity, and political integration of Spain's sixteenth-century global empire was limited in many respects (Kamen 2008:96–125), and the influence of Native leaders was more restricted still, some measure of international and interregional *cohesion* and *connectedness* can be seen in reviewing entrada histories in the Southwest and the Southeast.

At an international scale, for example, changes in Crown policy concerning *encomienda* privileges and the conduct of entradas during the 1540s, and again in the 1570s, appear to have had significant effects throughout the Americas (Mathers, this volume). Equally, Spain's major financial crisis in the 1570s, combined with large-scale megadroughts in the northern Borderlands and Mexico, and decades-long conflicts in Northern Europe seem to have contributed to the hiatus in both terrestrial and maritime expeditions in the Southwest and Southeast during that period. Other more localized events within the Americas emphasize how developments in one specific area could have broader implications. Examples include:

The Mixtón War and Vázquez de Coronado Expedition. These developments had their origins in Nueva Galicia in the 1530s (Altman 2007, 2010) and had some reciprocal effects on one another. The withdrawal of individuals from major regional centers such as Compostela and Culiacán as a result of recruitment for the Vázquez de Coronado entrada left some areas of Nueva Galicia more vulnerable to attack during a major Native uprising that erupted soon after the expedition departed for Tierra Nueva (Altman 2010). In turn, once it was underway, the Mixtón War may have redirected personnel and materials that might otherwise have been available to assist and relieve members of the Vázquez de Coronado expedition.

Impacts of Native Support on Entradas and Frontier Defense. In areas such as the Valley of Mexico, Nueva Galicia, Nueva Vizcaya, Tierra Nueva, La Florida, Yucatan, Guatemala, and Peru, political and military alliances with Native leaders were critical to the success of Spanish-led entradas. Native Mexica, Nahua, Tlaxcalan, and other leaders were also instrumental in supplying auxiliaries for campaigns hundreds, and even thousands, of miles away from their home territories (Altman 2007; Bratten 2009; Chuchiak 2007). In other contexts, particularly in the later half of the sixteenth century, negotiated agreements with Native communities, such as the Tlaxcalans, made it possible to establish strategic colonies of Native allies in frontier regions as a buffer zone (Powell 1977:147–159; Simmons 1964:102–104), a tradition that continued into the eighteenth century in Northern New Mexico with Genízaro settlements (Ebright and Hendricks 2006; Swadesh 1974:39–47).

Wider Impacts of the Pizarro and Soto Expeditions. News of Francisco Pizarro's successful entrada against the Inca in the early 1530s encouraged the departure of significant numbers of Spaniards and others for more lucrative opportunities in Peru. These developments had important economic and demographic consequences for settlement and colonization efforts in areas as far afield as Honduras-Higueras (Chamberlain 1953:37) and Yucatan (Chamberlain 1948:47). In a similar vein, Duncan (1995:226–239) describes the broader, regional effects of Hernando de Soto's 1539–1543 entrada into the American Southeast—particularly the impact of its provisioning requirements on the inhabitants and economy of Cuba.

Competing Entrada Schedules. Meachem (1968:75) indicates that in 1558 the viceroy of New Spain, Luis de Velasco, delayed further exploration of Copalá (the frontier area formed by present-day northern Mexico and the American Southwest) in favor of a more pressing entrada in the Southeast commanded by Tristán de Luna y Arellano.

Raids by Pirates/Privateers and Renewed Exploration of New Spain's Northern Frontier. Rumors concerning the Strait of Anian (or Northwest Passage) had been circulating among seafaring European nations from the beginning of the sixteenth century (Brigden 2000:275–277; Reinhartz 1998:135). Spanish attempts to locate this ill-defined geographic feature intensified in the later sixteenth century with the appearance of the first cartographic representations of the straits in the 1560s (Reinhartz 1998:135), with initiation of a piratical war by English privateers beginning with Francis Drake in 1570 and pursued into the early 1590s (Hakluyt 1969:158–203; Kamen 2002:228–232), and with the persistence of such raids into the early seventeenth century by Dutch corsairs (Kamen 2002:262–263). These and other contemporary developments, noted above, helped stimulate renewed interest in both maritime and terrestrial exploration across a wide area of Northern New Spain in the late 1500s (Figure 1.1).

As its territorial interests expanded, the maintenance and extension of Spanish imperial power clearly became a more complex business of balancing competing priorities and investments. Native communities and Spanish colonists also weighed their options carefully—whether to acquiesce, negotiate, or resist, and where to draw the line between peaceful relations and personal gain. As the chapters in this volume remind us, the broad, interregional connections between different spheres of the Spanish empire and Native polities in the Americas all have important implications for our understanding of sixteenth-century entradas and their lasting impacts.

Clearly, we still have much to learn from the rich macro- and microhistories of the different ethnic groups, regions, and processes connected with early entradas. Much remains to be done with the archival

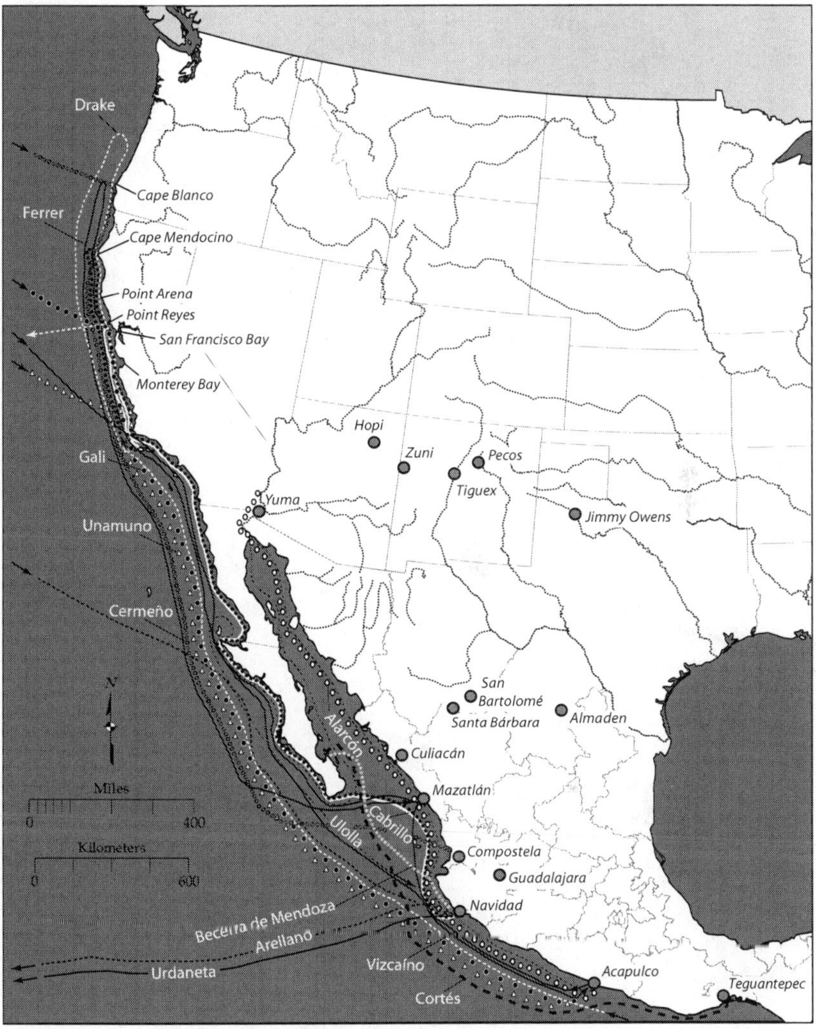

FIGURE I.1. Maritime Entradas and Expeditions in the Sea of Cortés and the Pacific Coast (1533–1603). Diego Becerra de Mendoza (1533); Hernán Cortés (1535–1536); Francisco de Ulolla (1539–1540); Hernando de Alarcón (1540); Francisco de Bolaños (1541-1542); Juan Rodríguez Cabrillo (1542–1543); Bartholomé Ferrer (1543); Alonso de Arellano (1564-1565); Andrés de Urdaneta (1564–1565); Francis Drake (1578–1579); Francisco Gali (1584); Pedro de Unamuno (1587); Sebastián Rodríguez Vermeño (1595–1596); Sebastián Vizcaíno (1602–1603).

and archaeological records to explore these connections further, particularly if we seek to analyze entradas processes (and as *chaînes opératoires*), rather than as discrete events. In examining early entradas more comprehensively—from planning and execution to long-term consequences—there are a variety of promising avenues for future research. First, our understanding of entradas would be greatly enhanced by a more detailed archaeological understanding of the provincial capitals and entrêpots that launched and supported Spanish entradas. Similarly, ethnohistorical and archaeological studies of settlements and frontier colonies established by Native allies and auxiliaries (Altman 2010; Card and Matthew 2009) will have much to tell us about the longer-term consequences of entradas for some of their primary participants. Although shipwrecks have been a rich source of information about many aspects of sixteenth-century commerce and material culture (Arnold and Weddle 1978; Brewer and Horvath 2004), their tremendous potential for understanding entrada-related planning, logistics, trade, and military conflict is only now beginning to be realized (Bratten 2009; Skowronek 2009; Worth 2009b). Other aspects of entrada history have been neglected more comprehensively, such as the Indian auxiliaries, Africans, and others who chose to remain in Native communities after the return of expeditions to their original points of departure/origin. Although there are an increasing number of publications devoted to the role of women in the early post-Columbian history of the Americas (Gaspar and Hine 1996; Martín 1983; McEwan 1991; Powers 2005; Schroeder et al. 1997), our understanding of their contribution to entradas remains poor, despite their notable contributions in roles such as financiers (Flint 2008:64), negotiators (Townsend 2006), and advisors (Pocock 1967:92–93). A similar research focus is beginning to reveal the significant role played by Africans in sixteenth-century entradas and early colonial society—as expedition leaders, conquistadores, rebels, and skilled laborers (Altman et al. 2003:204–222; Carroll 2001:62–64; Gerhard 1978; Restall 2003:52–63, 2005; Restall and Fernández-Armesto 2012:108–110).

As our perspectives develop, and as more sixteenth-century sites, assemblages, and archival materials emerge from the Southwest and Southeast, and as new methodological and theoretical approaches are developed to address them, we can look forward to a more nuanced and variegated understanding of all of these entrada-related subject areas, from class, gender, and ethnicity, to planning, frontier strategies, and community coalescence. In recent years archaeologists and historians have made progress in modeling the composition and variability of entrada assemblages and in extracting valuable predictive conclusions from these data (Bratten 2009; Cook 2009; Mathers et al. 2008, 2010; Mathers and Haecker 2009; Worth 2009b). Equally, quality assessments of archaeological and documentary data by way of reflexive and comparative critiques are helping to improve our understanding of thematic and geographic data gaps, as well as the interpretive limits of our source information (Ethridge et al. 2009; Galloway 1997b, 2006; Mathers 2011). Adopting these more systematic approaches to entradas will enable us to better understand the life cycle of individual expeditions, as well as to comprehend their overall efficacy and application as a tool of empire. Although they proved to be useful as an initial device for creating the territorial framework of empire, by the latter part of the sixteenth century entradas and *conquistas* were increasingly replaced by colonization-based settlement and religious conversion efforts. Within little more than a century, entradas had transitioned from an expedient to an expendable tool as the Spanish Crown consolidated its New World domains. Charting this historically embedded process, with its deep-rooted antecedents and long-term, broad-based repercussions, remains a formidable and engaging challenge in the Southwest and Southeast, as it does elsewhere.

SECTION I

Native Perspectives

2

Crossing the Corn Line

Steps toward an Understanding of Zuni Communities and Entradas in the Sixteenth-Century Southwest

Kurt E. Dongoske and Cindy K. Dongoske

From prehistory to the present day, the Zuni region of west-central New Mexico has continued to occupy a place of special significance for Pueblo communities and others. For centuries before the first Spanish-led entradas began to arrive in the area, Ancestral Zuni Pueblos were located in fertile river valleys west of the Continental Divide and along the Zuni-Acoma trails—a series of key routes for communication, travel, and commerce from the Prehistoric Period into the later Historic Era. These trails connect the Zuni region to the Pueblo of Acoma and the Rio Grande Valley to the east, and to the Hopi Mesas to the west (Ferguson and Hart 1985:54–55).

As Spanish-led entradas began to enter the northernmost frontiers of New Spain in the sixteenth century, the Zuni area assumed particular importance as an economically prosperous and well-populated resource zone. Referred to by sixteenth-century Spaniards as Cíbola or Cívola, these economic and demographic characteristics made the Zuni area an attractive prospect for sixteenth-century expeditions (Mathers and Mitchem, this volume).

For a variety of reasons, an appreciation of Zuni cultural traditions, oral histories, and cultural interactions with others (past and present) is critical to a wider understanding of Native responses to Spanish contact and a more comprehensive appreciation of the Early Historic Period in the Southwest generally. In particular, there are approximately six historical developments at Zuni that make it especially relevant to a discussion of early entradas and Native–European–African interactions. These developments include:

1. The first contact between Africans and the Pueblo world took place at Zuni in the spring of 1539 (Flint and Flint 2005:72–76; Kennedy and Simplicio 2009; Mathers et al. 2011).

2. The first large-scale contact between the Pueblo world and Europeans occurred at Zuni in the summer of 1540 with the appearance of the Vázquez de Coronado entrada (Kennedy and Simplicio 2009).
3. The Zuni region also represents one of the largest concentrations of early sixteenth-century sites with evidence of Native–European contact currently known in the United States (Clay Mathers, personal communication 2010).
4. The Zuni area is believed to have been visited by most of the major expeditions in the American Southwest during the sixteenth century, including Esteban the Moor (1539), Vázquez de Coronado (1540–1542), Sánchez Chamuscado and Rodríguez (1582), Espejo (1583), and Oñate y Salazar (1598, 1605) (Mathers, this volume). Zuni also saw some of the longest-sustained occupations by sixteenth-century expeditions in the Southwest (Mathers, this volume).
5. In addition, the Ancestral Zuni Pueblo of Hawikku represents the site of one of the earliest known battles between Native Americans and Europeans in North America, and is one of the best documented to date with respect to both historical and archaeological evidence (Damp 2005; Mathers, this volume).
6. Finally, some of the earliest major anthropological and archaeological investigations in the American Southwest were conducted in the Zuni region (Bandelier 1890, 1892; Cushing 1896; Fewkes 1891; Hodge 1918; Kroeber 1917; Mindeleff 1891; Parsons 1918; Stevenson 1887). Furthermore, the 1917–1923 excavations by the Hendricks–Hodge expedition at the Zuni pueblo of Hawikku (1917–1923) (Damp 2005; Smith et al. 1966) and by the 1919–1923 Clarke expedition at Kechiba:wa (Mathers et al. 2009), as well as survey work at Kyaki:ma (Damp 2005:101–121), all produced material evidence of the Vázquez de Coronado expedition.

Initial contact between Zuni communities and African/European expeditionaries took place in the late spring of 1539 when a small scouting party led by Esteban the Moor entered Zuni territory. Shortly afterward, major conflict between these two groups and the death of Esteban led surviving members of this reconnaissance group to withdraw from Zuni territory. Following this brief encounter, Zuni communities were again confronted with a foreign expedition in July 1540— in this case represented by the much larger entrada of Francisco Vázquez de Coronado. Composed of Spaniards, Mexican Indians, Africans, and others, this expedition moved steadily north from Nueva Galicia (west-central Mexico) in search of large Native population centers. The first major encounter with the Vázquez de Coronado entrada took place at the Zuni ancestral village of Hawikku, which at the time was one of the largest of the occupied Zuni villages (Damp 2005:1). The encounter between the Zuni and this Spanish-led expedition did not go well. Initial contact between the two groups was followed by open conflict, and the result significantly affected the history of the Zuni people.

There are many reasons why this first meeting ended in armed conflict. The most common explanations have focused on the tendency of Spanish-led entradas to employ force against Native groups, to cause unusual stress on the local available food and natural resources, and to force Native inhabitants to supply labor and other valuable resources (Mathers, this volume). While these explanations are often based on multiple documentary sources and contemporary accounts written by Spanish expeditionaries, descriptions of these interactions are frequently biased and one-sided. Absent from many such explanations is the Native perspective on these intruding, uninvited, and boorish visitors.

Throughout the Southwest, the Native groups that experienced Spanish encroachment were preliterate societies. As a result, they did not create parallel historical narratives comparable to the voluminous documents generated by Europeans. Thus, contemporary scholars have been forced to speculate about how the Native inhabitants viewed and reacted to these foreigners. One approach to understanding the Native perspective is through oral tradition. Oral tradition has been demonstrated to be a valid means of passing on cultural information from generation to generation and often entails the accurate transmittal of esoteric, historic, and cultural information (Vansina 1985; Whiteley 2002; Wiget 1982).

In this chapter we endeavor to provide an active Zuni voice to the understanding of this major historical encounter between Zuni and the earliest Spanish-led expeditions. We acknowledge that history is written generally by victors or literate members of a society, and such has been the case for the Spanish historical documents that chronicle the interaction between sixteenth-century entradas and Zuni. Zuni, historically a preliterate society, documents its history through the transmission of oral tradition.

As Mathers and Mitchem (this volume) point out, until recently an understanding of the Early Historic Period in the American Southwest has largely been an exercise in European and American scholarship, with relatively little attention being paid to the active roles played by Native communities in affecting the trajectory of these interactions (see also Ethridge, this volume; Flint and Flint, this volume; Mathers, this volume). The absence of Zuni and other Native perspectives in history has tended to skew not only the directionality of historical interpretations but also the quality of scholarship on this subject. Moreover, the exclusion of tribal voices concerning Contact Period history has deprived many tribal members of their legitimate place in shaping interpretations about significant events that define their own histories. In recent years, however, research by Native scholars (e.g., Agoyo 2002; Kennedy and Simplicio 2009; Sando and Agoyo 2005; Suina 2002) and partnerships between Native and non-Native scholars (e.g., Liebmann and Toya 2010; Mathers et al. 2009, 2011) have begun to alter the balance and nature of research on the early Historic Period in the Southwest.

In spite of the fact that we are non-Zuni authors, we were approached by the editors of this volume to contribute an essay reflecting the Zuni point of view on this significant historical event. In agreeing to participate, we want to make it clear that our sole intent is to attempt to convey a Zuni perspective by building on the past research of Zuni scholars and colleagues (e.g., Ed Ladd and Dan Simplicio). Their work has been fortified and enhanced through numerous conversations that we have had with the Zuni Cultural Resource Advisory Team (ZCRAT) and other Zuni individuals concerning this issue.

The ZCRAT was officially established in 1991 by Zuni Tribal Council Resolution No. M70-91-L164. The ZCRAT was charged by the Zuni Tribal Council to provide advice and guidance relating to Zuni cultural preservation issues, natural resource concerns, and places of traditional cultural importance relevant to federal and state laws. The ZCRAT is an integral and vital aspect of the functioning of the Zuni

Heritage and Historic Preservation Office and also counsels the Zuni Cultural Resource Enterprise regarding issues involving important Zuni traditional cultural properties, places, and resources located on the Zuni reservation.

The Pueblo of Zuni

Today, the Pueblo of Zuni is the largest of New Mexico's nineteen Pueblo communities, with a population of more than eleven thousand enrolled members, the vast majority of whom live within the village. The Pueblo of Zuni lies at an elevation of approximately sixty-four hundred feet on the Zuni River in west-central New Mexico. The Zuni Indian Reservation covers a land area of more than six hundred square miles.

Prior to the arrival of the first Spanish-led entradas, Ancestral Zuni Pueblos were located throughout the Zuni River basin and its environs. As early as A.D. 900, small habitation sites in the Zuni drainage appear that suggest these communities were organized around a large public building with an associated Great Kiva, a very large ceremonial chamber (Ferguson and Hart 1985:26). The Village of the Great Kivas along the Nutria River is one example of this kind of community center (Roberts 1932).

Between A.D. 1250 and 1300, a major change in settlement pattern occurred in the Zuni area as people began to aggregate into very large, well-planned pueblos ranging from 250 to 1,200 rooms (Ferguson and Hart 1985). In the Zuni drainage alone, there were thirty-six large, plaza-oriented pueblos constructed between A.D. 1250 and 1540, extending from Atsinna (located in El Morro National Monument east of the Zuni Indian Reservation) to Hawikku (situated near the current border between New Mexico and Arizona). By the end of the Pre-historic era, the Zuni people concentrated their settlements into a tightly clustered group of six to seven pueblos along the Zuni River in an area with optimal land and water resources for agriculture.

According to Ferguson and Hart (1985:27), the core area of Zuni settlement was surrounded by a much larger sustaining area used for hunting and collecting wild plants and animal resources. The Zuni pueblos at this time served as a nexus in a widespread regional trade network connecting the Colorado River area to the west with the Great Plains to the east, and the Colorado Plateau on the north with the deserts of southern Arizona, New Mexico, and northern Mexico (Ferguson and Hart 1985).

The number of ancestral pueblos at Zuni suggests this area was one of the richer agricultural locations in the Southwest and represented one of the larger and more aggregated centers of population in the region. A long-standing Spanish myth regarding seven rich cities, known as the Seven Cities of Cíbola, was further fueled by the reports of Álvar Núñez Cabeza de Vaca and his colleagues following their harrowing journey from the Florida and Texas coasts, across Northern New Spain, and finally to Mexico City, between 1528 and 1536 (Adorno and Pautz 1999). Rumors circulated that in lands to the north copper was worked in foundries, people were clothed in cotton, and the land was full of cultivated corn (Ferguson and Hart 1985:29). Whatever the actual stories, in 1539 they inspired Viceroy Antonio de Mendoza to sanction a reconnaissance of northern territories and a search for the Seven Cities of Cíbola, led by Friar Marcos de Niza and accompanied by Esteban the Moor (Ferguson and Hart 1985:29). It is perhaps this strong Spanish belief in seven rich cities and the anticipation of financial wealth that shaped how they treated the Native inhabitants, which gave cause for the Zuni response.

At the time of the Vázquez de Coronado expedition to Zuni in 1540, there were probably only six occupied Zuni villages: Hawikku, Kwa'kin'a, Halona:wa, Mats'a:kya, Kyaki:ma, and Kechiba:wa; although it is possible that the Zuni village of Chalo:wa, located some two miles northwest of Hawikku, was also inhabited (Ferguson and Hart 1985).

Documentary History of the Spanish Contact with Zuni

When Esteban and his advance party arrived at Zuni in the spring of 1539, it is claimed that Esteban had taken to wearing an affected costume, adorned with feathers and bells, and carrying a gourd rattle, in an effort to impress any Native people he might encounter (Ferguson and Hart 1985). Unfortunately for Esteban, his dress and demeanor do not appear to have found favor with the Zuni who executed him when he allegedly tried to appropriate Zuni women and valuables. Friar Marcos de Niza, who in all likelihood did not make contact with any Zuni Pueblos, quickly returned to Mexico, where he supposedly confirmed the tale of the Seven Cities and elaborated on the wealth contained there.

Spurred by the accounts of Marcos de Niza, Viceroy Antonio de Mendoza, Francisco Vázquez de Coronado, and other interested parties began to organize a major expedition northward to explore Tierra Nueva and the Seven Cities of Cíbola. The first Zuni village reached by Vázquez de Coronado was Hawikku, where he was met by some 250 Zuni warriors.

Damp (2005) recounts that prior to the Battle of Hawikku, Vázquez de Coronado sent an officer and some soldiers to a pass along a trail near the lower course of the Zuni River. This advance party was attacked by a small group of Zunis during the night, but they continued on toward the villages of Zuni the following day. As the advance party moved toward Zuni they observed "smoke signals" off to the south. The late Ed Ladd, a Zuni Tribal member and an anthropologist, concluded that the trail utilized by Vázquez de Coronado's advance party paralleled a spiritual lifeline between the sacred lake at Ko:thluwala:wa and the villages of Zuni, and that when Vázquez de Coronado's expedition arrived at Hawikku, it was during an important event in the Zuni religious calendar, the summer solstice (Ladd 1997:231).

During the summer solstice Zunis make a pilgrimage to Ko:thluwala:wa and return. No one is permitted to cross the path of the pilgrims. Ladd considered this important because when the Spanish arrived, the religious Bow Priests and their party were guarding the trail. Ladd postulated that the attack on Vázquez de Coronado's advance party was a symbolic statement by Zunis signifying, "Don't cross the trail." When on the following day, Vázquez de Coronado and his expedition arrived at Hawikku, the Zuni people were assembled there because, as Ladd postulated, Hawikku was the village sponsoring the pilgrimage for that year. The Zuni were assembled on the rooftops, looking to the west the direction from which the pilgrims would return (Ladd 1997:231). The smoke signals that were observed by the Spanish were part of the ceremony performed by the little fire god (Shu'la:witsi) and had nothing to do with the coming of the Spanish. Ladd noted that, in front of the assembled Zuni people and out of the smoke (a symbol for rain and clouds), there "came a cloud of dust with all kinds of animals, waving flags, and shining armor." Vázquez de Coronado stumbled into Zuni, uninvited, during important ceremonies, with his ambition set high on the acquisition of wealth and the conquest of Cíbola.

Vázquez de Coronado's intentions notwithstanding, the Zuni people apparently did not approve of this uninvited visitor, or his entourage of armed men and horses, appearing at this important ceremony. The Zuni attempted through their Bow Priests to convey to Vázquez de Coronado that he was unwelcome while this ceremony was taking place, making indications by drawing a line of cornmeal on the ground that Vázquez de Coronado's expeditionaries were not to cross over. The combination of this religious ceremony, the arrival of a large armed force, the memory of a similar expeditionary force the previous year led by Esteban the Moor, and the possibility that Vázquez de Coronado was leading a slave-raiding party all led to major tensions (Ladd 1997). Vázquez de Coronado interpreted the actions of the Zuni people at Hawikku as a threat, the Zuni people did likewise, and the events that ensued led to the first known battle between Europeans and Native Americans in the American Southwest (Damp 2005:1–2).

The results of this conflict were a number of Zuni warriors killed, a serious head injury to the Spanish commander, Vázquez de Coronado, and the Zuni abandonment of the village of Hawikku. Using Hawikku as their base of operations for a period of more than four months, the Vázquez de Coronado expedition began to reconnoiter the Zuni River basin, as well as regions further afield such as the Hopi Mesas, Grand Canyon, and the Upper Middle Rio Grande valley. While some Zuni communities fled to the well-defended mountaintop refuge of Dowa Yalanne, a short time later some rapprochement appears to have taken place between the two groups. Documentary and archaeological evidence of exchange between the expedition and the caciques of several large Zuni villages such as Mats'a:kya and Kechiba:wa (Flint 2002:281–282; Mathers et al. 2011) suggests an improvement in relations, at least temporarily and with some Zuni communities, or components of them. By December of 1540 the last of the expedition's companies, under the command of Tristán de Luna y Arellano, appears to have departed the

Zuni area for the Southern Tiwa region (Tiguex) in the Middle Rio Grande valley farther east (Flint and Flint 2005:401).

Zuni Perspectives of the Spanish Encounter

Our Zuni colleague Dan Simplicio conducted a number of interviews with Zuni tribal members and reported the results of his research in a paper delivered at the annual meeting of the Society for American Archaeology in 2009 (Simplicio 2009). The details outlined below are based on his research.

One of Simplicio's interviews was with a forty-five-year-old Zuni woman who recalled a story regarding the Zunis' initial encounter with Esteban. She stated that "without having any experience in dealing with foreigners, Zuni people could only compare his arrival with the mythical period of the Kachina wars." Simplicio's informant recounted the story of a black-faced kachina that used a gourd rattle to fight against the Zuni kachinas. The rattling of the gourd caused it to rain, which resulted in breaking the Kachinas' bowstrings. By this means, the Zuni Kachinas were overcome by alien beings. Thus, when Esteban arrived at Hawikku holding a gourd rattle and making demands on the Zuni people, they believed it was a sign of impending calamity. Esteban made the fatal mistake of not understanding or appreciating the religious beliefs and social values of the Zuni. The informant commented that "the first encounter was about fear and apprehension." The same fear and apprehension reemerged at Zuni with the arrival of the Vázquez de Coronado expedition a year later. This entrada was large, numbering some 2,800 individuals and several thousand animals (Mathers, this volume). According to Simplicio's informant, "Most Zuni families knew in advance of Vázquez de Coronado's arrival, and had sufficient time to move to distant villages, but the men remained at the village of Hawikku to face Vázquez de Coronado's army." Simplicio's informant further observed that the arrival of this armed force severely disrupted the Zuni ceremonial calendar. Vázquez de Coronado's arrival occurred just after the summer solstice ceremony and the beginning of the summer rain dances. As a result of the Battle of Hawikku there was the disruption of the Zuni religious calendar for the remainder of the year.

Zuni religious and ceremonial activities are intended to nurture life, and they are the antithesis of taking life. Simplicio's informant also stated that "it seemed that the world view of the Old and New Worlds were dramatically different in terms of the intent to conquer and exploit the resources of other people." She made the observation that "this may have been the reason why the Aztecs aligned themselves with the Spaniards, since they also relied on the dominance of others through fear." She emphasized that "the fear component still resonates today and that she doesn't feel safe around men who are not Zuni knowing that Zuni men have a different protective value for the women."

Simplicio also interviewed a sixty-five-year-old man, a fifty-five-year-old woman, and a thirty-eight-year-old woman. He first presented to them a general history concerning the arrival of Vázquez de Coronado's army at Zuni, and then asked each of them about their impressions of this event. The male elder commented on the sheer size of Vázquez de Coronado's army and the strange sight of hundreds of people mounted on horses. To the Zunis, a man on a horse was simply one alien being. There were also the hundreds of Aztec warriors dressed in battle regalia, the thousands of animals grazing on the lush landscape, and the trails created by the advancing army. As both sides prepared for this battle, the Zunis watched in amazement how quickly these mounted beings could move. They had never before experienced the viciousness of war dogs, which could be commanded by these foreigners. Zuni warriors had also never seen the deadly objects hurled at them from a distance. The elder also mentioned the dress of the Franciscan priests in robes and hoods. They were seen by the Zunis as supernatural beings that practiced witchcraft. The battle-hardened members of this alien army could not be stopped by the Zuni warriors. Never before had the Zuni suffered as many deaths in a single battle. The elder continued, saying, "This is the historic trauma that has kept the Zuni silent about this event, and why shouldn't they? It's just as if you were healthy one day and then you were stricken by sickness. When, after several weeks you finally get better again, you don't want to recall the sickness. Death and destruction are not part of our lifeway and when they occur we have to take care of the situation through ritual."

The fifty-five-year-old woman emphasized Zuni religious values after the contact with Vázquez de Coronado's army. The foreigners eventually forced their religious beliefs on the Zuni people by building a church on Zuni burial grounds. This was an extreme violation of Zuni burial practices. The thirty-eight-year-old woman recounted her experience as a child, when she visited the statue of Santo Niño. This iconic figure has been incorporated into the Zuni religion. It is considered a supernatural figure by some Zunis, one that offers well-being and prosperity to those who worship it, but the worshipper needs be a good person to obtain the benefits. Simplicio's informant believed that if she viewed the saint as being old, then she would also have a long life. However, if the saint should appear to her in the form of a child, then she would die at a young age. She then stated, "Can you imagine how scared that made me, to believe that this statue was directly out of a horror movie?" The male elder continued this line of thought by stating that a whole belief system was created and incorporated into the Zuni clan system, by designating who would be the caretaker of the saint. All of these religious beliefs were taught without conveying any of the traditional Zuni beliefs. And the result was to create fear if you failed to worship this saint.

Zuni Cultural Resource Advisory Team's Perspective

The authors met with the Zuni Cultural Resource Advisory Team prior to one of their regularly scheduled meetings with the Zuni Heritage and Historic Preservation Office. The topic of the Vásquez de Coronado entrada and the Zuni reaction to the Spaniards was presented to the ZCRAT, whose response was surprising. The ZCRAT stated that the Zuni encounter with the Vásquez de Coronado expedition happened a long time ago and that they did not have any particular thoughts to express about the subject.

This ZCRAT response was unanticipated, and in reflection we provide three possible explanations for their lack of a detailed response or discussion with us about this topic. The first is that they really had no specific thoughts to express on the subject, which ended the discussion. However, this explanation seems highly unlikely given our past interactions with this group of august gentlemen who normally willingly express their Zuni traditional erudition on many diverse subjects. The second possible explanation involves the ZCRAT, individually and/or collectively, having thoughts about this historical event but being unwilling, for whatever reason(s), to share their perspectives with the authors. While this explanation is plausible, it is also not consistent with our past experience in dealing with the ZCRAT, who reliably demonstrate an openness and willingness to discuss many issues, especially those that concern Zuni. The third explanation, which appears to be the most likely, is that the topic was presented to the ZCRAT in a far too general manner. Asking general, nonspecific questions promoted general, nonspecific responses. Further conversations with the ZCRAT regarding this issue are anticipated, however. These will employ a methodology to elicit specific responses to increasingly focused questions about the Vázquez de Coronado entrada and will create a structure for generating Zuni narratives concerning these important historical events.

Other Possible Factors Influencing Zuni/Spanish Interaction

The following factors are identified as future discussion topics with the ZCRAT and will be part of the ongoing effort of the Zuni Heritage and Historic Preservation Office to construct the Zuni historical narrative.

Climate and Environment. Native groups throughout the Southwest were, and continue to be, adept at utilizing a wide range of resources, both cultivated and wild. As several chapters in this volume have emphasized, Spanish-led entradas tended to rely heavily on Native groups as their economic fallback, since these communities were more familiar with the range of local resources available as well as seasonal and spatial fluctuations in their availability (see Blanton, Chapman, Ethridge and Mitchem, this volume; Mathers and Mitchem, this volume; Worth, this volume). The value of Indigenous knowledge about the ecosystem to Spanish-led expeditions in the Southwest would have been significant, particularly in a semiarid landscape, and in the extreme conditions that prevailed during harsh winters such as those of 1540 and 1541. Major stores of food and other resources (such as turkey-feather blankets), together with a local knowledge of emergency plant and animal resources, may have been critical to the viability and survival of large expeditions (like those of Vázquez de Coronado), as well as smaller ones in the later sixteenth century (such as Sánchez Chamuscado and Rodríguez, Espejo, and Oñate y Salazar).

Strategies of Deception, Deflection, and Confrontation. As elsewhere in the Americas (Clay Mathers, personal communication 2010), it appears that the strategy (actively and passively) of directing or deflecting Spanish entradas to other regions may have been pursued at Zuni during the more than four-month occupation by the Vázquez de Coronado expedition. The Spanish chronicler Pedro de Castañeda de Nájera, for example, indicates that following the Battle of Hawikku a small Spanish-led party was taunted at a safe distance and then disrupted by a group of Natives (Flint and Flint 2005:393). Events of this type suggest that tactics of harassment were being pursued by at least some Zuni communities (or subgroups within them) during the protracted Spanish occupation by the Vázquez de Coronado expedition. Other tactics, such as abandoning villages, temporarily removing Native food stores and potential labor, rustling horses and livestock, and possibly raiding expedition camps and small task-related groups (such as fuel-gathering parties), may have contributed to the overall malaise of the expeditionaries as their occupation at Zuni wore on. Ferguson (2002:36–37) reports that Zunis employed tactics similar to these in the aftermath of the Pueblo Revolt of 1680, including the poisoning of water supplies. Continued harassment of the expedition, the lack of portable wealth and valuable resources promised by the reports of Marcos de Niza, and the onset of a bitterly cold winter may all have eventually contributed to the expedition's departure from Zuni to Tiguex in late 1540. When well-organized Zuni warriors were unable to best Spanish forces and their allies at Hawikku, some of these more subtle tactics may have been employed by Zunis instead of, or perhaps in addition to, more belligerent and bellicose strategies.

Political Organization and Spanish-led Entradas. Major expeditions such as those of Vázquez de Coronado and Oñate y Salazar were clearly in search of large population aggregations with centralized authority structures (see also Ethridge and Mitchem, this volume; Mathers and Mitchem, this volume; Worth, this volume). More mobile and dispersed communities—such as the Chichimecs in northern New Spain or mobile hunter-gather groups in what is now Sonora, Mexico, and along the Arizona–New Mexico border—were of considerably less interest, except as a potential military threat (Mathers, this volume). The three major foci of the Vázquez de Coronado expedition in the American Southwest (i.e., Zuni, Tiguex, and Hopi) were consistent with the Spanish goals of targeting large population centers with significant stores of resources and major potential pools of Native labor (Mathers et al. 2011).

Coalescence and Multicultural Identities in the Early Historic Period. As Mathers and Mitchem point out, one of the interpretative challenges in evaluating the impact of sixteenth-century entradas, at least in the Southwest, is the presence of a number of Mexican Natives and Africans who remained in Pueblo communities once the entradas returned to Mexico. At Zuni there is compelling evidence to suggest that several of Vázquez de Coronado's Mexican allies remained behind in the Zuni region after the expedition departed for Mexico City in 1542. Found by members of the Espejo party in 1583, these Spanish-speaking Mexican auxiliaries had lived for more than four decades among the pueblo communities at Zuni (Hammond and Rey 1967:93–95; Mathers and Mitchem, this volume). The role and influence of these Mexican Natives has yet to be assessed. Like other aspects of community formation and reformation during this period, there are many dimensions of cultural identity and coalescence that await future research.

In the meantime, it is clear that Zuni communities played a critical role in shaping the initial encounters with Spanish-led entradas as they entered the northern Southwest in the sixteenth century. In many senses, this complex history of interaction, coalescence, support, and resistance remains incomplete and poorly understood. It is our hope that by integrating the deep histories of Zuni (and other Native) oral tradition and cultural practice, future analyses of sixteenth-century Native–European contacts will begin to address some of the missing elements in archaeological approaches to this subject. With our colleagues at Zuni and elsewhere, we look forward to contributing to that ongoing challenge and dialogue.

SECTION II

Historiography

3

Catch as Catch Can

The Evolving History of the Contact Period Southwest, 1838–Present

Richard Flint and Shirley Cushing Flint

For much of its course, study of the Contact Period of the American Southwest and northwest Mexico has been frozen in concepts and paradigms long ago superseded by scholars in other fields. Centuries-old historical frameworks have survived in strictly narrative, triumphalist accounts of "great men" and "great events" that have flashed across the region. For far too long, the sole criterion of worthwhile history of the Southwest has been "the declaration of true things in order set foorth" (Cooper 1578).

As far as that goes, that is an admirable, if extremely limited, goal, one that ignores an equally ancient desire for understanding the past and using that understanding to guide the present. As long ago as the seventeenth century, the English biographer of Elizabeth I, William Camden (1630), put it this way:

> Take away from History Why, How, and To what end, things have been done, and Whether the thing done hath succeeded according to Reason, and all that remains will rather be an idle Sport and Foolery, than a profitable Instruction.

The historical study of the sixteenth-century Southwest began as a simple, naïve narrative told from an essentially European perspective, and it has, in large measure, continued in that vein. Broader study and analysis have taken a backseat to drama, adventure, glorification, and entertainment.

For the English-speaking United States, what was to become the American Southwest was a dim and largely irrelevant quadrant of the continent until the nineteenth century was well under way. It was the vast, remote, and amorphous north of New Spain and then Mexico, of interest primarily for its celebrated wealth of silver. Until 1838, it was unlikely that anyone could have been found in the United States who had reliable information about events and people of the preceding three hundred years in northern New Spain. In that year, though, the collector and bibliophile Henri Ternaux-Compans (1838) published the ninth volume in his series *Voyages, Relations et Memoires Originaux pour Servir a l'Histoire de la Découverte de l'Amérique.* This publication offered French translations of Spanish-language *relaciones* (firsthand accounts) by Fray Marcos de Niza and Pedro de Castañeda de Nájera of the Vázquez de Coronado expedition from Mexico City to present-day Kansas and back between 1538 and 1542. The expedition resulted in the first contact between Europeans and Native Americans of the Southwest and extreme northwest Mexico.

French being the international language of the day, Ternaux-Compans's volumes were soon read by educated Americans. As in all of his volumes, Ternaux-Compans simply presented firsthand narrative accounts of European "adventurers," as he called them, in their wondrous activities among the peoples and places of a "new world." His emphasis on documents that told of glamorous and stirring actions by intrepid European men in a wealthy land dovetailed easily with the belief of many Americans of the day that their "manifest destiny" was to spread across the continent and exploit its resources.

That westward expansion had already been under way for years by 1838, with decades of aggressive filibustering by American frontiersmen, the paper annexation of Louisiana by the United States in 1803, and the American-ex-patriot-led Texas rebellion of 1836. American imaginations lusted wildly after the remainder of the Mexican north and were hungry for news of its mineral wealth. Although many Americans generally had cultivated a dislike of Spaniards and Mexicans for decades, tales of the "heroic deeds" of the first conquerors, Spaniards or not, were hot sellers in the United States and served as promise of the North American future.

Consequently, Ternaux-Compans's translations soon inspired books and pamphlets in English. After peace was negotiated following invasion of New Mexico and California by United States armies in 1846 and 1847, military surveyors of the Corps of Topographical Engineers were anxious to locate, among other things, the places and peoples that figured in the published accounts of the Vázquez de Coronado expedition. Some carried copies of Ternaux-Compans's translations to guide their search.

One of those surveyors was Lieutenant (years later, Brigadier General) James H. Simpson. As a young man he performed a geographical reconnaissance of the Navajo and Zuni country in 1848. More than twenty years later he published his findings in *Coronado's March in Search of the "Seven Cities of Cibola" and Discussion of their Probable Location* (Simpson 1872), one of many contemporary publications dealing with that topic. As the title of his article implies, Simpson's effort was mostly to correlate documentary descriptions with known geographical locations and to assess previous speculators' placement of those locations. The precise geographical position of places mentioned in the reconnaissance and conquest narratives has remained a preoccupation of many students of the subject.

Those who have not been as focused on geographical questions as Simpson have slowly enlarged the pool of primary documentary source material and have little by little clarified and fine-tuned the storyline first told to Americans by Ternaux-Compans. Typical of those was W. W. H. Davis, whose publication *The Spanish Conquest of New Mexico* appeared in 1869, the same year Simpson wrote his article for the Smithsonian (Davis 1869). Davis was US Attorney for New Mexico and spent several years in New Mexico in that capacity beginning in 1853. His book is the largely unquestioned repetition of the contents of the then known, relevant sixteenth-century Spanish documents and therefore presents Spanish viewpoints as the complete and true record of the region's past. He called his subject "this field of early adventure and . . . one of the most interesting relations of incidents to be met with in the record of early explorations in the New World (Davis 1869:v)."

Those two characterizations of early European–Native American contact in the American Southwest and northwest Mexico as "adventure" and "exploration" have been typical of much historical writing on the subject. Even as recently as 1992, Douglas Preston's best-selling *Cities of Gold: A Journey Across the American Southwest in Pursuit of Coronado* (Preston 1992) has revisited those themes, albeit with a nod to more modern sensibilities. Without the emphasis on adventure, it doubtless would not have been the hit it was.

A hundred years before Preston, Adolph Bandelier was different. He lived an adventure, but that is not what he wrote about. Instead, he followed three distinct lines of research for years in an effort to understand what happened between Spaniards and Indians in the Southwest during the sixteenth century and who those people were. One line of inquiry was archaeological, taking him from Pecos Pueblo to central Chihuahua and Sonora in Mexico. A second line of research was ethnological, involving talking with and observing hundreds of American Indians from many different tribes and entering the life of Catholic Hispanos. And a third line of investigation involved indefatigable research into the archives and private collections of ancient documents written by participants in, and observers of, the events that fascinated him. That last task took him from Santa Fe to Spain, Peru, and Mexico.

In 1888, he wrote his *History of the Colonization and Missions of Sonora, Chihuahua, New Mexico and Arizona to the Year 1700* (Bandelier 1888; Rodack 1988) as a gift to Pope Leo XIII. This work was, to that point, unparalleled. It was an incredibly rich, seven-volume manuscript accompanied by 502 drawings, paintings, and photographs that included "many interesting theories" about what had happened in the colonial past. Bandelier expanded exponentially the evidence available for study of the Spanish colonial Southwest and brought to bear on the subject different types of evidence than had ever been employed before. Bandelier and his second wife, Fanny, probably did more than any individual or team before or since to broaden the scope and increase the depth of study of the Contact Period. Some of the fruits of their labors were not made public until after their deaths, when in 1923 Charles Wilson Hackett published three volumes of their documentary research titled *Historical Documents Relating to New Mexico, Nueva Vizcaya, and Approaches Thereto, to 1773* (Hackett 1923–1937).

Since Bandelier's pioneering work, others have also energetically pursued his twin passions for the search for more, and nonnarrative, primary source documents and what has come to be known as ethnohistory. Most notable among these have been George Parker Winship (1896), with his publication of *The Coronado Expedition, 1540–1542*, and the team of George P. Hammond and Agapito Rey, who produced three influential source books: *Narratives of the Coronado Expedition,*

1540–1542 (1940), *Don Juan de Oñate: Colonizer of New Mexico* (1953), and *The Rediscovery of New Mexico, 1580–1594: The Explorations of Chamuscado, Espejo, Castaño de Sosa, Morlete, and Leyva de Bonilla and Humaña* (1966). Our own *Documents of the Coronado Expedition, 1539–1542: "They Were Not Familiar with His Majesty, nor Did They Wish to Be His Subjects"* (Flint and Flint 2005) and *Great Cruelties Have Been Reported, the 1544 Investigation of the Coronado Expedition* (Flint 2002) fall within this category also. Some of this documentary work was materially facilitated by the archival research conducted by Lansing B. Bloom in the 1920s and 1930s. (Microfilm and photographic copies of hundreds of documents obtained by Bloom at the Archivo General de Indias at Sevilla, Spain, and the Archivo General de la Nación in Mexico City are curated by the Center for Southwest Research, Zimmerman Library, University of New Mexico.)

In the seventy years since the centennial of Ternaux-Compans's publication of the narratives of Castañeda de Nájera and Fray Marcos, in 1938, US and more rarely Spanish and Mexican historians in the now professionalized academic field have produced a series of books covering the first century of the Spanish colonial Southwest and northwest Mexico. Usually they have retold and expanded the story of the increasingly familiar Spanish narratives. Often those narratives have been extensively contextualized with data concerning the Indigenous side of the contact equation, and sometimes they have offered alternative visions of the colonial past from Native perspectives. A number of these authors have striven to legitimize and even celebrate history of the Hispanic and Indian past within fields long dominated by Anglo-American centrism. Included within this group must be A. Grove Day (1940), Herbert E. Bolton (1949), John Francis Bannon (1970), Stewart Udall (1987), Marc Simmons (1991), David J. Weber (1992), Carroll L. Riley (1995), John L. Kessell (2002), and Julio César Montané Martí (2002).

In addition, there have been a few historians and ethnohistorians who have framed the history of the sixteenth-century Southwest from markedly distinct theoretical vantages. Perhaps one of the most influential of them to date has been Edward Spicer, who in *Cycles of Conquest: The Impact of Spain, Mexico, and the United States on the Indians of the Southwest, 1533–1960* addressed the following question: "What are the chief ways in which Indians have responded to Western civilization and what has happened to their cultures as a result of contact?" (vii). Although he devoted little of his book to the sixteenth century, Spicer's notion of a "culture of conquest, . . . a distillation of the culture of the Spaniards" as the primary vehicle of culture change among colonized American Natives in the Southwest has been very influential.

Patricia Nelson Limerick (1987) provided an equally powerful framework in her book *The Legacy of Conquest: The Unbroken Past of the American West.* She rightly insisted that "One skill essential to the writing of Western American history is a capacity to deal with multiple points of view. . . . Seldom are there only two parties or only two points of view" (Limerick 1987:39). Legitimate histories of the Southwest and other regions could no longer, according to her, be written solely from a single cultural viewpoint nor with the assumption of innocence on any side of what was a devastating, multidirectional clash.

Richard Flint's *No Settlement, No Conquest: A History of the Coronado Entrada* (2008) has been governed by a standard very similar to Limerick's. It has been his goal to treat as equally human all parties to the cultural encounters that occurred in the American Southwest and northwest Mexico between 1540 and 1542. As such, each party deserves the historian's utmost effort to reveal their different motives, strategies, and fates.

To this end, it is imperative that we realize that the potential evidence for study of the interplay between Indigenous American, European, and African cultures in the sixteenth century has by no means been exhausted. We are confident that we still know less than what remains to be learned. The disclosure, integration, and analysis of new evidence from all manner of perspectives can only help us approximate an adequate and truly useful, if always provisional, understanding of events, forces, and people that have brought us to where we are today. That means more documents of all sorts are needed, more traditional accounts, more ethnology, more archaeology, more geography, more linguistics, more findings from less well-defined, emerging, and yet-unknown fields.

At the 2005 meeting of the American Society for Ethnohistory in Santa Fe, Neil Whitehead posed an extremely provocative question: "Who should decide what additional documentary evidence is brought forward by historians and ethnohistorians?" For the sake of human understanding, the answer to that question, and similar questions about other sorts of evidence, must be that unfettered individual researchers must direct their own choices. We must encourage the production of new evidence from every imaginable source. There certainly must be no universal, automatic stricture on what evidence can and cannot be introduced into the ongoing dialectic of history. The flip side of that imperative, though, is that it is the responsibility of those who bring forward new evidence to make a good-faith effort to assess the reliability, worth, and bias of that evidence, not simply to drop unexamined novelties into the intellectual hopper as though that action carried no consequences. Coupled with an expanding evidence base, the range of research questions to which that evidence is applied needs to be maximized, with the aim of avoiding cultural or disciplinary tunnel vision. At a minimum, researchers need to be forever aware that their conclusions are only as valuable as their questioning has been thorough and wide ranging and as their evidence net has been commodious and fine meshed.

Our own thirty years of expansion and reexamination of the documentary evidence for study of the Vázquez de Coronado expedition have led us to gradual recognition that long-held assumptions about sixteenth-century Spanish-led reconnaissance and conquest are erroneous and seriously interfere with understanding that particular enterprise and other similar ones of the era. In accordance with a long-entrenched characterization of Spanish-led expeditions, for many decades the Vázquez de Coronado expedition typically was styled as "a small army of Spanish knights in clanking armor dispatched by the king of Spain to look for gold" (Flint 2005:204).

But if we look carefully at the growing documentary record, it is apparent that characterization is badly distorted. In fact, it is grossly inaccurate on every count. The Vázquez de Coronado expedition, as revealed by the contemporaneous documentary record, was instead a very large, only quasimilitary group composed, in its European component, primarily of civilian investors self-organized for the principal purpose of obtaining Indian tribute.

For the remainder of this chapter we devote ourselves to one aspect of the more up-to-date quasimilitary conceptual model and its older distorted counterpart. We show that the Vázquez de Coronado expedition had an only faintly military complexion, and that the older assumption that it was a full-fledged army by modern standards has interfered with its archaeological investigation.

In the first place, and most importantly, the expeditionary troop was a miscellaneous, ad hoc group, assembled principally for the purpose of taking economic control of a presumably large and prosperous Indigenous polity known as Cíbola. And it was disbanded when that place proved far inferior to its reputation. It was not a preexisting troop, drilled and schooled to specific practices, welded into a smoothly operating fighting unit. Instead, it came to be over the course of months beginning in the fall of 1539, as groups and individuals joined. The troop grew by accretion as it progressed from Mexico City to San Miguel de Culiacán and beyond, picking up members and constituent units in Michoacán, Jalisco, Nayarit, Sinaloa, Sonora, Arizona, New Mexico, Texas, and Kansas. And it disintegrated in an equally haphazard way on its return from the north, arriving in Mexico City almost three years after it had departed "with fewer than a hundred men" (Flint and Flint 2005:430).

The force was far from a coherent and cohesive body. Its population of some two thousand to twenty-eight hundred people represented at least a dozen ethnic and national sources, from Scotland to Tzintzunzan, from Mudéjar slaves to Ópata-speaking traders. They shared little besides their physical goal. The group was a polyglot of languages, traditions, motives, and practices. It was only nominally under the leadership of Francisco Vázquez de Coronado. It certainly shared no military culture, in fact very few, if any, cultural elements at all.

Two-thirds to three-fourths of its members were Native Americans with a variety of tribal affiliations. Some belonged to groups antagonistic to others who were on the trek to Cíbola. They were largely autonomous and adhered to their own organizational and tactical standards. They often acted independently, even leaving the expedition entirely when that suited them. As an indication of the independence of the Indigenous contingent of the expedition, it is worth pointing out that, according to court testimony of some of its leaders, the Native contingent joined the expedition voluntarily. These *indios amigos* were incorporated into the expedition as groups under their own traditional leaders, rather than as individual enlistees (Flint 2009). Incentives for joining, such as cash payments, bestowal of honors, reduction of tribute, and perhaps the right to keep prisoners, were provided by the viceroy and his representatives.

Despite their unpredictability, the *indios amigos* probably represented the expedition's most experienced and practiced fighters, most of them coming from cultures in which warrior prowess was the most common means to social advancement and combat was an activity engaged in periodically by most men. But those *indios amigos* certainly abided by no manual of military conduct of the sort later used in Europe and around the world; they camped and fought according to their own customs, with a wide array of equipment and gear. All of this implies that attempts to locate the remains of their presence in Tierra Nueva, as the greater Cíbola region was known, are doomed to failure if predicated on searches for patterns typical of recent European and American professional military campaigns (Flint 2003; Flint 2008:58–62).

Lack of adherence to formal military procedures was true also of the expedition's European contingent. They, the presumed "knights" in earlier visions of the expedition, comprised approximately four hundred free men, at least an equal number of mostly African slaves and servants, and an unknown number of women and children. If we look only at the free men, we see, by examining evidence of their activities both before and after the entrada, that they were not, with a single exception, professional soldiers. In fact, most had no known military experience and no formal military training. They inhabited an age and place, Spain in the sixteenth century, in which boys and men of upper social ranks routinely practiced swordplay, and a fair number were accomplished horsemen.

Practicing the martial arts, though, was neither the experience nor the ambition of most members of the Vázquez de Coronado expedition. By and large, they had civilian occupations and professions, which they practiced before the journey to Cíbola and afterward as well. Typical of many, Tomás Blaque, a Scotsman whose true name was probably either Thomas Black or Thomas Blake, was a *calcetero*, a seller of men's hose at the time he enlisted in the expedition, and he continued to be a merchant for the remainder of his life after returning to Mexico City from Cíbola and Quivira (AGI 1546; Mijares Ramírez 1997).

Most did not embark on other entradas after the conclusion of the Cíbola expedition. There were exceptions to that general statement, though: an estimated group of thirty-six or so who joined the Villalobos voyage to the Philippines in 1542; a group of about eight who just weeks after returning from Cíbola agreed to set out to intervene in the civil war in Peru in 1547; and another group about that same size that went to La Florida with former Vázquez de Coronado expedition captain don Tristán de Luna y Arellano in 1559. Only one former member we know of, Pero Hernández, El Leal, frequently engaged in military activities after the Vázquez de Coronado expedition, in Peru. Even Juan Troyano, who had run away from home at age fifteen to fight in Spain's wars in Italy, became a professional soldier, and was an artilleryman during the Vázquez de Coronado expedition, gave up that calling after the expedition's return to Mexico City in 1542. Thereafter, he built *bergantines* (brigantines) and operated a small shipping business on Lake Texcoco, as well as filled low-level government posts (Flint 2002:162–163; AGN 1550; AGI 1559; Flint and Flint 2011).

A relative few did have military, or quasimilitary, experience before the expedition to Cíbola. Among them were twenty-five men who had served in Viceroy Mendoza's personal guard. But that was a largely honorary and symbolic office, the chief criteria for admission to which were loyalty to the viceroy and robust health. Service in the guard undoubtedly offered the opportunity to hone one's facility with sword and dagger. The very fact, however, that so many of the guardsmen were permitted, perhaps even dispatched, to go on the expedition to Cíbola is testimony to their not being essential to the viceroy's safety, confirming their primarily symbolic and ceremonial role, militarily speaking. With potentially more impact on the military capacity of the expedition were three of its captains who were veterans of the conquest of Nueva Galicia, conducted under the direction of Nuño Beltrán de Guzmán between 1529 and 1532. They had at least learned something about fighting Indians from various groups in what is now west-central Mexico and had acquired campaign habits, which they conveyed to their respective companies. But, all told, such individuals made up only a small fraction of the Europeans who went to Cíbola (Flint 2008:49–55; Flint 2005:206–207; S. Flint 2002).

In contrast, many of the Vázquez de Coronado expeditionaries had the most rudimentary martial skills and experience. That lack of skill was evident on a number of occasions during the entrada. For example, consider this description of the expedition by expeditionary Pedro de Castañeda de Nájera as it departed from Compostela in February 1540, immediately following its muster:

> Since each person was compelled to carry his belongings on horseback and not everyone knew how to harness [a horse] and [since, further,] the horses were wide and fat when they set off, there was great difficulty and annoyance during the first days' travel. Many [persons] left behind many costly objects and gave them, at no charge, to who[ever] wanted them, in order not [to have] to load them. [But], in the end and with time, necessity (which is a teacher) made masters of [the inexperienced]. From that point on, many caballeros could be seen [who had] turned into muleteers, and anyone who rejected that work was not held to be a man. (Flint and Flint 2005:391)

Inexperience even proved dangerous later in that year when Zuni warriors menaced the expedition's advance guard one night not far from the pueblo of Hawikku in what is now west-central New Mexico. Again in Castañeda de Nájera's telling:

> The next day at night, two leagues from the pueblo, a number of Indians taunted [them] from a safe place. Although the troop had been warned, some [of them] became so flustered that there were some who put their saddles on backwards. These were persons [who were] untried. (Flint and Flint 2005:393)

A factor contributing to this situation was that the expeditionaries were for the most part very young, in their teens and twenties. Based on the 108 European members of the expedition whose ages are known, we estimate that 48 percent of the free men were twenty-five years old or less—that is, at or under the formal age of majority at that time. That includes 13 percent who were teenagers. Their young age gave them little chance to acquire practical combat experience, and most had not been in the Western Hemisphere long enough to engage in conquests previously.

Upon reaching the northernmost Spanish outpost of Culiacán in March 1540, the members of the Vázquez de Coronado expedition engaged in a mock battle with the residents of the town. The town's "defenders" arrayed themselves "according to the practices of war in squadrons." During this ritualized and stylized event, the men's lack of experience was again exposed. An artilleryman's hand was blown off when a cannon's fuse was lit before he had removed the ramrod (Flint and Flint 2005:391).

The nomenclature used to designate the leaders of the Vázquez de Coronado expedition suggests a military hierarchy: captain general, *maestre de campo* (field commander), captain, and *alférez* (standard bearer). Yet the persons who occupied those positions generally did not have the skills or experience today implied by their titles. Twenty-nine-year-old Francisco Vázquez de Coronado, for example, was captain general. His only known prior official duty had come in 1537 following the suppression of a revolt of African slaves at Amatepeque. In this episode, young Vázquez de Coronado was sent after the fact as *visitador*, or reviewing judge, to determine whether Indians had been complicit in the uprising. He was apparently unable to reach a decision. His promise as an able administrator and his personal ties to Viceroy Antonio de Mendoza were his qualifications for being tapped as captain general, that and his and his wife's family's large financial investment in the expedition. There is no hint that he possessed military skills or a record of such service (AGI 1537).

As did many other participants in the entrada to Cíbola, the captain general revealed his military inexperience in the course of combat. On the day in July 1540 when the advance guard reached the "first *ciudad* of Cíbola," Vázquez de Coronado had a formal summons read to the Zuni warriors there, in accordance with royally mandated protocol. When, understandably, the Zunis responded in a hostile manner rather than submitting to Spanish rule, he first ordered a charge by mounted lancers. And when that did not gain their submission, a frontal assault on the pueblo followed. The captain general personally led the attack, rashly rushing into a trap by scaling a ladder that seemed to have been left accidentally leaning against an outer wall of the pueblo. Exposed and vulnerable on the ladder, Vázquez de Coronado was immediately attacked from the roof by warriors bombarding him with heavy stones and others firing arrows. As expeditionary Pedro de Ledesma later remembered, the Zunis

> struck the general down with a great many rocks they threw at him from above. And they might have killed him, if several captains had not thrown themselves over him. He was brought out wounded in the nose and one leg and bruised all over and he remained unconscious for more than three hours. (Flint 2002:236)

The man designated as *maestre de campo*, or field commander, Lope de Samaniego, was another matter. He was one of the three veterans of the Guzmán expedition mentioned earlier. And he had been in New Spain since probably 1523, so he was a true veteran. Unfortunately, his knowledge and experience were lost to the expedition when he was killed at Chiametla only a few days into the journey, possibly in retaliation for his earlier activities in the conquest of the area under Guzmán. Samaniego's successor, don García López de Cárdenas, on the other hand, was a twenty-six-year-old Madrileño, who evidently had served briefly as a very young man fighting in Germany and Italy before traveling to the New World in 1535. Thus, he may have gained fighting experience in the king's army, which, along with his high social status, recommended him for his post during the expedition to Cíbola (Flint and Flint 2005:391; Achúe Zapata 2011).

The captains were Hernando de Alvarado, age twenty-three in 1540; Diego López, age twenty-five; García López de Cárdenas, age twenty-six; Diego Gutiérrez de la Caballería, age thirty-nine; Rodrigo Maldonado, age twenty-seven; Tristán de Luna y Arellano, age twenty-eight; Diego de Guevara, age nineteen; Pedro de Tovar, age twenty-two; Juan de Zaldívar, age twenty-six; Velasco de Barrionuevo, probably in his twenties; and Pablo de Melgosa, age twenty-eight or older. Only Alvarado (with Cortés in reconnaissance of the Mar del Sur), Tovar (with Guzmán as a teenager), and Zaldívar (also with Guzmán as a teenager), in addition to López de Cárdenas as discussed above, can now be confirmed as having had expeditionary experience prior to the Vázquez de Coronado expedition. It needs to be pointed out that being a captain generally hinged on social status, providing funding, and bringing associates along on the expedition, rather than on military know-how.

There were, thus, individuals scattered through the expeditionary corps who had formal military knowledge and experience, but the great majority of the European contingent were raw civilians. They were expected to fight if need be, but that was not an activity ingrained in them by training and combat. As we have written elsewhere, the expedition essentially was an imperial town seeking a site for itself, rather than a force dedicated to fighting. If a military analog is to be sought for the expedition, it would be a makeshift, untrained civilian militia, which a group of variously experienced combat veterans did their best to field with military effect (Flint 2008:2).

The group's sketchy and unregimented military background was matched by the ad hoc miscellany of its gear and equipment, including arms and armor. As revealed by the expedition's muster roll, prepared just as its northward trek was about to begin in February 1540, the expedient nature of its combat materiel is clear. Of the 287 men included on the list, fully 35 percent (101) possessed no European arms or armor at all, instead only Native weapons and armor (such things as obsidian-edged *macanas* and quilted cotton tunics). Lacking any traditional European weapons and armor, these men could hardly be judged as professional soldiers. And more than another 55 percent of the European men-at-war carried Native arms and armor to complete rare pieces of European metal war gear (a sword or a helmet or a piece of chain mail). Again, it seems unreasonable to portray this group as professional soldiers either. Certainly they possessed nothing like a "standard issue" kit (Flint and Flint 2005:139–151).

The issue of how such a troop of "accidental" men-at-arms would travel and camp is one for inductive archaeological research. There are features of the expedition's makeup and organization, which are a matter of documentary record, that would have influenced the arrangement of its travel, but there is no textual "snapshot" of the expeditionaries on the road or in camp. For example, the European contingent was composed of at least three distinct major divisions. The first was the captain general and his entourage comprised of *los sobresalientes*, those individuals whose social status and/or close connection to Vázquez de Coronado set them beyond subordination to captains. That subgroup totaled some thirty-nine persons, who together probably constituted the core of the captain general's *casa*, or traveling household. In camp they and their servants and slaves likely occupied a tented compound, or *real*. Typically, such a shelter consisted of a large circular or rectangular enclosure formed by a massive peripheral tent, leaving an interior *plaza* in which was erected the large campaign tent housing the captain general and his intimate staff and associates (Flint and Flint 2005:140–141).

The second division of men on the muster roll consisted of the European horsemen, 184 individuals, initially, partially divided into six companies. Other companies were established later. Documentary evidence shows that on the road the companies traveled separately with intervening distance between. It seems likely that a similar detachment was evident in their camping also. It is possible that each company occupied a *real* of smaller scale than the one of the captain general (Flint and Flint 2005:141–148).

The third division was made up of sixty-two undifferentiated footmen under the command of Pablo de Melgosa. (Melgosa, by the way, returned to Spain immediately after the expedition and worked in various accountancy offices for the remainder of his life.) How the footmen traveled and camped is not suggested by the known documentary record (Flint and Flint 2005:148–150).

Families on the expedition, and there were at least several, may have occupied separate tents in camp and were likely integrated into the appropriate companies while on the march. Like *criados* (retainers), slaves and servants undoubtedly occupied quarters near their masters. Juan de Contreras, the captain general's head groom, for instance, testified in 1544 that he was "always personally with Francisco Vázquez, because he was his head groom. He always ate and lived in his house and slept at the entrance to his tent" (Flint 2002:109).

Even this scant detail is available only for the European component of the expedition. The Mexican Indians (*indios amigos*) are completely in the dark in this regard. Their traveling formations and the possible patterns of their camps are unmentioned in the contemporaneous documents. Any attempt at reconstructing their practices must take into account the work done by Ross Hassig regarding pre-Conquest Mexica/Aztec traditions (Hassig 1988, for example). Excavation at LA 54147 near Bernalillo, New Mexico, in the 1980s, and recent investigations at the Kuykendall site in southeastern Arizona may provide some hints (Brasher 2009; Vierra 1989; see Mathers and Haecker 2009:3–17 for an initial attempt to model camp organization and social distinctions for Vázquez de Coronado camp locations).

That the Vázquez de Coronado expedition adhered to very few conventions typical of more formalized military units of the day should be no surprise. Spanish expeditions throughout the Western Hemisphere were usually equally ad hoc affairs, making their way "by the seat of their pants." Their practices represented a grab bag of elements learned from earlier experience and formulations of innate intelligence. Each expedition, thus, had its own peculiar character and its own idiosyncratic procedures that, over time, became its standard modus. Writing near the end of the sixteenth century, former leader of expeditions in northern South America Bernardo Vargas Machuca confirmed this state of affairs. He lamented,

> Those who have written [about government of the Indies] have only addressed the conquests, the deeds of the famous captains and soldiers, the qualities, lands, and locations, without revealing the method and practice of the militias our Spaniards have formed there, which now results in many poor choices with troublesome results, and yields many who lack all training and theory. (Vargas Machuca 2008:25)

It is with this in mind that sixteenth-century Spanish expeditionary sites in the Americas need to be approached, rather than with assumptions of more modern military stereotypes. Instead, a new model must be formulated by reading what the sites have to tell. We think that it is this kind of reassessment and reformulation of old models, a shift from a military to a quasimilitary paradigm, made possible by an expanded suite of evidence, that can move us toward more accurate understanding of the past, whether investigated by means of documents or seemingly mute traces in and on the ground.

4

Contact Era Studies and the Southeastern Indians

Robbie Ethridge

In the past twenty years a profound change has occurred in the study of the Native peoples of the American South—the bridging of prehistory and history. This important breakthrough now allows scholars a way of fashioning a seamless social history from the earliest Paleoindian period to contemporary Indian life. Such a deep historical perspective has revealed that Southeastern Indian life underwent a dramatic transformation between the pre-Contact Mississippian Period and the Colonial Era. Awareness of this transformation has given scholars a way to frame and analyze the critically important years after contact. The scholarship underlying this change comes from many directions, but much of the groundwork can be attributed to Charles Hudson and his colleagues who worked on reconstructing the routes into the South of the Spanish explorers Hernando de Soto, Tristán de Luna y Arellano, and Juan Pardo (Pluckhahn et al. 2006:1).[1] Hudson began this work in the late 1970s. Therefore, to understand the profundity of the paradigm shift that occurred with the Soto project, one has to look at the state of Southeastern Indian ethnohistory in the 1960s and 1970s.

At that time, Southern history was mostly about the antebellum era and the Civil War. And, except for some notable exceptions such as Herbert Bolton (1925), Verner Crane (1929), Grant Foreman (1932), Angie Debo (1934, 1941), Robert Cotterill (1954), David Corkran (1962, 1967), and a few others, Southern Indians simply did not figure much into the history of the South (Usner 1998:4). This is not to say that Indians were not on the scholarly radar. At this time, for many complex reasons, the study of non-Western peoples was mostly done in anthropology, not history. But anthropology in the 1960s and 1970s did not provide the intellectual framework needed to study Indigenous people historically. At that time, anthropology was committed to studying contemporary

Indigenous peoples, and they had concentrated on developing synchronic frameworks for thinking about culture and society. Theoretical frameworks such as Lévi-Straus's structuralism, the British school of structural-functionalism, ethnoscience, cultural ecology, culture area studies, cultural materialism, and other varieties of anthropological theory were popular. Anthropology also thought of itself as positivistic and scientific, and, therefore, none of these paradigms took history seriously, and some were actually hostile to it. When they did consider change over time, they did not speak of history, but "culture change," and they viewed this change usually through grand theory or through simplistic models such as assimilation, acculturation, and cultural decline (Pluckhahn et al. 2006:4).[2]

Nowhere was this more apparent than in Southeastern Indian ethnohistory. Until the late 1970s, Southeastern Indian studies were dominated by the anthropologist John R. Swanton. Born in 1873, Swanton had done most of his work in the first half of the twentieth century, and he died in 1958, but his influence in Southeastern Indian ethnohistory continued into the 1970s. Swanton was not particularly interested in history. Rather, he wanted to piece together Southeastern Indian culture, and to do so he used the culture area paradigm, wherein culture was understood to be "a bag of particulars, all parts of which were tacitly assumed to be more or less equally weighted" (Charles Hudson, personal communication 2004). Within the culture area paradigm, cultural analysis consisted of discerning "pristine" cultural traits among Indigenous people, or those traits that had not been "degraded" through acculturation. But the Southeastern Indians posed a particular problem. At the time, scholars and lay people alike understood the Southeastern Indians to be the most acculturated Indians in North America. They were even called collectively the "Five Civilized Tribes." So Swanton, in his search for "pristine" cultural traits, understood that those could be found in the historic documents where he hoped to uncover "real" Southeastern Indian cultural traits—that is, those traits that existed before contact with Europeans. And through fieldwork with contemporary Indians, he sought to identify those pure cultural traits that had survived into the twentieth century (Pluckhahn et al. 2006:5; Usner 1998:2–3).

Swanton pored over historical accounts spanning over three hundred years. Of these, he took special interest in the accounts of the early explorers into the Southeast, as he reckoned these accounts would be those most likely to contain evidence for the "pristine" cultural traits he sought to find. Accounts from these early expeditions, most notably those from the Hernando de Soto expedition between 1539 and 1543, have been published in both the original and in translations over the past several centuries. From these accounts, historians have penned numerous histories detailing the trials and tribulations of these early expeditions into eastern North America. However, none of these conventional histories took Native people as central to the stories, and they typically used Native experiences as backdrops against which to place European actions.

Swanton, however, began to compile the ethnographic information on Southeastern Indians contained in the accounts left by these expeditions in order to reconstruct something about Native life. Swanton's interest in the historical documents was novel for an anthropologist at the time. Still, as Steven Hahn (2004b:xxiii) has noted, while Swanton pioneered the use of historical documents in his ethnographies, his research methods were "less than meticulous." More importantly, Swanton's work was flawed by his use of the ethnographic present, an anthropological convention by means of which one depicted cultures synchronically in the present that were, in fact, wholly or partly defunct, and it also assumed historical continuity between the late prehistoric inhabitants of the Southeast and the societies of the eighteenth and nineteenth centuries (Galloway 1997a:285; Hahn 2004b:xxiii; Pluckhahn et al. 2006:5). Swanton's use of the ethnographic present led him to collapse more than three hundred years of history into a synchronic snapshot of Southeastern Indian culture.

The weaknesses of Swanton's approach to the past are most evident in his reconstruction of the route of Soto (Swanton 1985). Swanton used the four known chronicles of the expedition—three first-hand accounts (Elvas 1993; Hernández de Biedma 1993; Rangel 1993) and one second-hand account (Garcilaso 1993) to reconstruct Soto's route through the Southeast. Assuming that Indian towns and polities did not move between the sixteenth and eighteenth centuries, Swanton used contemporary place names to anchor the locations of polities encountered by Soto, an analytical technique that led his reconstruction astray (Pluckhahn et al. 2006:6; Smith 2000:82).

Swanton's portrayals, as important as they have been, obscured most of the significant social transformations for Native peoples that took place following European contact, and hence failed to untangle the connections between prehistoric Southeastern Indians and historic Southeastern Indians. In all fairness to Swanton, though, these transformations and connections were lost on most anthropologists, archaeologists, and historians at the time. One need only look at the way classes on the Southeastern Indians were taught in the 1960s and early 1970s to see that prehistory and history were disconnected. Courses on the Southeastern Indians, usually taught in anthropology departments, were of two types. There were North American archaeology courses that dealt with the prehistory of Native culture areas. And there were courses about the historic Indians of the Southeast organized around specific groups, such as "The Cherokees," "The Creeks," "The Choctaws," "The Timucuans," and so on. As Pluckhahn et al. (2006:6) recently noted, "That there was a connection between the prehistoric Native groups and the historic Indians, while not altogether lost on these professors, did not seem like a question that could be addressed profitably. In short, there was an intellectual disconnect between pre-1500 and post-1600."

Charles Hudson was trained under this paradigm, but this disconnect had puzzled him even as a graduate student. And he still did not have the solution to this intellectual problem when he wrote his seminal work, *The Southeastern Indians* (Hudson 1976). Hudson included beginning and ending chapters on Southeastern Indian prehistory and colonial history, but mostly the book is organized around the synchronic concept of culture that prevailed in anthropology at the time. *The Southeastern Indians* largely consists of detailed, "equally weighted" sections on such cultural traits as art, music, recreation, belief systems, social organization, subsistence patterns, and so on. Hudson realized, even as the book went to press, that it had a profoundly important unanswered question in it (Pluckhahn et al. 2006:11). As he recently stated, "When this book went into print, I was acutely aware of not having the foggiest understanding of how the Etowah, Moundville, Cahokia, and Spiro mounds that dominated the Southeast in the late prehistoric Mississippian era were connected to the Cherokees, Creeks, Choctaws, Chickasaws, Catawbas, and Seminoles" (Hudson 1993).

Others also recognized this in the book. For instance, the archaeologist Jeffrey Brain (1978), in his extended review of *The Southeastern Indians* for *American Antiquity*, faulted the book for its broad generalizations on Southeastern Indian culture. He also commented on the book's failure to integrate prehistory and history, although he underscored that the latter was difficult if not impossible because, as he wrote, "the archaeology and the ethnography cannot be successfully integrated because there are too many imponderables and contradictions in the data" (Brain 1978:312). Brain's comment reflects the thinking at the time: "The breach between the sixteenth and eighteenth centuries—between prehistory and history, and in a broader sense between archaeology and history—was simply too great to be bridged" (Pluckhahn et al. 2006:12).

However, things were beginning to change. In 1953, the American Society for Ethnohistory (ASE) was founded. The emergence of ethnohistory and the ASE certainly inspired historians and anthropologists to do Indian history, but most of them focused on regions other than the South (Usner 1998:4). And although striving for a new way to put American Indians into American history, most ethnohistorians in the 1960s and 1970s used the conventional narratives on war, treaties, and policy for their framework (Usner 1998:4–7). Then, in the late 1970s, this beginning merged with a larger movement in history to produce what would become known as the "New Indian History" (Berkhofer 1971). The New Indian History developed within history when social historians, influenced by the French *Annales* school, opened up historical inquiry to subjects and people that theretofore had been deemed unimportant or ignored altogether—groups such as women, African Americans, and Indians. The subsequent outpouring of work on Indian–European relations in the Northeast, especially on the Iroquois, prompted Southern historians to take a fresh look at Southeastern Indians. Concurrently, studies of slavery during the Colonial Period led to a growing awareness that sources were available that allowed for serious study of groups other than elite Europeans. All of this work not only challenged many of the entrenched ideas on American history and the Indians' place in it but it also offered a new look at Indian communities as societies both formed out of and integral to the American colonial experience.

Ethnohistory also advocated an interdisciplinary method, something quite novel for the time, and many ethnohistorians began to combine cultural anthropology, archaeology, and history. Still, in Southeastern Indian ethnohistory, most ethnohistorians preferred work dealing with the eighteenth, nineteenth, and twentieth centuries. They usually treated prehistory and the Contact Era in brief opening chapters presenting synchronic snapshots of Indian life based on a smattering of archaeology, but mostly on Swanton and, after the publication of *The Southeastern Indians*, on Hudson. Their innovations came from their work on the eighteenth, nineteenth, and twentieth centuries, and they did not, and perhaps could not, reach across the prehistory/history divide (Pluckhahn et al. 2006:12).

It was archaeologists who began to look across this divide. In the 1970s, American archaeology received a major stimulus with the passage of landmark legislation concerned with historic preservation. This legislation generated numerous large-scale surveys and excavations, and helped fund graduate programs across the country, including those in the South (Johnson 1992). During this active and productive period, Southeastern archaeologists began to make considerable progress in identifying elements of the complex Mississippian Period, which, in turn, led them to look across the prehistoric/historic divide. In particular, work by Jeffrey Brain, Alan Toth, and Antonio Rodríguez-Buckingham (1974) in the Mississippi Valley opened archaeological eyes to the fact that one might be able to study early European artifacts as an adjunct of sixteenth-century Indian sites. University of Georgia archaeologists, most notably David Hally and Marvin Smith, were investigating the sixteenth-century Indian community known as the King site, and they had looked to the Soto narratives as a way to interpret the site as well as for a secure chronological marker. Smith (1976) had even written a short paper in which he attempted to trace part of Soto's route primarily using Spanish artifacts. Steve Baker (1974) wrote a Master's thesis on the chiefdom of Cofitachequi, a polity visited by Soto. Meanwhile, Jeffrey Brain was also promoting the reprinting of the Swanton report on the Soto expedition and a general rethinking of the route. Even though the overviews of Southeastern archaeology written in the 1980s stopped at the Soto entrada, the tide was obviously turning (Pluckhahn et al. 2006:13; Smith 1985; Steponaitis 1986).

Hudson was quite aware of the new currents running through Southeastern archaeology and ethnohistory. After writing *The Southeastern Indians*, he took a sabbatical year as senior fellow at the Newberry Library in Chicago (Hudson 1997:466; Pluckhahn et al. 2006:11–12). While at the Newberry, Hudson succeeded in identifying that the Soto–Luna y Arellano–Pardo routes were the key to the puzzle over the connection between the Mississippian world and the colonial world. Hudson recalls that it "just made sense to use the Soto route to interpret the late Mississippian Period. People were already doing it" (Pluckhahn et al. 2006:14). However, Hudson's intent was never to simply retrace the footsteps of Soto, Luna, and Pardo. As Hudson puts it today, "The entire Soto-Luna y Arellano-Pardo project was conceived within the context of the [*Annales*] social history paradigm of Fernand Braudel and [world systems theory of] Immanuel Wallerstein" (Pluckhahn et al. 2006:15). Using the *Annales* paradigm, Hudson realized that by tracing the route of Soto, Luna y Arellano, and Pardo, one could reconstruct a protohistoric benchmark of the social geography of the Late Mississippian Period. "With a late Mississippian benchmark in place one could then move backward in time to better understand the dynamics of the Mississippian world and also forward in time to begin to understand the structural transformations that occurred when the Native peoples of the Southeast came up against the modern world system in the sixteenth and seventeenth centuries" (Pluckhahn et al. 2006:18).

Hudson had studied Swanton's reconstruction of the Soto route and saw that, because of the state of archaeology at the time, Swanton did not have the archaeological confirmation for the location of the towns on his version of the route. Yet, to reconstruct the route with more precision, Hudson would need to pinpoint the places that Soto had visited. This could only be done through archaeology. Hudson then enlisted the aid of archaeologists, especially Marvin Smith and Chester DePratter. As they began to follow Soto's route, they sought the aid of other scholars. The reconstruction of the Soto route—while led by Hudson—became a truly collaborative effort, drawing together the work by archaeologists, historians, geographers, and linguists (Pluckhahn et al. 2006:18–22).

After almost thirty years of work on the Soto project, this protohistoric benchmark is now in place, and it has made clear that the Indians of the sixteenth-century South were quite different from the Indians of the eighteenth-century South. We now know that the Indian societies of the eighteenth-century South, the ones with which we are most familiar—the Creeks, the Cherokees, the Chickasaws, the Choctaws, the Catawbas, and so on—were formed out of the collapse of Southeastern chiefdoms such as Coosa, Mabila, Chalaque, Cofitachequi, and all the other chiefdoms of the Southeast at the time of the European invasion. In other words, the Indians that the early Spanish explorers to the Native South encountered were very different from the Indians living there 150 years later. To quote Hudson, "A profound social transformation occurred among the Native people of the Southeastern United States between the time of the earliest Spanish exploration and the early decades of the eighteenth century. The people who stood on either side of this great transformational divide were organized into quite different kinds of societies" (Ethridge and Hudson 1998:34). We still do not have an adequate vocabulary to describe the Southeastern Indian societies of the eighteenth century. They have been called "confederacies," "tribes," "nations," and so on. For convenience we now call them "coalescent" societies because they were all, in varying degrees, coalescences of people from different societies, cultures, and languages.

The next question, then, as formulated by Hudson, is simply this: "What shaped the Indians of the eighteenth-century South? That is to say, what historical forces, trends, and events were attendant to the formation of the Indians of the colonial South?" (Hudson 2002:xii). Hudson and his colleagues have already identified some of these forces—military losses at the hands of early explorers and destabilization of the chiefdoms, the introduction of Old World diseases and the subsequent demographic losses, and the political and economic incorporation into the capitalist market system (Hudson 2002:xxii).

Hudson's question also directs current research on the Contact Era. As this research progresses, it is becoming increasingly clear that the Contact Era was not a time of absolute disconnect, as some archaeologists have proposed (some recent works on the Contact Era include Cobb 2003b; Ethridge 2010; Ethridge and Hudson 2002; Ethridge and Shuck-Hall 2009; Ewen 1996; Lapham 2005; Milanich and Milbrath 1989; Wesson 2008; Wesson and Rees, eds. 2002; Worth 1998a, 1998b). The Mississippian world assuredly collapsed, but the people did not disappear, nor did they reconfigure everything about life. Rather, people used old methods and devised new ones for coping with the opportunities and stresses that came with European contact. They rebuilt their lives and societies using some Mississippian structures that could be linked to a capitalist market system and colonial circumstances such as the household and township structures. In some cases, they put Mississippian devices of diplomacy and warfare in service to colonial demands. And some things changed dramatically, such as political leadership and trade. Mississippian *micos* were living representations of gods. Historic *micos* were savvy mortals. Likewise, artisans stopped using the elaborate religious iconography typical of the Mississippian Period. And a new array of goods entered Indian towns and homes through an exchange with Europeans in a nascent market system.

Influenced by the writings of Alfred Crosby (1972) on disease exchanges with contact between the Old and New Worlds, one of the most important questions to emerge from this work was the question of the introduction of Old World diseases and the consequences for Mississippian chiefdoms. Initially, these scholars attributed much about the changes in Native life during the first hundred years of European contact to the introduction of Old World disease and the subsequent catastrophic loss of life. More recently, however, as these scholars continue to debate and refine their ideas, they are understanding that disease was but one factor, and they are developing a multicausal model that includes such contributing agencies as slaving, internecine warfare, declining fertility rates, migration, violent colonial strategies such as genocide, and a general cultural and social malaise resulting from colonial oppression (Baker and Kealhofer 1996; Crosby 1972; Ethridge 2009; Galloway, 1995:134–141, 159–163; Hutchinson 2006; Hutchinson and Mitchem 2001; Kelton 2007; Larsen 2001; Perttula 1992:148–182; Ramenofsky 1987; Ramenofsky and Galloway 1997; Smith 1987:129–147, 2000:112–122, 2002; Stojanowski 2004, 2005; Worth 1998b:1–37).

The Soto project also inspired an intense collaboration between historians, anthropologists, and archaeologists working on Spanish Florida, which one historian recently marked as one of the most important modern developments in Southeastern Indian ethnohistory (Usner 1998:9–10). As Eugene Lyon (2009) recently noted, lengthy treatments for almost all of the Native people who once lived in present-day Florida have been published (Davidson 2001; Hann 1988, 1991, 2006; Hann and McEwan 1998; Lyon 1967; Marquardt 1987; Milanich 1996; Milanich and Proctor 1994; Wheeler 2000; Widmer 1988; Worth 1998a, 1998b). Dictionaries and a grammar of the Timucuan language now exist (Granberry 1993; Milanich and Sturtevant 1972). Lengthy investigations have been undertaken at St. Augustine and Pensacola (Clune and Stringfield 2009; Deagan 2008). As John Worth demonstrates in this volume, scholars can now ask quite refined questions about Native life during the early Spanish Colonial Era.

Scholars also are examining more closely the effects of commercial slaving as causes of the Mississippian collapse and how such commercial forces continued to shape the subsequent social and political reorganizations (Braund 1993; Ethridge 2010; Ethridge and Hudson 2002; Ethridge and Shuck-Hall 2009; Gallay 2003; Hudson and Tesser 1994; Saunt 1999; Snyder 2010; Wood et al. 1989). Some are turning their attention to the diffusions, amalgamations, and social transformations that led to the formation of the coalescent societies—for example, mapping the widespread dislocation and migrations that occurred after the fall of the chiefdoms and identifying which Native groups coalesced together. They are also discerning whether or not there were any pre-Contact precursors to post-Contact alliances (Ethridge 2010; Ethridge and Shuck-Hall 2009; Hahn 2004a; Jenkins 2009; Regnier 2006a, 2006b; Smith 2000).

Archaeologists and ethnohistorians are beginning to distinguish between coalescent societies and to recognize other social types that formed after the Mississippian decline. Some are concerned with tracking the cultural continuities across the Mississippian into the Historic Period (see, for example, Carson 1999; Ethridge 2003; Hahn 2004a; Jackson 2003; Milanich 1996; O'Brien 2002; Perdue 2004; Pluckhahn and Ethridge 2006; Smith 2000; Usner 1992, 1998). One of the most exciting developments has been the historicizing of prehistory—as scholars have begun to understand the Mississippian Period not only in terms of trends and processes, emergence and collapse but now also in terms of the histories of chiefdoms (Cobb 2003a, 2003b; Jenkins 2009; King 2003; Knight and Steponaitis 2007; Pluckhahn 2003; Regnier 2006a, 2006b, 2009). These are just a few examples to convey the complex picture of the Contact Era that is now emerging.

It should be obvious that the nature of the evidence for the Contact Era requires researchers to be comfortable with both archaeological and documentary evidence. One reason for this is that in the Southeast the archaeological and documentary records are inversely proportional. In other words, the amount of documentary evidence on Southeastern Indians decreases as one goes farther back in time. There is a relative abundance of documents for the twentieth and nineteenth centuries, fewer for the eighteenth century, even fewer for the seventeenth century, yet even fewer for the sixteenth century, and none for the pre-Contact Era. Conversely, the archaeological data available increase as one goes further back in time. Generally speaking, there is much more archaeological information on the protohistoric and prehistoric Mississippian Period Indians than on seventeenth-, eighteenth-, and nineteenth-century Native communities.

Such disproportionate evidence prompted Bruce Trigger (1982, 1984), in the 1980s, to delegate the Contact Era to archaeology. His reasoning was that the Contact Era had so little documentary evidence that the only way we could truly understand the culture change that occurred with contact was through archaeology. In more recent years, others have seconded Trigger's assessment (Dunnell 1991; Galloway 1993:106–108; Loren 2008:1–28; Wesson and Rees 2002:4). And indeed, for the Southeast, archaeologists have staked their claim to the Contact Era. Except for a handful (Ethridge 2010; Hall 2009), scholars researching the Southeastern Indian Contact Era are mostly archaeologists (for examples, see Brose et al. 2001; Cobb 2003b; Ethridge and Shuck-Hall 2009; Ethridge and Hudson 2002, Loren 2008; McEwan 2000; Milanich and Milbrath 1989; Thomas 1989–1991; Wesson and Rees, eds. 2002).

All of these archaeologists use both archaeological and documentary evidence in their work, and Southeastern archaeologists are quite comfortable with documentary evidence. In fact, Patricia Galloway (1993:92–98) notes that Southeastern archaeologists have had a long tradition of using documentary evidence. During the WPA days, Southeastern archaeologists mined the published historical records (especially the massive compilations of historical data that John Swanton published at the time) to reconstruct prehistoric lifeways. And although contemporary archaeologists still frequently cite Swanton, they are much more careful in their use of his compilations and have become quite proficient in the use of unpublished documents, as well.

These archaeologists have also been engaged in methodological discussions about the use of documents since the 1980s (see Galloway 1991, 1993, 1997a; Jeter 2002; Lightfoot 1995; Nassaney and Johnson 2000; Pauketat 2001; Rogers and Wilson 1993; Waselkov 2001). In addition to heeding the pitfalls that ethnohistorians have pointed out, such as biases, misunderstandings, and so on, they have also developed their own methods for combining the documents with archaeology. For instance, they have devised a modern version of the "direct historical approach," which is basically tying archaeological sites to historic Indian groups for which we have documentary evidence. They have also developed sophisticated approaches to the use of Historic Period maps. Generally speaking, they have gone far in disentangling what Samuel Wilson (1993:20) calls the "mixed epistemologies" of archaeology and history.

On the other hand, ethnohistorians have known for some time that undertaking Indian history poses some peculiar problems, and they have long insisted on an interdisciplinary approach using anthropology, history, linguistics, oral tradition, and archaeology (Axtell 1982; Berkhofer 1971; Calloway 1988; Horsman 1979; Hudson 1974; Trigger 1982). They also have been involved in discussions about the benefits and problems in doing interdisciplinary work (Fixico 1997; Krech 1991; Shoemaker 2001; Smith 1999; Thornton 1998). Most of these discussions, however, have revolved around oral tradition, anthropology, and history. Archaeology is notably absent. For the most part, ethnohistorians seem uncomfortable with raw archaeological data. Most do not know how to "read" a site; most cannot make heads or tails of the multiple tables and graphs portraying archaeological phases, seriations, ceramic types, and so on. Although they seek out and read archaeological reports and essays, many have trouble deciphering their importance and relating them to their own work. Moreover, I fear that many American ethnohistorians are reluctant to study archaeology because of the ongoing controversy between many Native groups and archaeologists. Given the current state of enthnohistory in the Southeast, and despite a few recent efforts to incorporate archaeology, most ethnohistorians continue to use archaeological data sparingly—and then only to verify or contest the documentary record. Their questions are not derived from archaeology, nor is archaeology integral to their arguments.

But the problems are more than those arising from separate methods and training. There are also deep conceptual problems that derive from the long and complicated intellectual disconnect between prehistory and history, which I can only summarize here. As the western academy formed in the nineteenth century, the study of Native people fell to anthropology, which was, as a discipline, decidedly ahistorical for much of its own history. Thus, conventional history failed to consider American Indians and other non-Western people in their narrative, and anthropologists failed to historicize Native life. In short, anthropology took the "savage slot" and history chose to not deal with Natives (Trouillot 1991). The result was the construction of Native people as *Other*, people existing outside of history, unchanging, static, bounded cultural entities, subject to natural laws and not to the forces of history. As we have seen, in the last twenty or so years, however, scholars have begun to reconsider and rectify this construction, and in the process anthropologists are beginning to find their way out of the savage slot. They have joined with historians to historicize Native peoples and more recently have turned to world systems and globalization theory to take a hard look at the colonial and modern experiences of Native people. Today, American Indians are usually included in American histories, and one can no longer portray American Indians as static, unchanging, and passive "people without history" (Wolf 1990).

Anthropology seems to be finally finding its way out of the savage slot, but as Charles R. Cobb (2005) recently noted, archaeology has inherited it. Cobb (2005:563) acknowledges that the scholarship to understand the forces of modernism, capitalism, and globalization on Native societies has gone far in deconstructing the Native as *Other*, but he insists that this has been done "at the expense of reifying a homogenized past of traditional, static societies." In other words, for many nonarchaeologists, the prehistoric past of Indigenous people was a time of unchanging, traditional, premodern ways. Cobb further argues that anthropologists and historians uncritically use this static concept of prehistory as a baseline for measuring the impact of colonialism and thus conclude that the changes in Native life only occurred once Europeans set things in motion. All of this serves to reinscribe the notion of an unchanging, traditional prehistory. As Cobb puts it, we, in fact, have not dismantled the *Other*, we have simply construed it into a *pre-Columbian Other*. Cobb goes on to demonstrate archaeology's complicity in this conundrum, but he then offers an archaeological solution by drawing on recent innovations in the study of the history of Southeastern Mississippian chiefdoms to show that change, migration, displacement, and what he calls "emplacement" were at work long before Europeans came on the scene.

The developments of the Mississippian Period summarized above by Cobb link to recent development in Southeastern Indian Contact Era studies. For example, recent work by Southeastern archeologists Ned Jenkins and Amanda Regnier on the origins of the Creek Confederacy indicates that the confederacy initially coalesced in the seventeenth century around chiefdoms on the Alabama, Tallapoosa, and Chattahoochee rivers (Jenkins 2009; Regnier 2006a, 2006b, 2009). These chiefdoms were founded before contact by the descendants of the Middle Mississippian chiefdoms of Moundville and Etowah after they declined. The Alabama, Tallapoosa, and Chattahoochee chiefdoms collapsed sometime in the late sixteenth/early seventeenth centuries, most likely due to the disruptions caused by Soto's expedition and also subsequent disease episodes. However, unlike other collapsed chiefdoms, Native peoples remained in these river valleys. Here, they began to take in migrants from more distant chiefdoms that were also breaking apart after the disintegration of Contact Era chiefdoms, such as Coosa, Mabila, Apafalaya, and perhaps others. Archaeological evidence also indicates that all of these more distant chiefdoms had pre-Contact associations with the Tallapoosa and Chattahoochee chiefdoms, some perhaps originating during the Middle Mississippian Period. All of this indicates that in the case of the Creeks, when the Mississippian world began to fall apart during the Contact Era, people reformulated their social alliances along pre-Contact lines.

In fact, if Jenkins and Regnier are correct, coalescence may not have been invented during the Contact Era and may have been employed as a reorganizing device throughout the Mississippian Period as chiefdoms rose and fell. The outcome of a coalescence during the Mississippian Period was the formation of a new, "multiethnic" chiefdom.

In the post-Contact colonial world, however, the old chiefdom structures could not work, and the outcome of coalescence during the Historic Period was a different kind of political order. Works such as those of Jenkins and Regnier sketch a history of Native life from the Middle Mississippian Period into the late Colonial Period, informing our understanding of the late eighteenth-, early nineteenth-, and even twentieth-century Creek Confederacy. This is indeed deep history.

This example of Mississippian chiefdom histories, Contact Era coalescence, long-term Indian alliances, and the emergence of colonial Indian polities is intended to demonstrate that the issues surrounding what happened during the Contact Era require one to look on both sides of the divide, and force the nonarchaeologist as well as the archaeologist to look at prehistory in a new way (Lightfoot 1995). In part, many questions relating to the Contact Era concern single events set within the larger contexts of the European invasion. They are matters that relate to the workings of the Mississippian world, as well as to processes, trends and structures of the *longue durée*. Such questions cannot be answered solely by either archaeological or documentary evidence. Equally they cannot be addressed by merely using first one line of evidence and then another. Rather, we must strive for a true synthesis—conceptual and methodological—because only a synthetic approach can give us the mechanisms and processes by which disintegration, integration, and coalescence took place. Such a synthesis may be, as Charles Hudson recently remarked, "akin to joining the edge of a piece of silk cloth to the edge of a sheet of aluminum" (Pluckhahn et al. 2006:20). Be that as it may, the state of the field of Southeastern Indian studies today is such that we are ready to stitch this suture as we turn our attention to investigating both the proximate and ultimate causes for the transformation of the Southeastern Indians during the Contact Era.

SECTION III

Climatic Influences and Impacts

5

The Role of Climate in Early Spanish–Native American Interactions in the US Southwest

Carla R. Van West, Thomas C. Windes, Frances Levine, Henri D. Grissino-Mayer, and Matthew W. Salzer

Archaeologists describe and reconstruct past environments for two reasons. First, we describe the physical setting, climate, and environmental resources of a particular area and time period because they convey a mental image to our readers and form the background for subsequent narratives and interpretations. Second and more importantly, we reconstruct past environmental conditions because we know that factors such as the length of a growing season or access to dependable water often establish the limits within which a given set of human behaviors can occur. After environmental reconstructions are developed, we attempt to identify the economic opportunities, constraints, options, and risks present to various human groups, given their economic organization, technological capabilities, and population characteristics.

We describe in this chapter how we reconstructed past climate in the Middle Rio Grande basin of north-central New Mexico during the sixteenth and seventeenth centuries. We then describe how climate variation likely influenced natural resource productivity and food production in the Middle Rio Grande basin, which, in turn, influenced living conditions for its Indigenous populations and non-Native explorers. Although we understand that climate was but one of a number of important factors that influenced the events of the Spanish entrada (A.D. 1539–1598) and Early Colonial periods (A.D. 1598–1680), we contend that extremes in climate played a decisive role in permitting or inhibiting sustainable settlement for both Natives and newcomers.

Background: Why the Middle Rio Grande Basin?

Following orders issued by Captain General Francisco Vázquez de Coronado to explore lands to the east of the Cíbola province, Captain

Hernando de Alvarado and a party of twenty-three men-at-arms, an unknown number of Indian allies, and at least one Catholic priest were led from Hawikku by Pecos Pueblo emissaries to the Tiguex province along the Middle Rio Grande valley in early September 1540 (Flint 2008:130). What these explorers found was the largest concentration of settlements anywhere in Tierra Nueva—some twelve closely spaced pueblos stretching from what is now Albuquerque north to Bernalillo along both sides of the Rio Grande, housing many thousands of people. Within months, the remainder of Vázquez de Coronado's large expeditionary force at Hawikku had moved to the Tiguex province. There, they took up residence in and around at least one of the province's largest villages, Coofor (Flint 2008:141–144), after displacing its Native inhabitants and forcibly appropriating its stores of food, clothing, and fuel. These actions, as others in this volume discuss (Flint and Flint, this volume; Mathers, this volume), initiated the process of population dispersal, settlement abandonment, and demographic collapse in the Middle Rio Grande Valley from which these pueblo populations never fully recovered. This chapter, then, focuses its efforts on the reconstruction of climate in that portion of the Middle Rio Grande basin that was home to the Southern Tiwa-speaking peoples of Tiguex province.

The Study Area: The Middle Rio Grande Basin

Setting

The Rio Grande flows 1,887 miles from southwestern Colorado to the Gulf of Mexico and drains a basin of approximately 637,137 square kilometers. In its course, it traverses four geomorphic provinces of the United States and Mexico. Within central New Mexico, the lands bordering the river are assigned to the Mexican Highland or Basin and Range geomorphic province. This reach of the Rio Grande is referred to as the Middle Rio Grande Basin (MRGB), and it extends from the area near present-day Cochiti Lake and Cochiti Pueblo on the north to present-day Elephant Butte Reservoir near Truth or Consequences on the south. Within the MRGB are contained two subbasins—the Santo Domingo basin to the north, and the Albuquerque–Belen basin to the south—and numerous north–south oriented mountain ranges. Elevations range from about 1,524 m along the river to 3,255 m at Sandia Crest. The Tiguex pueblos occupied the northern portion of the Albuquerque–Belen basin.

Climate

The climate of the MRGB is arid overall and characterized by a summer dominant precipitation pattern. Elevation strongly controls the amount of moisture received. Whereas the lowland basins of the MRGB typically receive between about 230 to 300 mm of total precipitation per year, the upland ranges receive an average annual total of between 380 and 560 mm. Precipitation is delivered unevenly throughout the year, with more than half of the annual total delivered during the period between July and October as brief, heavy, and spatially patchy thunderstorms. These summer and early autumn monsoonal storms develop as moist air over the Gulf of Mexico is brought inland from the southeast in response to the shifting position of the Bermuda High Pressure Zone. In contrast, late fall, winter, and spring storms derive from moisture over the eastern Pacific Ocean, and these are greatly influenced by the periodic occurrence of the El Niño/Southern Oscillation (ENSO) phenomena. Under average, non-ENSO conditions, winter storms are prolonged, light, and widespread, due to the fact that they drop most of their moisture over more western regions before they reach the MRGB. However, when the ENSO is in its warm phase (El Niño), considerable amounts of moisture can be delivered to central New Mexico during the normally cool season as snow and in the warm season as heavy monsoons. In contrast, when the ENSO is in its cold phase (La Niña), areas that normally receive winter and/or summer moisture can experience extended periods of little to no moisture.

Monthly and annual temperature trends in the MRGB are similar to monthly and annual temperature trends elsewhere in the US Southwest. Average monthly temperatures are lowest in January (mean minimum ranging from −7 to −5°C) and highest in July (mean maximum ranging from 33 to 34°C). The length of the average frost/freeze period ranges from about 204 days near Bernalillo (April 17 to October 22) to 220 days near Albuquerque (April 1 to Nov 19), with each station having a sufficient number of Corn Growing Degree Days (CGDD)[1] to bring corn plants to maturity. The average May 1 through September 30 "growing season" for corn in the northern portion of the Albuquerque–Belen basin ranges from 2,939 CGDD units in Bernalillo to 3,241 CGDD units farther south in Albuquerque—well above the minimum threshold of 2,500 CGDD units needed for successful corn harvests (Adams et al. 2006). North of the Albuquerque–Belen basin, growing-season moisture increases but CGDDs decrease, whereas south of the basin, growing-season moisture decreases but CGDDs increase.

Pre-Contact Farming Practices

Not long after arriving in the Tiguex province, Captain Alvarado sent a message to General Vázquez de Coronado, describing the valley as, "wide, level, and fertile, planted with cornfields," and its inhabitants as "excellent, more like farmers than warriors" and having "much food: corn, beans, melons, and turkey in great abundance" (Flint and Flint 2005:305–306). The message was the signal that the general needed to hear; there was a good land not far away where he and his large expedition could come and survive the winter (Flint and Flint 2005:303). Alvarado clearly was describing the Middle Rio Grande Valley in a successful year when the various Native crops were beginning to ripen. But what foods other than corn, beans, and melons (probably pumpkin-type squash) were being grown, where, and by what methods? We simply do not know from this earliest eyewitness account.

Archaeological evidence from late prehistoric and early historic sites in Albuquerque suggests that the inhabitants of the Tiguex region were subsistence farmers whose agricultural way of life revolved around the intensive cultivation of corn, beans, squash, and cotton. These basic items were supplemented by the procurement of numerous weedy annuals (e.g., goosefoot, pigweed, purslane) and a variety of seasonally and locally available grass seeds, piñon nuts, fruits, and succulents (Toll 1992).

Researchers have not found reliable evidence that the Tiguex communities and other northern Rio Grande Pueblo peoples constructed large-scale, Iberian-type irrigation systems prior to sustained Spanish settlement (Anschuetz 1998; Biella and Chapman 1977a; Wozniak 1987).

Researchers currently working in the MRGB, however, increasingly suspect that many small-scale and rather ephemeral irrigation systems once existed along the Rio Grande (Kurt Anschuetz, Eileen Camilli, and Scott Worman, personal communication 2010). Anschuetz and Worman both draw on Espejo's 1582 observations that Piro communities near present-day Socorro planted corn, beans, calabashes, and other crops dependent on seasonal rainfall or irrigation from ditches, and that sandy stretches along both sides of the Rio Grande were cultivated (Hammond and Rey 1966:220–221). Based on his research near the MRGB site of Alameda Pueblo, Worman (2009) hypothesizes that these small, expediently constructed canals diverted water from the braided channels of the Rio Grande and irrigated fields at the floodplain margins. He also suggests that these systems were highly productive, sustained large MRGB populations, and were critical for food production during periods of drought.

In landscape positions above the floodplains, researchers suggest that many ingenious farming techniques were used to grow crops in diverse settings where stored soil moisture and harvested floodwater could be used to augment the patchy and often unreliable summer rains. Fields made productive by means of agricultural features (e.g., terraces, grids, gravel mulch) and strategic positioning (e.g., at arroyo mouths, at the base of gentle slopes, oriented toward or away from strong sunlight) were located in both upland and lowland settings. These strategies can be classified as forms of dryland, runoff, floodwater, and water-table agriculture, as well as hand-water "kitchen gardens" (Doolittle 2000; Doolittle and Mabry 2006). Locating fields in this way helped to reduce the risk of significant food shortfalls in any given year resulting from the often unpredictable occurrence of droughts, floods, midseason frosts, and short growing seasons.

Methods: Reconstructing Climate in the Middle Rio Grande Basin

Two existing and independent tree-ring chronologies were used to reconstruct annual precipitation and temperature patterns in the MRGB. The precipitation reconstruction (MRGB, A.D. 622–1992) was prepared by Grissino-Mayer et al. (2002) using a tree-ring chronology constructed from several species of long-lived conifer trees[2] from the Sandia Mountains east of Albuquerque, the Magdalena Mountains west of Socorro, and the lava fields of El Malpais National Monument south of Grants. The San Francisco Peaks temperature reconstruction (SFP, 663 B.C. to A.D. 1992) was developed by Salzer (2000a) based on an upper-elevation tree-ring chronology comprised solely of bristlecone pine[3] growing on the San Francisco Peaks near Flagstaff, Arizona.

For each tree-ring chronology, Grissino-Mayer et al. (2002), Salzer (2000a), and Salzer and Kipfmueller (2005) used standard methods to create or update their chronology (Fritts 1976; Stokes and Smiley 1996). This involved sample collection and preparation, cross-dating, measurement, as well as statistical verification for accuracy of measurement and cross-dating procedures. In addition, standardization of each ring-width series was accomplished through a curve-fitting process that removed age- and size-related variability and retained climate-related variability in the resulting tree-ring indices. Finally, all of the tree-ring series were combined using a mean value function to create an overall mean site chronology. Thereafter, statistical tests of modern climate and tree-growth studies were conducted with the goal of producing mathematical equations that would allow them to estimate the climate variable they wished to retrodict. The interested reader is urged to consult the dissertation research of Grissino-Mayer (1995, 1996) and Salzer (2000a), the articles by Salzer (2000b) and by Salzer and Kipfmueller (2005), and the report issued by Grissino-Mayer et al. (2002) for the MRGB reconstruction for a complete description of methods used to build each chronology and to develop their respective dendroclimatic reconstructions. Underlying both of these dendroclimatic reconstructions is the statistically demonstrated relationship that tree growth is strongly associated with climate (Fritts 1976; Fritts et al. 1965). It is this basic principle that allows dendrochronologists to transform the trends in tree-ring chronologies into reconstructions of given climate variables once tested and verified.

We use the MRGB chronology to represent local precipitation trends within the MRGB and the SFP chronology to represent regional temperature trends. As a first step, we converted the annual MRGB precipitation values expressed as Palmer Drought Severity Indexes (PDSI)[4] and the SFP temperature values expressed as mean maximum annual temperature values to standard deviation units (*Z*-scores)[5] so as to make these two datasets comparable (Appendix A). Second, we plotted these reconstructed values against the actual annual values recorded for the longest and most reliable weather station in the northern portion of the Albuquerque–Belen basin—the Albuquerque WSFO Airport (Station 29024). This was done to evaluate whether or not we were justified in using these two chronologies as proxies of past climate in the Middle Rio Grande Valley. Satisfied that the MRGB and SFP chronologies were reasonable proxies of past climate trends, we then plotted the annual values and trends displayed in these two chronologies to help us understand in what ways the sixteenth and seventeenth centuries may have differed from other centuries in the last millennium. Finally, we paired and plotted these two climate records and annotated these graphs with significant historic events as they are currently known for the sixteenth and seventeenth centuries. With these data we are able not only to characterize climate during these two centuries relative to preceding or subsequent centuries but also to identify specific years and intervals when climate conditions were unusual in their magnitude or duration. For example, periods of either extreme or persistent warmth or coolness, coupled with either drought or relative wetness, have likely consequences for crop growth, food supply, human health, and sustainable settlement. Observations recorded in dated historic documents are used to support or refute the overall accuracy of these reconstructions.

Results: Correlating Climate and Human History in North-Central New Mexico Moisture Variation

The first half of the sixteenth century was moderately moist, fairly predictable from year to year, and favorable for crop production (see Figure 5.1a). Immediately after the single wettest multiyear interval during the last millennium (1553–1557), however, climate conditions rapidly and dramatically deteriorated in the MRGB. What resulted was the most severe and persistent multidecadal drought in the entire reconstruction (1571–1593, although it started earlier and continued later). The most pronounced period of this long drought has been referred to as

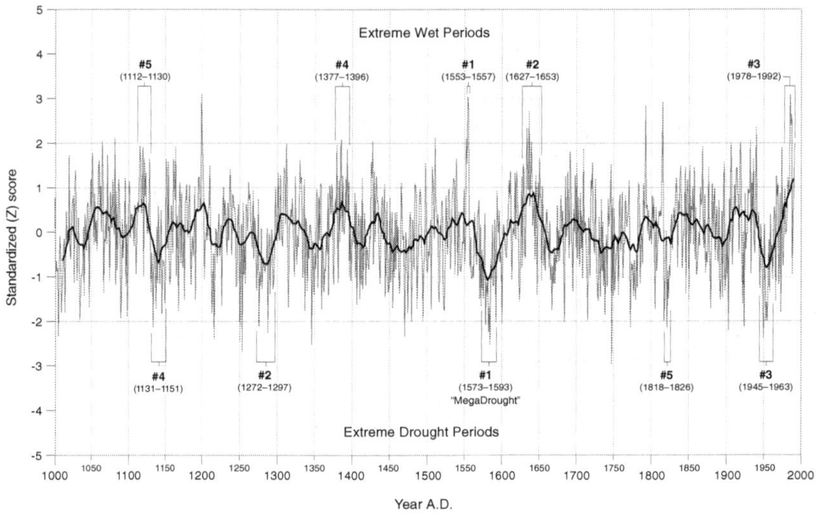

FIGURE 5.1A. Reconstructed PDSIs (reexpressed as *Z*-scores) for the Middle Rio Grande Basin, New Mexico, for the period between A.D. 1000 and 1992. PDSIs are proxy values for precipitation. Needles are reconstructed annual values; trend line is a twenty-year, standard, weighted, running mean. The five most extreme wet and dry intervals in the millennium are identified (Grissino-Mayer et al. 2002:1, Table 4, Table 5).

the "megadrought" of the last one thousand years, and it appears in many North American tree-ring chronologies (e.g., Blanton, this volume; D'Arrigo and Jacoby 1991; Hughes and Brown 1992; Stahle et al. 2000; Woodhouse and Overpeck 1998). Historians, anthropologists, geographers, and medical researchers, among others, have associated the effects of the sixteenth-century megadrought with numerous cases of famine, disease, significant environment change, and dramatic population declines across the United States and Mexico (e.g., Acuna-Soto et al. 2002; Marr and Kiracofe 2000; Stahle et al. 1998).

In contrast, the seventeenth century was unusually wet. Beginning in 1606 and lasting until 1713, the MRGB was favorably moist, with one pronounced period of extreme wetness between 1627 and 1653. Only one interval of prolonged drought, from 1664 through 1674, punctuates the record of moisture. Nevertheless, year-to-year predictability in precipitation was quite low in the first half of the century, despite the increase

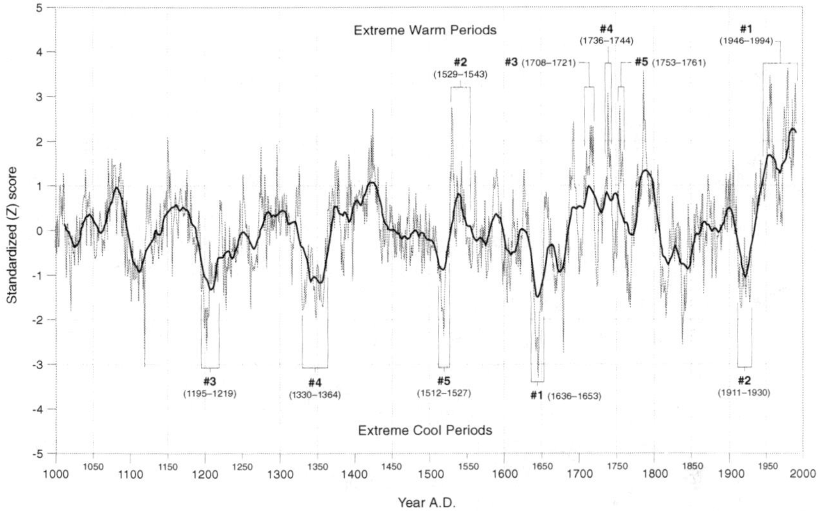

FIGURE 5.1B. Reconstructed mean maximum annual temperature (re-expressed as *Z*-scores) on the San Francisco Peaks, Arizona, for the time period between A.D. 1000 and 1992. Needles are reconstructed annual values; trend line is a twenty-year, standard, weighted, running mean. The five most extreme warm and cool intervals in the millennium are identified (Salzer 2000:Table 7).

in moisture over the previous century. Year-to-year predictability returned in the second half of the century.

Temperature Variation

The sixteenth century was moderately cool overall. Two brief intervals of extended warmth occurred, however, the first dating from 1529 to 1543 and a second dating from 1586 to 1593 (see Figure 5.1b). The longest and coldest interval of the sixteenth century took place between 1512 and 1527. This sixteen-year-long interval of cool growing seasons, however, was minor in comparison to the severe cool-to-cold conditions that persisted for most of the seventeenth century.

The seventeenth century began cool (1599–1612), then warmed for fifteen years, and thereafter plunged into the most extreme cold interval for the entire one-thousand-year period. An extended interval of coolness persisted from 1636 to 1683, with very few individual warm years. Annual mean maximum temperature only began to approach normal and warmer-than-normal after 1684. This cold period's most extreme expression took place between 1636 and 1653, which Salzer (2000:187) identified as the single coldest interval during the last millennium. Salzer (106–126) suggests that numerous and strong volcanic eruptions occurring between 1599 and 1683 released gases and ash of a sufficient quantity to significantly reduce sunlight and contribute to global cooling. Although he does not suggest that volcanism caused the seventeenth-century cool period, he does suggest that large volcanic events at least enhanced the persistent temperature effect. Other researchers (e.g., Eddy 1981) have suggested that this intense cool period is a response to a long period of sunspot minima known as the Maunder Minimum (A.D. 1645–1715). Whatever the atmospheric and terrestrial causes, there is no question that the mid-seventeenth century cold period was severe and widespread.

A Combined Record of Precipitation and Temperature

When we overlay these two tree-ring reconstructions, we are able to examine the paleoclimatic record in yet a different, and perhaps more interpretable, manner. Figures 5.2a–5.2d represent the combined records of reconstructed precipitation and temperature for the MRGB. Each annotated graph portrays the annual trends for a fifty-year period of time.

Figure 5.2a depicts the first half of the sixteenth century. The fairly persistent coolness of the early 1500–1530 period gave way to two decades of unusual warmth between 1530 and 1550. It was during this period that Fray Marcos de Niza and Francisco Vázquez de Coronado ventured north to Tierra Nueva. Perhaps not coincidentally, Vázquez de Coronado's large expedition made its way north during one of the few exceptionally warm and wet intervals of the sixteenth century. Such conditions likely encouraged the warm-season growth of grass and browse that supported the many thousands of animals that accompanied the expedition. Similarly, the unusual combination of warm and wet climate probably encouraged the growth of corn and other crops for the Native peoples of the region. Nevertheless, the unusual wetness

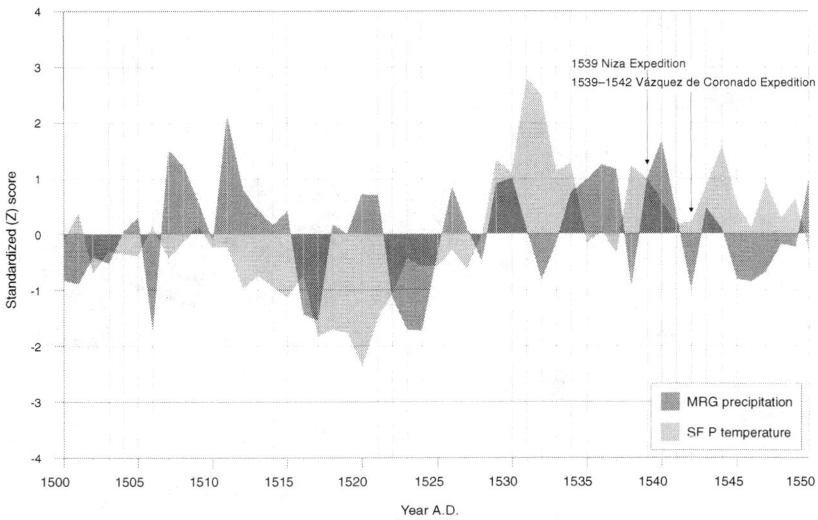

FIGURE 5.2A. Middle Rio Grande Basin climate, A.D. 1500–1550. Long-term mean is 0.00; each unit above and below the mean is equivalent to one standard deviation unit. Positive values represent increasing wetness and greater warmth. Negative values represent increasing drought and cold.

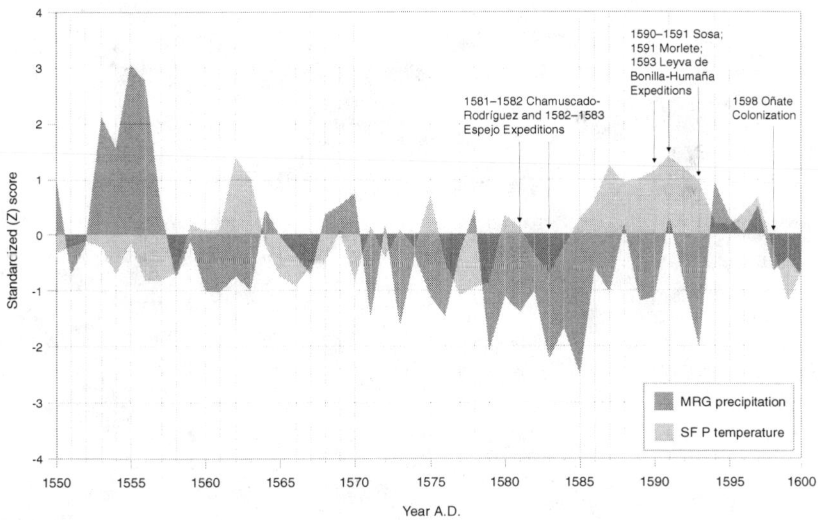

FIGURE 5.2B. Middle Rio Grande Basin climate, A.D. 1550–1600. Long-term mean is 0.00; each unit above and below the mean is equivalent to one standard deviation unit. Positive values represent increasing wetness and greater warmth. Negative values represent increasing drought and cold.

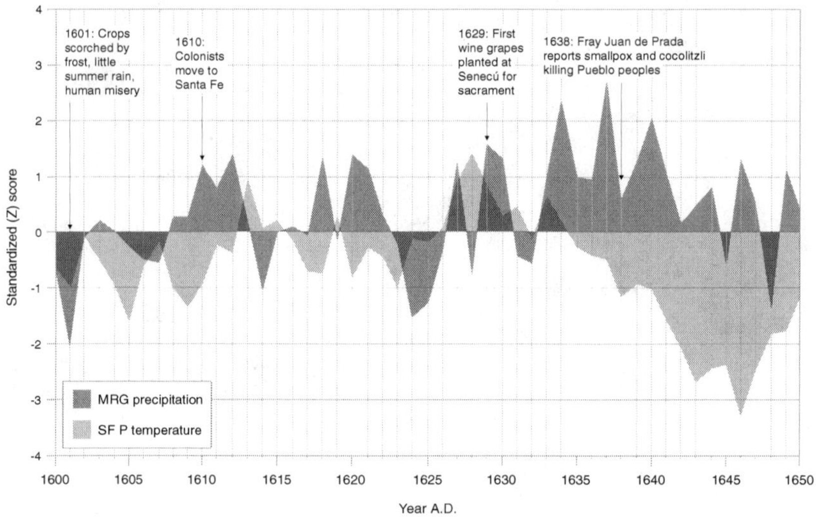

FIGURE 5.2C. Middle Rio Grande Basin climate, A.D. 1600–1650. Long-term mean is 0.00; each unit above and below the mean is equivalent to one standard deviation unit. Positive values represent increasing wetness and greater warmth. Negative values represent increasing drought and cold.

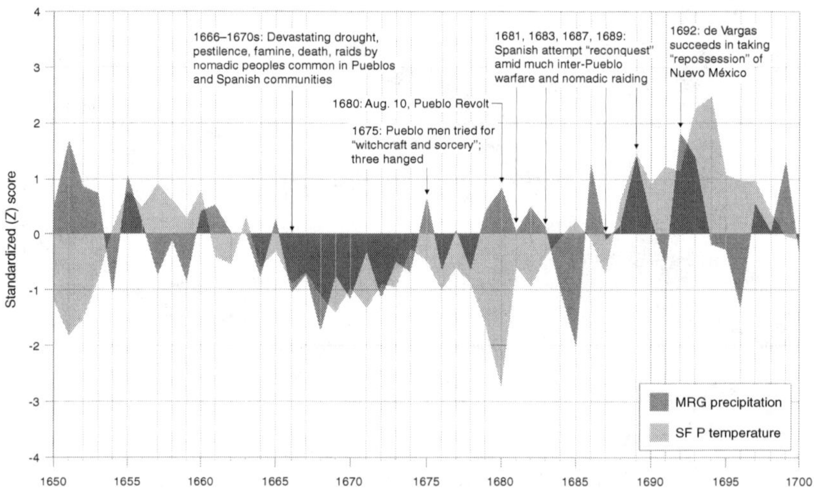

FIGURE 5.2D. Middle Rio Grande Basin climate, A.D. 1650–1700. Long-term mean is 0.00; each unit above and below the mean is equivalent to one standard deviation unit. Positive values represent increasing wetness and greater warmth. Negative values represent increasing drought and cold.

had its drawbacks; snowfall was probably greater, and summer monsoons may have been more intense, with the possibility of frequent floods and high water in normally low-flowing streams. Corroborative evidence from other paleoclimate records suggests this may have been so. For example, Quinn (1992, 1993) has reconstructed a record of strong El Niño events for the 1525–1987 period. His data suggest that years 1539, 1540, and 1541 experienced especially strong El Niños, which likely reached eastward to the MRGB. In addition, Richey and his colleagues (2007) have created a decadal-scale record of sea surface temperatures in the Gulf of Mexico using deep-sea cores and radiocarbon-dated foraminifera. The similarity of this foraminifera-based data set to the El Malpais tree-ring precipitation reconstruction (Grissino-Mayer 1995, 1996) suggests that both are proxy records for the history and strength of the summer monsoon (Poore et al. 2005).

Historic documents tell us that Vázquez de Coronado and his remaining party departed from the MRGB in April of 1542. With many of their villages greatly damaged by the large group of intruders, we can imagine that the remaining inhabitants of Tiguex vigorously attempted to cultivate the land and restock their once-large stores of corn, beans, squash, and cotton. Unfortunately for the Native peoples of this region, 1542 appears to have been warm and rather dry, and this moderate drought persisted for two decades.

Figure 5.2b depicts the second half of the sixteenth century. The deterioration in climate observed by both Grissino-Mayer et al. (2002) and Salzer (2000) is visible first as a cool and intensely wet interval between 1553 and 1557, followed by a dramatic trend toward arid conditions, often accompanied by cool weather. The sixteenth-century megadrought was near its maximum expression when Spanish explorers returned in 1581–1582 with the Chamuscado-Rodríguez and 1582–1583 Espejo parties. In those particular years, it was not only extraordinarily dry but also frequently cold—a climate condition that worked against raising successful crops in almost all landscape settings, high and low. When the Sosa, Morlete, and Leyva de Bonilla-Humaña expeditions of the 1590–1593 period arrived, they experienced the final warm and dry phase of the megadrought. That these expeditions were not particularly well received seems no surprise from an examination of the paleoclimate record. Native populations probably struggled to bring in a harvest, which was increasingly subject to raids from and theft by Plains Indian populations. Demands by outsiders, no matter how few, surely must have been unwelcome, although there are reports (cited by Schroeder and Matson 1965:145–160) that Sosa's party did receive food from various pueblos. Climate alone cannot explain why Oñate y Salazar and his colonists were able to establish a settlement near Ohkay Owingeh (San Juan Pueblo) in the Northern Rio Grande valley, but climate conditions likely contributed to the failure of the colony when colder conditions set in after 1598 (see below). Nonetheless, it is interesting to note that he and his party arrived after the only warm and wet interval of the late sixteenth century. Both this paleoenvironmental reconstruction and historic documents show that the Northern and Middle Rio Grande valley was cold and dry by the time they arrived, and these conditions continued for the next four years.

Figure 5.2c depicts the first half of the seventeenth century. The few years of occupation near the Pueblo of Ohkay Owingeh were years of great hardship for Oñate y Salazar and his colonists. Barrett (2002:17, citing Hammond and Rey 1953:696) describes a letter written to the viceroy by Fray Juan Escalona for supplies. Escalona tells the viceroy that frost had scorched the corn fields that year, and in recent years, drought had caused the fields to dry up. As a result, he writes that in the three years the Spaniards had been in New Mexico, they had consumed all the maize that the Pueblo Indians had stored during the previous six years. Although the colonists did experience relief from the extreme cold drought by 1603, the climate of the early 1600s was often cool and wet. A brief warm and wet interval from 1626 to 1631 permitted the successful cultivation of wine grapes in at least the southern MRGB pueblo of Senecú in 1629. By 1635, though, conditions took a turn for the worse, and a long interval of extremely cold and wet conditions set in. Numerous reports of epidemic disease and death are recorded by midcentury; the total census of Pueblo population was only a fraction of what Alvarado saw in 1540.

Figure 5.2d depicts the second half of the seventeenth century. Midcentury wet and cold conditions were broken by a decade or so of relatively benign conditions that alternated between warm-wet and warm-dry climate (A.D. 1654–1663). But in 1664 the MRGB apparently experienced one of the most severe and persistent cold droughts in the entire millennium. These harsh conditions initiated around 1664 and continued, almost unbroken, through 1678. As with the cold drought of 1598–1603, this extremely cold and dry interval resulted in much suffering for the inhabitants of central and northern New Mexico. Hackett (1923–1937:17) cited historical documents describing the famine that beset the Pueblo Indians and the Spaniards, who only escaped starvation by eating hides and the straps of carts that they prepared as food, boiling them with what little corn, herbs, and roots they could find. Hackett also cited reports that a great "pestilence" had killed many people and cattle by 1671. It was during this period of environmental strife that Governor Treviño tried forty-seven Pueblo men in 1675 and hanged three for practicing religious rituals that Spanish colonists believed were witchcraft and sorcery (Hackett and Shelby 1942:xxii). By the end of the 1670s, total Pueblo population in New Mexico had diminished markedly and many pueblos were abandoned, including all in the Estancia basin and most in the Albuquerque–Belen basin (Barrett 2002:67–70; but see Ramenofsky and Kulisheck, this volume).

The Pueblo Revolt of August 10, 1680, took place after nearly two decades of unimaginable hardship. Adverse climatic conditions that negatively impacted agricultural endeavors; devastating epidemics; massive population decline; constant raiding; Spanish policies related to population aggregation, tribute, and Native religious practices; and growing intolerance on the part of Native populations coalesced in the successful routing of the colonists and Spanish sympathizers from New Mexico (Barrett 2002). Although there was sufficient cause for staging such a coup well before the late summer of 1680, we suspect that a particularly destructive freeze took place that summer and may have contributed to the timing of the revolt. The evidence for this crop-damaging freeze takes the form of a "frost ring" that appears not only in the SFP temperature chronology but also in other high-elevation tree-ring series in western North America. According to Salzer (2000:91), frost-damaged rings displaying cellular damage from ice formation develop during the growing season of a tree when at least two nights of subfreezing temperatures occur. If this happens early in the growing season, then the earlywood (large, thin-walled cells) of the tree is affected. In contrast, if a hard freeze occurs later in the tree's growing season, the damage will take place in the latewood (smaller, thick-walled cells that show up at the outer margin of the tree's annual ring). Thereafter, with improved weather conditions, the tree continues to grow and produce new wood. Given that bristlecone pines in the Rocky Mountain region put on new growth from late June to late August or early September (Salzer 2000:92), we suspect that this destructive frost took place at a point in the corn-growing season when it was too late to replant at lower elevations.[6] The frost-damaged section of the SFP ring of 1680 is located within or near the latewood rather than in the earlywood. It is likely that this destructive freeze took place in early August during a year *and* a multiyear interval of exceptional cold. Our guess is that this "event" was a contributing factor to the timing of the revolt.

Concluding Remarks: The Role of Climate in Early Spanish–Native American Interactions in North-Central New Mexico

Our review of this paleoclimatic record suggests that different types of multiyear periods described as either "warm and wet," "cold and wet," "warm and dry," and "cold and dry" often have outcomes that can be anticipated. Multiyear intervals that were both relatively warm and wet are rare in this reconstruction. Of all combinations of temperature and precipitation trends, these last are the most favorable for aboriginal Pueblo subsistence. In the MRGB, farming both on the Rio Grande floodplain and adjacent valley slopes would have been possible. Although the typical spring runoff may have been larger than usual, warmer-than-normal conditions may have lessened the limiting effects of cool air drainage in the floodplain and encouraged the use of small-scale irrigation systems. In upland settings, such as Albuquerque's West Mesa, enhanced precipitation would have allowed recharge of soil moisture and facilitated summer runoff irrigation. We suspect that when warm and wet conditions prevailed, successful crop production was possible in many settings using a variety of agricultural water-harvesting techniques, surplus could be generated and stored, and long journeys to Tierra Nueva with many participants and livestock were possible. These were the climate conditions surrounding the Vázquez de Coronado expedition of 1539–1542, the initial arrival of Oñate y Salazar and his colonists in 1598, and even the "reconquest" by Vargas in 1692.

Multiyear intervals characterized by moderate to extreme cold accompanied by wetness are far more frequent in this paleoclimate record. Successful harvests would have been possible only from well-chosen locations with good drainage protected from the adverse effects of cold air flowing down from the Sandia Mountains into the fertile river valley. Cool and wet conditions would favor crop production in upland settings where direct precipitation supplemented by runoff irrigation was possible but would thwart successful agricultural production in the floodplain. Planting in the floodplain would have been delayed until after the spring floods diminished and temperatures rose sufficiently to support seed germination. Furthermore, the total acreage of arable settings and the possibility of producing significant crop surpluses likely would have been reduced. We also suspect that the intensity and duration of these two conditions influenced health as well as economic conditions for all inhabitants of the region. For example, when persistently wet and intensely cold conditions prevailed, disease, illness, and crop failures were not uncommon. Such was the case of the long cold and wet period of 1635–1653, when Father Juan de Prada reported in 1635 that New Mexico was a land of extremes in cold and heat (Hackett 1923–1937:108), and that Pueblo people were dying of smallpox and cocoliztli; Acuna-Soto et al. (2002) interpret this disease to be hemorrhagic viral fever.

We also note that multiyear droughts were common during these two centuries. Prolonged warm-dry periods, as well as cold-dry periods, were particularly frequent in the sixteenth century. During these two centuries, droughts usually lasted from six to eleven years, but a few were longer. Depending on their magnitude and duration, the effects of these droughts varied considerably. Although warm droughts could be very severe, harvests usually could have been secured from fields in the Rio Grande floodplain using small-scale irrigation techniques. It is likely, however, that the quantity of floodplain fields was diminished, given the reduced number and altered distribution of braided channels within the Rio Grande. These same warm-dry conditions would have extensively limited production in arable upland settings due to low soil moisture and fewer runoff events.

In contrast, cold droughts added more constraints associated with short growing seasons, growing-season frosts, and problems associated with cold-air drainage in lowland settings. Cold and dry conditions impeded successful aboriginal crop production in all landscape positions.[7] Although floodplain settings had access to irrigation water, low temperatures, shortened growing seasons, and the ever-present danger of crop-killing frosts were significant hindrances. Arable settings in the uplands probably suffered from a lack of winter-moisture recharge needed for seed germination and early growth, as well as summer moisture, which was required for tasseling, silking, and continuous growth. Historical documents written during drought periods suggest that suffering was greatest during the cold droughts. The best example of a prolonged cold drought was the one that occurred in the 1664–1678 interval, when open display of traditional ceremonies to rebalance the world and bring warmth and moisture resulted in the trial and hanging of Pueblo leaders in 1675.

By pairing two independent, statistically verified tree-ring chronologies (see Appendix A) and comparing them to historic reports, we have been able to reconstruct a paleoclimate record for the sixteenth and seventeenth centuries in the MRGB. As students of human behavior, we readily acknowledge that the relationship between culture and environment is complex. We do not propose that climatic conditions determined any particular outcome. Instead, we suggest that complicated interactions among environmental, behavioral, and demographic factors (Dean 1988, 1996) operating in the 1500s and 1600s in what is now New Mexico resulted in the events recorded in the historical documents of the period. Weather conditions that influenced the abundance or dearth of food resources and other critical economic resources most certainly should be considered in the mix of factors that help historians and anthropologists explain cultural events.

Acknowledgments

We wish to thank Richard Poore for sharing his Gulf of Mexico foraminifera data with us, Cindy Elsner Hayward for preparing our figures for publication, and our colleagues Kurt Anschuetz, Jeff Dean, Ron Towner, and Scott Worman for carefully reading our draft and providing important comments that improved its content.

6

The Factors of Climate and Weather in Sixteenth-Century La Florida

Dennis B. Blanton

While the Southeastern United States does not share the reputation of the arid Southwest as a place of climatic extremes, recent experience in the region reminds us that historical averages do not imply a steady state. Severe drought in the last few years has sorely tested the sustainability of modern human systems in the Southeast, and with the benefit of a paleoclimatic record extending many centuries back, it is amply clear that periodic, extended deviations from the average condition are the norm (Cook et al. 2007; Seager et al. 2009). Moreover, it is evident from historical and archaeological sources that drought and other climate-related conditions sometimes challenged human societies (Blanton 2000, 2004; Blanton and Thomas 2008; Pauketat 2007; Saunders 2000; Stahle et al. 1998; Worth 1999).

In this chapter I will describe the paleoclimatic record for the Southeast, focusing first on sixteenth-century conditions in today's south Atlantic states of South Carolina, Georgia, and Florida, as well as in the Gulf coastal states and the lower Mississippi River valley. My summary will only review briefly the detailed record teased from diverse, proxy sources such as tree rings, chemical isotopes, and historical documents. Yet, impressively, they extend our reach backward about one thousand years, sometimes with interannual precision. Readers will discover that the region experienced a range of climate and weather extremes during the sixteenth century, and I offer examples of the ways climate and weather affected or could have affected early exploration and settlement in the Southeast. In the process, I seek to impart a sense of the complexity surrounding human responses to those conditions.

Overview of Climate Trends in the Sixteenth-Century Southeast

Few proxy sources of paleoclimatic information inform us specifically on conditions in the Southeast. A host of reconstructions, however, address broader trends, mainly at the hemispheric scale (Briffa et al. 1998; Mann 2001a, 2001b; Mann et al. 1998, 2000). While we must not overstate the relevance of these records, it is appropriate to judiciously take their trends into account. Thus, my presentation will progress from a discussion of generalized patterns, presently evident at only broad spatial or temporal scales, to those regional data sets exhibiting better precision.

Temperature patterns of the premodern era specific to the Southeast are difficult to establish precisely. For even a basic approximation we must consult reconstructions of low-frequency hemispheric patterns such as for solar irradiation or the incidence of volcanic eruptions. Recent estimations assign great influence to those two factors, since together they may account for 40–60 percent of reconstructed variability (Briffa et al. 1998; Crowley 2000; deMenocal 2001:668). Derived from fluctuating levels of radioactive isotopes, reconstructions of irradiance reveal multicentury, broad-scale trends like the so-called Medieval Warm (ca. A.D. 900–1300) and Little Ice Age (ca. A.D. 1400–1850) periods, as well as also shorter spans of warmer or cooler temperature (Fagan 2001; Mann 2001c, 2001d). Extrapolating from these sources, it is reasonable to propose that portions of the Southeast experienced cooler-than-average spells during the fifteenth through seventeenth centuries, as did most of the northern hemisphere. However, actual conditions would have varied across the region, especially from more northerly to more southerly latitudes.

Effects of volcanic eruptions in far-flung places can be consequential for the Southeast. The ash and gas that spew into the atmosphere affect air quality and, thus, levels of solar irradiation. As it happens, numerous major eruptions are documented around the world between the end of the sixteenth century and the end of the seventeenth century (Bradley and Jones 1995; Briffa et al. 1998; Robertson et al. 2001; Silva and Zielinski 1998). We would rightfully be dubious of the relevance of these events for the Southeast were it not for the case of the famous

Tambora eruption of 1815 in Indonesia. That eruption was cause for the infamous Year with No Summer in eastern North America, when it was reported as far south as Virginia and North Carolina that frost occurred in every month except August (Post 1977). Obviously such conditions would wreak havoc on food crops. A case in point for La Florida may be the great famine of the last decade of the seventeenth century (Bushnell 1994:184–185), likely attributable in part to the effects of three major eruptions in 1693–1694, one in Iceland, one in Indonesia, and one in Japan (Siebert and Simkin 2002). The latter part of the sixteenth century was marked by two powerful eruptions, one in Mexico in 1585 and one the next year in Indonesia. Their effects in the Southeast would have been most apparent over the subsequent year or two, when stratospheric aerosol concentrations were high and hemispheric temperatures fell (Briffa et al. 1998; Robertson et al. 2001).

A phenomenon known as the North Atlantic Oscillation (NAO), a pattern of atmospheric circulation linked with sea surface temperatures, also influences prevailing temperature in eastern North America, especially in wintertime (Durkee et al. 2007). A NAO reconstruction based on multiple proxies now extends back to A.D. 1400 (Cook et al. 2002) and reveals how cooler winter conditions were probably persistent in the eastern United States during the middle of the fifteenth century, the middle of the sixteenth century, and the latter half of the seventeenth century. Specifically during the sixteenth century, between 1521 and 1530 and between 1582 and 1589, the NAO was in a prominent positive mode conducive to warmer conditions. The NAO was strongly in the opposite mode, when cooler conditions would have likely prevailed, between 1503 and 1507 and for an extended period between 1560 and 1574, and then moderately so from 1534 to 1544. Modeling of NAO effects has established that they are more strongly felt at higher latitudes, but the phenomenon has some direct influence over Southeastern weather. The work of Durkee et al. (2007:59–61) documents, first, a strong correlation between positive NAO phases and "stronger than normal south-southeasterly flow of warm moist air into the southeastern US" and, second, that "more cold air intrusions into the southeastern region" occur during negative phases. Recent climate modeling also reveals how NAO teleconnections, especially in the positive (warm) phase and in conjunction with cool Pacific Ocean surface temperatures, may be a major driver in the incidence of large-scale "megadroughts" in North America (Cook et al. 2009; Feng et al. 2008).

The potential effects of the El Niño Southern Oscillation (ENSO) must also be considered since the southern United States has been described as a "prime ENSO-sensitive area" (Allan 2000:28; see also McCabe and Muller 2002:95) where the phenomenon seems to have an influence on regional temperature and precipitation, especially during the stronger events. In reconstructions back almost to A.D. 1500, the period of the sixteenth through mid-seventeenth centuries is recognized for especially frequent, strong ENSO events in the La Niña phase (Gergis and Fowler 2006:177; Ortlieb 2000; Quinn and Neal 1995). The La Niña phase is often cited as a factor suppressing rainfall in the subtropical Southeast (McCabe and Muller 2002:96), so Ortlieb's (2000) reconstruction identifying eighteen La Niña occurrences over this span, rated as extreme or very severe, may help explain why the era was prone to anomalous dryness. During one unusual period early in the sixteenth century, three extreme or very severe La Niña events occurred in short succession between 1528 and 1533. The El Niño phase of ENSO can have its own set of effects in the Southeast, usually cooler and wetter conditions in fall and winter (Allan 2000:31; Dettinger et al. 2000:119; McCabe and Muller 2002:96; Ropelewski and Halpert 1986; Seager et al. 2009). There is also indication that stormy conditions correlate positively with El Niño events in the Gulf region, especially in association with increased frontal activity, with the opposite pattern holding under La Niña conditions (McCabe and Muller 2002:100). No unusually strong El Niño events occurred during the sixteenth century, but moderately strong events developed at regular intervals, usually on the order of every ten to twenty years. Making the link between ENSO and precipitation patterns in the Southeast requires caution, however, as some of the latest models now describe the La Niña effect on winter precipitation as weak, and that of El Niño as suspect (Seager et al. 2009).

The highest quality reconstructions of past climate conditions are derived from dendroclimatological data and from historical documentary records. The region boasts several stands of ancient, living bald cypress trees, some of which exceed one thousand years in age, as well as old-growth pine, cedar, and oak up to several centuries in age, and

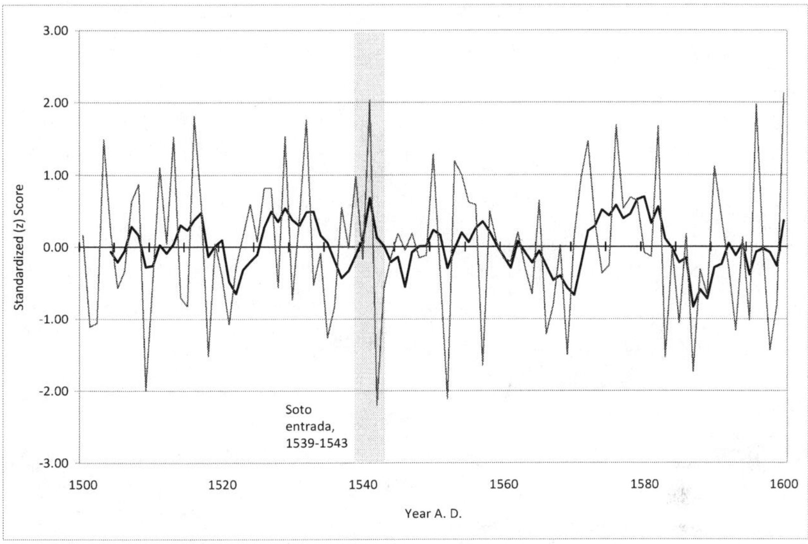

FIGURE 6.1. Tree-ring reconstructed spring-season precipitation record for the sixteenth century in North Carolina, South Carolina, and Georgia (after Stahle et al. 1992). Trend line represents five-year moving average and shaded bar brackets interval of the Soto entrada (A.D. 1539–1543).

these trees feature ring patterns that correlate closely with patterns of precipitation. University of Arkansas researchers, in particular, have compiled extended precipitation histories for many southeastern locations, the most prominent of which are found in North Carolina/Virginia, South Carolina/Georgia, and in the lower Mississippi River valley (Anderson et al. 1995; Blanton and Thomas 2008; Cleaveland 2000; Cook et al. 2007; Stahle 2006; Stahle and Cleaveland 1992; Stahle et al. 1985; Stahle et al. 1988; Stahle et al. 1998). In the aggregate, the records (Figure 6.1) give a sense of year-to-year patterns of growing season rainfall with very specific measures for particular data locales (Stahle and Cleaveland 1992). Calibrated against modern instrumental data, dendroclimatic time series are especially useful for gauging the spring rainfall patterns so critical for farming economies (Anderson 1994; Anderson et al. 1995). Continent-wide assessment is even possible now by means of an integrated North American Drought Atlas based on a network of hundreds of tree-ring data sets (Cook and Krusic 2004; Cook et al. 2008).

Traditionally, the Southwest has been the laboratory for climatologists and archaeologists seeking to explore the intersection of aridity and culture (Van West et al., this volume). However, stressful dry periods across the Southeast in recent years have drawn overdue attention to the causes of its own drought history (Seager et al. 2009). Studies confirm the sense that climate in the area has been punctuated by periodic spells of deep drought considerably worse than those experienced in living memory. In addition to extreme Medieval Warm Period dryness, the new analyses conclude that "a strong and uninterrupted drought occurred in the eastern plains between 1555 and 1574 and also affected the Southeast" (Seager et al. 2009:5039). The findings also reveal that the occurrence of drought in La Florida is linked to distinctive sets of factors. The oceanic–atmospheric–continental teleconnections that drive conditions elsewhere in North America have different or even nominal effects. Seager et al. (2009:5042) were left to conclude that while the causes of drought in the Southeast remain poorly known, it appears that the wintertime ENSO linkage is weak at best, and that they are "correlated to only internal atmospheric variability in the summer half-year."

Pertinent to the time frame of interest is a series of drought periods (Figure 6.2) exemplifying the unusually variable and often extreme conditions that characterized intervals of the sixteenth century (Seager et al. 2009; Stahle et al. 2000). Because patterns of precipitation across the region are seldom uniform, I summarize the known trends according to particular localities. The discussion will follow a geographical path that begins at the northern reaches of Spanish Florida—in Virginia and North Carolina—runs southward along the Atlantic coast, and then westward to the lower Mississippi valley. The notable absence of high-quality precipitation reconstructions for Florida, the veritable ground zero of Spanish incursions, stems from the effect of its more tropical climate on tree growth. Simply put, the distinct seasonal growth patterns of trees in more temperate northerly latitudes better register perturbations in available moisture, especially during the growing season (Stahle et al. 1985:530).

Taking advantage of old-growth bald cypress stands, a thousand-year-long record of annual precipitation has been constructed for the lower Chesapeake area of southeastern Virginia and northeastern North

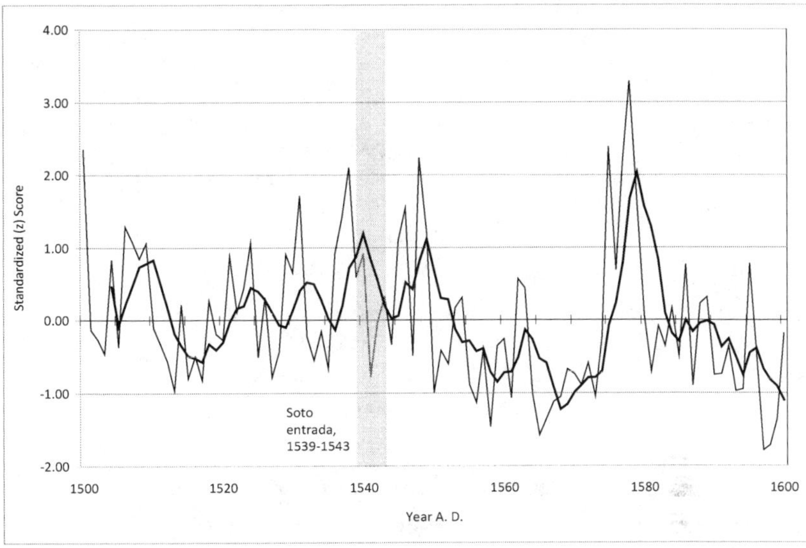

FIGURE 6.2. Tree-ring reconstructed spring-season precipitation record for the sixteenth century in the lower Mississippi River valley (Black Swamp, Arkansas; after Stahle et al. 1985). Trend line represents five-year moving average and shaded bar brackets interval of the Soto entrada (A.D. 1539–1543).

Carolina (Blanton 2000; Stahle et al. 1998). Sixteenth-century conditions there are largely exemplary of those farther south, to the extent that they were punctuated by a relatively high incidence of downturns in rainfall. Drier-than-average conditions occurred in the first half of the century between 1534 and 1539. Known Spanish activity in the Chesapeake began later during another dry spell, between 1562 and 1575, that brackets an attempted Jesuit mission settlement in 1570 (Blanton 2004:13; Lewis and Loomie 1953; Stahle et al. 1998). The area also became mired in a brief but severe dry interval between 1587 and 1589, referred to as the Lost Colony Drought. Two decades later, a more prolonged dry period (1606–1612) contributed to the hardship surrounding settlement of Jamestown (Blanton 2000; Stahle et al. 1998).

A similar bald cypress reconstruction has been generated for the lower Atlantic coastal plain, conforming to today's southeastern South Carolina and eastern Georgia (Anderson 1994; Anderson et al. 1995; Blanton and Thomas 2008; Stahle and Cleaveland 1992). At the beginning of the sixteenth century a notable dryness is evident between 1510 and 1515, but drought conditions became more prevalent later. Two multiyear dry periods are apparent, one between 1564 and 1571 and another from 1585 to 1595, in close accordance with downturns noted for the Chesapeake area. Thus, independent tree-ring studies along the Atlantic seaboard conclude that late sixteenth-century climate was especially subject to precipitation extremes, and that that these periods were linked to extraordinarily severe, continent-wide dryness (Blanton 2004; Cook et al. 2007; Stahle et al. 2000).

Multicentury precipitation reconstructions based on bald cypress have also been completed for parts of the lower Mississippi valley, most prominently for eastern Arkansas (Stahle et al. 1985). Here, again, the record documents regular occurrence of significant droughts during the latter half of the sixteenth century, and at times they are consistent with some of the dry intervals evident in Atlantic state reconstructions. Three dry periods of at least ten years' duration are established: one around 1555, one around 1570, and the final one around 1595. The authors of the reconstruction made the pertinent observation that, statistically speaking, the period between 1549 and 1577 represents the "worst June drought period for Arkansas in the past 450 yr" (Stahle et al. 1985:3). In a companion study, they note that area streamflows were markedly reduced at the same time, between 1563 and 1571 (Cleaveland 2000:37). They also point out that the amplitude of moisture anomalies was exceptionally great prior to 1650, and markedly so during the sixteenth century, placing emphasis on the fact that conditions were highly variable. In fact, the longest period of exceptionally high streamflow is recorded between 1575 and 1578.

It is useful to close this overview of sixteenth-century precipitation patterns in the Southeast with a decade-by-decade summation drawn from the integrated tree-ring data network of the North American Drought Atlas (Cook et al. 1999, 2004, 2007, 2008). The Web-based compilation allows queries specific to intervals of time for virtually all of North America (Cook and Krusic 2004; Cook et al. 2008). In the opening decade of the sixteenth century, somewhat dry conditions prevailed throughout the Southeast as part of a widespread pattern extending across most of today's United States. Although these low-level dry conditions lingered in the lower Mississippi valley through the second decade, the region-wide pattern from 1510 to 1529 approached that of the historical average. The balance of the century was marked by below-average precipitation, but those conditions did not always uniformly affect the region. From 1530 to 1539 the entire Southeast experienced somewhat dry conditions, and over the next two decades the dryness contracted, first to encompass the Gulf states and the lower Mississippi valley from 1540 to 1549, and then to cover only the lower valley and most of the midsection of the continent from 1550 to 1559 (Burnett and Murray 1993:235). Significantly drier conditions affected large sections of North America for the three decades between 1560 and 1589. During the 1560s all of the area eastward of the Mississippi River suffered from dryness, but those conditions moderated in the east over the following two decades as they intensified west of the Mississippi. In the Southeast, only the lower Mississippi valley was experiencing marginal rainfall during the 1570s, but dry conditions expanded again in the final two decades to encompass the entire region.

The climate record for the Southeast is also routinely punctuated by short-lived, extreme weather events. Notorious are tropical storms most prone to strike between July and October, and those reaching hurricane strength are capable of devastating effects. The Southeast is affected annually by a tropical storm pattern, and unquestionably it became a singular challenge to trans-Atlantic and Caribbean-area colonizers. Presently, our storm record based on documentary sources extends well into the sixteenth century, but because reconstructions of early storm events are dependent upon written sources, they are understood to be incomplete. Still, they speak clearly to the fact that warm-season storms loomed large in the New World experience, certainly in the absence of a sophisticated forecasting system.

Strong tropical storms and hurricanes are documented for eighteen years during the period between 1500 and 1700 in Florida, Georgia, and the Carolinas, and in two of those years multiple storms are recorded (Barnes 1995, 1998; Ludlum 1963; Sandrik and Landsea 2003). For the period preceding 1550, the paucity of good records limits our ability to chart the relative frequency and intensity of tropical weather events. Many more events were recorded over the subsequent period, and the mere increase in colonial activity can partially explain that pattern. However, judged against later times, one is left with the impression that the latter half of the sixteenth century was a particularly active storm period. For example, ten of the eighteen years between 1500 and 1700 with storm activity occur in the second half of the sixteenth century, and after that period notable storms are not recorded again until 1638.

Implications of the Record for Sixteenth-Century Exploration and Colonization

For an archaeologist, the easier part of exploring the relationship between people and climate is compiling the kind of basic paleoclimatic record just described. More difficult is explaining the human response to periods of extended drought, or extended cool, or catastrophic storms. In this section I consider some of the specific implications for people in the Southeast of periods of climate or weather extremes during the sixteenth century. In many instances, we cannot be certain of the direct effect, if any, on either Native or colonizing groups, but at the very least questions about the nature of those responses can be more precisely framed. The narrative will expose the unevenness of human responses under extreme natural conditions, drawing attention in part to the fact that humans, either as individuals or as groups, will react to stressful natural conditions according to their own unique historical and cosmological perspectives (Dean 2000; McIntosh et al. 2000).

Conditions at the Time of Initial Contact

Weather observations were rarely recorded in early sixteenth-century documents, and, where they do exist, they usually describe severe weather at sea. On the one hand, the dearth of sources is the obvious effect of a low level of activity, but it is also a function of the related issue of European inexperience in the region. None of the newcomers had sufficient firsthand knowledge to know which of the conditions in the Southeast were anomalous; consequently, they had a weak basis for making comparative judgments. To some extent, we can accommodate for the deficit of recorded observations by consulting other proxy sources, and with proper caution it is sometimes possible to infer something of the conditions from indirect commentary in the accounts. In this opening section, emphasis is placed on understanding conditions during the latter part of the 1520s when two of the initial Spanish incursions took place, the competing colonizing ventures of Lucas Vázquez de Ayllón in 1526 (Hoffman 1994a, 2004) and of Pánfilo de Narváez in 1528 (Hoffman 1994b).

The prevailing climatic pattern of this period as determined from proxy sources is best characterized as wet and relatively warm. Those conditions are attributable to the NAO in a rather strong and persistent positive mode, in addition to a strong El Niño event in 1525–1526 followed quickly by a very strong La Niña event in 1528.

Both the Vázquez de Ayllón and Narváez ventures were hampered by storms. In the case of Vázquez de Ayllón's attempt to colonize the south Atlantic coast, his six ships had no sooner arrived offshore of present-day South Carolina in early August 1526, when a storm arose that caused their *capitana*, or command ship, to run aground (Hoffman 1994a:41, 2004:67). Very little about the storm is described, and, in fact, there are questions concerning the accuracy of the account (Barnes 1995; Ludlum 1963). Certainly the season was right for storm activity. ENSO conditions at this time might have contributed to the storm's location, since there is evidence that such events tend to track northward of the Gulf of Mexico under El Niño effects (McCabe and Muller 2002:101).

Firsthand commentary about other weather conditions is equally thin. Survivors' accounts from Vázquez de Ayllón's desperate and ultimately failed settlement of San Miguel de Gualdape include mention of discomfort from cold (Hoffman 2004:75), and we know that these were El Niño years that can bring cooler-than-average temperatures to the area in wintertime. However, temperatures in October and November even on Georgia's coast can dip close to freezing in normal years. The reports of extreme cold on the return voyage to the Indies are probably explainable in the same way (Hoffman 2004:79). All told, there is as much reason to believe the complaints about cold weather are explained by poor shelter and general privation as by unusually cool seasonal temperatures.

In the case of Narváez there is nothing illusory about the dangers posed by storms. His fleet, with plans to sail north and westward from Cuba to the north shore of the Gulf of Mexico, was actually plagued by two storm encounters. First, two of his six ships, under the command of Núñez Cabeza de Vaca, were lost at the port of Trinidad, Cuba, when a severe storm swept through in October 1527. Having eventually embarked from Trinidad for Havana in February 1528, intending to stop over there for resupply, the remaining four ships were blown seaward into the Gulf en route. This second storm denied Narváez an all-important opportunity to reprovision, and Hoffman (1994b:53–54) has suggested that it was only out of desperation for water and food that the fleet made its landing along peninsular Florida's west shore instead of the intended northern Gulf coast. Thus, a pair of storms, very possibly generated by a very strong La Niña event, literally steered the path of this early expedition along an unintended course.

Other kinds of weather and climate conditions are just as sparsely mentioned in the Narváez accounts as they are in Vázquez de Ayllón's. By inference, one might surmise that spring and early summer of 1528 in Florida were relatively wet. The chronicles report more than once how streams were flowing strongly and difficult to cross (Hoffman 1994b:58–59). On one hand, the normal flow of major streams in Florida can be significant, especially in rivers like the Withlacoochee and Suwannee, but difficult crossings would probably not be the rule assuming recognized fording places were used. On the other hand, springtime is the season of high water in many Southeastern rivers, so we cannot dismiss the possibility that the challenges were simply the result of a normal, seasonal streamflow pattern.

Conditions During the Entrada of Hernando de Soto

Even with the benefit of three separate chronicles devoted to Hernando de Soto's lengthy experience in the Southeast (1539–1543), there is precious little direct commentary about climate and weather. Referencing proxy sources, it is safe to conclude that the years Soto was moving through the region were consistently cooler than average but widely variable with respect to precipitation. The NAO was in a negative mode for the entire span (Cook et al. 2002), and the northern hemisphere temperature reconstruction registers temperatures well below the long-term mean (Briffa et al. 1998). The North American Drought Atlas indicates that during the period 1539 to 1543 most of the Southeast was receiving slightly less precipitation than normal. However, this characterization is highly generalized, and a year-by-year summary is more meaningful.

Referring again to independent proxy records, the first three years of the Soto entrada appear to have been the coolest and the wettest his party experienced. The NAO reconstruction and the northern hemisphere temperature reconstruction indicate that winter temperatures were probably below average. Rainfall amounts as determined from tree-ring data ranged from above average to moderately above average (Cleaveland 2000; Stahle and Cleaveland 1992; Stahle et al. 1985, 1988). The bald cypress tree-ring series for South Carolina and Georgia depicts 1541 as the third-wettest year during the sixteenth century, and the complementary Arkansas tree-ring reconstruction records the years 1539 and 1540 as relatively wet.

Conditions began to change sharply in 1541, and by 1542/1543 tree rings register precipitation amounts significantly below average. In the lower Mississippi River valley drought conditions became extreme in 1542, when much of the area farther west was also suffering through a severely dry year. Conditions improved somewhat the following year, but dryness of moderate severity is still measured. The area of South Carolina and Georgia underwent a tremendous reversal, shifting from one of the wettest (1541) to *the* single driest year of the century in 1542, followed by a somewhat dry year in 1543. In Arkansas dry conditions continued into 1542, but they moderated significantly, and by 1543 precipitation had increased to slightly above average.

So how does weather commentary in the Soto chronicles, meager though it is, square with the proxy determinations? The answer, all things considered, is that the correspondence is good. There is, for example, excellent corroboration of a brief but intense episode of drought in 1541 that extended through the next year with less intensity. In entries for June 1541, we discover the only explicit comment about drought, and it appears in each of the three Soto chronicles. The Gentleman of Elvas relates that an Indian leader from Casqui (present-day Parkin site, Arkansas) rejoiced at relief from a "great drought" that had threatened crops, Hernández de Biedma reports how the same chief had complained of want of rain, and Ranjel told how the chief expressed relief that overdue rain had "saved our cornfields and seed beds" (Robertson 1995:120; Worth 1995b:239–240, 302). As noted, the veracity of the accounts is secured with tree-ring data that record the worst single-year dry event of the sixteenth century precisely in 1541, with evidence that the conditions continued into 1542 with less severity. In addition, the NAO was in a strong negative mode in 1541, just as a strong La Niña ENSO event was occurring.

The varied records are also in agreement about the harshness of winter in 1540/1541 and 1541/1542. During the first of those winters, the Soto party was traveling in present-day Mississippi through the Native province of Chicaza (Hudson 1997). All of the chronicles remark on the difficult conditions, describing them in terms like "the snows and cold very great . . . it snowed with as much wind as if they were in Burgos" (Ranjel 1993) and "great hardship from cold . . . more snows fell there than in Castille" (Hernández de Biedma 1993; Robertson 1995:236; Worth 1995b:296). The following winter in the province of Autiamque/Cayas (present Arkansas) was hardly better, as accounts include such comments as "a month amid snow" (Elvas) and "the cold of the winter was greatly menacing" (Hernández de Biedma 1993; Robertson 1995:129; Worth 1995b:242). Because the NAO was in a relatively strong negative mode over that span, it might well have contributed to the severe winter conditions. Likewise, temperature models for the northern hemisphere record cool conditions, and especially so in 1542 (Briffa et al. 1998). However, models evaluating the effects of La Niña conditions in the Southeast, which were also occurring at this time, would predict warmer-than-average conditions. All told, it is not possible to reconcile the question of dominant causal factors here, and the contradictions in expectations serve to underscore the complexity of climate/weather modeling.

How weather and climate might have influenced the behavior of Hernando de Soto and his expedition is a question that is seldom asked. Obviously the entrada in and of itself created a host of challenges for both the Native people and the members of the exploring party, and weather extremes surely would have added to the stress of the situation. Because period commentators were quite selective about the details they chose to set down on paper, it stands to reason that the rare comments regarding weather were purposely included. Following this logic, I argue that the difficult winters were described with unusual detail because they affected events, or were perceived to. More than likely, the cold and hunger of those seasons took a significant toll on both the stamina and morale of Soto's group, leading to attrition in numbers and increasing desperation to find an exit strategy. Thus, difficult weather became a significant contributing factor as the party became increasingly vulnerable. The commentary concerning drought-induced food shortfalls of 1541 does not betray a direct challenge to Soto's plans but rather is among the numerous anecdotes that attempt to glorify and justify the events, correlating the erection of a cross with a seemingly divine end of the drought. At the same time, it is probably safe to suggest that the low maize yields of that period explain some of the Indian resistance they encountered.

Conditions in the Period of Early Sustained Settlement

Allusions to climate-induced hardship become more frequent after about 1560, when settlement began to achieve a degree of permanence. On one hand, the enriched commentary is the effect of a growing and seasoned populace, but the late sixteenth century also corresponds to a time of depressed precipitation and frequent tropical storm activity. Difficult protracted droughts occurred generally in the 1560s and again after 1580, but as before, the timing and severity could vary. Dryness affected the region relatively uniformly in the 1560s, when it was linked with continent-wide megadrought conditions (Cook et al. 2007, 2009; Stahle et al. 2000). Dry conditions occurred again in the south Atlantic states from about 1583 to 1589, and in the lower Mississippi valley throughout the 1590s. The rain shortfall of the 1580s was exacerbated by the cooling effects of volcanic explosions in 1585 and 1586.

The first ambitious attempt at settlement in La Florida following the Soto years was led by Tristán de Luna y Arellano (Hudson 1990; Hudson et al. 1991; Priestley 1928). Severe weather in the form of an August 1559 hurricane set the plan for a permanent colony back before it ever got started. All but three of the original eleven vessels in the Luna y Arellano fleet were lost soon after they arrived in Pensacola Bay. Losses were so extreme that survivors devoted themselves mainly to staying alive, essentially abandoning the original plan altogether. Ultimately, the troubling incident suspended official plans to colonize the west coast of Florida along with the east coast (Barnes 1998:43).

Luna y Arellano's situation became especially dire when Indians around Pensacola Bay resisted requests for aid. A contingent of the struggling party then headed inland to search for food in the Native province of Nanipacana (Alabama). It too met with limited success, since the Indians fled and in their wake destroyed or hid food stocks. Some of the group eventually reached the province of Coosa (Georgia), and while the reception was warmer, they were disappointed to find less surplus food than Soto had reported seventeen years earlier. The question has been asked whether drought accounted for the obvious decline in the prosperity of the interior Indian province of Coosa on which Luna y Arellano's colonists placed so much stake. Its reputation as a rich locale had obviously found a place in Soto-era lore, including in the memories of some Soto veterans accompanying Luna y Arellano (Hudson 1990; Smith 2000). I offer that drought is an unlikely cause of the change, since reconstructions indicate that the last significant drought to affect the Coosa territory, beyond the very dry year of 1542, occurred from 1551 to 1552, well before 1559–1560 when Luna y Arellano arrived (Cook et al 2008; Stahle and Cleaveland 1992). Precipitation was close to or above average throughout most of the Southeast during the Luna y Arellano years and had been, for the most part, since 1553. In fact, there is no mention whatsoever of dry conditions in the correspondence related to the Luna y Arellano events; to the contrary, several documents make mention of regular rains (Priestley 1928).

Epic dryness plagued the decade of the 1560s across most of the east. A well-known account from that period relating incidents associated with an excursion northward from St. Augustine by Governor Pedro Menéndez de Avilés in the spring of 1566, aimed mainly at establishing relations with leaders of the Guale and Orista chiefdoms, conveys a sense of those conditions (Barcia Carballido y Zúñiga 1951:112–119; Jones 1978:181). The Spanish party discovered tension between two of the chiefdoms on today's South Carolina coast, aggravated if not created outright by drought-induced food shortfalls (Saunders 2000; Worth 1999). In the words of one chronicler, "It had not rained for eight months in this country, and their corn fields and farming lands were all dry, whereat they were all sad, on account of the little food they had" (Solís de Merás 1964:170–171). Under the strain of privation, the Guale chief was threatening to attack the neighboring Orista, presumably to take what meager provisions they had left.

Tree-ring reconstructions confirm that 1566 was a severely dry year throughout the eastern United States, and southeastern South Carolina was among the driest areas (Cook et al. 2008; Stahle and Cleaveland 1992; Stahle et al. 2000). In fact, every year of the decade experienced below-average precipitation except 1565. Anderson (1994) and Anderson et al. (1995) have thoroughly examined the likely effects of those conditions and persuasively demonstrate how activity at Santa Elena was influenced by them.

Under the desperate circumstances, Juan Pardo was dispatched from Santa Elena to seek provisions among Indian communities deep in the interior (Anderson et al. 1995; Hudson 1990). He made the first of two trips between December 1, 1566, and March 7, 1567, and the next from September 1, 1567, to March 2, 1568. By this time the extreme dryness of 1566 had begun to abate, and in the period of his marches precipitation was only moderately to marginally below average (although 1569 proved to be even drier than 1566). Lessening of the drought could account for the absence of its mention in the Pardo narratives, but it is surprising there was little or no indication of it. Pardo gushed about the productivity and promise of the interior lands and gives no indication that his constant requests for maize were resisted because of a poor crop year. None of this brings the reality of the dry interval into question, but it does demonstrate how certain cultural interests might temporarily override economic ones. I am suggesting that the seemingly ready availability of maize in the interior provinces reflects the strength of a prestige economy among the Native societies. The Indian leadership was prepared, at least for a while, to exchange short rations of corn for metal, glass, and fabric. We must also be mindful of the seasonal dimension of precipitation and ask if winter snowfall in the mountains compensated to any degree for the dry growing season that is registered by tree rings.

A few years later, in 1570, Jesuits sought to establish a mission on lower Chesapeake Bay, at the northern limit of Spain's claim to La Florida. The tree-ring record for the area reveals that the six-year drought reported by the missionaries was actually nine years in duration, and that they arrived just after the worst part of it (Blanton 2000; Stahle et al. 1998). They reported, "Our Lord has chastised [the area] with six years of famine and death . . . many have died and many also have moved to other regions to ease their hunger . . . they have no maize . . . Neither roots nor anything else can be had, save for a small amount obtained with great labor from the soil, which is very parched" (Lewis and Loomie 1953). The outcome in this case was grim: within months all but one of the members of the religious enclave were killed by local Indians. And in this same year, a rebellion was sparked back at Santa Elena when colonists ordered local Native communities to deliver supplies of scarce corn (Anderson et al. 1995; Hudson 1990:23).

Drought conditions returned to the deeper Southeast in the 1580s (Anderson 1994; Anderson et al. 1995; Blanton and Thomas 2008; Stahle and Cleaveland 1992). There is very little direct commentary in documents about the dry conditions, but there is circumstantial evidence that may be indicative of its effects. First, Santa Elena was abandoned in 1587 in favor of St. Augustine. Anderson (1994) and Anderson et al. (1995) have suggested that the return of drought was a final blow to the struggling outpost. Also, the so-called Lost Colony Drought has been implicated as a factor in the failure of the English toehold on the coast of North Carolina (Stahle et al. 1998). It is not unreasonable to make these inferences since the dry conditions of 1587 through 1589 were the most severe of the entire tree-ring reconstruction for eastern Virginia southward to Georgia (Stahle et al. 1998).

Tropical storms were a common problem late in the sixteenth century, and losses of oceangoing vessels rose as ship traffic increased, including voyages of the Spanish treasure fleet operating out of the Caribbean and skirting the Florida peninsula. Laden with precious metals and other goods, it was customary for convoys of many dozen ships to attempt the Atlantic crossing together, and the sinking of just one vessel stood to affect the European economy. The fleet was functioning in high capacity by the 1560s and enjoyed a peak in precious metal exports in the last decade of the sixteenth century, a time when tropical storm activity appears to have been especially high. The complete toll from storms will never be known, but records document many losses. In just one example, Governor Menéndez sought compensation from the Crown for ships lost during the 1560s (Lyon 1995:211–213).

Establishment of St. Augustine, the long-time regional capital of La Florida, was partially motivated by the need for a haven from storms (Deagan 1983). Battered vessels routinely limped into the port city for repairs, and it was also common for shipwreck survivors to straggle in from points up and down the coast (Barnes 1998:43; Marx and Marx 1994:225–226). St. Augustine's existence was itself challenged on numerous occasions by land-falling storms that made direct hits or closely missed. In 1561 the nascent settlement was hit hard by a hurricane that forced temporary abandonment. It was struck again in 1565. The land-falling storm of 1571 accelerated coastal erosion so dramatically the town was moved the following year to a seemingly less vulnerable location. Still, the town was flooded by another hurricane in 1599 (Sandrik and Landsea 2003).

Other cases illustrate different effects of coastal storms on the region's early colonial history. One is the storm that dispersed and damaged Ribault's French fleet in early September 1565, bound for an attack on St. Augustine (Hoffman 2004:229–230; Ludlum 1963:8). The loss allowed Spain a quick retaliation by overland attack on the weakly defended Fort Caroline, ending the French presence in La Florida. Later, the Carolinas were struck by five heavy storms between 1583 and 1591. The storm season of 1591 was especially active and is well known for the headaches it caused for both English designs to settle the Outer Banks and on Spanish fleets offshore (Barnes 1995; Ludlum 1963; Sandrik and Landsea 2003).

Closing Comments

Within the last decade, the field of paleoclimatology has exploded with extended, detailed reconstructions and increasingly sophisticated understanding of the systems and teleconnections that account for observed conditions. While no one would describe the Southeast as a marginal environment, an outcome of the improved record is this: climatic variability is the rule in the region and over the long run it has been subject to periodic extremes.

Like examples worldwide, the case of La Florida reveals the complexity of both the global climate system and human responses to it. Working in the context of La Florida, it is plain to see that outright "collapse" has seldom if ever been a human response to climate stress. This is especially true of Indigenous societies, even those that have adopted the most narrowly focused agriculturally based economies.

Periods of drought may have been challenging for them, but not usually catastrophic.

Fundamentally, the Native response to drought is what we would predict. Under a relatively nimble traditional pattern, attention was directed more intently on the option of noncultivated Indigenous food resources, and, accordingly, population was dispersed to a degree. This was an especially viable plan in the coastal zone, where high estuarine productivity can be readily exploited given appropriate know-how (Thomas 2008). Also, consideration was given to raiding the stores of neighbors. In effect, we observe a more or less instinctual shift to ancient, proven alternatives to farming, albeit temporarily.

At the same time, the Spanish newcomers were struggling to gather useful intelligence and adapt more or less without local experience. They were paying attention to Native ways but it was a difficult learning curve. Nonetheless, under the growing sense that La Florida was—especially in their still inexperienced view—more a godforsaken place than a virtual Eden (Saunders 2002:39–41), a pattern emerged that was designed to expose the colonizers to minimal risk.

While the immigrants were not inclined to "go Native" in any literal sense, a tacit respect for the wisdom of Native economic practices took hold, arguably inspired by Indian success in the desiccated sixteenth-century environment. I suggest early struggles with the environment, set off by abnormal drought and storminess, did not determine but rather influenced the path La Florida was to follow for the next 150 years. European settlements were few, highly dispersed, and, where they did occur, were mapped directly onto Native communities (Milanich 1994:288). Native foodstuffs were staples and interaction with Indigenous people was constant. Arguably, local climate and Native cultural patterns influenced the Spanish model of existence more so than the reverse, and this course, ultimately, created a distinctive La Florida creole culture (Deagan 1985).

It is fascinating to explore less tangible aspects of the human response to climate conditions, including culturally influenced perception. In both the Spanish and the Indian case, conditions of climate stress were almost always attributed to a higher power, and most usually an unhappy one. Spanish remarks include references to a "chastised land" and an "angry God" (Lewis and Loomie 1953; Solís de Merás 1964). Surely this kind of thinking influenced behavior. On occasion these "acts of God" were subject to manipulation in the realm of ecopolitics. For example, in 1565 Governor Menéndez sought to convince an Orista chief that the dearth of rain was a result of God's anger because the chief had not behaved as a good Christian (Solís de Merás 1964:178–181). Clearly, all this was for the purpose of coercing cooperative behavior from the chief and his subjects. Coincidentally, no sooner had the chief sworn himself to Christianity than it began to rain heavily. This apparent feat of divine influence gave Menéndez a valuable reputation as a rainmaker that paid dividends for at least a time (Hann 1996:55). And, as others have noted, claims to powers of control over the weather were no less central to the practices of Native cultural leaders (Hudson 1976:337–338).

In the end, it becomes clear that people have struggled most when seemingly random events change the rules, effectively redefining limiting conditions. I would liken these situations to popularized "perfect storm" scenarios. A case in point is the context of contact itself. The Spanish Colonial Period created circumstances that increased the vulnerability of human systems in the region. It introduced a constellation of unprecedented factors that conspired to elevate routine challenges into supreme challenges. Bad timing put alien colonists face-to-face with Indigenous people during what was the most anomalous climatic period since the early thirteenth century. And because climate (drought and cool) and weather (storm events) were just some of many ingredients that brewed this storm, it meets expectations of what might constitute as transformative a situation as any we know.

In the context of our contemporary debate over climate change, investigation of the culture–climate connection deep into the past is a most relevant archaeological undertaking. Profound improvement in our ability to reconstruct paleoclimatic conditions provides the necessary basis and impetus, really for the first time, to ask sophisticated questions with a straight face. Yet the impressive span and precision of those reconstructions are hardly a silver-bullet solution to cracking the culture–climate code. The connection between climate and human affairs is anything but direct or simple. A natural event amply recorded in proxy data sets, like a drought or a major storm, may register only dimly if at all in the human record. What we are faced with is a far more nuanced account.

Finally, no one should draw the conclusion that climatic data sources relevant to the Southeast have somehow been exhausted. Dendrochronological data are yet to be systematically collected from subfossil trees in excess of one thousand years of age in an effort to extend the regional record across multiple millennia. And certainly ample opportunities exist to better calibrate the record of the last half-millennium based on shorter-lived species like pine and cedar, not to mention new work on other stands of bald cypress and building timbers. The prospects are equally encouraging in the realm of so-called historical climatology. Untold numbers of ship logs, personal journals, plantation journals, military records, and the like have never been examined for the purpose of compiling long series of climate data. Obviously most of the documents pertinent to sixteenth- and seventeenth-century La Florida are housed outside of the United States and require proficiency with archaic Spanish, but the payoff from pursuing that research would be tremendous.

SECTION IV

Disease

7

Regarding Sixteenth-Century Native Population Change in the Northern Southwest

Ann F. Ramenofsky and Jeremy Kulisheck

Historical and archaeological analyses across the North American Southeast have repeatedly shown significant sixteenth-century decline of Native populations, primarily from introduced infectious diseases, but assisted by warfare, exploitation, and nutritional stress (Hutchinson, this volume; Ethridge and Mitchem, this volume; Ramenofsky 1987). The repetition of this spatial pattern is a strong warrant for the inference that, in large parts of the Southeast, sixteenth-century Native populations had declined dramatically.

By contrast, there is no consensus regarding the nature of Native population change in the North American Southwest during the same century. Based on the demonstration of demographic collapses among Native populations elsewhere in the Western Hemisphere, several scholars have argued for significant sixteenth-century Native population decline caused primarily by infectious disease introduction (Dobyns 1992, 2002; Thornton 1987; Upham 1982, 1992). Others believe that the onset of demographic decline from warfare, disease, or both occurred a century later (e.g., Barrett 2002; Flint and Flint 2002; Kulisheck 2003, 2005; Ramenofsky et al. 2009; Reff 1991). Even given seventeenth-century decline, however, the relatively greater persistence of Native Southwestern societies into the present suggests that the loss was of a magnitude smaller than occurred across the Southeast.

Here we use documentary descriptions and archaeological settlement records to review the evidence that the northern Southwest, the heartland of the Pueblo peoples, was demographically stable through the sixteenth century. We analyze history and archaeology independently, and this separation is both deliberate and essential.

Archaeology and history differ in terms of scale and resolution. As scale (or scope) increases, resolution (or detail) decreases. The concepts not only account for major differences between the disciplines but also have implications for building knowledge of the period. Conquest documents are typically written by a single individual at a particular time and address specific events. Artifact distributions, by contrast, are the result of collective activity that accumulates over sometimes-substantial periods of time. As a result, historical writing is generally at a lower scale with high resolution. The archaeological record is the opposite. It is formed and survives at a higher scale with lower resolution. These differences between archaeology and history combined with the value placed on writing means that archaeological information can be lost between the lines of history. This we do not want to do.

The separation of archaeological and historical records allows us to compare the evidence from one record to the other. Happily, in the case being addressed here, the analyses are mutually confirming. While there are clear historical and archaeological demographic shifts in the northern Southwest during the 1500s, the regional-scale Pueblo trends are commensurate with the patterns of demographic coalescence and contraction that characterized Pueblo demography and settlement since the mid-twelfth century. For the Pueblos, the sixteenth century was a period of relative demographic stability. The arrival of the Spanish resulted in severe short-term disruptions and localized abandonments. However, significant population changes, including decline, did not occur until the early or mid-seventeenth century.

Historical Records

The Spanish explorer accounts of the northern Southwest are temporally confined to the period after A.D. 1538 and include the records of ten expeditions (Hammond and Rey 1940, 1953, 1966; Mathers, this volume). Although useful demographic information on the question of Native population stability or decline is embedded in most of these chronicles, there are also several methodological problems that dictate the most productive way to use the information. First is the issue of Pueblo population counts (Kulisheck 2005). All population figures mentioned in the documents are *estimates* made by unfamiliar observers as they traveled from one village to another. They are not equivalent to population counts taken from mission registries, tax rolls, or census counts, records that are amenable to quantitative verification of their accuracy. Second are the translations themselves. Except for Richard and Shirley Flint's research of the Francisco Vázquez de Coronado expedition (Flint 2008; Flint and Flint 2002), the translations of the other explorations are of a much earlier vintage (Hammond and Rey 1966; Hodge et al. 1945). Because historiographic methods and knowledge build over time, we do not know whether and how scholarly understanding postdating the Vázquez de Coronado explorations would change under the close scrutiny by contemporary historians.

Given that we cannot control for either problem, our documentary method is conservative. We seek consistency among the demographic indicators, including village counts, village descriptions, and population estimates. Substantial variation across the indicators will render one or more of these measures unreliable estimators of demographic trends. Agreement across the indicators, on the other hand, can suggest whether populations are numerically increasing, decreasing, or stable. Because Southeastern historians have used the lack of consistency across documentary accounts to indicate demographic decline, this measure also provides a point of contrast between the regions. We begin with that contrast.

In the interior Southeast, descriptions of Native society observed by the members of the 1559–1561 Tristán de Luna y Arellano expedition are dramatically different from those of the Hernando de Soto party made twenty years earlier. The contrasts are striking evidence of demographic change and collapse in that region (Hudson et al. 1989). Dávila Padilla, a member of the Luna y Arellano expedition wrote:

> Truly, the land was fertile, but it lacked cultivation. There was much forest, but little fruit, because as it was not cultivated the land was all unimproved and full of thistles and weeds. *Those they had brought along as guides, being people who had been there before, declared that they must have been bewitched when this country seemed to them so rich and populated as they had stated.* The arrival of the Spaniards in former years had driven the Indians up into the forests, where they preferred to live among the wild beasts who did no harm to them, but whom they could master, than among the Spaniards at whose hands they received injuries. (Smith 2000:43; emphasis added)

On the other hand, the accounts of the Spaniards in the northern Southwest are remarkably consistent in the numbers of villages as well as the physical descriptions of settlements.

Because there were basically only two routes that Spanish parties used to enter the northern Southwest, both earlier and later explorers traveled similar pathways and visited many of the same villages and districts (Barrett 2002) (see Table 7.1 and Table 7.2).[1] As seen in Table 7.1, there is certainly variability through time, with some regions showing fewer villages and others showing more. On balance, however, there is no dramatic change in the number of villages across the entire region through time. All regions continue to be populated throughout the sixteenth century.

This inference of stability is corroborated by observations that the Spaniards made regarding the size, layout, and construction of villages. For instance, in a 1540 letter to the viceroy, Vázquez de Coronado gave this description of villages in the Zuni district:

> They are . . . very good houses, of three, four and five stories. . . . The seven ciudades are seven small towns. . . . In this one [Hawikku], where I am now lodged, there could be some two hundred houses. . . . There is another neighboring town, one of the seven, [that] is somewhat larger than this one. [There is] another one the same size as this [one], and the remaining are somewhat smaller. (Flint and Flint 2005:259)

In 1582, Hernán Gallegos provided a similar description of the Zuni district: "[In] the valley of Zuni . . . there they found six pueblos with thirty, forty and up to one hundred houses. . . . The houses were similar to those of the other pueblos, two or three stories high, and built of stone (Hammond and Rey 1966:13)."

Various meanings have been assigned to consistency of descriptions. In the Southeast, Patricia Galloway has argued that redundancy in the format and structure of Spanish exploration chronicles reflects medieval Spanish literary traditions. It is possible, however, that redundancy in description is a function of a relatively stable population structure. This explanation seems more likely in the northern Southwest and is supported by consistent descriptions of Pueblo subsistence, economics, and political organizations within communities. Pueblos

Table 7.1. Explorer's village counts, by district

Year	Explorer	Zuni	Hopi	South Rio Grande	Salinas	Central Rio Grande	Santo Domingo	Acoma	Galisteo	Upper/ Lower Jemez	Chama/ Española	Taos	Pecos
1540 to 1542	Vázquez de Coronado	7	7	4	11	18	7	1	6 (7?)	7	6	1	1
1581 to 1582	Sánchez Chamuscado-Rodríguez	4(5)	5	9	11	21	6	1	7	10	NV	NV	NV
1583	Espejo	5	7(8)	10	11 (12?)	21	5	1	8	14	11	NV	1
1590 to 1591	Castaño de Sosa	NV	NV	NV	NV	15	6	1	7	NV	NV	2	1
1598 to 1601	Oñate y Salazar	6	7	10	7	17 (?)	11	1	5	16	4 (5?)	2	1

Note: NV = not visited

Table 7.2. Explorers' estimates of pueblo populations

Observer	Area	Date	Estimate
Castañeda (Vázquez de Coronado)	Northern Southwest	1540–1542	20,000 men
Sánchez Chamuscado–Rodríguez	New Mexico	1581–1582	130,000 people
Espejo	New Mexico	1583	233,000 or 248,000 people
Oñate y Salazar	Northern Southwest	1600	50,000–60,000 people

are routinely described as civilized, and Spaniards are just as frequently given corn, beans, squash, and, less often, turkey. We would expect such behavior to change if demographic catastrophes had struck the region.

Estimates of population are the one exception to the pattern of consistency. Across the fifty-five years of exploration, later counts suggest more rather than fewer inhabitants (see Table 7.3). The later and larger estimates, particularly those of Espejo in 1583, have been used as a baseline to establish large pre-Contact population sizes and to suggest that infectious diseases had winnowed Pueblo peoples early in the sixteenth century (Upham 1992). Embedded, here, however, is a logical contradiction. How can population loss from disease be invoked when the direction of population change is increasing?

Rather than assuming that the larger estimates are correct and retrofitting those back to the beginning of exploration, we take a simpler explanatory stance. The population figures in the accounts of different explorers made at different times are unreliable estimators of Pueblo population. While it is unlikely that Native populations were growing throughout the century, a more parsimonious explanation is that they were demographically stable but fluctuated within any given area.

Finally, our inference of regional demographic stability does not negate the significant short-term dramatic demographic impacts of Spanish exploration. As described in a later chapter (Mathers, this vol-

Table 7.3. Archaeological village counts, by district

Time Period Site Size (# Rooms)	South Rio Grande	Salinas	Central Rio Grande	Santo Domingo	Galisteo	Upper /Lower Jemez	Santa Fe /Pajarito	Chama /Española	Taos	Pecos	Total
Early Classic (1325–1450)	30	22	30	20	15	40	25	47	2	9	240
<100	7	8	10	5	2	24	4	8	0	4	72
101–500	15	6	10	7	5	9	12	11	0	4	79
501–1,000	5	4	3	2	3	2	2	9	1	0	31
1,001+	1	0	1	0	5	4	1	6	0	1	19
Unknown	2	4	6	6	0	1	6	13	1	0	39
Middle Classic (1450–1525)	15	11	17	11	9	23	15	34	2	3	140
<100	1	0	3	2	1	7	4	5	0	1	24
101–500	9	4	7	4	1	8	7	5	0	1	46
501–1,000	2	4	3	2	2	3	2	8	1	0	27
1,001+	1	0	1	0	5	4	0	5	0	1	17
Unknown	2	3	3	3	0	1	2	11	1	0	26
Late Classic (1525–1625)	22	14	16	9	11	26	6	19	2	2	127
<100	5	0	3	2	2	6	1	3	0	0	22
101–500	12	5	6	2	0	10	4	4	0	1	44
501–1,000	2	4	3	2	3	4	1	5	1	0	25
1,001+	1	0	1	0	5	5	0	4	0	1	17
Unknown	1	5	3	3	1	1	0	3	1	0	18

Table 7.3. (continued)

Time Period Site Size (# Rooms)	South Rio Grande	Salinas	Central Rio Grande	Santo Domingo	Galisteo	Upper /Lower Jemez	Santa Fe /Pajarito	Chama /Española	Taos	Pecos	Total
Historic (1625–1700)	14	12	12	6	8	16	5	9	2	2	86
<100	3	0	4	2	2	2	0	1	0	0	14
101–500	7	4	4	2	0	5	3	1	0	1	27
501–1,000	1	3	2	0	2	3	2	2	1	0	16
1,001+	1	0	1	0	3	5	0	2	0	1	13
Unknown	2	5	1	2	1	1	0	3	1	0	16
Total	38	26	31	23	18	57	26	48	2	9	278
<100	10	8	11	7	3	28	5	9	0	4	85
101–500	18	7	10	8	5	16	12	11	0	4	91
501–1,000	5	5	3	2	3	5	2	9	1	0	35
1,001+	1	0	1	0	5	7	1	6	0	1	22
Unknown	4	6	6	6	2	1	6	13	1	0	45

ume), the use of violence against Pueblo populations, especially in the central Rio Grande, is another consistency among the various Spanish entradas in the northern Southwest (Kulisheck 2005). Spaniards destroyed villages, and Pueblo peoples abandoned entire districts in advance of the Spanish once their reputation preceded them. Yet with the departure of the Spanish, Pueblo populations persisted in most districts. For example, at Zuni, even though Hawikku was the first recorded scene of Vázquez de Coronado's aggression against the Pueblos, the settlement continued to be a vital place until the Pueblo Revolt. In the seventeenth century, a mission was established there (Hodge 1937). A different pattern occurred in the Galisteo basin. San Marcos was briefly abandoned during Vázquez de Coronado's crossing of the Galisteo basin, but it was reoccupied by the 1580s (Flint 2008; Ramenofsky et al. 2009). On the other hand, several Galisteo basin pueblos, including Galisteo, San Lazaro, and San Cristobal, were apparently occupied throughout the sixteenth century (Hodge et al. 1945).

In essence, then, our reading of the sixteenth-century explorer accounts from the northern Southwest leads to two counterintuitive insights: local and severe disruption and even termination in the case of some villages in regions such as Tiguex, coupled with large-scale regional persistence. There is no clear-cut evidence of massive demographic loss within historic documents.

Archaeological Settlement

Settlement evidence (room counts and sizes, as well as settlement counts and sizes) is the most accessible proxy for measuring archaeological populations. In the centuries leading up to Spanish exploration, early modern Pueblo populations had shifted almost exclusively to an aggregated pattern of settlement, with most Pueblo peoples residing in towns of one hundred persons or more (Adams and Duff 2004; Adler et al. 1996). Although the predominance of aggregated settlements means that most Pueblo population centers occupied during the sixteenth century are known to archaeologists, reconstructing the sizes of population in those centers is exceedingly difficult (Kulisheck 2005).

To convert archaeological indicators of population into numbers of people involves knowing how many people occupied rooms or

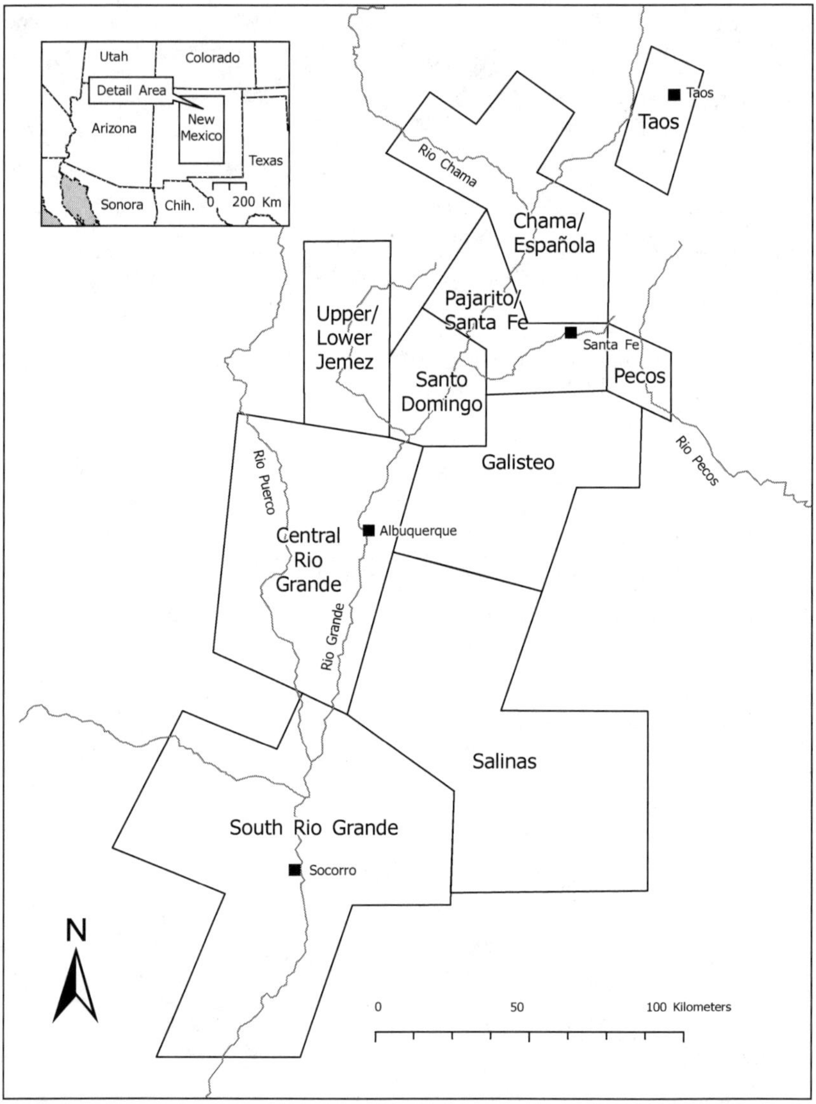

Figure 7.1. The districts of the Northern and Central Rio Grande region.

structures, the duration of structure use, the duration of settlement use, as well as patterns of residential mobility. Because uncertainty surrounds estimating any of these parameters, the resulting figures vary widely from one researcher to the next and, in the end, have little empirical meaning (Nelson et al. 1994).

Rather than converting archaeological parameters of population into numbers of people, we query the archaeological settlement record directly, tracking the direction of population change in the Rio Grande region through time (see Figure 7.1). In this examination, archaeological settlement counts are accumulated by the same geographic districts employed in the historical summary (see Table 7.1). To control for variation in settlement size and, therefore, population, settlements are separated into broad categories by the number of rooms by pueblo by district. Although coarse-grained, this examination agrees with the historical summary, as well as our earlier exploration of the issue (Ramenofsky et al. 2011). At both the scale of district or village, the 1500s were overall a period of relative demographic stability. Major demographic perturbations that took place in the region date to the mid-1400s and the early to mid-1600s.

Regionally, the settlement record from the fourteenth century through the seventeenth century demonstrates the continuing process of consolidation and coalescence that began much earlier across the northern Southwest (Adler et al. 1996; Hill et al. 2004). The maximum number of settlements of all sizes ($n = 240$) occurred during the Early Classic Period. The high settlement counts are likely a function of both intrinsic demographic growth and population migration/amalgamation that occurred as the Jornada, the Mogollon Highlands, and the Mogollon Rim were abandoned by early modern Pueblo peoples (Adams and Duff 2004; Adler et al. 1996; Duff 2002; Hill et al. 2004). From this high, the changes in settlement counts by group size follow a stepwise downward pattern.

The first major settlement decline occurred during the Middle Classic Period, when 42 percent of all settlements were abandoned. Because of aggregation, more small pueblos were vacated than larger ones. Across the late fifteenth century and sixteenth century (Middle through Late Classic), settlement loss continued but was minimal—and not statistically significant. Despite Spanish presence and evidence of severe drought episodes during the late sixteenth century (Van West et al., this volume), settlement counts suggest relatively stable populations. This trend, however, is not maintained in the seventeenth century. The second major decline of settlements occurs in the Historic Period when 33 percent of surviving villages are abandoned. Although sizable, the loss is not as great as during the process of abandonment and aggregation between the Early and Middle Classic.

At the scale of district, the sixteenth-century pattern is variable. The Galisteo, Salinas, and Southern Rio Grande show a net increase in settlements, but the Pajarito and lower Chama show a decrease. In the latter districts, the roots of these declines are apparently traceable to the population disruptions of the fifteenth century. On the Pajarito Plateau, populations began to decline in the late fourteenth century, and the decline became sustained after 1450 (Kohler et al. 2004). In the Chama valley, population levels likely peaked in the early 1400s, and they were in decline by the last decades of the fifteenth century (Fowles 2004). Ironically, both districts were largely abandoned during the sixteenth century but show some evidence of reoccupation during the seventeenth century, perhaps by refugees fleeing Spanish domination over the remaining occupied districts of the Pueblo world (Ramenofsky and Feathers 2002).

We are not the first to document this pattern of stability. Albert Schroeder (1992), using part of H. P. Mera's survey data (1940), showed attrition and consolidation of settlements between the early 1300s and the mid-1600s, with the greatest decline taking place in the mid-1400s. Elinore Barrett's (2002) settlement dataset, reliant on historic accounts to determine the occupation of villages in the sixteenth and seventeenth centuries, reached much the same conclusion, with nondirectional population shifts in the sixteenth century followed by a significant abandonment of aggregated settlements in the early to mid-1600s.

There has been, by contrast, no empirical settlement evidence for catastrophic collapse during the sixteenth century. Mark Lycett (1995) pointed to the terminal sixteenth-century abandonment of the Pajarito and the Chama as consequences of European arrival in the region, based on their coincidental occurrence. He insisted that the abandonment of some upland areas in the sixteenth century was inconsistent with previous centuries of population change, but this inference predates the research of the last decade and a half that has pointed to long-term population decline coalescence among the Pueblos from the mid-1100s onward (Adler et al. 1996; Hill et al. 2004). In a separate argument, Henry Dobyns (2002) suggests population collapse in the Southwestern settlement record, but he relies on novel ceramic dates not widely accepted by other researchers. The collapse that Dobyns points to follows the same contraction described by our Rio Grande settlement data during the early to mid-fifteenth century, some fifty years or more prior to the arrival of Europeans in the Western Hemisphere.

At this point, then, the weight of archaeological settlement evidence in the sixteenth-century northern Southwest argues for demographic stability. Village settlement histories are more nuanced, characterized by alternating cycles of abandonment and reoccupation. At the higher scale, shifting populations and community consolidation account for the pattern more completely than catastrophic decline. Despite local and severe Spanish depredations and fluctuating climatic conditions, the same regions occupied in the fourteenth century persisted until the early seventeenth century.

Exploring Cause

Having demonstrated that Pueblo populations in the northern Southwest were demographically stable during the sixteenth century, the obvious question is why? Were there factors unique to the Southwest that promoted Native survival but resulted in extinction in large parts of the Southeast? Were Native populations healthier in the Southwest, and were the tribute and other labor demands less onerous? Did the arid climate work against the diffusion of infectious diseases? Because warfare, forced labor, and infectious disease introduction were the principal causes of Native American mortality across the Spanish Empire, we limit our analyses to these variables.

Although Spanish brutality against Native populations was a widespread reality in the sixteenth century, Herbert Bolton (1949) argued more than fifty years ago that the Vázquez de Coronado entrada was peaceful by comparison with Soto's violence in the Southeast. Such a position is no longer supported by the evidence. Flint and Flint's (2005) analysis of the Tiguex War describes how Spaniards raped, tortured, and killed Native peoples, and burned Pueblo fields and settlements. In the wake of that destruction, the distribution and structure of Native settlements in the central Rio Grande changed. Unfortunately, because violence occurred in both the Southeast and the northern Southwest, it cannot be invoked as the cause of the differences in demographic patterns between the regions. In fact, given that there were more sixteenth-century recorded explorations in the interior Southwest than in interior Southeast, the reverse could be argued; the probability of aggression in the northern Southwest was greater than in the Southeast. Balancing this probability, however, is the fact that Soto's exploration in the Southeast was of longer duration than any exploration into the northern Southwest.

Our preliminary analysis of labor drafts, especially in mission settings, suggests that the differences between the two regions may have contributed to the patterns of Native decline or survival in the sixteenth century. In the Spanish colonies of Florida and New Mexico, forced labor, tribute requirements, and missionization began with settlement. These processes began in Florida in the 1560s, forty years earlier than in New Mexico, with labor drafts limited to *repartimiento*. The results expressed in skeletal series clearly suggest severe changes in work requirements for mission populations as well as in nutritional status (Hutchinson et al. 1998; Larsen 2001). These changes, in turn, affected the overall health of Native peoples and contributed to population loss.

In New Mexico, missionization and labor drafts that included both *repartimiento* and *encomienda* began with Juan de Oñate y Salazar's settlement in 1598. Although the documentary record is replete with descriptions of Native abuses in missions that, in turn, contributed to the Pueblo Revolt, the empirical evidence derived from archaeology is only beginning to accumulate. Katherine Spielmann's research in the seventeenth-century Saline missions (Spielmann et al. 2009) shows stress indicators of Native skeletons comparable to those that Dale Hutchinson, Clark Spenser Larsen, and others have documented for the Guale and Timucua in Spanish Florida. Although no less severe than in Florida, the timing of these changes among New Mexico mission populations was later. This temporal difference may have pushed forward into the seventeenth century the onset of Native Pueblo death from labor exploitation and/or inadequate diet.

Finally, infectious disease introduction, whether in mission or non-mission settings, also differentiates the demographic patterns of the Southeast and the Southwest. Although the extent of disease episodes across the Southeast is still under debate (Dobyns 1983; Ethridge and Mitchem, this volume; Hutchinson this volume), the available evidence from the northern Southwest is indisputable. There are no descriptions of disease outbreaks from the sixteenth-century northern Southwest. In fact, prior to the Pueblo Revolt, there are only two or three recorded epidemic episodes within the Pueblo world, and they occur in the seventeenth century (Palkovich 1985; Ramenofsky 1996). Although not mentioned in known documents, some researchers (Ramenofsky 1987; Upham 1986) have suggested that smallpox diffused north with exploring parties. The stability of settlement counts during the sixteenth century, however, coupled with the absence of disease descriptions, suggests this was not the case. There is no historical or archaeological evidence to suggest that smallpox or other pathogens gained a foothold in the region in the sixteenth century, leading us to infer that disease transmission was not a significant variable during exploration.

Why is this the case? Like other Native Americans, Southwestern peoples lacked immunity to European infectious agents. Yet they somehow escaped the disease events that so decimated Native peoples in the Southeast. The causes of this unexpected outcome are a function of disease ecology relative to the geography of the northern Southwest.

More than two thousand kilometers separated the Native populations in the northern Southwest from the centers of Spanish population in Mexico. Unlike the coastal Southeast, the distances were great and the travel was arduous and infrequent. Consequently, the remoteness and difficulty of access created a kind of geographic barrier against disease transmission between the Spaniards and Native Southwestern peoples (Ramenofsky 1987). In addition, the sizes of the exploring parties into the Southwest contributed to Native disease protection. After Vázquez de Coronado, Spanish legal reforms limited the size of entradas (Hammond and Rey 1966; Mathers, this volume); later Southwestern explorations were numerically too small to be reservoirs for the most common pathogens. Even if one or more viruses or bacteria managed to hitchhike on one or more explorers or their livestock, the probability of affecting more than one or a few communities was very low. Overall, as compared to the Southeast, Native population density in the northern Southwest was low and communities were widely scattered.

Domesticated livestock constitute the last potential pathway of infectious disease transmission into the Southwest. Although livestock was associated with entradas in both regions, the array of animals was different and may have indirectly protected Southwestern peoples. Southeastern livestock included cattle, horses, and pigs, but neither sheep nor goats (Ramenofsky 1987; Ramenofsky and Galloway 1997). Southwestern explorers brought cattle, goats, sheep, and horses, but not pigs. Because pigs do not sweat, they were not well suited to the hot, arid climate of the Southwest. Even after missionization, pigs were not common (Spielmann et al. 2009). Given the number of infectious agents transmitted from pigs to humans, their absence likely conferred an advantage to Southwestern Pueblo survival.

Conclusions

The shifts in Pueblo settlements extracted from the documentary record and archaeological settlement record of the sixteenth century concord with patterns of settlement change that had been taking place in the Pueblo world since the mid-twelfth century. In the four centuries that preceded the arrival of the Spaniards in the northern Southwest, Pueblo populations had gradually abandoned significant portions of the region and consolidated in ever-larger aggregated villages (Adler et al. 1996; Hill et al. 2004). At the same time, individual settlements remained demographically unstable, shrinking and growing throughout their life histories as populations flowed from one village and district to another (Kulisheck 2003; Ramenofsky et al. 2009).

In sum, we believe that the nature of Native–Spanish interaction in the northern Southwest was fundamentally different than in the Southeast, and those differences had demographic significance through the sixteenth century. Numerous factors made the diffusion of infectious agents unlikely. The region was geographically remote; encounters between Spaniards and Native populations were infrequent, even stochastic; Native populations were unevenly distributed across space;

excepting the Vázquez de Coronado entrada, the sizes of the exploring parties were small and their duration of stay brief; and domesticated livestock excluded pigs. Coupled with these factors was the later onset of missionization and labor demands imposed by the *encomienda* and *repartimiento*. The sum total, singly or in combination, inadvertently shielded Native peoples from the onslaught of European conquest and resulted in demographic stability.

This demonstration of stability is important in another regard. It emphasizes that the effects of European conquest and colonialism varied across Native North America and were contingent on both the nature of Indigenous demographic organization and the course of Native–European interaction. Using regional-scale settlement data from the lower Mississippi valley, Ramenofsky (1987) demonstrated a catastrophic decline of Native peoples during the sixteenth century. In the same century, Pueblo peoples of the northern Southwest were demographically stable. Although warfare, exploitation, and disease were the common variables that shaped the colonial encounter, understanding how these variables operated singly or in combination must be investigated on a case-by-case basis. Across the continent, there was decline to extinction as well as persistence, and the investigation of the causes and consequences requires the equal but independent analysis of history, archaeology, and biology.

Acknowledgments

The archaeological data in this chapter were developed from the paper files and electronic records of the New Mexico Historic Preservation Division's Archeological Records Management Section. This chapter also benefitted from the suggestions of our fellow participants in the 2009 Amerind Seminar. Carla Van West's comments, and the discussions with Dale Hutchinson, were particularly helpful. Any errors or omissions in the chapter are our own.

Disclaimer

Jeremy Kulisheck's institutional affiliation is listed for identification purposes only. The views expressed in this chapter are those of the authors, and do not necessarily reflect those of the US Department of Agriculture.

8

Entradas and Epidemics in the Sixteenth-Century Southeast

Dale L. Hutchinson

> Far more Native Americans and other non-Eurasian peoples were killed by Eurasian germs than by Eurasian guns or steel weapons. (Diamond 1999:29)

> Today the impact of European pathogens on the New World is undisputed. (Mann 2002:46)

> One cannot deny that following the arrival of Europeans in the Americas after 1492, a demographic decline of immense proportions began. And because the historical evidence is so overwhelming, one cannot deny that the introduction of Old World diseases played a major role in that decline. (Alchon 2003:148)

> Though the fact of demographic decline is widely acknowledged, its magnitude and timing have been a fruitful source of disagreement and debate. (Kunitz 1994:13)

The transformation of the New World that resulted from European exploration and colonization is undeniable. Native populations were subjected to forced labor, substantial migration, dramatic social change, and population declines. Thought once to have occurred primarily through the brutality of European conquerors, particularly the Spanish, reduction of Indigenous populations has been increasingly attributed for the past few decades to the introduction of Old World diseases.

For at least the past three decades, introduced infectious diseases have been emphasized as the primary cause of Native depopulation (e.g., Alchon 2003; Cook 1998; Cook and Lovell 1992; Diamond 1999;

Dobyns 1983, 1993; Ramenofsky 1987; Reff 1991; Smith 1987; Stannard 1992; Thornton 1987). Brought into "virgin soil populations"—those with no previous immunity—the new diseases are said to have swept through Native populations like a scythe reaping the nonimmune.

The disease impacts are often described as pandemics, universally affecting Native populations across vast spatial, social, and natural landscapes. Some who study the impacts of European migration emphasize the sweeping decimation brought about by the diseases they introduced as extending across all of the Americas, eliminating as much as 90 percent of the Native population in less than a century, essentially during the time of the Spanish entradas (e.g., Dobyns 1993).

There is no doubt that Native populations suffered the impacts of European-introduced diseases, but the speed and magnitude of their impacts is highly debated. While some hypothesize that the impact was immediate and widespread, others emphasize less immediate and more geographically restricted disease impacts (e.g., Kunitz 1994).

As with many theoretical issues, much depends on the data one is willing to accept as evidence for the impact of new diseases on Native populations and their resulting population declines. The question, simply put, is have we been able to demonstrate that epidemic disease ravaged Native populations, reducing them by as much as 90 percent, during the sixteenth century? A second question is this: What level of evidence are we willing to accept that demonstrates immediate population collapse due to introduced infectious diseases, and how demonstrable does that evidence have to be?

Two sources of data, demographic estimates of Native populations at the time of contact and ethnohistoric descriptions of disease epidemics, form the nucleus of the earliest conversations regarding Native population reduction. Those sources of data are still fundamental to our discussions, but archaeologists and bioarchaeologists inaugurated supplemental studies in the 1980s that use alternate methods and theoretical approaches to investigate the consequences of introduced diseases for Native populations.

Alternative approaches focus on three main types of evidence and interpretation of introduced disease: direct evidence, inferential evidence, and contextual variables that influence the maintenance and transmission of introduced disease. I would like to briefly discuss each and then focus on where I think we currently stand on the issue of disease epidemics among Native populations in the sixteenth-century Southeast.

Direct Evidence

Direct evidence in the form of pathological skeletal lesions has allowed us to make significant advances in the investigation of health and illness at the contact interface. For instance, numerous researchers have demonstrated declines in health for Southeastern populations following the increased reliance on maize (Hutchinson and Larsen 1988, 1990, 2001; Hutchinson et al. 1998, 2000; Larsen 1993; Larsen et al. 2001). Those skeletal lesions generally record the impacts of long-term infections, as well as behavioral impacts such as dental infection and decreased cortical bone mass.

The problem with using pathological lesions to investigate acute infectious diseases, like those that were introduced by Europeans, is that the new diseases likely killed those affected prior to the development of skeletal lesions. While studies of Mission Period populations in the Southeast have demonstrated long-term impacts on Native health (Larsen et al. 2001), there has never been much hope that skeletal remains would chronicle deaths that occurred very quickly, as in epidemics. Analysis of skeletal lesions caused by long-term infection following colonial policies that reoriented Native subsistence, residence, and mobility patterns has produced substantial evidence regarding changing lifeways brought about by European colonization, but not during the time of the entradas.

Direct evidence in the form of tuberculosis bacilli has been used in several studies (Allison et al. 1973; Braun et al. 1998; Brosch et al. 2002). Molecular evidence (aDNA) has also been used to indicate tuberculosis (Salo et al. 1994) and syphilis (Kolman et al. 1999). DNA extracts from teeth of fourteenth-century individuals buried near Provence, southern France, exhibit clear sequences for *Yersinia pestis*, supporting the presence of plague in the area during the fourteenth century (Drancourt et al. 1998).

Unfortunately, these methods have been limited in use and not applied, as far as I know, in the Southeast. Disputes about precision and quality of the samples are always issues, but more important is what the signature indicates. The signatures really only indicate exposure—not how serious the infection was, the duration, or whether death occurred as a result. Inferences must be made regarding the nature of the impact for the individual(s) and the distribution of the infection.

Thus, while there is some potential for direct evidence to give us signatures of infection, and perhaps specific types of infection, interpreting the impacts of that infection for Native populations remains the task of those who interpret the evidence. Our interpretive lens must still rely on the best contextual information at our disposal at the time of interpretation.

Indirect Evidence

Ethnohistoric descriptions of diseases and epidemics are made by direct and indirect observation. They are often made by secondhand reporting and then extended geographically based on the implication that if one group of people had a disease, then certainly everyone within large adjacent tracts of space must also have suffered.

Ethnohistoric sources also frequently lack the detail necessary to ascertain the specific disease. Descriptions such as "quick death" or "red spots," while offering some information, are not specific enough to interpret the full, or even the potential, impacts of a recorded disease epidemic. Furthermore, the diseases may have evolved and no longer have the same symptoms, or they may be diseases that are no longer familiar.

Demographic estimates have been another inferential method for demonstrating population decline due to epidemic disease. Derived from both archaeological and ethnohistoric sources, demographic estimates are probably the longest-standing source applied to the issue of Native population collapse. Most would agree that demographic estimates for different regions of the Americas show no single pattern of population decline. A number of demographic estimates have been made for the Americas, including the Southeast.

One of those estimates was made by Douglas Ubelaker (1988) of the National Museum of Natural History. Of note in his reconstruction are the varying patterns of response in populations across the Americas (see Figure 8.1). In no single population was the low point (nadir) immediate, and most demographers agree that Native population nadir was

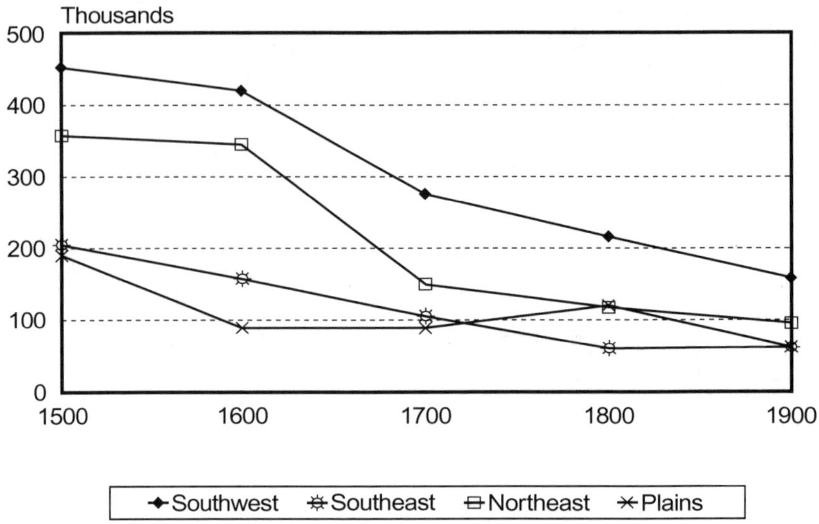

Figure 8.1. Depopulation in North America, 1500–1985. Based on quantitative data in Ubelaker, 1988: Table 2.

actually reached in the latter half of the nineteenth century. As you can see, Ubelaker's reconstruction indicates not an immediate loss of most Southeastern populations but rather a steady decline occurring over roughly three centuries.

Patterning in mortuary contexts has also been considered as an indirect method for investigating the archaeological signatures of disease epidemics. Deviations from "normal" (sustained) mortuary behavior such as aberrant mortuary patterns or mass burials seemed the most promising potential indirect marker of epidemics (Hutchinson 2006; Hutchinson and Mitchem 2001). Unfortunately, for both mass burials and aberrant mortuary patterns, there are many things that inaugurate deviations from sustained patterns of mortuary treatment. These include other types of mass disasters and conflict. The interpreting of mass burials due to intentional violence has seen immense study in the past three decades due to numerous documented conflicts. This body of research suggests that such conflicts should be recognizable in the archaeological record (e.g., Fiorato et al. 2000; Martin and Frayer 1997; Zimmerman et al. 1981).

Aberrant mortuary patterns, on the other hand, present interpretive challenges. Tatham Mound, an Early Contact Period mortuary locality in central Gulf Coast Florida, serves to illustrate the difficulties in using the indirect evidence of mortuary patterning. At Tatham, we excavated 339 burials from the upper (Contact) stratum of the mortuary site. Of the interments, 94 were primary burials, 93 secondary burials, and 152 were derived from the Minimum Number of Individuals (MNI) of unassociated elements. European artifacts associated with several burials at the site allowed us to provide a tight basal date for the Contact Period stratum of 1525 to 1550. Reconstructions of the route of the Hernando de Soto expedition place the mound directly in the route of those Native groups who would have potentially been in contact with those Europeans. At the time of our excavations, a large number of primary burials occurred near the mound summit, and they appeared to be largely later in date due to the inclusion of European artifacts with a number of them (see Figure 8.2).

Comparisons of late prehistoric and protohistoric burial position and form, however, yielded no conclusions about aberrant mortuary patterns. The individuals interred at Tatham did not vary distinctly in position or form from other mortuary localities in the eastern United States (Hutchinson 2006:Table 4.11). Patterns of artifact inclusion, however, were illuminating.

Most European artifacts were included with primary burials, and individuals interred in some burial positions had more artifacts associated with them. European artifacts were more often interred with females and children, whereas those of Native origin were more frequently interred with males. This pattern was not, however, unique to Tatham Mound. The Early Contact Period sites of Tram and Cameron in the northeastern United States, for instance, exhibited similar patterns; children possessed the most European artifacts, followed by females and then males (Wray et al. 1991).

Another factor in our interpretations was the presence of a greasy, black lens of soil approximately twenty to thirty centimeters thick (Feature 6) that lay directly underneath the Contact Period burials. Our working hypothesis has been that the soil feature was made by the accumulation of human body fats.

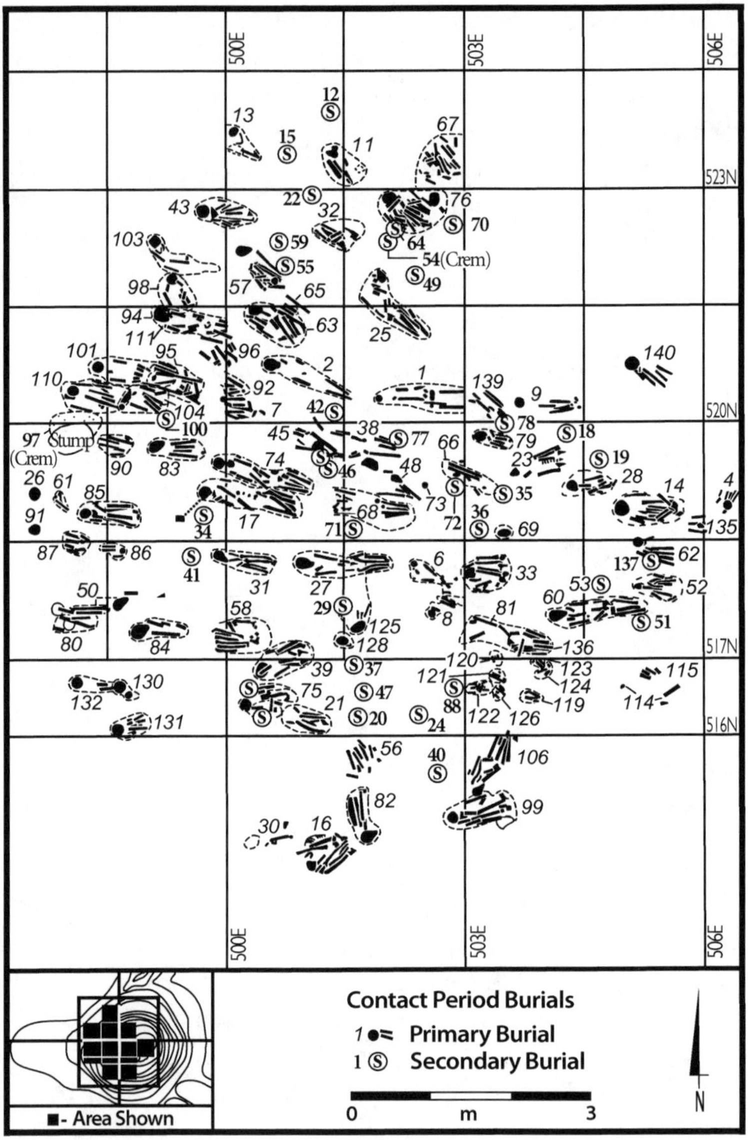

FIGURE 8.2. Plan map of Tatham Mound showing post-Contact burials by burial position. Reprinted by permission of University Press of Florida.

One hypothesis for the combination of data from Tatham is simultaneous death within a short period of time, possibly from a disease epidemic. There are other competing hypotheses though, such as accumulation of burials through the continuous use of mortuary space.

Ritual cycles of a number of stages are very common in the death and burial of dead ancestors. Many ethnographic observations and archaeological excavations have shown that primary burials (articulated at the time of burial) often represent a first stage of mortuary treatment in a ritual cycle where they will, after a number of years, be disinterred, cleansed, and placed in a final mortuary setting as disarticulated remains (secondary burials). Primary burials in the context of ritual cycles represent a snapshot in time, those individuals who have not yet been afforded the final process for whatever reason (Hutchinson and Aragon 2002).

In the Southeast, we are most familiar with the charnel house, as well as with the accompanying rituals described by Father Gabriel Sagard (Wrong 1939) and Father Jean de Brebeuf (Kidd 1953; Thwaites 1896–1901, Vol. 10:279–305), both descriptions of the Huron. Le Page Du Pratz provides an additional description of the closure of a ritual for the Natchez following the death of its leader, Tattooed Serpent (Le Page Du Pratz 1972, original account 1774).

Because mortuary spaces are used over lengthy periods of time, large numbers of primary and secondary burials often accumulate. Often altered during the process of further ritual use, collective mortuary spaces see frequent alteration, and the original context of those placed within a mortuary space is often in question. Delineating habitual use of a collective mortuary space from aberrant mortuary patterns will be difficult.

Abandonment of a region has been used as another indirect indicator of depopulation. Again, as with mass burials, the challenge is to determine one cause as compared to another (or multiple causes). In La Florida the historic narratives frequently mention migration to another region as a response to the incursion of Spanish entradas. Migration was undoubtedly inaugurated by a number of variables that included fear or avoidance of conflict; economic, social, and political unrest; and other fragmentation of societal structure (Hann 2003). While disease remains one possibility, it is only one among many.

I think the reason the ritual cycle ended at Tatham was the arrival of European explorers and colonists. Ethnohistoric documents for Florida describe the tremendous amount of migration inaugurated by increased pressure from Europeans as the early European exploratory parties gave way to the frequent movements of increasingly common and well-populated urban centers such as St. Augustine (Hann 2003). I think that those interred at Tatham were afforded a final mortuary ritual, an observation supported by a number of projectile points found in the surface of the mound and a row of Busycon cups that ran in a line over the top; the use of both types of objects is well documented in ethnohistoric descriptions of burial in the Southeast. The fact that no Mission Period ceramics or artifacts are found suggests that the site was abandoned prior to the seventeenth century. The primary burials represent those who had not gone through the final ritual cycle.

Contextualizing Epidemic Disease and Changing Health

It would seem that if we continue to stress a model of Native population collapse that occurred during the time of the entradas (within a century or so) and was brought about primarily by epidemic disease, then we need to do a few things. First, we must delineate adequate archaeological signatures of epidemic disease. Given that a rapid-impact disease model stresses short-term contact between Europeans and Natives—or that the movement of epidemic diseases into those populations likely occurred without direct contact with Europeans—it appears that as archaeologists and bioarchaeologists we have our work cut out for us.

There are a few sites in the Southeast where disease epidemics may have occurred during the sixteenth century (e.g., Tatham Mound; Hutchinson 2006; Mitchem 1989), but disease remains one hypothesis among several that could explain the archaeological remains present at these locations. Indicating that the cause of one signature or another "could indicate epidemic disease" is simply speculative and inadequate. We need to be able to arrive at a conclusion through the systematic elimination of competing hypotheses. I would say that at present there are no conclusive archaeological assemblages that support the notion that epidemic diseases decimated Native populations in the first century of contact in the Southeast.

The more we search for evidence of epidemic disease associated with the entradas of the sixteenth century, the less it seems that such evidence exists. I suggest that the strength of the evidence is in the direction of a Native population collapse that did not happen in a hundred years, but rather over the course of 300 to 350 years. I propose that rather than a single-effects approach of introduced infectious disease, we focus on a multiple-effects model. If the nadir for Native populations occurred during the mid- to late 1800s, and many scholars contend that it did (e.g., Ubelaker 1988), then the question simply put is this: What happened during the period between 1500 and 1850 that facilitated the maintenance and transmission of infectious diseases among Native populations?

New diseases introduced by Europeans were undoubtedly a significant force in the changing health of Native populations during the sixteenth century and beyond. But there are a number of things lacking in many versions of the disease hypothesis that weaken its explanatory power.

One troubling issue with the disease hypothesis as it stands is the supremacy given to disease, and the absence often of factors that facilitated transmission and maintenance of diseases and epidemics. Diseases are processes, not things, and the prevailing disease model seems often to leave out most of the social, political, and economic factors that facilitated the maintenance and transmission of new diseases. The problem is that epidemics are highly visible events that catch people's attention. Consequently, there is likely to be a bias toward recording them, as opposed to more mundane, everyday incidents (e.g., economic transactions or social rituals).

More troubling perhaps is the presentation of the uniqueness of the event. Epidemics occurred throughout Eurasian history after about 500 B.C., and there was no uniqueness about them. They were circumscribed to particular regions and populations, and while mortality was high, complete decimation was never an outcome. After all, the Black Death, arguably the most devastating epidemic in history, did not leave Europe completely depopulated. Certainly many people died, but Europe went on.

A number of variables contributed to the Black Death of 1347–1349. By the mid-thirteenth century, social and climatic changes in Western Europe resulted in crop failures and famine (Gottfried 1983:23–30; Hays 1998; Karlen 1995). During the 1290s, Europe was struck by another series of famines (Karlen 1995). Conditions deteriorated even further between 1300 and 1347. A succession of crop failures and food shortages continued and would not come to an end until after the Black Death. In 1316 and 1317 harvests improved, but from 1316 until 1322 a series of livestock epidemics decimated what remained of Europe's cattle population. The pattern of crop failures continued until bubonic plague began to expand throughout Eurasia.

Bubonic plague has broken out several times in the past two centuries, always associated with war, deforestation, natural disasters, or other severe disturbances of the ecological balance (Fritz et al. 1996; Gregg 1978; Ruiz 2001). One recent example, the Vietnam War, serves to remind us that when the cultural/biological interface is disturbed, plague can flare into epidemics quickly. Tens of thousands of cases of bubonic plague occurred during the 1960s and 1970s in refugee-swollen Saigon and the disturbed countryside of South Vietnam (Gregg 1978; Meade and Earickson 2000:76).

I began with a quote from Jared Diamond's *Guns, Germs, and Steel* (Diamond 1999). A view like that espoused by Diamond separates germs from the ecological and behavioral context in which they occur. In fact, one cannot understand the impact of Eurasian germs without also considering the concomitant role of Eurasian guns or steel weapons. The collapse of Native population health and population numbers was caused not only by the arrival of new diseases but also by a suite of landscape and behavior alterations that increased Native susceptibility to ill health and disease.

A number of archaeologists and bioarchaeologists have argued that there was no single landscape of introduced disease transmission, but rather that numerous variables such as spatial organization, economy, political structure, and population density influenced the maintenance and transmission of infectious disease (e.g., Ramenofsky 1990; Ramenofsky et al. 2003). Others, such as Alfred Crosby (1972, 1986), have long looked at the much larger picture of ecological reconfiguration and biological exchange that occurred coincident with colonization of the New World. Such efforts contextualize the arrival of new diseases within the constraints of populations differing markedly in a number of features.

The past two decades have seen substantial revisions to the traditional disease hypothesis. There has been a tempering of thoughts about the magnitude of impact, largely through the recognition that differences in natural and social landscapes acted to differentially influence the transmission and maintenance of infectious disease. Our ability to decipher the signatures of infectious disease is improving, but we need to continue to develop new methods of detection and to improve our interpretive lens. As we develop new analytical approaches and methods of detection, we should likewise direct our efforts toward examining the contexts created by the Spanish entradas that facilitated diseases in Native populations.

SECTION V

Political Organization

9

Sixteenth-Century Indigenous Settlement Dynamics in the Upper Middle Rio Grande Valley

Richard C. Chapman

The earliest entrada-related activities in the desert Southwest were undertaken by Esteban the Moor, Fray Marcos de Niza, and Melchoir Díaz/Juan de Zaldívar—who reached areas of present-day New Mexico and Arizona in 1539. The later and far larger expedition of Francisco Vázquez de Coronado encountered and then attacked the Zuni inhabitants of Hawikku in July 1540, and subsequently moved to the Middle Rio Grande valley for a more extended occupation. Unlike the small and short-lived path-finding expeditions of Esteban, Niza, and Díaz/Zaldívar, the Vázquez de Coronado party—numbering some two thousand to twenty-eight hundred individuals and more than seven thousand livestock—camped in the Zuni area for more than four months, and in the Albuquerque–Bernalillo area for a more protracted period of more than a year (Flint 2008; Mathers, this volume).

The advanced guard of the Vázquez de Coronado expedition, under Hernando de Alvarado, reached the Middle Rio Grande area in the late summer of 1540. Here, they found a particularly dense cluster of large pueblos situated in an expansive, well-watered floodplain and with seasonal resources available at different elevations in the nearby Sandia and Manzano mountains. The Spanish referred to this region as the Tiguex province, which was anchored by large communities such as Kuaua in the north, with more than 1000 rooms, and the Pueblo of Isleta in the south (Figure 9.1).

The Pueblo Indian settlements of the Upper Middle Rio Grande valley encountered by Spanish-led entradas are described as a series of provinces consisting of large residential villages, each containing multistoried adobe dwellings and storage rooms, plazas, and *estufas* (subterranean chambers). Implicit in these chronicles is an assumption that

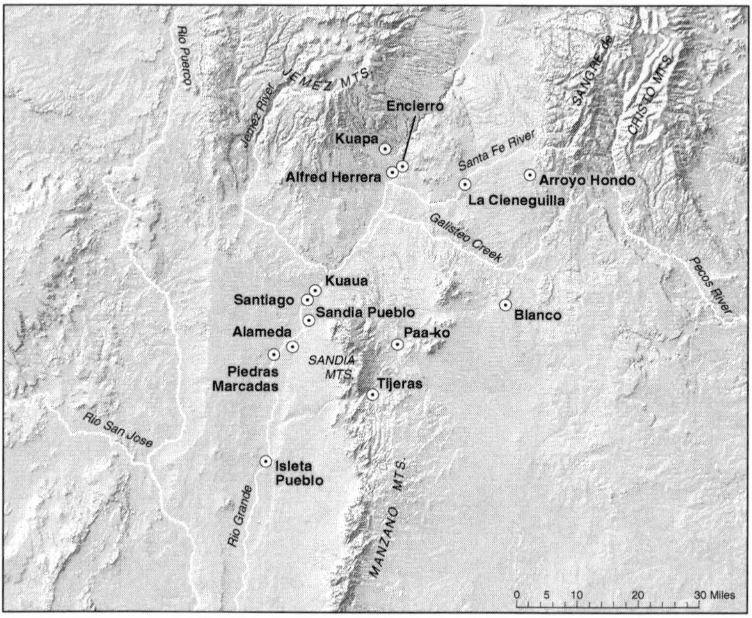

FIGURE 9.1. Map showing locations of Indigenous Pueblo village sites referred to in text (by Ronald Stauber).

these villages served as year-round residences for local groups that had long histories of continuous occupation at each village. Entrada accounts further characterize Indigenous settlements as consisting of groups of linguistically similar villages (termed provinces) that were organized into political polities. In this chapter it is argued on the basis of archaeological research that a very different settlement dynamic actually characterized Ancestral Pueblo occupation of the region at the time of the earliest European contacts—a pattern that had its origins deep in Pueblo history.

For the period from A.D. 1300 to 1540, archaeological survey and excavation data point to an annual cycle of aggregation during winter at these larger village centers, with a corresponding population dispersal across the landscape from spring through fall at numerous small field houses, ramadas, and open camps. At these locations the Native inhabitants of Tiguex and neighboring regions engaged in agriculture, hunting, gathering, and other resource procurement activities. Furthermore, the large residential centers themselves were characterized by frequent abandonment and rebuilding episodes reflecting population relocations among major villages over multiannual cycles.

This pattern reflected an effective adaptation to a region characterized by patchy habitats, extreme fluctuations of unpredictable rainfall, and noncontiguous small tracts of land suitable for horticulture—all of which required the development of a subsistence economy geared to exploitation of numerous, often widely dispersed small floral and faunal habitats, as well as patchy arable landscapes. Effective pursuit of this form of subsistence for large regional populations necessitated flexible social institutions and arrangements that allowed for an annual cycle of population dispersal across the landscape from village centers, while at the same time facilitating frequent relocation of population segments among village centers (i.e., on both seasonal and interannual cycles).

It can be argued that Contact Period Indigenous communities in the Middle Rio Grande were characterized by a "village-based" settlement system involving an annual cycle of dispersal of the residential population from spring through fall. When employed widely throughout the region, this strategy would have enabled Southern Tiwa and other neighboring Pueblo groups to take maximum advantage of wild and domestic food resources, to aggregate both people and accumulated food stores (in winter) to facilitate redistribution of resources, and to maintain the religious and ritual activities necessary for the well-being and social integration of their communities—each characterized by a large population center.

Coupled with this pattern of seasonal mobility and broadly based subsistence was the existence of a flexible set of family, clan, and perhaps moiety relationships across the larger region. The latter helped to facilitate easy relocation of family or larger groups from one center to another in response to the local cycles of drought and adversity in both agricultural and nonagricultural floral and faunal productivity. The ability to quickly abandon areas stricken by drought, and to relocate where agricultural production was not impaired, provided settlement stability over a wide region during multiyear cycles.

Seasonal Dispersal and Aggregation of Village Inhabitants

The early history of archaeological investigation into Classic Period Ancestral Pueblo occupation in the Upper Middle Rio Grande and environs was characterized by a focus on large-scale excavations at major village centers (e.g., the pueblos of Pecos, Kuaua, Santiago, Paa-ko, Pueblo Encierro, and Alfred Herrera, as well as Nelson's extensive testing research at the Galisteo basin pueblos). In all but a few cases, emphasis on survey and excavation in the vicinity of these village sites was modest until the advent of cultural resource management projects in the late 1960s and early 1970s. In one of these early survey projects at Cochiti Reservoir (Biella and Chapman 1977b), many small Pueblo IV sites were identified that were contemporaneous with the known larger village settlements in the near vicinity—such as Pueblo del Encierro, Alfred Herrera, and Kuapa. These small sites included open campsites, camp locations with dry-laid masonry wing walls or boulders for protection, and actual field houses constructed of masonry, some with small habitation and storage rooms. Comparison of room sizes and analysis of suitability for winter occupation of the sites or long-term storage revealed these were not, for the most part, winter-worthy constructions (Biella 1979:122–128). A diversity of economic practices characterized the small sites as well, including hunting, gathering, and horticulture, although the sites contained little evidence of food preparation involving the milling of maize.

In comparison, room sizes at large village sites like Pueblo del Encierro were consistently larger, constructed to be habitable in cold weather, and contained numerous storage rooms suitable for long-term bulk storage of foodstuffs (Biella 1979:136–137).

Recent archaeological research directed toward discovery and analysis of the "small site" component of Classic Period village occupation in the Upper Middle Rio Grande valley has revealed substantial evidence of seasonally occupied campsites, ramadas, masonry rooms, and agricultural facilities such as terraces, check dams, and diversion channels in the environs of large village sites. These include projects at Pueblo Blanco in the Galisteo basin (Kurota 2006a), surveys and excavations on La Bajada Mesa on the north side of the Santa Fe River near La

Cieneguilla Pueblo (Gerow and Doleman 2002; Gerow and Hogan 2005; Gerow and Kurota 2004), and surveys on the south side of the Santa Fe River in the same general area (Kludt 2005). Finally, a patchwork of surveys and small-scale excavations on Albuquerque's West Mesa above Piedras Marcadas, Alameda, and Santiago pueblos undertaken over the last fifteen years by numerous CRM firms to facilitate the rapid urban expansion of the communities of Albuquerque and Rio Rancho have revealed a similar set of small open campsites and small rooms contemporaneous with occupation of nearby large Pueblo IV village centers (Chapman and Estes 2004; Chapman and Stauber 2009; Cordero 2007, 2008; Kurota 2006b; Kurota and Chapman 2008; Kurota and Hogan 2009).

The picture that emerges for Classic Period occupation prior to European contact is one of a biseasonal settlement system, involving population dispersal across the landscape during the spring through fall to engage in subsistence activities (including agricultural production). This system also seems to have been characterized by aggregation at large village sites during winter. We speculate this pattern not only would facilitate a broadening of the subsistence base of the populations during the spring through fall seasons but also would encourage the redistribution of hunted, gathered, and agriculturally produced resources at the central places (villages) during winter (Figure 9.2). The presence of plazas and kivas at these larger pueblo communities suggests a range of social activities and ceremonial practices that also would have helped to integrate the larger groups assembled at these sites.

The utility of this suite of settlement and economic strategies may have been in part to accommodate the lack of large acreages of agriculturally suitable lands in the immediate vicinity of any given village. As a result, Pueblo agricultural practices in the region needed to be fine-tuned to target small, noncontiguous tracts of arable land at greater distances from larger village locations. This dispersed strategy of production could also help to counter the unpredictability of climate regimes and their associated effects on agricultural production from year to year. In addition, these approaches would have taken advantage of the considerable biotic diversity available in the Rio Grande, Galisteo, and Santa Fe basins. Finally, these dispersed seasonal strategies would help to facilitate a broad-spectrum hunting and gathering economy,

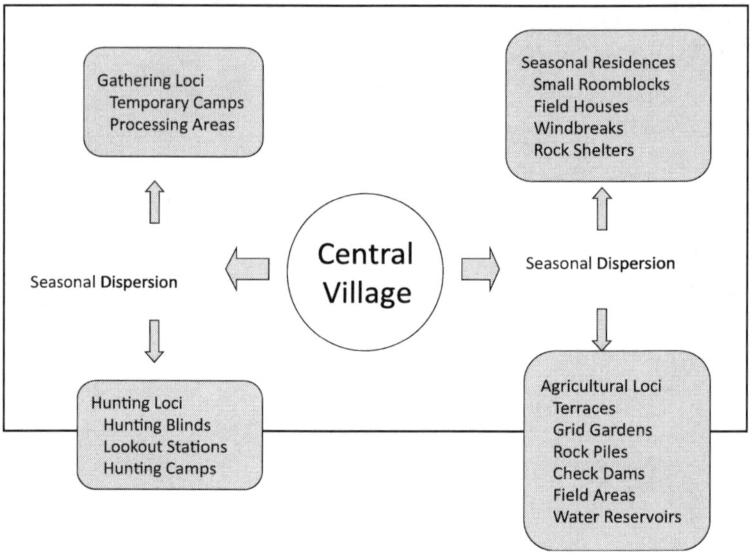

FIGURE 9.2. Schematic of seasonal settlement model (by Alex Kurota).

which would either buffer, or was buffered by, complementary agricultural production.

Hints that this archaeologically documented seasonal strategy of dispersed settlement during the warmer months was still operating in the sixteenth century are found in the Hernán Gallegos account of the first encounter with Ancestral Pueblo Indians by the Chamascado-Rodríguez expedition. In August 1581, from the general area somewhere south of present-day San Marcial, five members of the party decided to follow a trail they had found the day before, which traversed a plain for two leagues (presumably away from the Rio Grande itself) to reach a "sierra," or mountain range. "On entering the mountainous territory, we saw an Indian brave and two inhabited huts. Taking our horses and arms we went in that direction and discovered many people, who fled toward the mountains when they saw us approaching" (Hammond and Rey 1966:80–81). The party was subsequently informed about the existence of inhabited pueblos further upstream.

It seems possible that the "two inhabited huts" encountered by the Chamascado-Rodríguez party were field houses, and that the "many people" who fled at their approach were the inhabitants of the upstream pueblos, engaged in seasonal farming and subsistence activities near the mountains flanking the Rio Grande in late summer (August 1581).

Two days later and further upstream, Gallegos writes that the party "came to a pueblo of many houses three stories high, but found no inhabitants. They had left the night before because they had noticed our approach" (Hammond and Rey 1966:82).

While Gallegos attributes the absence of population solely to the arrival of the party, it is tempting to suggest that most of the village inhabitants may still have been residing at distant field locations such as those encountered earlier by the party some two-days' march downstream. After the passage of an unspecified amount of time, Gallegos states: "We endeavored to locate the people in order to calm them and bring them to us peaceably, which we managed to do" with the result that after the news of their arrival spread "there was not a day when we were not surrounded and accompanied by more than twelve thousand people" (Hammond and Rey 1966:82).

Population Movement Between Village Centers

Another facet of this settlement equation relates to longer-term cycles of village center occupation and the relocation of population segments among different village centers within the greater region. Because many earlier archaeological excavations were directed toward large Pueblo IV village sites, we have a significantly improved understanding of how each of these villages was physically constructed and how they evolved architecturally and historically. Overall, these excavations reveal an interesting and consistent pattern of multiple events reflecting roomblock construction, abandonment, and rebuilding characterizing the "architectural life history" of each construction episode. These construction phases occur both horizontally at times, with new roomblocks (enclosing new plazas) being added to the existing suites of rooms. In other cases, there is evidence of overlapping, vertical construction, with older roomblocks being abandoned, used for refuse disposal, and then leveled off for new construction above them. Sometimes as many as four or five vertical episodes of reconstruction are evident, and individual sites seem to go through apparently idiosyncratic expansions (Figure 9.3). In some

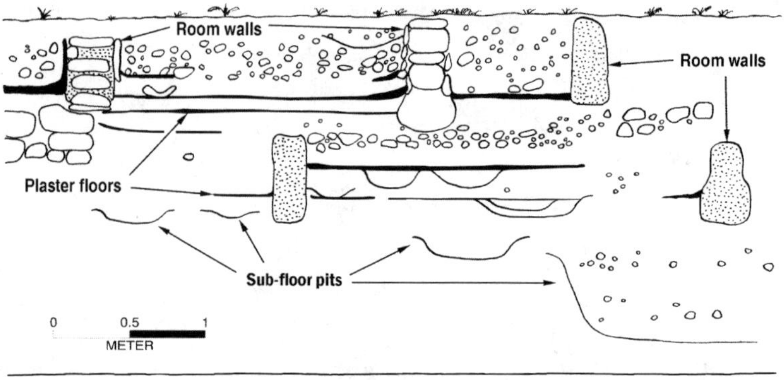

FIGURE 9.3. Typical archaeological profile of Pueblo roomblock construction stages (adapted by Ronald Stauber).

cases, these expansion phases are characterized by large groupings of new roomblocks constructed simultaneously; at other times, more modest household-sized constructions are added. Such multiple construction episodes have been well documented through excavations at Arroyo Hondo (Creamer 1993:134), Tijeras Pueblo (Cordell 1980:11), Pueblo del Encierro (Snow 1976:xvi–xvii), and Qualacu (Marshall 1987).

Entrada accounts contain several observations that this multiyear process of abandonment and reoccupation of all or portions of village sites was still a characteristic of Ancestral Pueblo settlement at the time of first contact. One of the earliest references to this is found in Pedro de Castañeda de Nájera's report for the Vázquez de Coronado expedition in 1540: "Between Cicuye and the provincia of Quirix there is . . . another *pueblo* almost entirely depopulated, of which only one section is inhabited. . . . It seemed as if it had recently been destroyed" (Flint and Flint 2005:420). While this probably refers to a site in the Galisteo basin east of the Tiguex province, it is certainly consistent with archaeological evidence of periodic partial abandonment at these sites.

Gallegos, reporting on the Chamuscado-Rodríguez expedition in 1581, notes: "We came to an abandoned pueblo that had been inhabited by a large number of people. . . . The said pueblo was walled in; and the houses had mud walls and were built of adobes, three stories high, so it appeared, though they had crumbled from the rains and seemed to have been abandoned for a long time" (Hammond and Rey 1966:81). Evidence for new construction is provided in Gallegos's final listing of settlements encountered by the expedition, for the area south of modern-day Isleta Pueblo: "Along this river we found another pueblo containing twenty-five two-story houses. We named it Pueblo Nuevo because its construction had just begun" (Hammond and Rey 1966:103).

Diego Pérez de Luxán's account of the Antonio de Espejo expedition the following year (1582) traces the same general route taken by the Chamuscado party and notes two abandoned pueblos south of present-day Socorro: "We found an abandoned pueblo with the houses in ruins . . . after going about three leagues, we came to another abandoned pueblo" (Hammond and Rey 1966:171). It is likely that these are the ruins noted by the previous Chamuscado expedition in the same area a year earlier. As the party moved farther upstream, still in the Piro region, Luxán writes, "On our way we found four large pueblos in ruins and abandoned, and a small hamlet of twenty houses" (Hammond and Rey 1966:173); even farther upstream, he notes, "There were some small pueblos and many deserted ones on this trip" (Hammond and Rey 1966:176).

Taken together, these accounts spanning four decades provide tantalizing glimpses of a settlement system apparently characterized by a cycle of village abandonment and reconstruction throughout the Upper Middle Rio Grande and Galisteo basin regions.

Social Implications of Construction Episodes at Village Sites

Another intriguing commonality observed among the prehistoric excavated sites is a possible pan-regional pattern of room construction and use, which might be interpreted as having a social correlate. At Pueblo del Encierro, Snow (1976:1) notes, for example, that "contiguous rooms were apparently built in units of up to seven or eight, with an effort being made to continue the linearity and alignment of walls already in place in adjacent room clusters," and he draws attention to several such room clusters at different locales within the site. At Arroyo Hondo, Creamer (1993:150) observes that "rapid construction was accomplished cooperatively with several rooms being built in a single construction episode," and she illustrates several room complexes with interconnecting doorways, which she terms residence units. Biella (1979:144) takes these observations a step further to posit that the basic seven-to-eight-room residential unit identified by Snow in the Classic Period village sites can be suggested to have its parallels in the earlier Coalition Period sites. She further suggests that this residential unit may reflect a fundamental social unit within ancestral Pueblo society that persists over the long term and constitutes a more or less economically self-sufficient component of larger local and regional groupings.

Entrada accounts are sparse with respect to details of household organization, but one intriguing observation is offered by Gallegos in 1581 in describing a marriage ceremony: "The first thing given the couple is a house in which to live. . . . The house is two, three, or four stories high, with eight or ten rooms" (Hammond and Rey 1966: 101). More detail on room function is provided for households at Pecos Pueblo as recounted in the Sosa Memoria in 1591: "Each floor of every house has three or four rooms, so that each house, as a whole, counting from top to bottom, has fifteen or sixteen rooms . . . every house is equipped with facilities for grinding corn, including three or four grinding stones mounted in small troughs and provided with pestles." (Hammond and Rey 1966:277). Both accounts seem to describe contiguous room arrangements much like those documented in archaeological excavations.

A Model of Indigenous Settlement during the Period of Spanish Entradas

It is argued here that the apparent patterning in residential construction episodes at these large Classic Period village sites reflects a basic organization of families into households, and that the cycles of construction, occupation, and abandonment that characterize each of the large village sites in the Upper Middle Rio Grande reflect a process of relocation of households among village centers. It is proposed that this Indigenous Pueblo "village-based" settlement system was characterized by an annual dispersal of the resident population from spring through fall to take maximum advantage of wild and domestic food resources, on a nuclear family rather than an extended household basis. Winter aggregation of both people and accumulated food stores at village centers facilitated the redistribution of intracommunity resources and maintenance of religious and ritual activities necessary for the well-being and social integration of such large population centers. In addition, flexible sets of family, clan, and perhaps moiety relationships across the larger region permitted easy relocation of family units or larger groupings from one center to another. These flexible relationships were developed in response to the local cycles of drought and decline in nonagricultural floral and faunal productivity. As a result, the ability to quickly abandon areas stricken by drought and to relocate to more advantageous agricultural areas was not impaired, providing settlement stability over a wide region during multiyear cycles.

This model envisions winter village centers distributed across the landscape to maximize access to both agricultural lands as well as hunting and gathering territories, with arable lands being dispersed and patchy. At the present time there is no evidence of any major reliance on primary drainages such as the Rio Grande for irrigation. Instead, Pueblo communities in the Middle and Northern Rio Grande valley appear to have based their agricultural production on a variety of slopewash runoff controls such as check dams, diversions, and terraces at the margins of the floodplain. These approaches would have maximized the harvesting and storage of rainfall through techniques such as gravel mulching. Evidence of probable agricultural use of the Rio Grande floodplain itself seems to have focused on "recessional agriculture" emphasizing planting in areas made available by receding spring flood waters, the locations of which would be expected to change from year to year (Worman 2009). The agricultural component of this subsistence system was critically dependent upon a fine balance of climatic and other environmental parameters. As a consequence, one or two years of poor crop production could lead Pueblo groups to relocate rapidly to other parts of the landscape and to other village centers.

Implications for Indigenous Political Organization at the Time of the Entradas

If this model fairly represents the underlying economic determinants of annual and interannual village occupation, a region-wide social system permitting the ready movement of household-size and multi-household-size social units could be seen operating for a very long period of Pueblo history. Indeed, it is tempting in this context to draw parallels between the Coalition Period and the Classic Period residential units and the Prudden Unit Pueblo complex recognized over one hundred years ago as a "building block" of Anasazi settlement in the Four Corners region (Prudden 1903). One unresolved issue here, however, is positing the composition of such a household unit and the processes by which a single unit could readily "detach" itself from one village community and "reintegrate" into another.

In a recent presentation, Ford (2009) offers an insightful discussion of Tewa household organization termed *maatui'in* (relatives), which are characterized as complex households consisting of a number of nuclear and extended, multigenerational families that function as both economic and social units, headed by an elder. Ford argues that the *maatui'in*, because of their control over land, provision of house sites, and role in food redistribution and religious life, are the unit of Tewa society that can respond most quickly to exigencies such as crop failure, internal social friction, or external aggression. According to Ford, "They can move out, make an adjustment, and at an appropriate time return to the community. Stories reveal these were not uncommon occurrences" (2009:6). Ford argues that most movements by Tewa populations were undertaken by *maatui'in*, and that because of their integration into larger social entities such as sodalities and moieties, their integration into existing or new villages "can occur almost spontaneously" (2009:7).

The preceding discussion argues that Pueblo economic organization in the sixteenth century, and in earlier periods, was characterized by seasonal dispersal and aggregation on an annual basis at each village center. It also suggests that the basic household units comprising the population inhabiting each village were analogous to Tewa *maatui'in*, who were essentially coalesced at particular villages on a multiannual basis. If those propositions are correct, then the fundamental political organization of villages encountered by the first Spanish-led entradas can be argued to be quite different from that sometimes articulated by the earliest Spanish expeditionaries and chroniclers.

Entrada accounts in fact present two quite different perceptions of Indigenous political organization. One view is first articulated in Castañeda de Nájera's account of Indigenous governance at Cíbola (Zuni) during the early stages of the Vázquez de Coronado expedition where he states, "There are no lords like [those] throughout Nueva España. [Instead], they are governed by a council of the oldest [persons]" (Flint and Flint 2005:417–418). Castañeda repeats this observation regarding governance at the pueblos of the Tiguex province: "They are [all] governed by a council of the oldest [persons]" (Flint and Flint 2005:418).

Additional insight into the nature of governance among the Pueblos is offered by a passage in the Benavídez account of Vázquez de Coronado's negotiations with one of the *principales* of the pueblo of Tiguex at the beginning of the 1540 winter occupation of the province. The Spaniards had named this individual "Juan Alemán." Vázquez de Coronado demanded Alemán "to furnish him three hundred pieces of clothing or more. . . . [Alemán] said that was not for him to do, but rather for the governors, and that above all it was necessary to engage in consultation and to distribute [the burden] among the *pueblos*. Further [he said] that it was necessary to make the request individually to each *pueblo*" (Flint and Flint 2005:402).

These observations of political structure are echoed by Luxán's account of the Espejo expedition some forty years later. In describing the inhabitants of pueblos in the Cochiti area, Luxán notes, "These people are governed by caciques, as they do not have any ruler who has authority beyond his own pueblo" (Hammond and Rey 1966: 179), and he goes on to say that the pueblo of Zia "was governed by three caciques" (Hammond and Rey 1966:180). Later, during the expedition's travels to Hopi, Luxan writes, "Every Pueblo in this province is ruled by three or four caciques and the cacique has as little power as the ordinary Indian; hence they are all equal" (Hammond and Rey 1966:193–194).

However, an alternative picture of Pueblo political organization is also presented in the narratives, first by Alvarado concerning his initial contact with representatives from the Tiguex province in advance of the main Vázquez de Coronado occupation in 1540: "The next day the *principales* and people came from twelve *pueblos*. [They came] in order, those from one [*pueblo*] behind the other" (Flint and Flint 2005:305). This implies a much more structured and hierarchical set of relations among the different villages in the Tiguex area than articulated by Benavídez.

A similar, more hierarchical view of governance among the peoples of the Piro region (directly south of the Tiguex province) is offered by

Antonio de Espejo in his final summary report of his 1582–1583 expedition: "All the pueblos have caciques, allotted according to the number of inhabitants. Thus there are the principal caciques, who in turn have other caciques under them, that is to say, their *tequitatos*, the latter functioning like sheriffs to execute the orders of their superiors in the various pueblos, exactly as in the case of the Mexican people. When the Spaniards ask for something from the principal caciques of the pueblos, these officials summon the *tequitatos*, who then proclaim the order aloud throughout the pueblo concerned and in a very short time all bring what they may have been asked to provide" (Hammond and Rey 1966:220). These summary observations are in clear contrast to the chronicler Gallegos's account of the same encounters.

Conclusion

Espejo makes an intriguing summary observation near the end of his deposition, when discussing the Indigenous populations of the Pueblo region: "They are an intelligent and orderly people. There are attractive pueblos with plazas, and well-arranged houses. This indicates that the inhabitants would learn quickly any matter dealing with good government" (Hammond and Rey 1966:230). It might be argued that the Gallegos account of pueblo governance is perhaps closer to the facts, whereas Espejo's summary is trying to put a "spin" on the potential suitability of the Indigenous populations to be incorporated into a subsequent colonial empire. The Spanish *encomienda* policy for colonial control of Indigenous populations in the New World was premised on an expectation of a Native population organized much like Espejo's summary—an orderly, intelligent populace with a hierarchical structure of governance capable of learning quickly and taking direction. Further, effective imposition of *encomiendas* presumed that the local populations being subjugated were stable and concentrated year-round in village centers.

It is suggested here that the reality of Pueblo settlement and political organization was significantly at odds with these requirements. Instead of year-round occupied villages, a nearly abandoned village was the normal state of affairs for many months of the year, since the population was widely dispersed across the landscape engaging in seasonal hunting, gathering, and horticultural activities. Instead of a hierarchically organized central government at each village, individuals treated by the European expeditionaries and their allies as political leaders might well have been just one of several *maatui'in* elders at the village at the time of their encounter—individuals who had no specific political power over other social units at the village. Finally, the resident population at any given Pueblo village was not stable from year to year, but rather fluctuated in response to multiyear cycles of climate, agricultural potential, and natural resource productivity in the environs of each village.

Despite the fact that hardly any of the requisite conditions existed in the Pueblo provinces for effective imposition of an *encomienda* strategy, the subsequent Spanish colonization efforts in 1598 were founded on exactly those premises articulated so elegantly, and erroneously, by Espejo and others. The *encomienda* system began to collapse in the mid 1600s, and ultimately met with tragic failure in 1680, to join the history of such quests based on false perceptions.

10

The Interior South at the Time of Spanish Exploration

Robbie Ethridge and Jeffrey M. Mitchem

As the only early sixteenth-century Spanish expedition to travel extensively through the Southeast, the 1539–1543 entrada of Hernando de Soto made contact with more Native American polities than any other expedition in the region.[1] The expedition entered the interior South during the Mississippian Period, a time period between roughly A.D. 900 and 1700, during which Southeastern peoples organized themselves into a particular kind of political organization termed chiefdom. "Mississippian world" refers to the fact that none of these chiefdoms existed in isolation. The Mississippian world was oftentimes one of much political strife and conflict, but the chiefdoms were tied together in myriad ways—through trade, travel, information, marriage ties, exchange of war captives, and so on.

Southeastern Mississippian chiefdoms were not uniformly alike across space and time. Archaeologists distinguish between simple, complex, and paramount chiefdoms. A "complex chiefdom" was a political organization in which one large chiefdom exercised some sort of control or influence over smaller chiefdoms within a defined area. Archaeologists call the smaller chiefdoms "simple chiefdoms," in that they were polities in which the elite only controlled the towns connected to that chiefdom (Steponaitis 1978). Simple chiefdoms were clusters of about four to seven towns, with one of these having usually only a single mound and serving as the center of the chiefdom. These towns were small, with an average population of 350 to 650 people, and a simple chiefdom, as a whole, had an average population of between 2,800 and 5,400 people. The territorial domain of simple chiefdoms was modest, with an average diameter of about twenty kilometers, while the average distance between simple chiefdoms was thirty kilometers (Anderson 1994:4–9; Hally 1993; Hally et al. 1990).

In the Late Mississippian Period (A.D. 1350–1600), complex and simple chiefdoms existed side by side, and in a few cases single, especially charismatic leaders forged an alliance of several complex and simple chiefdoms into "paramount chiefdoms." Archaeologists are not in agreement as to the specific organizational mechanisms that held a paramount chiefdom together. According to anthropologist Charles Hudson, one can think of a simple chiefdom as a

> hands-on, workaday administrative unit under the aegis of a particular chief, the paramount chiefdom may have been little more than a kind of non-aggression pact, and the power of a paramount chief may have been little more than that of first among equals. (Hudson et al. 2008:467)

In other words, paramount chiefdoms were political entities that could have ranged from strongly to weakly integrated and paramount chiefs could have possessed power *or* merely influence. The concept of the paramount chiefdom, then, implies a less centralized administration than larger, state-like organizations, but a larger area of geographic influence than that of simple or even complex chiefdoms, sometimes spanning several hundred miles (Beck 2003; Hally 2006; Hally et al. 1990). In at least one case in northwest Georgia, Soto encountered a powerful chief named Coosa who had built an alliance of several chiefdoms into a paramount chiefdom that spanned an area from present-day East Tennessee into northern Georgia and eastern Alabama (Smith 2000).

If one looks at Soto's route, one can see that he traveled through much of the Mississippian world, and, in fact, that when he came to the edges of it, he had to turn back and again enter into it (Figure 10.1). The reason for this is simple. It was common practice for Spanish-led expeditions not to take along their own food supplies but rather to depend on plundering the stored provisions of Native communities en route. Only in the Mississippian world did people grow enough surplus at the local level to feed such a large expedition when they passed through their towns (Hudson 1997:14). To the north, the growing season is considerably shorter; hence, although Indian people grew corn and other crops there, they could not produce a large surplus. To the

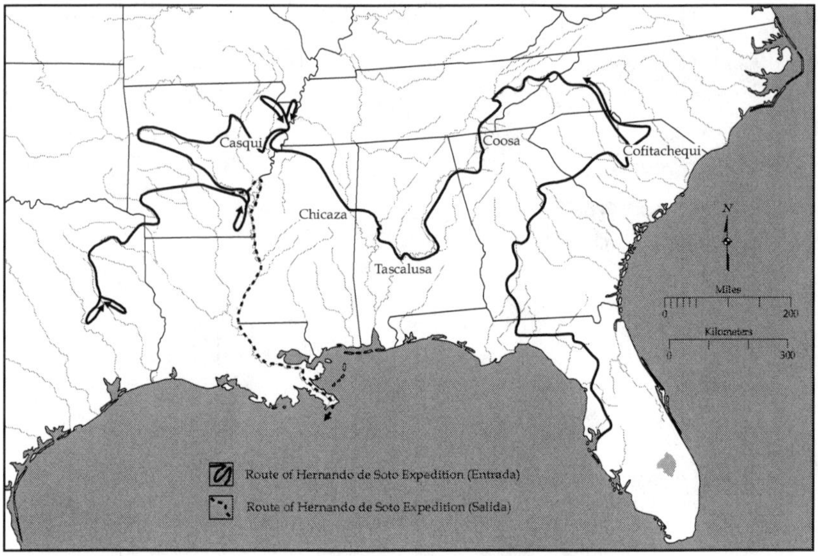

FIGURE 10.1. Generally accepted route of the expedition of Hernando de Soto, A.D. 1539–1543, with approximate locations of chiefdoms discussed in the text. Map drawn by Clay Mathers, adapted from unpublished map entitled "The Hernando de Soto Expedition, 1539-1543," January 1996, in possession of Charles Hudson.

west, the precipitation declines to the point where corn agriculture can only be maintained at a minimum level and one also enters the Great Plains, the home of the buffalo hunters, who traveled on foot. This environment and the hunting and gathering lifestyle of the Native people could not sustain a large group of foreign travelers.

Although Soto and his expeditionaries focused their movements within the Mississippian world, they did not pass through the territories of all the extant Native polities in the South at the time. For instance, archaeological evidence indicates that chiefdoms existed on the lower Chattahoochee River at the time of the entrada; however, Soto had decided to head northeast from Florida, in search of Cofitachequi, which was renowned for its supposed riches. Hence, he did not visit the polities on the Chattahoochee. Later, when he departed from Mabila in present-day central Alabama, Soto traveled to the northwest, away from the Gulf coastal areas and therefore away from the polities that made up what archaeologists call the Pensacola culture. Likewise, when he left Chicaza in present-day northeast Mississippi, Soto continued northwest, away from another famed province to the west called Caluça by the Chicaza. Still, Soto and his men did see much of the Mississippian world, and by combining a more accurate retracing of his route with modern archaeology, scholars have been able to reconstruct much about the people and places that made up the Late Mississippian South, as well as something about the relationships among chiefdoms and their people. Here, we highlight the encounters between the early Spanish explorers and five Mississippian chiefdoms—Cofitachequi, Coosa, Tascalusa, Chicaza, and Casqui. By so doing, we aim to provide a glimpse at the geopolitics of the interior South in the mid- to late sixteenth century.

Cofitachequi

Soto had heard about Cofitachequi soon after landing in Florida, and he believed he would find gold, pearls, and other wealth there. That is why he was determined to move northwest from Florida, to find Cofitachequi. After departing from the province of Ocute on the Oconee River in present-day Georgia, Soto and his expedition passed through an expansive uninhabited zone for seventeen days before coming to the first towns of Cofitachequi around the beginning of May 1540. Archaeologists believe that Cofitachequi was a paramount chiefdom that administered a territory of large towns and hamlets along the lower Wateree watershed, centered most likely at the Mulberry site near present-day Camden, South Carolina, and probably corresponding to the Mulberry ceramic phase (DePratter 1994). They also suggest that its prominence from A.D. 1450 until the arrival of Soto had a dampening effect on the expansion of polities in other portions of the South Carolina Piedmont, making it the most prominent polity in the region at the time (Beck 2009:115–116). About twenty years later, when Juan Pardo traveled from Santa Elena, located on present-day Parris Island, South Carolina, into the lower Piedmont, he, too, encountered Cofitachequi in the same location reported by members of the Soto entrada. At the time of the Pardo expedition (A.D. 1566–1568), the polity was composed of the chiefdoms of Cofitachequi (also called Canos in the Pardo documents) on the Wateree River, Guatari on the middle Yadkin River, and Joara (the Burke phase, and undoubtedly the Berry site) on the upper Catawba River. Between Cofitachequi and Joara, a polity that Soto called Chalaque (perhaps the Low phase) was located on the lower and middle Catawba River, although it is unclear whether or not Chalaque was subservient to Cofitachequi (Hudson 1990:68–73). Interestingly, the archaeology of the lower and middle Catawba River indicates that this section of the river valley was sparsely but continuously populated and lacked a hierarchical political structure. Perhaps it could represent a buffer zone between Cofitachequi and Joara that had been settled by people living outside of a chiefly order. Pardo passed through this region, stopping at the town of Yssa while here, whose people later became known as Essaw or Nassaw (Beck 2009:118–119; Fitts and Heath 2009:147–148, 153–154).

From the Pardo accounts it is obvious that the lower Piedmont was still densely inhabited even though some sort of political reshuffling had occurred since 1540. Cofitachequi appears to have still been intact, although in a somewhat diminished form, and perhaps no longer representing a paramount chiefdom within the region. The center of power seems to have been shifting from Cofitachequi to the previously subordinate chiefdoms of Joara and Guatari. Archaeologists surmise that Cofitachequi's paramountcy prior to 1540 inhibited the political ambitions of chiefs along its borders. By 1567, though, Cofitachequi was significantly diminished, and Joara and Guatari were flourishing. The Soto records hint that disease was present in Cofitachequi prior to 1540. This development could help account for the shifting political fortunes, since such an episode would certainly have strained chiefly authority. Nevertheless, the dense Native population in 1567 would indicate that any disease episode would have been a localized event. Soto's presence could also have precipitated such political changes in the region, especially if these challenges came directly on the heels of a major disease episode. Conversely, such shifts were common enough in the Mississippian world, and they may have derived purely from existing agencies and processes within Native communities (Anderson 1994).

Coosa

The Coosa chiefdom was one of the largest and most powerful Native groups encountered by the Soto expedition. The Spaniards made a habit of naming principal towns and "provinces" after the paramount leaders in the area. Hence the name "Coosa" applies to the paramount chiefdom, the main town, and the name of the chief. The main town of Coosa was located in northwest Georgia, but at the time of Soto's visit in 1540, the chief controlled most of the territory at the eastern end of Tennessee, the northwest corner of Georgia, and portions of northeast Alabama (Hudson et al. 1985; Smith 2000:3). As a paramount chiefdom, Coosa had hegemony over much of the Tennessee River and Coosa River drainages, areas that were important because of their abundant fertile soil for agriculture and their strategic importance for traveling through the region. Towns that were subject to Coosa were arranged along these river drainages like beads on a string.

When the Soto expedition crossed the Appalachian Mountains into East Tennessee in 1540, they learned that the first town they visited, Chiaha, was a subject town of Coosa, or Coça (Elvas 1993:85). As the expedition members traveled around the territory, they encountered several other towns also under Coosa's hegemony, although the fact that some were not indicates that Coosa was not all-powerful in the region. Eventually the expedition reached the main town of Coosa, where they were met by the paramount chief, who was carried out of the town on an elaborate litter borne by sixty or seventy of his principal men, along with accompanying flute players and singers. The chief was dressed in a robe or mantel of marten skins and had a headdress of feathers (Rangel 1993:284). When Soto had the opportunity, he took the Coosa chief hostage and captured a number of his people to use as bearers of his supplies. When the expedition continued their trek to the south and west, the chief (and his sister), as well as Coosa bearers, were taken along. At the town of Talisi (apparently the edge of Coosa territory), the chief was released and Soto moved on to the west (Smith 2000:37–38).

Archaeological evidence indicates that the Coosa chiefdom developed prior to European contact and was probably at its peak when Soto passed through the area. But contact with Soto did not lead to political collapse in the region. The expeditions of Tristán de Luna y Arellano in 1560 and Juan Pardo in 1566–1568 visited the principal town of Coosa (in Luna y Arellano's case) or experienced the effects of Coosa's ongoing political power decades later (Hudson 1990; Hudson et al. 1989; Smith 2000:38–48). Later iterations of Coosa still existed in the 1700s, although in a much less powerful and more dispersed form (Smith 2000:50–81). Based on geographical and archaeological factors, the Little Egypt site (9MU102) has been proposed as the principal town of Coosa (Hally 1979, 1980; Smith 2000:84). Extensive excavations at Little Egypt and the contemporaneous King site (Blakely 1988; Hally 2008) in northwest Georgia have yielded several sixteenth-century Spanish artifacts, including an intact sword, sword fragments, and a brass bell (Smith 2000:90, Plates 2 and 3). Study of the distribution of these and other datable sixteenth-century Spanish artifacts in the region has allowed archaeologists to confidently identify the extent of the Coosa realm in Tennessee, Georgia, and Alabama (Hally et al. 1990; Hudson et al. 1985).

An alternative argument is presented by Little (2008:229–238), identifying the Etowah site (9BR1) in northwest Georgia as the location of the principal town of Coosa. His discussion of the distribution of sixteenth-century Spanish artifacts in the region adds support to his contention, and archaeologists will no doubt continue to debate the exact location for many years to come.

Tascalusa

After Soto's expedition traversed the entire extent of the paramount chiefdom of Coosa, in early October of 1540 they crossed into present-day central Alabama and the province of Tascalusa. By all accounts, Tascalusa was a powerful chief. His chiefdom, Tascalusa, was most likely on the upper Alabama River in present-day Alabama, just south of its confluence with the Coosa and Tallapoosa rivers. There are both documentary and archaeological indications that Tascalusa may have been in the process of putting together his own paramountcy at the time of Soto's visit by forging an alliance with the adjacent polities of Mabila and perhaps Piachi to the west and by enticing the polity of Talisi, which lay on Tascalusa's eastern boundary, away from Coosa, with whom it was aligned at the time (Hudson 1997:231). Tascalusa also orchestrated a surprise attack against Soto at the palisaded town of Mabila. Although Tascalusa and his allies did not destroy the Spanish expedition in this now-famous attack, they did succeed in doing them much harm, killing and wounding a number of the soldiers, killing several horses, and destroying many of their supplies. In hindsight, one can also see that they succeeded in pushing the Spaniards out of their provinces (Elvas 1993:96–105; Hernández de Biedma 1993:232–236; Rangel 1993:291–294).

The province of Tascalusa coincides with the archaeological ceramic complex known as the Big Eddy phase (which dates to A.D. 1450–1575) and is most likely represented by a cluster of Late Mississippian sites on the upper Alabama River. The central town of Tascalusa, Atahachi, was probably located at the Charlotte Thompson site (Jenkins 2009:214–216, 221, 223; Sheldon 2009:120; Waselkov et al. 2009:230–231). The Mabila and Piachi provinces may be represented by the archaeological ceramic complex known as the Furman phase (A.D. 1400–1575), which begins southwest of the Coosa–Tallapoosa confluence and extends along the upper and middle Alabama River. Although Furman phase sites are located all along the upper and middle Alabama, archaeologists divide the sites into two clusters—one, known as the Wilcox cluster, is centered around the mound site of Matthew's Landing in present-day Wilcox County, Alabama, and the other, known as the Cahaba cluster, is a cluster of Furman phase sites centered around the Durant Bend site in present-day Dallas County. Archaeologists are in general agreement that the province of Mabila is most likely represented by one of these clusters, although they have yet to determine which one. The town of Piachi, likewise, may be represented by one of these Furman phase sites, with Durant Bend being a likely candidate (DePratter et al. 1985:122; Jenkins 2009:222; Regnier 2006a:128; Sheldon 2009:120–23; Waselkov et al. 2009:232–233). The Talisi chiefdom, which was allied with Coosa at the time, most likely corresponds to the archaeological ceramic complex known as the Shine II phase (A.D. 1400–1575) and extended from the big bend in the Tallapoosa River to just east of the confluence of the Coosa and Tallapoosa rivers (DePratter et al. 1985:120; Jenkins 2009:198–208, 220–221; Waselkov et al. 2009:229–239).[2] Archaeologists also have been able to reconstruct something about the history of these polities in central Alabama. The upper Alabama River and lower Tallapoosa River were only sparsely occupied during the Middle Mississippian Period. At this time, populations were congregated in the grand Middle Mississippian sites such as Etowah, Moundville, and Bottle Creek (located in the Mobile-Tensaw delta region). However, all of these large Middle Mississippian polities failed sometime in the late fifteenth century, at which time groups from these fallen chiefdoms and elsewhere began to congregate in the upper Alabama and lower Tallapoosa river basins. Recent archaeological investigations indicate that, unlike their Middle Mississippian predecessors, Talisi, Tascalusa, Mabila, and Piachi were not homogenous, monolingual political entities but rather multilingual, heterogeneous polities wherein the descendants of people from various fallen Middle Mississippian chiefdoms lived side by side in the same towns. We know this because Lamar, Moundville, and Pensacola ceramics (representing populations from present-day northeast Georgia, the Alabama Gulf Coast, and the Black Warrior River) are found together at Late Mississippian sites here (Sheldon 2001:23; Jenkins 2009:200–216; Regnier 2006a:128, 2006b:6, Figure 4, 128, 243–251, 2009).

Chicaza

After the battle of Mabila on October 18, 1540, and in dire need of supplies before the winter, Soto sought out Chicaza, which he had heard was a bountiful province. Soto and his expedition spent a hard winter at Chicaza during which they ransacked Native supplies and antagonized the people of Chicaza. The chief of Chicaza launched a surprise attack on March 4, 1541, and seriously debilitated the army. Afterward, Soto moved on toward the Mississippi River, where he would soon encounter the grand chiefdoms of the Mississippi Valley (Elvas 1993:109–110; Hernández de Biedma 1993:236–237; Rangel 1993:297–298).

Although the site of Chicaza has not been found, archaeologists agree that the province was most likely located in present-day northeast Mississippi in the physiographic region known as the Black Prairie. The Black Prairie, which is an upland prairie underlain by a long, narrow deposit of chalk and marl filled with ancient fossil shells, forms a distinctive geological and vegetative arc that swings down through

Alabama and into eastern Mississippi. In present-day Mississippi it cuts west across the Tombigbee River and then north into the Tupelo area (Atkinson 2004:7; Johnson 2000:88; Rafferty 2003:169, 190). Researchers believe that the central area of the Chicaza province may have been located somewhere within the Black Prairie on the watersheds of Mogawah Creek, Catalpa Creek, and the southern tributaries of Tibbee Creek, within the triangle formed by the present-day Starkville–Columbus–West Point area, just west of the Tombigbee River. The main town of Chicaza may have been in present-day southwestern Monroe County, central or eastern Clay County, eastern Oktibbeha County or Lowndes County, or even northern Noxubee County, Mississippi (Atkinson 1987:4–9; Hudson et al. 1990:194; Morgan 1996:5). In addition to Chicaza, two or perhaps three other polities—Sacchuma, Alimamu, and Talapatica—were adjacent to Chicaza. Hudson et al. (1990) suggest that the Lyon's Bluff site, a single-mound site located on Line Creek in Oktibbeha County, may be the principal town of Alimamu. Recent C14 dates from Lyon's Bluff indicate that it was occupied from A.D. 1200 to 1650 but that the main building stage occurred between A.D. 1390 and 1420, during the Middle Mississippi Period (Peacock and Hogue 2005). Archaeologists have not yet proposed archaeological correlates with Sacchuma and Talapatica.

Scholars are in disagreement over whether or not the province of Chicaza was a chiefdom with a hierarchical social and political structure, or an egalitarian, tribe-like organization. Archaeologists have not found the town of Chicaza, or any of its related towns, and they argue that the Soto narratives can be interpreted either way (DePratter 1983:56, 208; Johnson 1997:302). Those who interpret the current archaeological data as indicating that Chicaza was not a hierarchical, chiefdom society but a decentralized, egalitarian one argue that around A.D. 1450, when many of the chiefdoms located in the bottomlands of the central Tombigbee and its tributaries were abandoned, people moved northwest, into the Black Prairie uplands. They note that the sites dating to the sixteenth century in the upland prairie are all small hamlets, and that there are no upland prairie mound sites. They interpret the absence of mound sites to mean that there were no central administrative centers typical of chiefdoms, and hence, that the people were not under the political organization of a chiefdom (Johnson 1997, 2000; Johnson and Sparks 1986).

Conversely, others have proposed that the sixteenth-century hamlets scattered through the uplands were part of the local center-farmstead settlement patterns typical of the Tombigbee chiefdoms (Blitz 1993). In this case, the people in the uplands would have kept up their affiliations with mound centers that were operating on the Tombigbee and its tributaries in the sixteenth century (Hogue and Peacock 1995; Jenkins 2009:229–230; Peacock 1995; Rafferty 2003). Examining solely the documentary records, Ethridge (2010) recently argued that Chicaza was a ranked society and chiefdom. Ethridge's close reading of the Soto documents show that the army Chicaza assembled to battle Soto and their methods of warfare were consistent with those of a ranked social order, that Chicaza *mico* clearly had subordinate chiefs from neighboring polities, that the ceremonial greeting between Soto and Chicaza were indicative of his high rank, and that Chicaza *mico* bore himself like a man of high status, including being presented to Soto borne on a litter carried by many of his principal men (Ethridge 2010).

Casqui

In June 1541, the remaining members of the Soto expedition crossed the Mississippi River. Although the exact crossing place is unknown, most scholars agree that it was most likely south of Memphis, Tennessee (Dye 1993:36–39). Shortly after making that crossing, they were told of two powerful rulers to the west and north, Casqui and Pacaha (Dye 1993:45–46). In late June, they set out to make contact with these groups.

Based on geographical and archaeological factors, Dan and Phyllis Morse (1990) suggest that the archaeological Parkin phase may be analogous to the Casqui chiefdom and that the Nodena phase may correlate with the Pacaha chiefdom. Both of these eponymous domains were ruled by powerful men who controlled a number of towns along rivers in northeast Arkansas. The expedition narratives indicate that these rulers were at war with one another, and had been for a long time, possibly for generations. This long-term warfare is reflected archaeologically by the fact that all of the Late Mississippian sites in northeast Arkansas are fortified, nucleated sites. Small, scattered farmsteads are absent: everyone had to live in the fortified towns for safety (Morse 1981). Their extensive cornfields were located nearby along the rivers. The Casqui chiefdom extended along the St. Francis and Tyronza rivers, and the Pacaha chiefdom was located on the west bank of the Mississippi River to the east and northeast of Casqui territory.

Casqui refers to the chief, his capital town, and his domain, and likewise for Pacaha. Reference is made in the expedition narratives that Pacaha was the more powerful of the two (Rangel 1993:303). When the Soto expedition entered northeast Arkansas, they first made contact with Casqui. They were surprised (and suspicious) to be welcomed with open arms. This welcome was most likely based on Casqui's belief that the Spaniards could help him defeat Pacaha, but we cannot know for sure. After remaining adjacent to Casqui's main town for a few days, Soto traveled to Pacaha, where their arrival at the main town created a panic. Pacaha and his followers fled, and Casqui and his subjects raided the town, desecrating temples and stealing all they could carry. This infuriated Soto, who went to considerable effort to establish peace between the two chiefs (Rangel 1993:302–303). While he did succeed in calming things, it is unlikely that he settled their differences for good. In fact, the circumstances and events surrounding his presence may have resulted in the defeat of one of the two chiefs. This inference is supported by evidence of dismantling of the defensive palisade at the Parkin site (3CS29), the presumed location of the capital of Casqui (Mitchem 1996b).

Archaeological evidence of sixteenth-century Spanish contact in northeast Arkansas is scant. The Parkin site has yielded the best evidence. A Clarksdale bell was excavated from the neck of a child burial by a casual digger in the 1960s, and a seven-layer faceted chevron bead was recovered during excavations by the University of Arkansas Museum in 1966. Excavations by the Arkansas Archeological Survey in the 1990s produced two lead shot and two Clarksdale bell fragments (Mitchem 1996a). None of the other Parkin phase sites has yielded any Spanish artifacts. In the Nodena phase area, three lead shot of varying calibers have been found at the Bradley sites (3CT43 and 3CT7), which have been suggested as promising candidates for the principal town of Pacaha. However, recent lead isotope studies indicate that the Bradley items may be from later occupations (Alyson Thibodeau, personal communication 2010). The Bradley sites cover a large area and have been investigated only sporadically, so the isotope data do not rule out that they may be the location of Pacaha.

When the Soto expedition left northeast Arkansas in the summer of 1541, they continued west, exploring at least as far as the Ouachita Mountains, but eventually headed back to the Mississippi River, probably in present-day southeast Arkansas. There, Soto died on May 21, 1542 (Hudson 1997:349). The survivors decided to abandon further exploration, and eventually made their way to Mexico, after considerable hardship (Hudson 1997: Chapters 17 and 18).

Aftermath of Soto and the Shatter Zone

After the Spanish entradas of the sixteenth century, many of the interior groups in the South did not have direct or sustained contact with Europeans for over 130 years, yet the next Europeans to witness the interior South saw something quite different than what Soto, Luna y Arellano, and Pardo had observed. Exactly what happened to Cofitachequi, Coosa, Tascalusa, Chicaza, Casqui, and the many other chiefdoms after the Soto entrada is only now beginning to come to light. Between 1540 and 1700, in case after case across the American South, chiefdoms collapsed and people restructured their political and social systems along new lines, creating a new geopolitical landscape by the early eighteenth century.

Most scholars agree that the military losses at the hands of the early explorers and destabilization of Native chiefdoms had a profound effect on many Mississippian polities. Soto and his men represented a formidable military force, and in the cases of those chiefdoms that experienced intense combat, the direct military assault of the Spaniards may have precipitated their collapse. This was probably the case at the chiefdom of Napituca in northern Florida, Anilco in Arkansas, and Tascalusa in Alabama (Hudson 1997:110–115, 238–249, 266–274, 336–338).

Soto's prolonged stay and ransacking of the region for food would have seriously depleted local stores. Although Mississippian people knew much about utilizing wild plant and animal foods, such a shortage of stored cultivated crops would have meant hardship for all and starvation for some. The leadership of chiefdoms partly derived from leaders being able to procure and secure stores of food for just such emergencies, and if a leader failed on this count, then that polity would have been subjected to political unrest (Blitz 1993:69–97, 123–125, 176–178, 180–181; Wesson 1999:157–158). Mississippian polities were no strangers to internal political stresses that could easily break into full-scale rebellions. Factions oftentimes developed within ruling lineages and between lineages, resulting in a continuous jockeying for power within a polity's political order. If, as suggested above, Soto's depletion of local food stores created civil unrest, there would have been any number of factions ready to exploit the situation.

It is likely that Soto's presence upset the balance of power in other ways as well. Records from the expedition across the South describe several instances when *micos* of simple chiefdoms were challenging and defying the authority of a chief under whose power they had fallen, as at Chicaza when Sacchuma refused to pay tribute. Similar episodes occurred at Tascalusa, Cofitachequi, Coosa, and Casqui (Hudson 1997:179–180, 228–229). In these political struggles, the more powerful *mico* often enlisted Soto's influence and military aid to extinguish the rebellion, as did Chicaza. In some cases, a savvy lesser *mico* used Soto to bolster his authority in challenging the overarching *mico*, as at Casqui. In either case, given the fragile nature of the ties binding simple chiefdom alliances, complex chiefdoms, and paramount chiefdoms, the presence of a new and powerful ally could easily upset the balance of power resulting in a reshuffling of authority.

Most scholars agree that the introduction of Old World diseases into virgin-soil populations of the Americas resulted in a demographic collapse on the order of 90 percent across the hemisphere. However, scholars are still not certain about the exact diseases that were introduced, when they were introduced, or their specific pathologies, among other things. Moreover, in recent years, the idea that disease alone was responsible for the dramatic loss of Indian life in the first hundred or so years after contact has come into question. Today, scholars agree that disease was but one factor in the demographic collapse, and all point to contributing factors such as slaving and increased warfare.

Certainly the Spanish expeditions of the sixteenth century and the later permanent Spanish presence in La Florida impacted Native life in various ways. But these were followed by other colonial shockwaves generated from the Atlantic seaboard, and the combination would rend the Mississippian world. Two other contributing factors came with the European invasion—the introduction of Old World diseases and the introduction of commerce in Indian slaves and deerskins between Europeans and Indians. Soto's presence disrupted much, and that, along with subsequent disease epidemics and cultural exchanges with the Spaniards of La Florida, had profound impacts on Native life during the sixteenth and early seventeenth centuries. But these disruptions, epidemics, and exchanges, in and of themselves, were not fully transforming. Rather, it was the mid-seventeenth-century introduction of a new economic system ushered in by a commercial trade in Indian slaves that completed the constellation of forces that created what Ethridge (2006, 2009a) has called the "Mississippian shatter zone."

In the American South, the Spanish regime did not prove transforming for Native people. Not until they became engaged in the world economy through contact with the English, French, and Dutch did Southeastern Indians revamp their social, political, and economic orders to adapt to the new world in which they now existed. The commercial trade in Indian slaves and animal skins and the consequent intensification and spread of violence and warfare were among the fundamental causes for the collapse and transformation of the Mississippian world and for the shaping of the new geopolitical landscape that emerged.

Throughout the seventeenth century, England, France, Spain, and Holland established "beachheads of empire" along the Atlantic seaboard and into the Gulf of Mexico (Gallay 2006). These four European colonizers struggled to establish empires in North America, and each employed different strategies to engage and incorporate Native allies into their imperial designs. Like the Spanish, the English, Dutch, and French colonial projects in North America had political, religious, and military dimensions. However, by the seventeenth century, Spain was in decline as a commercial world power, and the Dutch, French, and English colonial projects carried significant commercial dimensions—they came to North America to make money. As soon as English, French, and Dutch settlers landed on North American shores, they set about this business, and they brought with them strong commercial connections in the nascent global economy. The initial form of this commerce was a trade in Indian slaves and armaments. The result was the spread of militarized slaving societies across the South and out-of-control slave raiding and intra-Indian violence that lasted for about sixty years and resulted in the widespread dislocation, migration, amalgamation, and, in some cases, extinction of Native peoples (Ethridge 2010; Gallay 2003).

Cofitachequi and the other lower Piedmont chiefdoms were some of the first polities to feel the effects of slavers. In the Carolina Piedmont, other than two brief mentions of Joara and Cofitechequi in some Spanish accounts in 1605 and 1628, the Carolina Piedmont Indians disappear from the documentary record until 1670, and by that time Cofitechequi and the other polities, besieged by armed Indian slave raiders working for Virginia and Carolina traders, were in a process of dispersal and coalescence (Beck 2009:130–137). By 1675 Cofitachequi was gone, and refugees from Indian slavers were pouring into the lower Catawba River valley, where they would eventually form the Catawba of the eighteenth century. In 1540, when Soto had passed through Coosa, eyewitnesses described it as an expansive, fertile province, with numerous large towns and abundant agricultural fields stretching from town to town. Twenty years later, when a contingent from the Luna y Arellano expedition surveyed Coosa, they were disappointed to find only small towns, many abandoned agricultural fields, and a much smaller population. In 1600, the inhabitants of the once expansive paramount chiefdom began to disperse. Over the next eighty years, these descendants of the famous Coosa made a series of strategic moves south into present-day central Alabama, in part to be closer to the European trade emanating from Spanish Florida and later Carolina, and in part to evade Indian slave raiders from the east. In the early eighteenth century, they would join the Creek Confederacy as the Abihka towns (Smith 2000).

The battle of Mabila was costly to the Indians of Tascalusa, and, assuming they recruited warriors from their allies, it was costly for Mabila, Piachi, and Talisi as well. Spanish reports of Indian casualties were undoubtedly exaggerated (over three thousand men), but any large number of dead and wounded would have been a devastating blow to all of the towns and polities that participated (Elvas 1993:104; Rangel 1993:294). Even so, Tascalusa's losses at Mabila apparently did not spell immediate disaster, as people continued to put earthen mantles on the mound at Atahachi at least until around 1560. We know this because some of the gifts brought by Luna y Arellano's men when they visited there were buried in the mound. However, the Luna y Arellano reports on Tascalusa are skimpy, and the archaeology shows that several of the surrounding mound sites and small farming communities were abandoned, all of which suggests that Tascalusa was no longer the noteworthy paramountcy that Soto had encountered. The archaeology suggests that the paramountcy, and perhaps the chiefdom of Tascalusa, disintegrated at least fifteen years later, by 1575, if not earlier (Galloway, 1995:161; Hudson et al. 1989:36–39; Jenkins 2009:224–227; Priestly 1928:291; Regnier 2006a:127–28, 2006b:97–98, 103–104, 2009). Still, the survivors migrated slightly upstream to the confluence of the Coosa and Tallapoosa rivers. Here they would form the core of the Alabama Indians, taking in refugees from present-day Tennessee, Georgia, Alabama, and Mississippi (Ethridge 2010). They would form part of the Creek Confederacy in the eighteenth century.

The fate of the Mabilians after the battle with Soto is unknown, but the archaeology attests to some dramatic settlement shifts. In the Wilcox cluster of the Furman phase, the mound center at Matthew's Landing and the surrounding farmsteads were abandoned almost immediately following the battle and soon after were replaced by a series of large nucleated towns. Ceramic analysis from one of the large towns, the Liddell site, shows an amalgam of people from present-day western Alabama, eastern Mississippi, the Gulf region, and the lower Mississippi valley joining together at the town. At Durant Bend in the Cahaba cluster, people stayed at the site after the battle of Mabila, and the Furman phase ceramics were replaced by a local manifestation of Alabama River phase ceramics. Recent analysis of the Durant Bend ceramics reveals that people from other areas moved to the site, indicating absorption of migrants. Then, sometime in the early seventeenth century prior to 1650, all of these sites associated with Mabila and Piachi were abandoned. Archaeologists suggest that those in the Wilcox cluster moved downstream into the Mobile-Tensaw delta, where they became part of the historically known Mobilians, and that those from the Cahaba cluster moved northeast to join those citizens of the former Tascalusa chiefdom at the Coosa and Tallapoosa confluence. The middle Alabama River would not be reoccupied again until after the American Revolution (Jenkins 2009: 224–227; Regnier 2006a:128–132, 2006b:131, 132, 146, 259, 2009).

We have relatively little information about Chicaza's history in the first few decades after the encounter with Soto, but we do know that the people of this polity began a series of migrations that led them away from the Tombigbee and eventually into the vicinity of present-day Tupelo, Mississippi (Johnson 2000). Once there, they became known as the Chickasaws, and by the late seventeenth century they had entered into trade agreements with Carolina and became highly militarized slavers, slaving across the lower South and destabilizing much of the region (Ethridge 2010).

The fates of Casqui and Pacaha are unknown after the Soto expedition. No other Europeans were in the region for at least 135 years; consequently, there is no specific description of Native groups in the area. Excavations at the Parkin site have not revealed evidence of massacre or attack on the town, but the aforementioned evidence of dismantling the palisade suggests that the long-term internecine conflict may have ended, perhaps with the death or surrender of either Casqui or Pacaha. At the time of the Soto expeditions, the central and lower Mississippi River valley was home to some of the most powerful, populous, and impressive polities through which the Spaniards had passed. One hundred-thirty-five years later, French explorers paddling down the Mississippi did not encounter any of these. Several scholars have proposed that high losses from introduced disease precipitated the collapse and abandonment of the polities in the central and lower Mississippi valley, although they also acknowledge that the subsequent changes in Native life were not solely due to disease, but also to contributing factors such as slaving and increased warfare. Most recently, Ethridge (2010) argues that shockwaves from the Indian and European trade system penetrated far beyond the Atlantic beachheads of empire and affected Native polities on the Mississippi River, setting in motion a sequence of events, movements, opportunities, and failures that changed Indian life before the French and their Indian allies canoed down the Mississippi River.

The Soto expedition cut a swath through the entire Mississippian world, destabilizing many chiefdoms and thus making regional readjustments and recovery difficult. Still, the Mississippian world was in the process of recovery from the Soto expedition when it was assaulted again by the introduction of Old World diseases and Indian slave raiders. Chiefdoms then began to collapse in quick succession, thus interrupting the processes that regulated regional stability. The Mississippian world could neither withstand nor recover from the region-wide and unprecedented succession of chiefdom failures in the first 190 years of contact.

11

Inventing Florida

Constructing a Colonial Society in an Indigenous Landscape

John E. Worth

Beginning with the 1513 discovery of Florida, Spanish explorers and colonists embarked on a lengthy process to incorporate the American Southeast into the expanding Spanish colonial empire. Despite multiple false starts over the course of the next half-century, it was ultimately the colony of San Agustín de la Florida, established in 1565 by Pedro Menéndez de Avilés, that set the stage for the successful integration of southeastern North America into Spain's global colonial system. The mechanism by which this occurred was not dissimilar to that which resulted in the spread of Spanish influence across much of the New World and across the Pacific Ocean, namely, the structural assimilation of Indigenous local polities into a vast overarching political and economic system administered in Spain. Part and parcel to this strategy was the assimilation of living, functioning Indigenous societies on a local scale, and the structural linkage of these societies into the broader political and economic milieu that was the emerging Spanish colonial system of the sixteenth and seventeenth centuries. Even though the effects of internal demographic collapse and external slave raiding ultimately doomed the Spanish Florida experiment to failure by 1706, it nonetheless stood in marked contrast to other colonial endeavors elsewhere in eastern North America during the same period, shaping the trajectory of the European colonial era across a broad region.

The Spanish colonial system differed fundamentally from that of other European colonial powers such as the English who principally sought unoccupied land for immigrant settlers and generally interacted with Indigenous groups at a distance, commonly through bilateral trade. In Florida, as elsewhere in the Spanish colonial world, local Native American groups ultimately became part of a newly formed, multiethnic colonial society that, although clearly dominated in a political and military sense by immigrant Spanish settlers, was demographically more Native American than Spanish (e.g., Bannon 1974; McAlister 1984; Weber 1992). The difference between these two colonial approaches is perhaps best viewed in terms of the primary resources of value in each system. In the Spanish system, colonial expansion was measured more in terms of human resources, whereas in the English system, it was measured in terms of territorial resources. Spanish Florida grew by assimilating people, not simply land. The growth and success of the Florida colony would ultimately be measured by the extent to which it harnessed the labor of Indigenous groups, and its ultimate failure by the early eighteenth century was in large part a result of demographic collapse among those same groups (Bushnell 1994; Hoffman 2001; Milanich 1999; Worth 1998a, 1998b). For Spanish Florida, colonial success depended not on dispossessing Indigenous groups of their land and populating it with immigrant settlers but instead on assimilating those groups into a new colonial society. This strategy was founded on the vertical integration of Native American and Spanish populations into a new political and economic relationship based on human labor and the product of that labor. As such, the colonial system of Spanish Florida ultimately depended on winning and maintaining the voluntary cooperation of Indigenous groups within that broader system.

While this system only reached its full development in Spanish Florida during the middle decades of the seventeenth century, at the height of the Franciscan Mission era (McEwan 1993), the groundwork for the system was laid during the sixteenth century, when first contact was made between Spanish explorers and would-be colonists. It was during the sixteenth century that Spanish authorities first began to learn about the social and physical geography of the American Southeast, and when initial experiments were conducted regarding the most effective strategies for assimilating Indigenous groups in different regions (Hoffman 2001; Milanich 1999; Skowronek 2009; Weddle 1985). Indeed, I would argue that at the dawn of the seventeenth century, many of the most ineffective strategies had already been tried and failed, leaving only that strategy which ultimately led to the successful expansion of Spanish Florida into the interior and across the Florida peninsula to link the Atlantic and Gulf of Mexico. In this sense, it is instructive

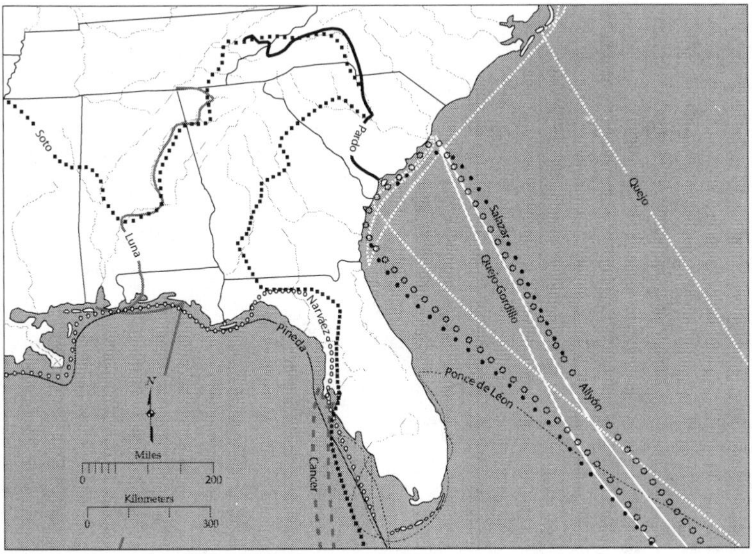

FIGURE 11.1. Sixteenth-century Spanish expeditions to Florida, A.D. 1513–1568 (created by John Worth and prepared for publication by Clay Mathers).

to explore the origins of this strategy during the exploratory and early colonial phases of Spanish Florida's development during the sixteenth century.

During the first quarter-century after Juan Ponce de León's 1513 accidental discovery of the Florida peninsula, the vast majority of the American Southeast remained an unknown frontier on the edge of Spanish awareness. The earliest Spanish contacts during this period were almost exclusively with coastal groups, with only the briefest penetration of the near-shore interior in the Apalachee province along the northern Gulf of Mexico (see Figure 11.1). Until 1537, the Spanish Crown subdivided the Southeast into two colonial territories, one on the Gulf Coast known as La Florida, as visited and explored by Juan Ponce de León, Diego Miruelo, Alonso Alvarez de Pineda, and Pánfilo de Narváez between 1513 and 1528, and one along the lower Atlantic coast known as the Tierra de Ayllón, as explored by Pedro de Salazar, Francisco Gordillo, Pedro de Quejo, and Lucas Vázquez de Ayllón between 1514 and 1526 (Hoffman 1980, 1990, 1992, 1994b; Lawson 1946).

Though a number of these early expeditions were initially motivated by slaving, two early attempts were officially licensed by the Spanish Crown in order to establish colonies along the coasts of these territories (Spanish Crown 1514, 1523). Both resulted in rapid failure, including a 1521 settlement attempt by Ponce de León in southwest Florida and a 1526 attempt by Vázquez de Ayllón in southeast Georgia. The 1528 landing of Pánfilo de Narváez near Tampa Bay was accidental (his original goal was to settle far to the west along the margins of New Spain; Spanish Crown 1526), but it nonetheless resulted in a similarly spectacular failure during the expedition's attempt to return westward (Núñez Cabeza de Vaca 1989). Within fifteen years of Florida's first discovery, three successive would-be colonial leaders had perished in the attempt to claim southeastern North America for Spain.

Less than a decade later, and just a year after the only four survivors of the Narváez expedition had been rediscovered in northern New Spain, a new expedition was authorized in 1537 that explicitly combined the two earlier territories—Ponce's Florida and the land of Ayllón—into a single, vast region within which Hernando de Soto was to explore and select a two-hundred-league stretch of coastline which he would subsequently govern (Spanish Crown 1537). A successful and wealthy veteran of the Pizarro conquest of the Inca, Soto associated riches with mountains, and over the course of four long years, his expedition plunged deep into the interior of North America, probing the boundaries of the geographically extensive Southeastern culture area from the Carolinas to Arkansas and Texas (Hudson 1997). Commonly employing brutal tactics with Indigenous populations, the survivors of this ill-fated expedition never returned to the planned coastal rendezvous at Pensacola Bay, and the survivors and a number of captive Indians eventually fled by sea to Mexico, leaving Soto's body behind as the fourth Spanish leader to die in the attempt to settle greater Spanish Florida. Nevertheless, despite the failure of any of these early expeditions to establish a permanent Spanish colonial presence, by the mid-sixteenth century Spanish authorities had gained a broad, if coarse-grained, portrait of the social and physical geography of the American Southeast, and this knowledge would ultimately shape all future colonial endeavors in the region.

One of the most important details gleaned from Soto's expedition was the fact that there appeared to be no readily available sources of gold or silver or other intrinsic wealth in La Florida, nor densely populated Native empires on the scale of the Aztec or Inca of Central and South America. The importance of this fact cannot be overstated from the point of view of the eventual assimilation of Indigenous societies across the American Southeast. Lacking the profit motive to encourage private settlement and local economic development within a colonial context, the territory of Spanish Florida was effectively relegated to a marginal role within the broader Spanish empire and was eventually colonized primarily for its strategic value in protecting the returning New World treasure fleets. While this ultimately ensured a relatively stable source of royal funding to maintain the Florida colony over the long term, it also meant that Spanish colonists in Florida would have to rely even more substantially on local Native American populations to buffer against interruptions in external supply lines for their presidial garrisons (Bushnell 1994; Sluiter 1985; Worth 1998a, 1998b).

Another important change that had occurred during Soto's expedition was the promulgation of the "New Laws of the Indies" by the Spanish Crown in 1542 (Mathers, this volume; Santa Cruz 1923:222–236). These laws explicitly outlawed Indian slavery and overtly abusive treatment of Native groups, and ultimately marked a watershed change in Spanish imperial policy with respect to the Indigenous peoples of the New World. The failure of all previous Spanish expeditions to settle Florida prior to 1542 meant that when Florida was finally colonized more than two decades later, events would unfold under far different circumstances than might otherwise have been the case. Nevertheless, when Spanish settlement did finally occur, it was not under the wholly pacific circumstances envisioned by Dominican idealist Fray Luís Cancer, whose 1549 expedition to Tampa Bay was originally designed as a catalyst for the purely "spiritual" conquest of Florida, manned by only four Dominican priests and a single Spanish farmer (Lowery 1911:411–427; Weddle 1985:234–246; Worth 2009a). The murders of the farmer and two of the priests, including Cancer himself, not only marked the end of Cancer's novel experiment (and the death of the fifth Spanish expedition leader to Florida) but also ensured a consistent military presence in future expeditions.

Subsequent attempts to establish a Spanish foothold in southeastern North America were ultimately framed within a rising fear of French settlement in the very same region. The first attempt under Tristán de Luna y Arellano in 1559 was financed largely by the Spanish Crown and launched from New Spain. This enterprise was originally designed to establish a Spanish foothold at Ayllón's renowned Atlantic port of Santa Elena by tracing Hernando de Soto's route across the Appalachian summit and connect the Gulf and Atlantic coasts from modern Pensacola, Florida, to Port Royal Sound (Santa Elena) in South Carolina (Hudson et al. 1989; Priestly 1928). Taking the explicit advice of four Indian women brought out by the Soto expedition two decades earlier, the supplies for Luna y Arellano's expedition included substantial stores of food loaded onto a total of eleven ships in the colonial fleet, in order to ensure that there would be no need to rely upon Indigenous populations for food or other supplies for the colony.

Pivotal to Luna y Arellano's effort was the Indigenous chiefdom of Coosa located in northwestern Georgia (Smith 2000), intended to be the lynchpin in the anticipated Spanish road across the interior Southeast. The importance of Coosa only increased after the unexpected devastation of Luna y Arellano's fleet and food reserves in Pensacola Bay just five weeks after their arrival, leaving some fifteen hundred soldiers and colonists both stranded and hungry. Nevertheless, when veterans of the Soto expedition finally led a military detachment northward to Coosa in 1560, finding only minimal surplus food in contrast to their recollections from two decades earlier, the last hope for Luna y Arellano's interior road was dashed, and even a brief maritime expedition to Santa Elena by Luna y Arellano's successor was unfruitful. Tristán de Luna y Arellano was the sixth to fail in the settlement of Florida, but the first leader to survive the attempt, even though he lived out the rest of his days in relative poverty in Mexico City.

In the aftermath of Luna y Arellano's failure, it would be Pedro Menéndez de Avilés who in 1565 established what would become the hub of all subsequent Spanish expansion into the American Southeast from St. Augustine (Lyon 1976). Concurrently attempting to establish colonial bases all along the coast and to penetrate and fortify the vast interior, Menéndez initially embarked on a strategy that focused heavily on the military occupation of Indigenous administrative centers in strategic locations, albeit within the context of the 1542 laws ensuring good treatment for Indigenous peoples and thus with explicit permis-

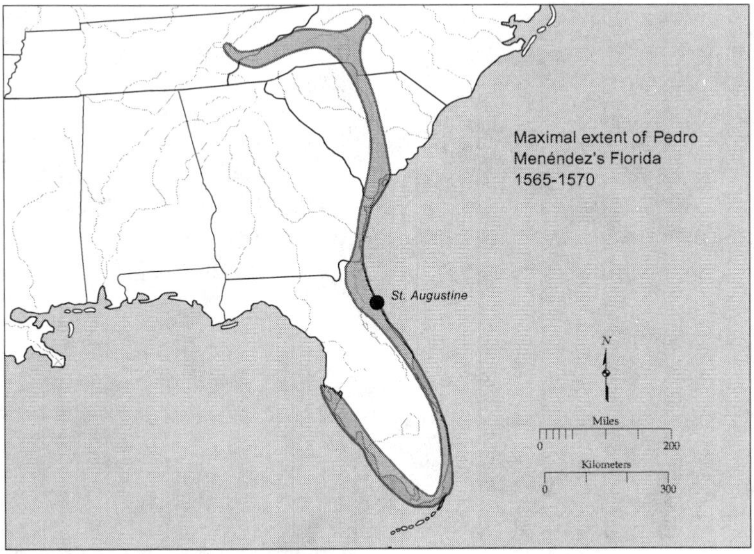

FIGURE 11.2. Maximal extent of Pedro Menéndez's Florida, A.D. 1565–1570. (Created by John Worth and prepared for publication by Clay Mathers.)

sion from all Native leaders. Apart from establishing a second Spanish colonial port city at Santa Elena in Port Royal Sound, between 1566 and 1568 he stationed Spanish garrisons at the capital towns of all major Indigenous coastal chiefdoms allied to the Spanish along the Atlantic coastline and the entire Florida peninsula. These garrisons included Orista and Guale to the north, and Ais, Tequesta, Calos, and Tocobaga to the south, not to mention the besieged garrisons stationed successively at San Mateo and San Pedro in the French-allied Mocama region between Guale and St. Augustine (Hann 1996, 2003). From Santa Elena he also dispatched an exploratory expedition under Juan Pardo in yet another attempt to cross the Appalachian summit and establish a direct connection to New Spain (Hudson 1990). Though Pardo's expedition turned around due to rumors of an ambush by a coalition of chiefs led by Coosa, he managed to leave a string of garrisoned forts in the capital towns of deep interior chiefdoms at Olamico, Cauchi, Joara, Guatari, and Cofitachequi. All told, Pedro Menéndez established some fifteen fortified garrisons across Spanish Florida (see Figure 11.2), distributing a handful of secular priests and Jesuit missionaries to promote conversions in these newly assimilated communities (Milanich 1999:82–103). By 1570, only five years after St. Augustine's establishment, just two of these forts remained, virtually all the rest falling victim to Native resistance resulting in the slaughter or withdrawal of all Spanish garrisons except St. Augustine and Santa Elena. Santa Elena fell to Indian rebellion in 1576, and despite reoccupation it was finally withdrawn in 1587. The subjugation of Spanish Florida's Indigenous chiefdoms by military means was at an end, and a new era dawned toward the latter decades of the sixteenth century, one characterized by the primacy of Franciscan missionaries in the subsequent assimilation of chiefdoms from the single remaining Spanish port at St. Augustine.

The new strategy was simple and successful, and ultimately resulted in the structural assimilation of many tens of thousands of Native Americans living in local chiefly jurisdictions across the coastal and interior regions north and west of St. Augustine (Bushnell 1994:70–72; Milanich 1999:106–109; Worth 1998a:35–43). Indigenous leaders ultimately clamored to establish connections with the Spanish authorities at St. Augustine, receiving both diplomatic gifts as well as access to Franciscan friars. Once resident at Indigenous administrative centers, these missionaries acted both as religious practitioners and cultural brokers for Native American chiefdoms, whose autonomy was in theory only subject to the royal authority of the Spanish Crown through Florida's governor. In return for their formal "rendering of obedience" to the Spanish Crown, Indigenous chiefs not only augmented their own internal political authority over their own chiefdoms but also gained a powerful military ally in the Spanish garrison at St. Augustine. Moreover, chiefdoms increasingly gained access to Spanish markets for their labor and goods as the economy of Spanish Florida eventually focused on the production of corn both in the mission provinces and in the environs of St. Augustine itself. Linked into a multiregional political and economic structure centered at St. Augustine, Indigenous Florida chiefdoms became de facto members of a Spanish paramountcy in which Native American labor and staple foods supported the Spanish administrative center in exchange for Spanish luxury goods and military protection. The previous sixteenth-century landscape of competing autonomous local and regional chiefdoms was replaced in the seventeenth century by what might be referred to as a sort of *Pax Hispanum*, in which a diversity of local Native American societies were assimi-

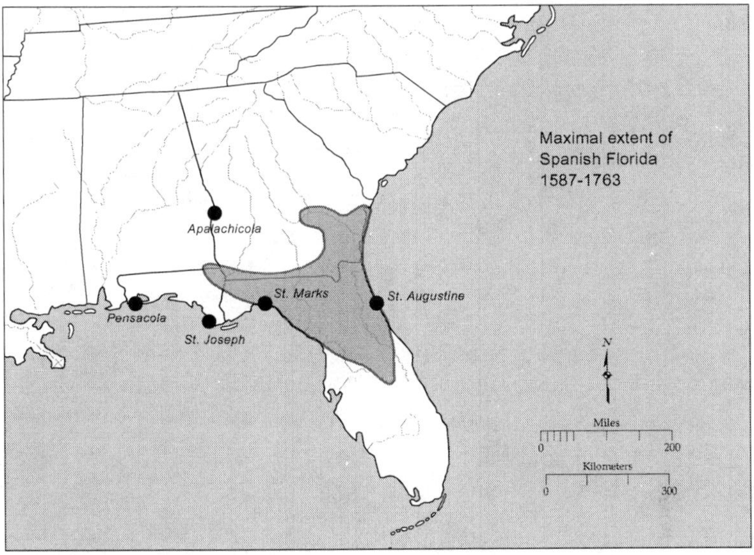

FIGURE 11.3. Maximal extent of Spanish Florida, A.D. 1587–1763. (Created by John Worth and prepared for publication by Clay Mathers.)

lated into a far-flung, multiethnic colonial society centered at the Spanish port city of St. Augustine (see Figure 11.3).

This new polity of greater Spanish Florida was probably larger than anything ever witnessed in the same region of the lower American Southeast, but it was built with the same building blocks that had characterized the late Prehistoric Period and maintained a considerable degree of internal autonomy for its constituent chiefdoms. In this sense, it reflected a unique accommodation between Spanish and Indian political and economic systems. The reasons for this are of course complex, but in part it was a direct result of the lessons learned during the exploratory and early colonial era of the sixteenth century. Many such lessons were learned as a result of the failures and occasional successes of this early period, but a few are worth highlighting here.

One lesson learned during the sixteenth century was the fact that the establishment of diplomatic relations with Southeastern chiefdoms was best accomplished within existing political structures, by dealing directly with chiefs. Moreover, political alliances of this sort were always facilitated by diplomatic gifts to chiefs and other principal leaders, normally including cloth, clothing, jewelry, and other items such as iron tools that could be worn or carried for their social value as sumptuary regalia. Documentary accounts of the Soto, Luna y Arellano, and Pardo expeditions provide ample evidence for the Spanish awareness of these facts, as do extensive records of Menéndez-era and later sixteenth-century Spanish interactions with Native leaders in Florida. Perhaps the most detailed record of Menéndez's use of gifts in establishing diplomatic relations is to be found in the official record of the Juan Pardo expedition into the Appalachian summit region, where great care was taken to record the names and gifts distributed at each meeting place along the route (Hudson 1990). The association of such gifts with Indigenous leaders is also supported by archaeological evidence for the burial of such gifts as elite grave goods, and the geographic distribution of such goods furthermore tends to indicate that they cluster in areas of Indigenous political power and do not simply reflect incidental proximity to the sources of such goods in Spanish colonies, shipwrecks, or expedition routes (e.g., Luer 1994; Smith et al. 2008; Worth 2005). Beyond the use of diplomatic gifts, the very pattern in which Indigenous communities and chiefdoms were ultimately assimilated into the expanding Florida mission system during the late sixteenth and early seventeenth centuries also reflects the Spanish understanding of Native power structures and the need to work from the top down within aboriginal chiefdoms (Worth 1998a:42–43). Ultimately, the pattern of interaction between Spaniards and Indians within and along the margins of Spanish Florida reflects a widespread recognition of the importance of Indigenous political structures in achieving the voluntary assimilation of such societies into the expanding colonial system.

Another lesson learned during the sixteenth century in Florida was the fact that sedentary agricultural societies were far easier to assimilate than foragers, in large part due to their infrastructural ties to specific plots of arable land, as well as the intimate relationship between political power and agricultural surpluses in such societies. Despite the pivotal position of the coastal fishing chiefdoms of South Florida with respect to Spanish maritime travel routes between Havana and St. Augustine, these areas were never effectively assimilated, as the rapid overthrow and withdrawal of all Menéndez-era forts in this region demonstrated. Moreover, the failure of the Franciscan mission system ever to push very far southward into central Florida was in part a reflection of the generalized foraging economy that allowed such groups simply to move away when pressured (Hann 1991, 1993a, 2003). When Spanish Florida finally grew and flourished during the early seventeenth century, it was among the agricultural populations of northern Florida and southeastern Georgia, and it was their labor and staple foods that fueled the Florida economy for a century (Bushnell 1994; Milanich 1999; Worth 1998a, 1998b). Moreover, the eventual configuration of broader Spanish Florida, extending west and north from St. Augustine toward the Apalachee and Guale provinces, was in large part a reflection of the fact that St. Augustine was poor in both arable soils and Indigenous populations to farm them, requiring the input of labor and food from the more distant provinces of Apalachee and Guale, which were nonetheless more densely populated and agriculturally productive (Worth 1998b:144–151). Once anchored to the Atlantic port of St. Augustine, Spanish Florida ultimately expanded only as far as needed to assimilate nearby chiefdoms with sufficient human and natural resources to provide a buffer against interruptions in external supply routes, but rarely beyond that point. In part, this was a result of yet another lesson learned during the sixteenth-century—namely, that direct military occupation of Native American villages was both ineffective and risky as a means of controlling Indigenous populations in the Southeast.

Pedro Menéndez's initial strategy of military fortification of the Florida coast and interior turned out to be an utter and complete failure. As a result, there were no fortified garrisons placed in the mission provinces for nearly a century, and then only in the face of English-sponsored slave raiding after 1659 (Worth 1998b:112–113, 2007:15–24, 2009c). For this reason more than any other, Spanish Florida ultimately grew slowly and over far shorter distances than the bold expeditions of the sixteenth century. Since Franciscan friars led the way and became the primary agents of societal assimilation in Spanish Florida, they only pushed as far as Spanish military aid could reach by land or sea from St. Augustine, and even then only with a few yearly visits by soldiers bringing supplies or recruiting laborers (Worth 1998a:171–175). After the peregrinations of Soto, Luna y Arellano, and Pardo, the chiefdoms of the deep interior remained blissfully devoid of any European presence for more than a century, and far beyond the more spatially limited

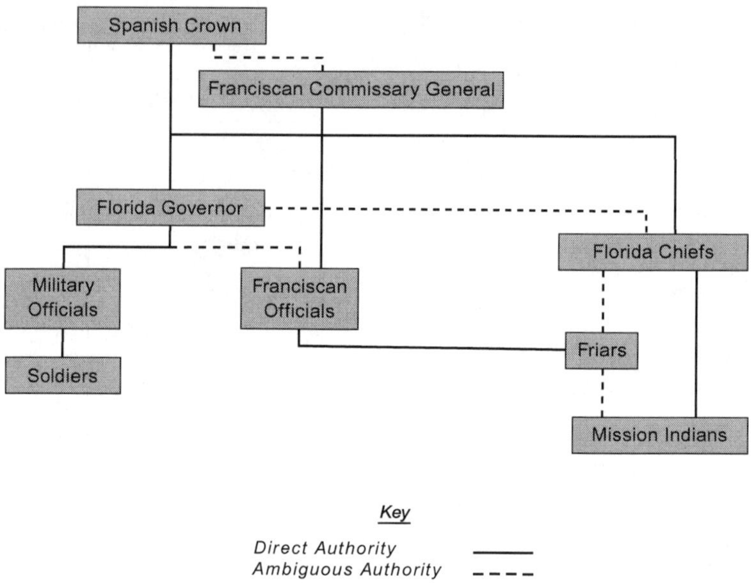

FIGURE 11.4. Schematic diagram of political relationships in seventeenth-century Spanish Florida.

colonial society comprising greater Spanish Florida. With few exceptions (e.g., Worth 1994), neither friars nor soldiers ventured very far beyond the established mission provinces.

In the end, Spanish authorities in Florida adopted a policy of quasi-autonomy for the assimilated mission chiefdoms within their nominal jurisdiction (see Figure 11.4). Chiefs ruled in secular local matters, albeit within the broader structure of Spanish military and ecclesiastical policy as related to the so-called Republic of Indians (Worth 1998a:77–80, 114–115). Resident friars supervised only in spiritual affairs, particularly after the disastrous Guale rebellion of 1597, in which five missionaries were murdered following their attempt to disinherit a chiefly heir, nominally over his refusal to abandon polygamy (Jones 1978). Indeed, during the seventeenth century internal matters of chiefly inheritance seem to have been outside the realm of any normal Spanish intervention, and even when practiced it was generally only to reinforce Indigenous norms and ensure the smooth transition of power (Hann 1986, 1993b; Worth 1998a:96–102, 1998b:192–197). Food and labor were always purchased, never appropriated or seized, in order to avoid the kinds of violent uprisings witnessed by the overthrow of Menéndez's forts and the Guale-Orista rebellion of 1576. The entire economic system of Spanish Florida was fundamentally based on the voluntary integration of missionized chiefdoms into an exchange network that funneled surplus labor and staple foods toward the administrative center at St. Augustine in exchange for goods and services provided via Native leaders to Indigenous populations (Worth 1998a:126–214).

While at any scale of analysis, one might argue that there was a certain amount of coercion and involuntary constraints on the freedom of action exercised by individuals and leaders living within the mission provinces of Spanish Florida, the entire system was predicated upon a mutually voluntary and negotiated relationship between colonists and Indigenous populations, one that bore only superficial resemblance to Spain's earliest and most overtly militaristic conquests during the early sixteenth century. Ultimately, it was this sort of accommodation that characterized the Spanish–Indian society that emerged in colonial Florida toward the end of the sixteenth century, and which resulted in the successful assimilation of many Southeastern chiefdoms into the Spanish Colonial world. The successful strategy ultimately employed in Florida did not arise untested, however, for it was in the turbulent exploratory and Early Colonial Period of the sixteenth century that the pattern for Spanish Florida's eventual growth in the seventeenth century was forged, including not only its eventual size and configuration on the Southeastern landscape but also its internal political and economic structure, as well as the fatal flaw—depopulation—that would eventually doom it to failure. The false starts and failures of the sixteenth century ultimately served their purpose and laid the foundation for a new kind of colonial polity, which though short-lived, marked a novel integration of Native American and Spanish political systems into something entirely new.

SECTION VI

Conflict

12

Contest and Violence on the Northern Borderlands Frontier

Patterns of Native–European Conflict in the Sixteenth-Century Southwest

Clay Mathers

From the early decades of the sixteenth century, the shifting northern frontier of New Spain became a theater for both exploration and conflict, as Spanish-led expeditions advanced tentatively into new, unknown territories (Altman 2010; Chipman 1967; Gerhard 1982). Small parties of Europeans, Native Mexicans, and Africans who had entered the *Tierra Nueva* of the American Southwest in the 1520s and 1530s met with extreme hardships (Adorno and Pautz 1999:212–231), lethal violence (Damp 2005:13–14,101–104), or the threat of it at the hands of Native communities (Rodack 1997:102–104). From the killing of Esteban the Moor and others at Zuni in 1539 to the large-scale violent confrontations between Pueblo groups and the expeditions of Francisco Vázquez de Coronado in 1540–1542 and Oñate y Salazar in 1599, sixteenth-century Native–European contacts in the American Southwest were punctuated by major and minor episodes of armed conflict. These military encounters and campaigns of Native resistance occurred well before the better-known Pueblo Revolts of 1680 (Hackett and Shelby 1942; Liebmann 2010a, 2010b; Preucel 2002; Wilcox 2009) and 1696 (Espinosa 1988). Throughout much of the Southwest, therefore, it appears that armed conflict had an important and continuous role in shaping, and reshaping, the relationships between Old World and New World communities from their outset.

Our understanding of these initial interactions in the Southwest has, and continues to be, informed largely by historical documents rather than physical remains. Furthermore, our evaluations of these largely literary sources have been profoundly affected by the relative abundance of recent research and new data (i.e., modern translations and additional documents) for the earlier part of the sixteenth century (e.g., Flint and Flint 2005). Far less historical and archaeological research in the Southwest, however, has been focused on the period from ca. A.D. 1550 to 1600.[1] As a result, the volume of modern translations, documents, and material evidence for the later sixteenth century is correspondingly smaller. Nevertheless, archaeological investigations at newly discovered sites in New Mexico suggest evidence of sixteenth-century military confrontations—both relating to the large Vázquez de Coronado entrada (Damp 2005; Mathers et al. 2007, 2008). Our discussion below attempts to bring together different sources of data bearing on these initial encounters and to place the early history of Native–European conflict in the American Southwest into a wider geographical, political, and historical context.

Throughout the sixteenth century, threats of violence and coercive force, as well as large-scale military conflict, were not unique in either the Old or New Worlds. In the eastern hemisphere, many European powers had sustained periods of warfare lasting decades or longer, as did the Aztec and Inca empires in the west. As medieval Iberia emerged from the *Reconquista* and began developing its empire, long traditions of social, political, and economic policy began to be transformed and reconfigured continuously as the frontier ceased to be peninsular and rapidly became global. These changes were accelerated considerably as the kingdoms of Castilla and Aragón extended their power westward to the Americas. Established patterns of social and military conduct underwent regular readjustment to cope with a new, unfamiliar landscape of risks and opportunities.

On the cutting edge of empire, early Spanish-led entradas borrowed from traditions of conflict and warfare extending over eight hundred years—from the Islamic invasion of 711 to the Italian Wars of the late fifteenth and early sixteenth centuries (O'Callaghan 2003; Tallet 1992). Faced with a variegated hemisphere of unfamiliar and often uncooperative Native communities, early Spanish-led expeditions found many medieval military precedents unhelpful and the need for rapid adaptation imperative. Although their initial military contact with Europeans often found Native communities unprepared and disadvantaged with respect to tactics and weapons, many quickly adjusted to the presence of European powers and the external threat to their communities. Building on traditions with their own significant historical roots, Native groups throughout the Americas began evolving a new and imaginative set of responses ranging from creative compliance, negotiation, and passive resistance to open conflict, guerilla warfare, and large-scale, sustained campaigns of armed confrontation (Anderson and Dibble 1978; Chamberlain 1953; Dye 2002; López Portillo y Weber 1939; Pohl and Robinson 2005; Restall and Asselbergs 2007). The result of this interaction profoundly shaped not only relations between Native and European communities in the American Southwest during the sixteenth century but also Crown policy across the empire and into later centuries.

Nowhere is this interaction between Natives and Europeans—with respect to military policies, weapons, tactics, and impacts—more complex and interesting than in the American Southwest. In focusing on this pivotal area, my discussion emphasizes the diversity of different actors involved in these relationships of conflict and negotiation, some of the strategies they employed, and the variety of long-term impacts for each party involved—from the Spanish Crown and their *adelantados* to a range of Native communities who both cooperated with and opposed the Spanish-led expeditions that had entered their territories. These social, economic, and military engagements helped to significantly alter the history of the American Southwest and the course of Spain's imperial designs.

Military Backgrounds: European, Native Mexican, and Native American

By the early sixteenth century, European military conflicts were becoming increasingly large, prolonged, and deadly affairs (Arnold 2001; Hall 1997). The competitive evolution of tactics and technology that began in earnest during the Italian Wars between 1493 and 1559 (Eltis 1995; Taylor 2006) was paralleled in eastern Europe and the Mediterranean between 1520 and 1536 (Reston 2009), and rapidly altered the conduct of warfare. These changes were reflected not only in Europe but also elsewhere—including the Western Hemisphere—as European powers engaged one another, *and* the wider world, in a violent clash over resources and empire.

Although Spanish-led entradas were led consistently by individuals who were neither professional soldiers nor trained as such (Flint and Flint, this volume; Restall 2003:27–43), several important points should be borne in mind when assessing the military conduct and impact of these campaigns. First, many of the written manuals and state-sponsored institutions that would later provide formal military training were developing during the 1500s, but they were not widespread until the latter part of the sixteenth century (Eltis 1995:20, 43–75). As a result, the fact that many members of Spanish-led entradas may have had little or no formal military training is not surprising. Second, after eight centuries of conflict during the *Reconquista* ended in 1492, the Spanish Crown rapidly became engaged in another six decades of nearly continuous warfare across southern Europe and North Africa. The strong military overtones of Late Medieval Iberian society were, therefore, carried forward and strengthened during the Early Modern Period. Throughout the late fifteenth and early sixteenth centuries, there were few individuals in the Iberian Peninsula who would not have had some exposure to military practice, either direct or indirect. Major Native and slave rebellions throughout Spanish territory in the decades both preceding and following entradas into North America, for example, underlined the importance of military preparedness (Chamberlain 1948:237–252; 1953:24,54–56; Chipman 1967:78–82; Himmerlich y Valencia 1998; Pocock 1967:54; Rausch 1984:420; Vinson and Restall 2005:21). Basing their actions on medieval precedents, and recognizing the widespread need and limited capacity of their armed forces in the Americas, the Spanish Crown passed *real cédulas* (royal decrees) in 1536 and 1540 requiring *encomenderos* and colonists, respectively, to raise local militia forces in defense of the wider colonial community and its interests (Vinson and Restall 2005:21). Also, while it was frequently the case that the commanders of New World entradas lacked direct experience in combat, it is equally true that some of their immediate subordinates were seasoned veterans of such encounters. Most of the captains associated with the Vázquez de Coronado expedition, for example, had served on other entradas—notably the earlier campaigns of Nuño Beltrán de Guzmán in Pánuco (Flint 2002:528). In any event, members of many entradas that were without military training initially, particularly in the American Southwest, did not have to wait long before gaining direct experience in battle. Finally, the significant degree of similarity in the military tactics used in Spanish-led entradas (Restall 2003:18–26)—from the uplands of Peru and coastal lowlands of La Florida to the high deserts

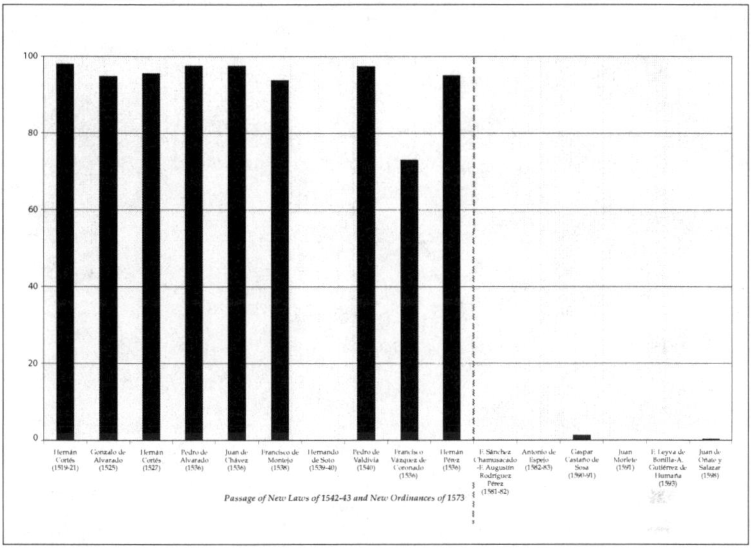

FIGURE 12.1. Percentage of Native allies for selected sixteenth-century expeditions.

of the Southwest—suggests a considerable sharing of information and intelligence between expeditions.

In many cases, the composition of Spanish-led expeditions and the casualty rates associated with them strongly suggest that the Native auxiliaries were the primary combatants and paid the price accordingly (Chuchiak 2007:219–220; Alva Ixtlilxochitl 1969:64, 116; Matthew 2007:107–108; Oudjik and Restall 2007:35; Restall and Asselbergs 2007:16). The composition of these entradas, especially in the first half of the sixteenth century, indicates that Native auxiliaries formed the overwhelming percentage of these expeditions (see Figure 12.1) and performed a wide variety of functions, from fighting and transportation of goods to cooking and shepherding.

Native Mexican auxiliaries fighting alongside the Spanish had their own long traditions of warfare—practices that had both intersections and important contrasts with their Iberian counterparts (Chacon and Mendoza 2007a; Hassig 1988, 2006; Matthew and Oudijk 2007). Many Mexica, for example, were formally trained in both ritualized and battlefield combat, some of them from a very early age in a type of instruction resembling that of modern Special Forces personnel. The historically significant role of combat and militarism in Mexica, Tarascan, and Tlaxcalan society made these well-trained warriors formidable opponents during the Spanish-led assault on the Aztec empire, as well as extremely valuable allies in the far-flung series of conflicts that followed Montezuma's defeat at Tenochtitlán. Initially at least, Spanish recruitment of Native auxiliaries recognized a distinction between well-trained warriors (such as Nahua) and others (such as Tabascans), and apportioned their tasks on expeditions accordingly (Chuchiak 2007:199). Native participation in these entradas was motivated by a number of factors, including *encomienda* requirements, marriage ties, relief from tribute obligations, coercion, battle honors, and the promise of economic/social advancement (Flint 2009; Restall and Asselbergs 2007:17–20; Schroeder 2007:19–23).

The role of Native Americans in both assisting and opposing Spanish-led expeditions is equally variegated and complex. Native communities throughout the Americas had a well-developed and wide-ranging set of strategies for defense, compliance, negotiation, misdirection, ambush, and combat, and frequently employed a variety of these approaches in blunting the impact of sixteenth-century entradas (Chacon and Mendoza 2007b; Ferguson and Whitehead 1992; Rice and LeBlanc 2001). Although conflict and competition appear to be common features of community life throughout the prehistoric, protohistoric, and early historic periods in the Southwest—judging by evidence from rock art (Schaafsma 2000), material and skeletal assemblages (Kanter 2004:170–171; LeBlanc 2001; Wilcox and Haas 1994), village architecture and regional settlement distributions (Connelly 1979:540–542; Plog 1997:159–160), ethnography (Ellis 1951; Titiev 1944:155), and historical documents (Sánchez 1992; Smith et al. 1966:48–49)—the regularity and intensity of warfare in the period immediately preceding European contact does not appear to have been unusual or to have involved extraordinary investments.

While the traditional suite of Native missile weapons in the Southwest (such as spears, arrows, rocks, ash pots, and sling stones; Sánchez 1992; Taylor 2001) compared poorly with European armaments on the battlefield, what Native combatants lacked with respect to weaponry, they frequently made up for with their numerical strength, knowledge of local terrain, and formidable village architecture. In particular, windowless, terraced pueblos of adobe were not only difficult to burn but also presented considerable obstacles to attackers unfamiliar with their irregular plan and access/exit points. In addition, despite their long experience and developed traditions of attacking well-fortified strongholds during the Crusades, *Reconquista*, and Italian Wars, Spanish-led forces sometimes found themselves confronting Native opponents in protracted sieges, rather than direct combat (Altman 2010:170–179; Chamberlain 1953:81–91; Flint 2002:571–573). Given that Spanish-led entradas often operated well inland where they could not be easily supplied by either maritime or riverine transport, their ability to damage or destroy strongly fortified Native villages (e.g., with heavy siege equipment or naval artillery) was severely limited. Tactics commonly employed by Pueblo communities during in the Early Historic Period included harassment via raiding, ambushing small parties, misdirection, and pitched battles (Hammond and Rey 1966:14, 26, 48–50; Schroeder and Matson 1965:56–57, 82–103, 160). Notwithstanding the evidence for disciplined troop dispositions (Damp 2005:92–95; Flint and Flint 2005:393) or the pervasiveness of military offices in Pueblo communities (such as War Priests; White 1935:37), the level of material and institutional investment in warfare by Native communities in the late protohistoric/early historic Southwest does not appear to have reached the same level of intensity as in contemporary areas of Mexico or the southeastern United States. In regions such as the Gran Chichimeca (Powell 1952, 1977), the valley of Mexico (Hassig 1988, 2006), and the Mississippian Southeast (Dye 1990, 2002; Larson 1972), for example, warfare appears to be characterized by qualitative and quantitative differences with communities in the early historic Southwest, including more sustained conflicts, the widespread procurement and display of body parts as trophies, and—particularly in the latter two areas—the development of complex webs of intra- and interregional tribute relations.

Crown Policy Toward Exploration and Military Campaigns

In the Southwest, sixteenth-century entradas clearly formed part of a wider campaign of *conquista* encouraged by the Spanish Crown and sanctioned by *asientos* (written contracts) that were broadly similar from region to region (Lyon 1976:1–18, 220–223). By the time the first major entrada reached the American Southwest in 1540, Spanish authorities had already begun to wrestle with the multitude of problems arising from these contracts. Throughout the Americas, the Crown faced a growing crisis over the largely unregulated activities of *conquistadores* and widespread abuses of the *encomienda* system, mining activities, slaving, and other related colonial enterprises.

In the Southwest, for example, sixteenth-century documents indicate that several members of the Vázquez de Coronado entrada were charged with cruelty toward Native communities when they returned to Mexico in 1542 (Flint 2002). New laws protecting the Indigenous population of the Americas were passed the same year (Wagner 1967:108–133). Charges and adverse judgments against sixteenth-century expeditionaries were not uncommon (Flint 2002; Simmons 1991:187), so when entrada leaders like Vázquez de Coronado, Oñate y Salazar, and others faced charges of cruelty from their own government, it is clear that the Crown needed to periodically regain control from expedition leaders who violated laws or defied explicit government policies concerning the conduct of expeditions. In new and distant lands, far from Spanish viceroys and their officious administrators, the latitude for establishing autonomous power bases was considerable. As a result, and with the prospects for vast fortunes in the offing, serious challenges to Crown authority and the economic stability of their newly acquired lands were commonplace. Examples of such challenges were widespread: from the open conflict between Cortés and his contemporaries (MacNutt 1977:277–284) and the Wars of the Captains in Peru (MacQuarrie 2007:270–304) to the internecine conflict between Spanish officials, *conquistadores*, and colonists in regions throughout the Caribbean and Central America (Chamberlain 1948:292–307, 1953:48–99; Chipman 1967:86, 94–95, 106, 153–164; Deagan and Cruxent 2002:47–70; Fernández de Oviedo 2006:60–64).

The regular use of military force, together with the unwelcome resource demands of many early expeditions and colonization efforts, often led to local resentment and frequently to major revolts and rebellions. Indeed, the need to wrest control of newly settled territories from some of their own citizens often represented a greater challenge to the

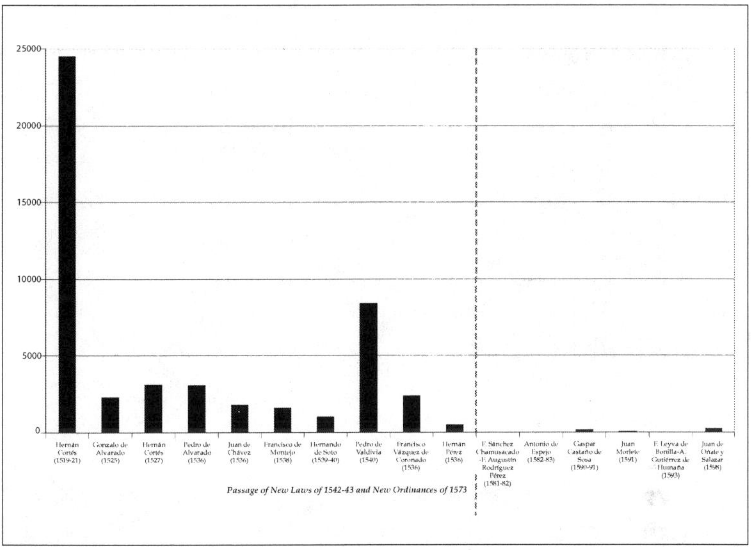

FIGURE 12.2. Overall number of expedition members for selected sixteenth-century expeditions.

Spanish Crown than the subjugation of Native communities in the same areas.

The substantive remedy for these problems came in the form of two landmark pieces of legislation: the New Laws of 1542–1543 (Hammond and Rey 1966:6–7; Simpson 1982:123–144) and the New Ordinances of Phillip II in 1573 (Tyler 1980). The impact of these laws had a profound (though not immediate) effect, not only on the size and composition of Spanish entradas in the later sixteenth century, but on their overall objectives and impacts as well.

When we compare early sixteenth-century entradas in the American Southwest with a range of other early expeditions in the Americas, a number of interesting patterns emerge (see Figure 12.2). First, these entradas consistently employed large numbers of Native auxiliaries (Chamberlain 1953:24, 54–56, 93–94; Flint 2008:112, 210–214, 2009; Matthew and Oudijk 2007; Restall 2003:44–63). Second, the percentage of these early (pre-1542) expeditions formed by Natives is remarkably consistent from region to region, regularly forming 90 percent or more of the overall total. Two important exceptions are worth pointing out: the Vázquez de Coronado expedition of 1540–1542 (Flint 2008), with a Native contribution of approximately 70 percent, and the more striking Hernando de Soto entrada of 1539–1543, with no Native auxiliaries at all (Clayton et al. 1993; Galloway 1997c; Hudson 1994, 1997; Milanich and Hudson 1993). Significantly, both expeditions set out only a few years before the passage of the New Laws in 1542–1543. The third point to be made in comparing these expeditions is that the large size of entradas in the first half of the sixteenth century gave way to smaller expeditions in the later 1500s, with significantly less representation by Native auxiliaries. In New Mexico, for example, the latter half of the sixteenth century is characterized by small expeditions that were primarily evangelical endeavors, illegal entradas, colonization efforts, or some combination of all of these. By the time entradas reentered the Southwest in the 1580s, important shifts had occurred in the size, composition, and purpose of Crown-sanctioned expeditions, that is, toward smaller, Spanish-dominated parties bent on religious conversion and colonization.

These marked changes in entrada policy, logistics, and orientation can be better understood by examining briefly the content of the 1542–1543 and 1573 laws. The New Laws of 1542–1543 were largely an attempt by the Spanish Crown to prohibit slavery and limit the power of *conquistadores* and *encomenderos*, particularly with respect to their treatment of Native populations. Together with the New Ordinances of 1573, these reforms were designed to not only curb some of the worst abuses of the *encomenderos* but also promote more benign treatment of Native communities. Chipman (1992:55) suggests that the 1573 legislation strictly licensed encounters between Spanish and Native communities, eliminated the term "conquest" from contracts, reinforced earlier injunctions against slavery, and recommended that if hostilities developed, Native populations be subdued with "as little harm as possible." Furthermore, according to Hammond and Rey (1966:6–7), these ordinances also made the following restrictions:

> Discoveries were to be undertaken "with peace and mercy," and there would be no excuse for any action that might injure the Indians. . . . Similarly, great care was to be exercised in the selection of the persons entrusted with new discoveries. They must be men of approved

> Christianity, of good conscience, lovers of peace who desired the conversion of natives; they had to be of the kind that could give absolute assurance that no harm would be done to the Indians. They must do them no wrong, must not take them away from their homes. . . . and of course they must not become involved in war or conquest or render aid to one tribe against another. . . . No one, not even the religious, would be permitted to explore or settle new regions without a license from the king, or from the viceroy in his name, under pain of death and loss of property.

The effect of these laws on military strategy and the conduct of expeditions in new territories such as the American Southwest was significant. Large expeditions and overwhelming military force had clearly been helpful in reconnoitering new, unknown territories, in establishing and maintaining a semblance of Spanish control, and in providing the security necessary to initiate colonization efforts (whether they were ultimately successful or not). After successive defeats in Yucatán between 1529 and 1535, *adelantados* like Francisco de Montejo knew only too well the cost of expeditions that failed to include a sufficient number of Native auxiliaries (Chuchiak 2007:179–180). Equally, Tristán de Luna y Arellano, who had been one of Vázquez de Coronado's captains during the 1540–1542 expedition to Tierra Nueva, did not repeat the Soto entrada's model of appropriating Native labor en route. Instead, from the outset, Luna y Arellano included a number of Mexica and Tlaxcalan allies, as well as a significant number of other personnel, in his 1559–1561 expedition to Pensacola Bay (Bratten 2009:109).

While overwhelming force had obvious advantages for expeditions in many contexts, it also created its own problems, particularly with respect to the provisioning of large forces far from their established terrestrial, riverine, or maritime supply lines. As in many other areas, the impact of large expeditions, such as the Vázquez de Coronado entrada in the Southwest, had serious social, economic, political, and military consequences for local communities and Spaniards alike. Moreover, de facto control of large numbers of Native auxiliaries was in the hands of Native leaders who participated in Spanish-led expeditions rather than European commanders, no doubt due to the small proportion of Europeans to Natives, the significant linguistic barriers involved, the logistics of battlefield communications, as well as the inexperience of many Spanish expedition members in actual combat. As a consequence, Native auxiliaries could often act independently, run amok, and inflame local populations against them and their Spanish allies (Chamberlain 1953:55, 64, 76; Chipman 1967:155).

With so many unknown variables at the outset, expedition planners faced an impossibly complex calculus. In the early sixteenth century particularly, anticipating the needs of specific entradas required a fine balance between creating a party that would be too small to avoid defeat or annihilation and forming a group so large as to become unwieldy, create dangerous resource demands, and generate major local hostilities. Such a balance was seldom achieved. Nevertheless, the difficulties inherent in these complex matters of entrada planning and execution appear to have led to some experimentation, which may help to explain the increasing variation in expedition numbers and composition on the eve of the passage of the New Laws.

In the Southwest, the hiatus between the economically disastrous Vázquez de Coronado entrada (returning in 1542) and the first tentative expeditions of the 1580s was filled with philosophical debate, legislative activity, considerable financial volatility, and major reorientations of government policies. Significant also is the fact that in northern New Spain this later period is marked by new approaches in unstable frontier areas, especially the Gran Chichimeca. This major shift in Crown political strategy and its relations with Native communities, which took place between the 1550s and early 1590s, represents a significant departure from early approaches. At the beginning of the Chichimec War, for example, military confrontations were characterized by small numbers of underfinanced troops that were regularly attacked and defeated by mobile foragers. The gradual introduction of a more conciliatory approach, backed by a program of Crown-financed gift exchange and a well-supported military presence with garrisoned troops (Powell 1952, 1977), brought success and eventually a region-wide peace. The Crown pursued similar strategies in La Florida and the Interior Southeast during the same period (Ethridge and Mitchem, this volume; Rodning et al., this volume; Worth, this volume). These developments mark a clear divide between the conduct of expeditions and patterns of conflict characteristic of the first half of the sixteenth century, as opposed to the second. Particularly important in this context is the shift in expedition focus from conquest and resource extraction to religious conversion and long-term settlement. A more detailed examination and comparison of conflict in the Southwest during these two periods is, therefore, appropriate.

Review of Entrada History and Conflict in the American Southwest

During the sixteenth century, a number of Spanish-led entradas entered the American Southwest and Southern Plains, making contact with Native communities from southwest Arizona to central Kansas. While there are likely to have been undocumented incursions of various types, sizes, and durations on the northern frontier of New Spain throughout this period (e.g., for slave raiding), the Spanish-led terrestrial expeditions and major reconnaissance parties known to have entered this area during the 1500s include four in the first half of the sixteenth century[2]: Esteban the Moor (1539), Marcos de Niza (1539), Melchoir Díaz and Juan de Zaldívar (1539), and Francisco Vázquez de Coronado (1540–1542); and six in the period after 1550: Francisco Sánchez Chamuscado and Augustín Rodríguez (1581–1582), Antonio de Espejo (1582–1583), Gaspar Castaño de Sosa (1590–1591), Juan Morlete (1591), Francisco Leyva de Bonilla and Antonio Gutiérrez de Humaña (1593), and Juan de Oñate y Salazar and Marcos Fárfan de los Godos (1598–1610). In addition, various seaborne reconnaissance efforts were undertaken along the Pacific coast (see Figure 12.3).

The dilemma for generations of Southwestern scholars is that, while they were well aware that conflict had taken place during the initial Contact Period in the Southwest and had been a component of expeditions throughout the sixteenth century, the general dearth of sites and materials made it extremely difficult to assess the *importance* and *impact* of that conflict. These interpretative difficulties extended not only to individual expeditions, and to their Spanish, Native Mexican, African, and other members, but particularly to the Indigenous communities of the Southwest. In recent years, however, the discovery of new sites and documents has begun to change our approach to, and perceptions of, Native–European conflict in this region.

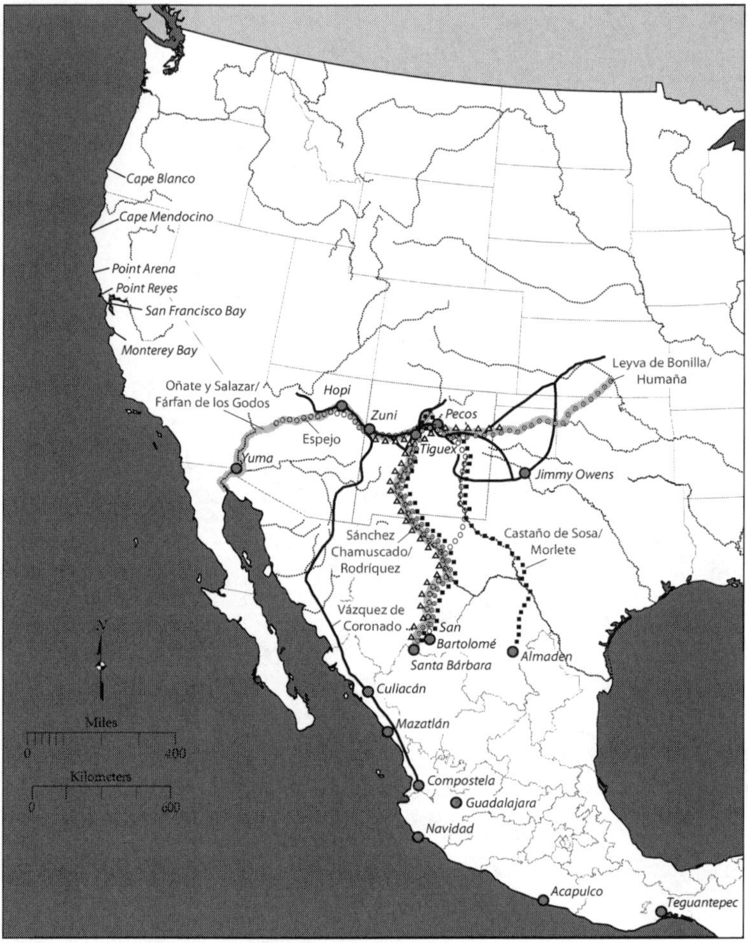

Figure 12.3. Major entradas and primary expedition routes in the American Southwest (1540–1610). Francisco Vázquez de Coronado (1540–1542); Francisco Sánchez Chamuscado and Augustín Rodríguez (1581–1582); Antonio de Espejo (1582–1583); Gaspar Castaño de Sosa/ Juan Morlete (1590–1591); Francisco Leyva de Bonilla and Antonio Gutiérrez de Humaña (1593); Juan de Oñate y Salazar and Marcos Farfán de los Godos (1598–1610).

By the end of the Italian Wars in 1559, Spanish military forces were some of the most formidable in Europe. The success of Spanish entradas and military campaigns in much of the New World was due, however, much more to the inclusion of large numbers of experienced Native auxiliaries than to any superiority in European tactics or firepower. The Vázquez de Coronado expedition was no exception, and recent documentary research suggests the number of their Native auxiliaries may have totaled some two thousand or more individuals (Flint 2009:73, 115). Large numbers of Native auxiliaries in elaborate, menacing costumes and well versed in the art of war made a compelling case for peace and consequently were employed regularly in entradas as a form of military theater designed to bring Native communities quickly to peace.

Theatrical displays of violence in the repertoire of Spanish tactics ran the gamut from the fairly benign and mildly farcical reading of the *Requerimiento*, together with shock and awe demonstrations of horsemanship and weapons, to more intimidating acts of captive taking (particularly Native leaders), and finally to more direct acts of terror and violence in the form of public mutilation and execution. When simple exhortations and theatrical displays were insufficient (using dogs, horses, weapons, or sham battles), expeditions often opted for more direct, belligerent tactics. Narrative accounts of the 1540–1542 expedition of Vázquez de Coronado and trial testimonies relating to the post-entrada prosecution of some of its principal leaders suggest that nearly all of these tactics were employed in some way, from the summary reading of the *Requerimiento* and iterative displays of firepower at the Zuni Pueblo of Hawikku to the burning/dismantling of settlements in Tiguex and the full-scale sieges of major pueblos such as Arenal and Moho (Flint 2008:148–149, 151–153). Brutal tactics of intimidation and terror, referred to by Restall (2003:24–26) as *display violence* and widely used elsewhere in the Americas, were regularly employed during the Vázquez de Coronado entrada. Examples include the severing of hands, noses, and tongues, the garroting of an uncooperative guide, and the burning at the stake of rebellious Natives (Flint 2002).

In campaigns throughout the Americas, theatrical displays and the overt threat of violence were often sufficient to discourage resistance and promote the cooperation of Native communities. Indigenous responses were by no means passive, however, and from Peru and Yucatán to the American Southeast and Southwest, Native communities developed countermeasures including techniques to combat cavalry charges, misdirect and ambush troops, trap and kill horses, frustrate waterborne assaults and sieges, employ poison arrows, and minimize the effects of crossbow and arquebus fire. Documents relating to the Vázquez de Coronado expedition indicate that a number of these techniques were employed by Native groups, particularly Pueblo communities in New Mexico. Some of these tactics included direct military confrontation and the ambush of small parties of Spaniards and allies at Hawikku, the use of poison arrows by Natives near Corazones in Sonora, as well as protracted sieges and the killing of large numbers of horses in the Middle Rio Grande. The variegated responses of Pueblo communities in the latter area (occupied by Tiwa, Towa, Keres, Piro, and Tano groups) underlines the complex relationships between different local Native communities and the expedition, including both feigned and genuine alliance, acquiescence, flight, misdirection, and violent confrontation—the latter ranging from periodic raids to sustained warfare.

While expeditions in the latter half of the sixteenth century in the American Southwest (following Vázquez de Coronado) were not without examples of conflict and lethal violence, the scale of death and destruction in this later period was considerably lower, both for Spanish-led expeditions and their allies, and for local Native communities as well. Many Natives fled as these later expeditions entered their territories, such as the Patarbueyes and Piro in advance of the Sánchez Chamuscado-Rodríguez party (Hammond and Rey 1966:10–12) and the Tompiro and Tiwa on the approach of the Espejo expedition (Hammond and Rey 1966:22–23). When confronted by the 1590–1591 expedition of Castaño de Sosa, other Native groups, such as the warriors at Pecos Pueblo, "were unwilling to match arms with the Spaniards and brought some food when the latter made a show of giving battle" (Hammond and Rey 1966:27). In a number of cases these later entradas, such as those of Espejo and Castaño de Sosa, were subject to small-scale raids and skirmishes directed at horses or livestock (Hammond and Rey 1966:20, 34). In the later sixteenth century, lethal violence was more unusual on both sides, but on occasions Native communities inflicted fatalities on small Spanish expeditions (e.g., the Sánchez

Chamuscado-Rodríguez and Espejo entradas; Hammond and Rey 1966:14, 26) or annihilated them outright (e.g., the Leyva de Bonilla-Humaña expedition; Hammond and Rey 1966:48–50). In other cases, Spanish expeditionaries attacked and killed small numbers of Natives, from several individuals at Pecos Pueblo (Castaño de Sosa in 1591; Schroeder and Matson 1965:88–95) to more than sixteen at the Pueblo of Puaray in Tiguex (Espejo in 1583; Hammond and Rey 1966:26). By comparison with the large numbers of fatalities suffered in protracted battles between the Vázquez de Coronado expedition and the Natives of Tiguex (upward of one hundred at Arenal and approximately two hundred at Moho; Flint 2002:148–153), the casualties associated with these later expeditions were significantly lower. This reduction in conflict and lethal violence in the second half of the sixteenth century appears to be related to several major factors, including the following:

- limited expedition size and resource requirements;
- greater expedition mobility (i.e., a shorter duration of stay in one location);
- greater balance of military power/coercive force between Natives and Europeans;
- an awareness by Native communities of the serious potential threat from European expeditions;
- the widespread tendency for local Natives to abandon villages and regions in advance of an expedition's arrival, and
- adoption of new laws/policies toward Native communities.

Catalysts for Conflict

One of the primary triggers for Native–European conflict in the Southwest, especially in the earlier sixteenth century, appears to have been the appropriation of major resources (including captives) from local Native communities by Spaniards and their allies. As Hordes (1989:214–217) points out, poorly provisioned Spanish expeditions in the Southwest regularly resorted to extorting food, blankets, shelter, and other provisions from Native groups. Many Indigenous communities were unaccustomed to such demands and could ill-afford to acquiesce without putting themselves at serious risk. On the other hand, they could not easily ignore the transparent menace and coercive force behind such insistent requests.

It is suggested here that the enormous size of the Vázquez de Coronado expedition placed a very substantial strain on local resources and communities wherever it remained for any significant period of time. The total number of people associated with this entrada (approximately 2,800) more than exceeded the population of the largest pueblo in both the Zuni and Tiguex areas. In addition, the considerable pressure created by the animals that accompanied this expedition (ca. 6,500 animals) would have added a further unexpected and unwelcome strain on local Native communities. The appropriation of other valued resources (such as blankets) during the cold winters of 1540 and 1541 would have further strained relations between Europeans and their Native Mexican/African auxiliaries on the one hand, and local Pueblo communities on the other. The Vázquez de Coronado expedition's extended stay in areas such as Zuni and Tiguex, for example, only worsened the situation. To compound matters, the failure of Hernando de Alarcón's naval contingent to resupply the Vázquez de Coronado entrada as planned—owing to the lack of navigable rivers inland—further exacerbated the deteriorating conditions for the expedition's base of operations in Tiguex. As Mathers et al. (2011) suggest, large population centers were the target of early Spanish entradas in the Southwest (such as Zuni, Hopi, and Tiguex), as they had been in La Florida and elsewhere. Large, aggregated populations not only promised short-term gains in the form of stored food and portable wealth but also longer-term prospects with respect to plentiful supplies of labor, productive agricultural land, and perhaps accessible mineral ores. Conversely, smaller, less militaristic expeditions entering the Southwest in the 1580s and 1590s placed fewer demands on local communities and generally faced less hostility as a consequence.

Archaeological Evidence for Sixteenth-Century Conflict in the Southwest

For scholars in the Southwest, the opportunity to evaluate early sixteenth-century conflicts in more material, tangible terms has come with the discovery of two apparent sites of armed conflict: one in 2003 at the Zuni

Pueblo of Hawikku in west-central New Mexico, and the other in 2007 at the Southern Tiwa Pueblo of Piedras Marcadas in present-day Albuquerque. Both sites appear to have been the scene of conflict between the Vázquez de Coronado expedition and Native Pueblo communities: Hawikku in July 1540 and Piedras Marcadas at some time between November 1540 and June 1542.

While a Vázquez de Coronado presence at Hawikku was strongly suggested by narratives related to this expedition, and copper crossbow boltheads were known from unpublished collections associated with the Harmon Hendricks–Frederick Hodge excavations at the site between 1917 and 1923 (Blakeslee et al. 1997:375, Figure 23.3), physical evidence of the 1540 battle was not confirmed definitely until metal-detecting surveys began at Hawikku in 2003 (Damp 2005). At Piedras Marcadas Pueblo there was no definitive documentary or archaeological evidence suggesting a connection with the Vázquez de Coronado entrada prior to 2007. Following geophysical prospection work at the site in 2007 carried out for the City of Albuquerque by Statistical Research, Inc., an unusual square structure (measuring ca. 10 × 10 m) was located beneath the surface. To determine whether this anomaly was likely to be a kiva or an early Spanish Colonial structure, I suggested that a brief metal-detecting survey be conducted. That work helped to identify a large concentration of metal objects at the site that are clearly connected with the Vázquez de Coronado entrada (Mathers et al. 2007).

In July 1540, after trekking along the Arizona/New Mexico border through a largely uninhabited, resource-poor region known as the *despoblado*, an advance element of the Vázquez de Coronado expedition approached the large cluster of Zuni pueblos from the south, exhausted and near starvation. Hernando de Alarcón was unable to resupply the Vázquez de Coronado entrada as planned, and as it would elsewhere, the need to provision large numbers of people and animals made the expedition's initial position at Zuni an extremely precarious one.

According to documentary sources, after a minor skirmish with Zuni tribal members, the expedition again confronted Zuni warriors on the outskirts of Hawikku. The Zuni then retreated behind the walls of their pueblo to await an attack, which subsequently came in waves of crossbowmen, arquebusiers, and cavalry, all of which were repulsed. A full-scale assault followed, which succeeded in killing some Zuni inhabitants and driving off the rest. The result was that Spaniards and their allies were left in possession of Hawikku and camped in the area for more than four months.

Materials found in several seasons of controlled metal detecting at Hawikku appear to indicate that the battle was concentrated on the pueblo's west side, as the narratives suggest (Damp 2005:96). Concentrations of horseshoe nails were found near passageway areas (entrances and exits) in the southwest and northwest corners of the site, which may suggest particular attention was focused on these strategic points (see Figure 12.4). Objects relating to this first major military encounter between Europeans, their Mexican/African allies, and Zunis in the Southwest substantiate, at least in general terms, contemporary accounts of this battle. Some of the early sixteenth-century horseshoes, nails, arquebus balls, scabbard tips, crossbow bolts, and chain mail from Hawikku appear to be associated with this short but significant military engagement. Military, trade, and other objects associated with the Vázquez de Coronado expedition are known from two other Zuni communities nearby: Kyaki:ma (a caret-headed nail, arquebus shot, a copper crossbow bolthead, and sheet-brass Clarksdale bells; Damp 2005:105–115), and Kechiba:wa (Nueva Cádiz short and long beads, seven-layer faceted chevron beads, a copper crossbow bolthead, Clarksdale bells, and a wrought-iron axe and awl; Billeck 2009; Mathers et al. 2009).

Another scene of conflict between the Vázquez de Coronado entrada and Native Americans in New Mexico appears to be the site of Piedras Marcadas, in what is now the city of Albuquerque. The site lies in the Tiguex province, a name given by the expedition to a series of large pueblos stretching from at least the Pueblo of Kuaua in the north to Isleta Pueblo to the south. Relations between the expedition and Native communities did not begin well in the early winter of 1540 and remained hostile until the Vázquez de Coronado party returned to Mexico in the spring of 1542. According to documentary sources, including detailed trial transcripts (Flint 2002, 2009), armed conflict erupted early and often between the two groups, involving major attacks, occupation of Native sites, public executions by fire, and other depredations. Precipitated again by shortages of food and supplies, as well as cold winters and assaults on Native women, a badly provisioned group of Europeans

FIGURE 12.4. Roomblocks and Vázquez de Coronado artifact distributions at the Ancestral Zuni Pueblo of Hawikku (Zuni, NM); after Damp (2005, Figure 5.1, Figure 7.7).

and their numerous auxiliaries pressed hard on Native communities for resources of all kinds. Under pressure throughout their territory, Tiguex communities resisted, revolted, attacked (in large and small groups), and were in turn besieged by an overwhelming force of Spaniards and their allies. The expedition's firepower and enormous fighting force were no match for Pueblo communities, accustomed as they were to more short-lived conflicts, a smaller and less persistent enemy, a more symmetrical balance of firepower, and less deadly, lasting consequences.

In 2007, it became clear that Piedras Marcadas might represent one of the earliest military encounters in sixteenth-century New Mexico. Following geophysical work, limited metal detecting, and surface survey, over one hundred artifacts of sixteenth-century date were recovered, all consistent with the Vázquez de Coronado expedition and with some form of military activity (Mathers et al. 2007, 2008). A relatively small area of the site was investigated initially (ca. four hundred square meters) and in a fairly preliminary fashion via metal-detector surveys. Nevertheless, the concentration of materials in one corner of the plaza and the small size of objects found in that localized area were of particular interest. Like concentrations of materials found at Hawikku, the dense clustering of artifacts in the southeastern corner of the southernmost survey unit may suggest that one of the focal points of conflict at Piedras Marcadas was a plaza area and the entrance and exit areas associated with it (Mathers et al. 2008). Attacks focused on enclosed spaces, and especially those targeting exits and entrances, are well documented in early sixteenth-century documents. This tactic had been employed in combat by both Spanish and Native forces at sites in Peru (Chaliand 2005:163–164; MacQuarrie 2007:207) and Mexico (Anderson and Dibble 1978:23, 43). In addition, during the initial work at this site, Mathers et al. (2008) suggested that the small size and fragmented nature of the objects found in the plaza area (such as small nail and brass bell fragments), as well as their concentration in a small, restricted space in conjunction with a considerable number of military objects, could indicate the possible use of such tactics by the Vázquez de Coronado entrada. Although preliminary, this evidence may also suggest the possibility that antipersonnel scatter-shot ammunition was being employed to assault the interior spaces of pueblos when protracted sieges failed and more precarious direct assault tactics became necessary (Mathers et al. 2008).

Epilogue: Long-Term Consequences

For the Spaniards and other Europeans who were either participants or investors in many sixteenth-century entradas in the Southwest, the results of their labors varied from mildly disappointing to disastrous. For those expeditionaries who survived, many faced a lifetime of financial ruin, including several entrada leaders who were tried for cruelties they inflicted on Native communities during their expeditions. Others returned to more mundane duties and professions, tried their fortunes again on later entradas in La Florida and the Philippines, or, like Castaño de Sosa and Oñate y Salazar at the end of the sixteenth century, led failed attempts to establish colonies.

For Native auxiliaries and allies, the results were also mixed. Large numbers had died from combat, exposure, and malnutrition. Most surviving expedition members returned with valuable military training and/or direct experience of the attitudes and culture of their Spanish counterparts. Groups such as Tlaxcalan elites gained considerable advantages for themselves and their communities, not simply token privileges such as horse riding and the right to wear Spanish dress, but eventually titles and *encomienda* privileges (Gibson 1952:162–169). Other Natives continued their labors as burden bearers, agricultural workers, miners, or servants in European households, many with duties largely unchanged from those they had carried out on campaign. A small handful of Mexican auxiliaries and Africans chose to remain in Tierra Nueva—an interesting but to date archaeologically invisible phenomenon associated with a number of Spanish-led entradas. By the final decades of the sixteenth century, loyal Spanish allies such as the Tlaxcalans were being employed successfully as buffer communities on the edge of the Gran Chichimeca (Powell 1977:147–159; Simmons 1963:102–104), a strategy that no doubt assisted in bringing peace ultimately to this region and in opening the Southwest to a new surge of colonial activity.

By the onset of the seventeeth century, *conquista* campaigns and the use of large numbers of *indios amigos* and Native auxiliaries for entradas had been replaced by colonial and military strategies predicated on settlement and defense, respectively. While Native groups such as Tlaxcalans continued to be employed as colonists in eighteenth-century Texas (Simmons 1963:105–107), no similar schemes appear to have been attempted in New Mexico. Instead, in much of the Southwest local recruitment of Native troops became increasingly commonplace by at least the 1630s (Kessell 2011:145–147), replacing earlier strategies of importing Native auxiliaries as the principal fighting force for entrada campaigns.

For the Pueblo world, and certainly the Tiguex region, the major impact of sixteenth-century entradas was to reconfigure the landscape of political and economic power, rearrange alliances, and redistribute centers of population. While some of these changes and disruptions were temporary, others were more lasting. Major villages were damaged or destroyed, many individuals were killed or wounded, and the landscape was scarred by the hard use of both expeditions and their voracious livestock. Recovery from the economic, demographic, and other impacts of the Vázquez de Coronado expedition, especially in the Tiguex region, was adversely affected by the megadrought affecting both North America (Van West et al., this volume) and Mexico (Acuna-Soto et al. 2002) in the later sixteenth century. Spanish-led entradas also introduced Native communities in the Southwest to a variety of new plant and animal resources, tools, technologies, raw materials, and trade goods. Despite many of the adverse impacts of European colonialism, Southern Tiwa, Zuni, and other Pueblo communities continued to maintain much of the social and spatial integrity of their communities into the later colonial period as missions, estancias, and towns were founded around them.

A little more than a decade after a renewal of Spanish interest in the Southwest (beginning in the 1580s), the megadrought and the Chichimec War both came to an end. At about the same time, major silver deposits were found in Northern New Spain and major settlements were established around them. With much of the northern frontier experiencing more sustained settlement, economic, and military activity, and its landscapes beginning to rebound somewhat ecologically, new entradas were contemplated once again—like Oñate y Salazar's at the very end of the sixteenth century. Because of the forward position of mining settlements such as Santa Bárbara, the point of depature for these expeditions was now east of the Sierra Madre Occidental in what is now Chihuahua, rather than to the west. Pioneering the route that would eventually become the Camino Real de Tierra Adentro, Oñate y Salazar and those expeditions that followed in the seventeeth, eighteenth, and early nineteenth centuries trekked north and south along the Rio Grande corridor. With Spanish settlement and missionary activity concentrated within this north-south riverine route, more distant Native communities such as Zuni and Hopi were less directly impacted by the growing effects of colonialism. Significantly too, the deep Native resentments and lasting consequences created by the Tiguex War of 1540–1542 helped encourage Oñate y Salazar and early seventeenth-century colonists to largely bypass the area near present-day Albuquerque, in favor of more northern areas, despite the shorter growing season and colder temperatures in the latter.

For much of the sixteenth century, the marginal nature of northern New Spain, in a political, economic, and military sense, helped deflect and postpone some of the most damaging effects of European colonialism on Native communities throughout the Southwest. In addition, the protracted warfare between Spaniards and Chichimec groups farther south, and particularly the acquisition of horses by Native communities in the Gran Chichimeca (Powell 1977:2, 80–81, 88), forced changes in military policy that slowed the progress of both commerce and settlement in the northern Borderlands. Decades of protracted warfare on the northern edges of empire against the Chichimecs, and centuries of conflict with the Araucanians on the southern fringes of Spanish territory in Chile (Pocock 1967:231–243), impacted imperial policies at a profound level and at an interregional scale. In the former area, the hit-and-run nature of Chichimec raids had been problematic enough for Spanish mining, ranching, and settlement activity in the 1550s and 1560s, but the later addition of horses to the military repertoire of Native communities in Nueva Galicia and Nueva Vizcaya nullified one of the primary advantages of Spanish armed forces. These developments also precipitated a strategy of frontier defense—in the form of small forts (*presidios*) with very modest Spanish garrisons (Moorhead 1975:7–14)—that would continue to be a military model in the region for centuries (Powell 1977:262–266). Such nodes of control and defense were isolated points in broad swaths of territory that remained largely, or wholly, under Native control. As Scholes (1930) and Moorhead (1995:28–35) have observed, Spanish settlements even in the seventeenth century continued to maintain their marginal character with respect to materials and communications, with supply caravans arriving at intervals of three to four years, and in some cases six to seven. Forging more sustained links between the American Southwest and the rest of New Spain would require continued efforts over the next three hundred years. The slow progress of colonization and commerce was to have a deep and lasting influence on both Native and Spanish communities throughout this period.

13

Conflict, Violence, and Warfare in La Florida

Christopher B. Rodning, Robin A. Beck, Jr., and David G. Moore

Native people and Spanish expeditions experienced several kinds of conflict in La Florida during the sixteenth century, some of which had roots in the prehistoric past, and some of which were new. Warfare in the Mississippian Southeast emphasized status relations within and between chiefdoms and the acquisition of war trophies rather than territorial conquest, and aboriginal warfare was often shaped by the interests and agendas of individual chiefs and individual towns. Members of Spanish expeditions launched attacks, or threatened violence in some instances, in attempts to acquire food and other resources, to capture slaves, to establish and to maintain Spanish hegemony in La Florida, and to create tributary relationships favorable to Spanish colonial interests. Here, we identify major types of conflict in the sixteenth-century Southeast, and the sources of those conflicts. Then, we consider the aftereffects of conflicts on Native and Colonial societies in the sixteenth-century Southeast, which compounded the problems and challenges posed by climatic developments (see Anderson et al. 1995; Blanton, this volume, 2000; Stahle et al. 1998) and, perhaps, some local cases of disease (see Hutchinson 1990, 2006, this volume; Kelton 2007). The combination of these developments created a "perfect storm" that dramatically altered the geopolitical landscape of the Native American Southeast, and the course of European colonial history in the Americas.

The colonial activities of primary interest here are Spanish entradas led by Juan Ponce de León (1513 and 1521), Lucas Vázquez de Ayllón (1521 and 1526), Pánfilo de Narváez (1527–1536), Hernando de Soto (1539–1543), Tristán de Luna y Arellano (1559–1561), and Juan Pardo (1566–1568), as well as mid-sixteenth-century attempts by the French to colonize the Southeast.[1] The routes and outcomes of these expeditions have been considered elsewhere, and we rely upon those treatments in developing our argument here (Adorno and Pautz 1999; Hally et al. 1990; Hudson 1994, 1997; Levy et al. 1990; Little and Curren 1990; Marrinan et al. 1990; Milanich 1990; Morse and Morse 1990; Scarry 1990). The last of these expeditions, those led by Juan Pardo, were dispatched by Spanish colonial governor Pedro Menéndez de Avilés to establish permanent settlements along an overland route connecting his capital settlement of Santa Elena, in coastal South Carolina, to New Spain, as well as to pacify Native American groups in the borderlands of La Florida (Beck 1997; DePratter and Smith 1980; Hudson 2005; Milanich 1995:155–163; Moore 2002:19–31). During and after the Pardo expeditions in the Carolinas and Tennessee, the focus of Spanish colonialism in the Southeast shifted from exploration and military installation to missionization and trade (Milanich 1996:68–82, 1998:132–170; Thomas 1988; Worth 1994, this volume).

Archaeological evidence of Mississippian warfare in the Southeast includes iconography on engraved shell gorgets, copper plates, and painted pottery; log stockades surrounding mound centers and villages; and some cases of burned structures and settlements.[2] The focus of Mississippian warfare was status and status relations within and between chiefdoms (Cobb and Drake 2008; Cobb and Giles 2009; Dye 1990, 2002, 2009; Knight 1986). Achievement of war honors and acquisition of tangible markers of warrior prowess were fundamental to the practice of power in Mississippian societies (Dye 2009; Hudson 1976). From the perspective of people from the Mississippian world, leaders of Spanish expeditions were probably seen as powerful chiefs—antagonistic, perhaps, but chiefs nevertheless—and chiefs who possessed valuable goods (Smith and Hally 1992). Many members of Spanish entradas in the Southeast were also warriors of sorts, and they offered opportunities for Native American chiefs and warriors to achieve war honors (Beck et al. 2011).

Manifestations of Conflict

Both archaeological and documentary evidence attest to cases of warfare in the Southeast during both the sixteenth century and late prehistory. Depictions of warriors, weaponry, scalps, and severed heads on copper, engraved shell, and pottery are clear indicators of the significance of violence to the structure of Mississippian chiefdoms and the cosmology of Native peoples in the Southeast (Dye 2004, 2007; Steponaitis and Knight 2004). The principles of "red" and "white" dualism—that is, dualism between war and peace, and the activities related to them seen in eighteenth-century tribal societies of the Southeast—are thought to have been derived from antecedents in late prehistoric and sixteenth-century chiefdoms (Dye 2009:160). Archaeologists have identified defensive log stockades at many Native American settlements and mound centers in the Southeast (Dye 2009:145–148; Smith 1987; Steinen 1992). The chronicles of Spanish entradas in La Florida record the presence of stout fortifications at numerous towns in eastern Tennessee, in the Central Mississippi valley, and elsewhere (Hudson 1997, 2005). In addition to war clubs, bows and arrows were very effective weapons in the hands of Native American warriors (Dye 2009:156; Hudson 1976:245), and many members of the Soto expedition discarded chain mail armor when an Apalachee archer demonstrated its ineffectiveness at protecting people from well-shot stone-tipped arrows (Ewen 1990:88–89). Spanish soldiers in La Florida carried weapons such as swords, daggers, crossbows, and matchlock guns (or arquebuses). Soto had warhorses and war dogs. Pardo lacked horses, but his sergeant, Hernando Moyano, had a war dog, and a chief of the Chiscas threatened to eat it and to kill Spanish expeditionaries in retaliation for Moyano's raids on Chisca villages in 1567.

Direct archaeological evidence of conflicts between Native American warriors and Spanish soldiers in La Florida is hard to come by. In contrast to growing knowledge about the sites of battles between the Vázquez de Coronado expedition and warriors from pueblos in the Southwest (Mathers, this volume), archaeological signatures of historically documented conflicts between Spanish soldiers and Native American warriors in La Florida are difficult to pinpoint. The general locations of many conflicts are known with varying degrees of accuracy and precision, but even the site of the epic battle of Mabila has not been identified archaeologically (Knight 2009). On the other hand, the Spanish colonial capital of La Florida, Santa Elena, was burned down in 1576, and archaeologists have found remnants of burned houses and the burned fort at Santa Elena, as well as remnants of the rebuilt fort dating from 1576 to 1587 (South 1988). Attacks by Native American warriors on Santa Elena followed successful assaults in 1568 on six forts established by the Juan Pardo expeditions, as well as attacks at the southern end of La Florida on Spanish outposts established by colonial governor Pedro Menéndez de Avilés (Hann 2003; Lyon 1976, 1990; Milanich 1996). Our investigations at the Berry site in western North Carolina have identified it as the location of the Native American town of Joara and the Spanish settlement of Fort San Juan, and we think that the five structures we have identified at the site were burned down during or after the attack on the fort (Beck et al. 2006; Hudson 2005; Moore 2002). Other sites offer evidence for conflict between Native groups and Spanish entradas, even if this evidence cannot be directly related to specific historically documented incidents.

The Tatham Mound is one of several burial mounds associated with the Safety Harbor culture in the vicinity of Tampa Bay, close to routes of the Narváez and Soto expeditions (Hutchinson 2006), and in the vicinity of settlements of the group known as the Tocobagas (Hann 2003). Archaeologists have found evidence for dozens of interments in the Tatham Mound, as is typical for burial mounds in that region, and the association of Spanish goods with some of those burials is clear evidence that they postdate early Spanish contact (Mitchem 1990:56). The number of people buried in the Tatham Mound who were killed by disease or by combat with Spaniards is not known with certainty, but at least two individuals at Tatham sustained premortem wounds from edged metal weapons, probably Spanish swords (Hutchinson 2006:146–152).

The King site is the location of an aboriginal town in the province of Ulibahali, in northern Georgia, founded shortly after either the Soto or Luna y Arellano expeditions traversed the province of Coosa (Hally 2008). Spanish goods have been found in six burials at King, including an iron sword, three iron celts or chisels, two iron knife blades, one iron wedge, and one iron rod (Hally 2008:222–223). The adult males buried with them may have received them as gifts from members of the Soto or Luna y Arellano expeditions. Known examples of Native chiefs receiving gifts from Spanish entradas include instances when Soto gave the chief of Casqui an iron knife (Hally 2008:461), when Narváez gave brass bells and glass beads to a Native chief in Florida (Hutchinson 2006:11–14), and when Pardo gave the chief of Joara several iron knives

(Moore 2002:237). On the other hand, people at King may have acquired Spanish goods through aboriginal trade networks (Waselkov 1989). It is also possible that they acquired these iron tools in battle (Hally 2008:460–462). When Soto visited towns in Ulibahali, there were several instances in which the Spanish soldiers took up arms in the presence of armed warriors from Coosa, but no skirmishes or battles in this particular area were recorded (Hudson 1997:224–229).

Types of Conflict

Chronicles of Spanish entradas and settlements in La Florida record at least eight types of conflict during the sixteenth century. These types of conflict include warfare between different Native groups, major battles between Native groups and Spanish expeditionaries, Native raids on Spanish expeditions, raids on Spanish encampments, Native raids on Spanish settlements, combined raids by Native warriors and Spanish soldiers on other Native groups, attacks on Catholic friars living in or near Native settlements, and battles between colonial rivals such as those between the French and Spanish.

One form of conflict includes the hostile receptions and stiff resistance that several Spanish entradas received upon entering a town or a province. Both the Narváez and Soto expeditions were attacked upon approaching the Apalachee province in Florida, and Pardo learned of plans by warriors from Coosa to attack his expedition before they could reach the province of Coosa itself. Even the Ponce de León expedition—the first recorded Spanish reconnaissance of Florida—encountered combative Native warriors, indicating there had already been contact between Native groups and Spanish colonists, such as Spanish slavers from the Caribbean (Hann 2003:13, 153). Preemptive responses by the Apalachee and Coosa to the Soto and Pardo expeditions make some sense, as there had been a history of interaction between those groups and preceding entradas. On the other hand, both Ponce de León and Narváez were the first recorded entradas in southern and northern Florida, respectively. It seems likely that in both of these areas there had been some earlier, unrecorded contacts between Native communities and Spanish or other European groups, perhaps in the form of slaving and slave raids. Ayllón captured slaves in 1521 and 1526 (Hoffman 1994a,

1994b), Ponce de León and Hernando de Soto both took hostages, Spanish slavers met surviving members of the Narváez expedition in Texas in 1536, and slaving became widespread in the Southeast during the 1600s (Bowne 2005; Ethridge 2006, 2010). Although direct documentary evidence of it is sparse at present, slaving activity may have led to the combative responses by many Native groups in the Southeast to entradas during the early 1500s, and hostage taking by the Narváez and Soto expeditions probably led to violent encounters as well.

Taking captives must have aroused enmity toward Spanish expeditions, and so also did the presence of friars. Violations of Native rules about gift giving and reciprocity led to the 1570 killings of Catholic friars at Ajacán, in coastal Virginia, close to where Jamestown was established in 1607 (Mallios 2006). Menéndez installed friars and soldiers at several Native settlements throughout La Florida during the late 1500s, but in several instances those friars and soldiers were killed, presumably when they had outstayed their welcome (Hann 1991, 1994, 1996:59–60, 2003).

Documentary sources demonstrate constant threats of violence at the southern edge of La Florida. Survivors of Spanish shipwrecks who were swept ashore in coastal Florida were often killed or enslaved (or adopted) by the Ais, the Calusa, and other Native groups (Hann 2003:78–79; Milanich 1995:156). In 1513, Calusa warriors in canoes challenged the Ponce de León fleet (Hann 2003:13). In 1568, Calusa warriors mobilized to confront Menéndez along the coast of modern southwestern Florida, the Tocobagas likewise challenged Menéndez during his visit to colonial outposts near Tampa (Hann 2003:172–173), and the Tequestas lured Spanish soldiers out of a garrison near Miami in retaliation for the murder of a former chief (Hann 2003:156–157). During the 1560s and 1570s, relations within and between Native villages at the southern edge of La Florida were closely related to the Spanish presence and Native responses to it. The Calusa chief Carlos, for example, first planned to attack Menéndez but, apparently, then decided that Menéndez would make a powerful ally (Hann 2003:170–174). Another Calusa chief, Felipe, a rival of Carlos, benefited when Spanish soldiers assassinated Carlos, a development that undermined Felipe in the long run, as it led to conflicts and violence between him and many local leaders in Calusa villages. As they did with Carlos, Spanish soldiers eventually assassinated Felipe, as well.

These events at the southern edge of La Florida involved both small groups and large numbers of people. Likewise, while aboriginal warfare sometimes involved small parties of warriors, large numbers of individuals and materiel were mobilized in some cases. As the Soto expedition traveled through Florida, some Spanish soldiers were killed by Native snipers. Small groups of warriors harassed the Soto expedition at its first and second winter encampments, with sporadic nighttime raids, during which they fired at soldiers, sometimes set fire to structures, and then quickly retreated.[3] By contrast, large numbers of warriors gathered to attack Soto at Mabila (1540), at Chicaza (1541), and at an Alibamo fort in the hinterlands of Chicaza (1541). Hundreds of warriors from Quigualtam pursued the Soto expedition, led by Luís de Moscoso, down the Mississippi River in 1543 in dozens of war canoes. The leaders of some chiefdoms clearly were able to mobilize large numbers of people, but combat also gave warriors chances to earn war honors. It is possible that some instances of attacks on Spanish expeditions gave Mississippian warriors and chiefs opportunities to claim that they bested the Spaniards in battle, or even conquered them.

Major battles between Spanish expeditions and Native American warriors were rare. Exceptions include the epic battle at Mabila in 1540, which greatly affected both Soto's army and the Native chiefdoms that participated in the battle, as well as the attack on Soto's winter encampment in Chicaza, just before the expedition was planning to depart in 1541. Other exceptions include the 1567 attack by hundreds of Timucuan warriors on vessels transporting some of Menéndez's soldiers to Santa Elena, the 1568 uprising during which Pardo's six forts were attacked and abandoned, and the 1576 uprising during which Santa Elena was attacked and burned by Native American warriors.

Although the outcomes of conflicts between Spanish entradas and Native American warriors had broader geopolitical implications, Native warfare in the Southeast traditionally emphasized status and status relations. Warriors from several chiefdoms pursued common strategic interests in attacking Soto's army at Mabila in 1540, but this alliance grew in part out of Tascalusa's attempts to consolidate his own power relative to neighboring chiefdoms such as Talisi and Coosa (Ethridge 2010:26–28; Hudson 1997:230–231). When the Soto expedition was building boats to cross the Mississippi River in 1541, after traversing the province of Quizquiz, they were visited every day for a month by warriors in two hundred to three hundred canoes from a chiefdom (Aquijo) on the west side of the river (Ethridge 2010:117–118; Hudson 1997:284–285). Warriors shouted at and shot arrows at the soldiers, soldiers fired back from foxholes near the river bluffs, and the fleets of canoes would then leave. These daily attacks, which harassed the soldiers but did not stop them from crossing the river, would have given Native warriors many opportunities to demonstrate participation in warfare. Given the significance of warfare, and the accomplishments of warriors to power and status in the Mississippian world, these daily attacks created theaters for warrior performance. The pursuit of Moscoso's canoes by hundreds of warriors from Quigualtam in 1543, during which the warriors sang war songs (Hudson 1997:390–394), likewise may have been a stage for warrior performance, even as warriors also drove the remnants of Soto's expedition out of their territory, and out of the Southeast.

Participation in warfare may have been the main point, in and of itself, from the Native perspective. Individual warriors could claim status from sniper attacks and from participating in sporadic harassment of Soto's (and, later, Moscoso's) expedition. Surely the Chicaza knew Soto was planning to decamp as winter gave way to spring in 1541, and warriors attacked the Soto expedition just before they departed, perhaps in an effort to claim that they had driven the Spanish out of Chicaza, after months of alternating diplomacy and conflict (Ethridge 2010:42–56; Hudson 1997:262–270). Soon after the Soto expedition departed Chicaza, they came to a small village called Alibamo, and in searching for food nearby, they encountered a fort with a series of concentric log stockades and hundreds of warriors (Ethridge 2010:56–59; Hudson 1997:271–274). Rather than bypassing this fort, Soto attacked, and the Spanish sustained heavy losses. Once the Spanish drove the Alibamo warriors out of the fort and across the nearby creek, they found that their horses could not cross the creek. There were neither houses nor stores of food inside the fort, which, presumably, was built to lure the Soto expedition into an area in which they were vulnerable. There is no doubt that battles at Chicaza and Alibamo hobbled the Soto expedition, but in these instances, as at Mabila and along the Mississippi River, there were also many chances for individual warriors to earn war honors, for themselves and their towns. Timucuan warriors harassed Menéndez's forts near the mouth of the St. John's River in 1567, dramatically affecting the fortunes of these forts (Hann 1996:60) and, again, giving warriors chances to achieve war honors. Timucuan warfare was, more typically, smaller in scale (Hann 1996:103–105), but large numbers of warriors were mobilized for some events, and warriors had chances to display evidence of success in combat during community events in council houses.

In contrast to status-related dimensions of Native American warfare in La Florida, motivations for Spanish participation in warfare were more materialistic. Ponce de León and Ayllón captured slaves and took hostages, and Soto threatened or committed violence to procure food, wealth, porters, and Native women. French colonists who participated in raids with Timucuan warriors on Potano villages in Florida in 1564 and 1565 specifically wanted to kill as many Potano warriors as they could, whereas Native chiefs and warriors were focused primarily on winning a battle against a rival and preparing their home villages for retaliatory raids (Milanich 1996:86). Not long afterward, having sacked the French settlements of Fort Caroline and Charlesfort, Menéndez established St. Augustine and Santa Elena in 1565 and 1566 as part of an effort to stake Spanish claims to La Florida in the aftermath of French exploration and settlement. His first settlement at St. Augustine was attacked by Timucuans, leading him to move St. Augustine to its current location soon afterward. During the 1560s and 1570s, Menéndez's men periodically launched punitive raids against Native settlements in retaliation for periodic raids on Menéndez's settlements and soldiers. Much later, in 1587, Sir Francis Drake attacked and burned St. Augustine, contributing to the abandonment of Santa Elena, the first capital of La Florida.

In contrast to violence and threats by many Spanish expeditions in La Florida, Pardo emphasized diplomacy as colonial strategy and practice. His sergeant, Hernando Moyano, however, raided Chisca villages in 1567 for reasons that are not clearly delineated in documentary sources but which may have been linked to relations between Joara and the Chiscas, as well as the presence of copper and mica in the areas where Chisca settlements were located (Hudson 2005:26–29). Whether the desired ends were land, people, metal, food, labor, or combinations thereof, Spanish colonists approached conflict and warfare differently than did Native peoples of the Southeast.

This is not to say there were no material motivations to aboriginal warfare in the Southeast. Members of the Soto expedition participated with Chicaza warriors in attacks on the Chakchiumas in 1541, the results of which were that the major town of the Chakchiumas was burned down and the Chakchiumas resumed paying tribute to the Chicazas (Ethridge 2010:39–41; Hudson 1997:266). Members of the Luna y Arellano expedition aided Coosa in raids on the Napochies in 1560, for the same reason (Ethridge 2010:62–64; Hudson 2005:102). When Menéndez met with the Calusa chief, Carlos, in 1567, Carlos requested Spanish help in attacking his rival to the north, the chief of the Tocobagas (Hann 2003:105). Menéndez declined, to Carlos's dismay. Similarly, in 1528, Narváez disappointed a Timucuan chief by not helping him in raids on the Apalachee (Milanich 1996:75). Even in these cases, and although tribute was involved, status relations within and between Native societies were at stake.

Sources of Conflict

The sources of some conflicts in La Florida can be traced back to the late pre-Contact (Mississippian) Period, and other forms of conflict developed in the course of cultural encounters between Native and colonial societies. Warfare was widespread in southeastern North America during the period just before and after early Spanish contact (Cobb and Drake 2008; Cobb and Giles 2009; Dye 1994, 1995, 2002; Lambert 2002; Milner 1999). Warfare shaped the history of major Mississippian mound centers such as Moundville, Cahokia, Etowah, and Spiro, and warrior imagery is present in iconography and material culture at these and other Mississippian centers (Dye 2004; King 2003; Knight 1986; Livingood 2008; Steponaitis and Knight 2004). In most if not all cases of Mississippian warfare, participants were involved in achieving status and in negotiating power relations between and within societies, rather than eliminating or displacing particular polities. Chiefdoms coalesced and collapsed throughout the Mississippian Southeast, but chiefdoms of varying scales and degrees of centralization dotted the cultural landscape of La Florida for hundreds of years before the Spanish entradas

(Anderson 1994; Beck 2003, 2006; Blitz 1999; Hally 1996, 2006). Cycles of cooperation and conflict, alliance and enmity, and warfare and peace contributed significantly to the history of Mississippian societies. These cycles shaped the Native societies of the Southeast that encountered Spanish expeditions. The history and ideology of Mississippian warfare guided strategic decisions about attacking Spanish colonists and colonial outposts, and about cooperating with or accommodating Spanish colonists and interests. On one hand, Spanish entradas in the Southeast changed everything, for everybody involved, including those only indirectly engaged. On the other hand, historical conditions and cultural practices in the Southeast affected the ways in which Native groups responded to Spanish contact and the situations created by these colonial encounters.

Threats or demands made by Spanish entradas in La Florida were probably the primary impetus for attacks by Native American warriors in some cases. Ponce de León took hostages from villages in southern Florida in 1513, perhaps contributing to the hostility he encountered when he approached Calusa villages (Hann 2003). Ayllón captured slaves in coastal Georgia or South Carolina in 1521, undoubtedly ensuring enmity toward his attempted colony five years later (Hoffman 1994a). Narváez captured several Native people during his march from Tampa Bay to the Apalachee province in northern Florida in 1528, which probably led to attacks by Native warriors on the Narváez expedition (Hoffman 1994b; Marrinan et al. 1990). Native interactions with the Narváez expedition likely also contributed to the stiff resistance to the Soto expedition upon reaching Apalachee in 1539 (Mitchem 1990). Soto often made demands on Native towns for food, porters, women, and for material wealth such as his expedition found at Cofitachequi (DePratter 1994). Soto took hostages both for their local intelligence and guidance, and for forcing Native groups to heed demands and threats placed upon them. He took Tascalusa hostage, for example, in advance of the battle that awaited him at Mabila, in 1540 (Hudson 1997:229–232).[4] Not long after Soto demanded porters from Chicaza, in 1541, warriors from Chicaza attacked his winter encampment (Hudson 1997:267–270).

As already noted, it is possible that slave raids by Spanish soldiers, by Native American warriors, or both, affected the geopolitical landscape of La Florida during the 1500s. In the 1600s, slaving activity had dramatic impacts on Native societies throughout eastern North America (Gallay 2002; Martin 1994). Given that Ayllón captured slaves, that Ponce de León took hostages, and that Spanish slavers were active in the Caribbean during the 1500s, it is not difficult to imagine that the slave trade and forms of warfare that developed along with it may have begun as early as the sixteenth century, although the supporting documentary evidence is not as clear-cut as it is for the slave trade in the 1600s (Ethridge 2006, 2009a, 2009b).

Threats and demands by Spanish entradas, the dynamics of chiefly warfare and rivalries among Mississippian towns and chiefdoms, and periodic shortages of food or other resources were all sources of conflicts in the Southeast during the sixteenth century. Menéndez traveled from Santa Elena to Guale and Orista villages in 1570, in an effort to ease growing tensions that had apparently arisen because of food scarcity and competition for resources in drought conditions. Droughts affected English settlement at Jamestown (Blanton 2000), the Spanish mission at Ajacán (Mallios 2006), and Santa Elena (Anderson et al. 1995; South 1988). When members of the Luna y Arellano expedition reached Coosa in 1560, it was neither as prosperous nor as powerful as it was when the Soto expedition visited in 1540, perhaps in part because of droughts that affected the productivity of farming and the ability of towns and chiefs to store and to mobilize surplus resources. Such developments may help account not only for the decline of Coosa between the Soto and Luna y Arellano expeditions but also, in part, for the apparent plans by Coosa to attack Pardo in eastern Tennessee, in 1567, before Pardo could reach Coosa itself.

Although Pardo placed greater emphasis on diplomacy and gift giving than did preceding Spanish entradas, the Pardo expeditions did lead to conflict. Pardo spoke with the leaders of Native communities and polities and gave them gifts such as iron axes, knives, chisels, wedges, glass beads, cloth, mirrors, and gilded ball buttons (Hudson 2005:134–141). Pardo did develop favorable diplomatic relations with many Native groups through gifting. However, there were places where he did not distribute any gifts, and he may have committed one or more diplomatic errors in what he gave (or did not give) to some chiefs as compared to what he gave to neighbors or to rivals. Supplies of gifts also did not last very long, and if Native people expected that they were forming relations of reciprocity and gift exchange with the Pardo expeditions, which seems likely, they would have been disappointed when provisions ran low and new supplies were not forthcoming, especially during the long periods when Pardo himself was in Santa Elena rather than at his outposts along the northern edge of La Florida.[5]

On the other hand, Pardo provisioned those forts with what supplies he could (Hudson 2005:141–153). All six forts were built at Native American towns. His primary outpost, Fort San Juan, was built beside the town of Joara, in the western North Carolina Piedmont (Beck et al. 2006).[6] It is not clear whether Native people frequented those forts or the houses built for Spanish soldiers, but they may have, and whether or not they did, they must have known that supplies were stored at Pardo's forts. Spanish material culture from Santa Elena includes weaponry, hardware, metal tools, pottery, scrap copper, glass beads, and other artifacts (South et al. 1988); very similar artifacts have been found at the Berry site, the location of Pardo's Fort San Juan (Beck et al. 2006). Such items probably were highly valued by the people of Joara and other towns in La Florida (Smith 1987; Waselkov 1989). Native people, especially warriors whose status depended upon war honors and tangible markers of their accomplishments, may have perceived the supplies known to be (or thought to be) stored at Pardo's forts as prestige goods, or war trophies, or even gifts that Native people thought they deserved in exchange for supporting Spanish garrisons and building houses for them. There are no historically known cases in which goods were stolen from Pardo's forts, but there are many instances in which Native people asked for gifts from Pardo himself.

During his talks with Native leaders, Pardo requested that Native groups build houses and set aside food (primarily maize) for his soldiers (Hudson 2005:141–146). It was common practice for Spanish expeditions to ask for or demand food from Native towns. Leaders of Spanish expeditions quickly learned to travel trails connecting large and powerful Native towns, where they could find large stores of food and powerful chiefs who could give them what they wanted or needed. Many entradas placed demands on towns they visited only briefly. By contrast, members of the Pardo expeditions lived for prolonged periods at Joara and other Native towns, and demands they made were placed on a single community, rather than on a series of towns for shorter intervals.

At first, favorable relations developed between Pardo and Native towns at the northern edge of La Florida. Talks took place and gifts were given, houses and forts were built, and Pardo became part of networks of chiefly tribute and diplomacy that were already in place. Fort San Juan was first built in January 1567, and by May 1568 news reached Santa Elena that Pardo's forts had been sacked and abandoned. Little is recorded in documentary sources about what transpired during attacks on Pardo's forts (which may have been burned down after soldiers were lured out of them), nor about whether attacks on different forts were part of a coordinated effort or even a revitalization movement, like the 1680 Pueblo Revolt in New Mexico (Liebmann 2008b; Liebmann et al. 2005; Preucel 2002). Perhaps inspired by these and other attacks in 1568, Native American warriors sacked and burned Santa Elena in 1576.

The "perfect storm" that ruined Pardo's forts and Menéndez's plans for settling La Florida and developing an overland route to the Spanish silver mines at Zacatecas was shaped by cultural, historical, and climatic trends. By 1568, there had been more than fifty years of Spanish exploration in La Florida and a long history of conflict and instability created by Spanish entradas. By 1568, there would have been few people still alive who had experienced what life was like before Spanish contact. Native people had learned that Spanish entradas could alter the fortunes of specific Mississippian chiefdoms and towns, for better or worse. Despite Pardo's emphasis on diplomacy, Moyano's raids on Chisca villages and his entry into the province of Chiaha contributed to regional instability and the vulnerability of Pardo's forts. Despite Pardo's emphasis on gift giving and alliance making, he could not sustain the stream of gifts to Native chiefs. Pardo specifically forbade any of his soldiers from bringing Native women into Fort Santiago, at the town of Guatari, when the fort was built in early 1568 (Hudson 2005:150–152), and there is some indication in documentary sources that soldiers at Fort San Juan committed improprieties with Native women from Joara during Pardo's long absence in 1567 (Hudson 2005:175–177). Pardo and his garrisons were dependent on local Native groups for at least some food (Hudson 2005:176), and, meanwhile, droughts and other unfavorable climatic conditions may have posed considerable challenges to chiefs in collecting and mobilizing surplus resources to support Spanish forts at the northern edge of La Florida (Anderson et al. 1995; Blanton, this volume;

Worth, this volume). It is likely that the chief or chiefs of Joara (as well as those of other towns) saw some benefit in forming alliances with Pardo—the power of Joara seems to have grown as the chiefdom of Cofitachequi waned during the years after the Soto expedition, and an alliance with Pardo probably bolstered Joara's hegemony (Beck 2009). Just as an alliance with Pardo was probably in Joara's interests in late 1566, the conquest of Fort San Juan (and the sacking of Pardo's other forts) probably served the interests of Joara and those of other towns whose warriors participated (Beck et al. 2011). Pardo's forts, the houses and storehouses built for him, the goods stored at them, and Pardo's men themselves may all have been perceived by Native warriors as war trophies.

Aftermath of Entradas

After the Pardo expeditions, the focus of Spanish colonialism in La Florida shifted to missionization and trade (Hann 1994; Hann and McEwan 1998; McEwan 1993; Worth 1994, 1998a,b). The colony was unable to sustain settlements along the frontiers of La Florida, and efforts were concentrated instead on settlements in Florida and neighboring areas of coastal Georgia (Milanich 1996; Thomas 1988). The inability, in the long run, for the La Florida colony to maintain a permanent presence north of modern Florida and Georgia created an opening for later French and English exploration and settlement of the Southeast. Had the Spanish found gold or silver (gold was discovered in Georgia and in North Carolina in the 1800s), had they built the road to Zacatecas, had Santa Elena and Fort San Juan endured, the English settlements at Roanoke and Jamestown may have had a very different history. What happened to towns and chiefdoms in La Florida in the wake of Spanish entradas? What impacts did conflicts with Spanish expeditions have on Native societies?

Some groups, such as Cofitachequi and Coosa, experienced diminishing power and prosperity in the aftermath of the Soto expedition (DePratter 1994; Hally 1994; Smith 1987, 2000), but others, like Joara, may have risen in status and prestige, at least temporarily (Beck 2009). Joara was still a major town, if not a powerful polity, in the early 1600s (Moore 2002:29–31), and some form of chiefly hierarchy endured at Cofitachequi through the 1600s (Beck 2009:136). Casqui benefited from an alliance with Soto in its rivalry with Pacaha, but there is some indication that Pacaha retaliated and raided Casqui after the Soto expedition left the Central Mississippi valley (Jeffrey Mitchem, personal communication 2009). Although many Native people were killed in conflicts with Spanish colonists during the sixteenth century, damage to the social fabric of Native communities was probably greater, and participation of Native warriors in conflicts with Spanish entradas probably had effects on status relations within Native societies that went unnoticed and unrecorded by Spanish chroniclers. Spanish contact changed the conditions from those in which Mississippian culture had developed, and conflicts within and between Native groups in La Florida compounded the effects of direct conflict and combat between Native American groups and Spanish expeditions.

Chiefdoms of La Florida were dynamic social and political formations. For several hundred years before Spanish contact, chiefdoms had formed, had reached their respective peaks, and had declined, in cyclical patterns. Centers of chiefly power shifted across the landscape, and relative statuses of Mississippian mound centers waxed and waned. Despite instability in *individual* chiefdoms, and despite *variation* in their structure of leadership and spatial extent, the general form of Mississippian chiefdoms endured. Spanish entradas and the conflicts sparked by them contributed to changes in the fortunes and status of individual chiefdoms (including the decline of Coosa and the rise of Joara), but they also led to the collapse of chiefdoms as a viable and a sustainable form of social and political organization. Mississippian chiefdoms experienced warfare, changes in trade networks, changes in environmental conditions, and changes in the capacity of chiefs and towns to mobilize surpluses, but chiefdoms had endured (Hally 2006). Spanish contact, on the other hand, created cycles of conflict and other conditions from which those chiefdoms could not recover in traditional forms, leading to the coalescence of the confederacies and tribal societies present during the eras of French and English exploration and settlement in the 1600s and 1700s (Ethridge 2006, 2009a, 2009b).

Acknowledgments

Thanks for guidance and encouragement from Charles Hudson, Mark Williams, Russell Skowronek, Patrick Livingood, Heather Lapham,

Gayle Fritz, Lee Newsom, Sarah Sherwood, Martin Gallivan, David Anderson, David Hally, Marvin Smith, Vin Steponaitis, Steve Davis, Brett Riggs, Linda Hall, Tasha Benyshek, Paul Webb, Bennie Keel, Trawick Ward, Tim Maxwell, Clay Mathers, Jeff Mitchem, Charles Haecker, Matthew Schmader, Robbie Ethridge, Charles Cobb, David Hurst Thomas, Stanley South, and Chester DePratter. Our research in western North Carolina has been supported by Warren Wilson College, the University of Oklahoma, the University of Michigan, the Tulane University Committee on Research, the Tulane University Research Enhancement Fund, the National Science Foundation, the National Geographic Society, the Burke County Historical Society, the Exploring Joara Foundation, and the Certified Local Government Grant program of the National Park Service.

SECTION VII

Discussion

14

Honor and Hierarchies

Long-Term Trajectories in the Pueblo and Mississippian Worlds

David Hurst Thomas

The symposium from which this book emerged took place at a most opportune time. The papers there provide fresh insights into the nature of Spanish entradas across the American Southeast and Southwest. But more than that, this conversation took place shortly after several paradigm shifts opened the door to new understandings on the earliest Native–European interactions in both areas. In this chapter, a first-order heuristic, I attempt to contextualize the various contributions by comparing and contrasting the entrada strategies, projected against long-term trajectories in the Puebloan and Mississippian worlds.

Encountering the Mississippian World

For decades, John R. Swanton dominated our understanding of the Native Southeast. Swanton pioneered the use of historical documents in Southeastern ethnography, but his reconstruction of Southeastern Indian society was flawed by a reliance on the myth of the ethnographic present, leading him to "collapse more than three hundred years of history into a synchronic snapshot of Southern Indian culture" (Ethridge, this volume). Such a portrayal glossed over the important social transformations that connected the Mississippian world of archaeology with eighteenth-century realities of Southeastern Indian life. The weaknesses in Swanton's approach are particularly evident in his reconstruction of Soto's entrada route (Swanton 1985), in which he assumed a continuity in place names between the sixteenth and eighteenth centuries.

The chapters addressing the entrada era in the American Southeast are framed within the paradigm shift precipitated by the groundbreaking ethnohistorical research of Charles Hudson and his collaborative cadre of archaeologists (see also Galloway 1995). Together, this multidisciplinary team bridged the gap between the ethnohistoric Mississippian world and its deeper historical roots.

Hispanic Honor and Hierarchy

More medieval than modern, the Soto expedition was all about honor and hierarchy, plus a favored few carrying out a divine mission (Hudson 1997:10). Social status was typically determined by a complex system of racial gradients and classifications (Wilcox 2009:81). The titled Spanish elite overarched the lesser nobility, those caballeros and hidalgos who were sometimes addressed as *Don* and enjoyed a life free of taxes and servitude. Shoring up the base of the Hispanic social pyramid was the peasantry—80 percent of the Castilian population—who paid the bills as backward farmers. Soto's parents were both hidalgos and he quickly rose to prominence in explorations of Central America and Peru.

Hernando de Soto organized his Southeastern exploration like many other contemporary expeditions launched throughout the Indies (Weber 1992:Chapter 2). A captain-general was tasked with overseeing the military operations, and three royal officials were enlisted to ensure appropriate taxes were collected for the Crown. Soto personally bankrolled his "Florida fantasy" with one hundred thousand gold pesos amassed during his Peruvian escapades, but he actually spent perhaps half that amount (Avellaneda 1997). Soto required that each man pay his own way (although he was unusually generous in underwriting the arms and horses of some immediate relatives).

In setting out to conquer Florida for the Spanish king, the initial goal was to locate gold, treasure, and tribute. But once the realities of the Southeastern landscape quashed that dream, Spain shifted objectives to simply holding the land due to its strategic importance with little potential for Spanish settlers or colonists supporting themselves. Christopher B. Rodning, Robin A. Beck, Jr., and David G. Moore (this volume) stress the degree to which the Spanish entradas were motivated by the need to secure supplies, to capture slaves, and to establish tributary relationships as well as lasting colonial hegemony comparable to that experienced in Peru and Mexico.

Mississippian Honor and Hierarchy

The Mississippian world was also about honor and hierarchy, but these concepts played out very differently among the heirs of the multilingual and heterogeneous yet brittle polities at Etowah and Moundville. Writing about the "Mississippian transformation," Hudson (1990:58) predicted that "within the geographic area where corn horticulture came to be practiced, certain traits should have appeared seriatim: (1) first corn horticulture, then (2) dependency on corn, then (3) organization into chiefdoms, and finally (4) the elaboration of symbols of hierarchical status, including the construction of substructure mounds."

Although population growth is commonly viewed as an unintended consequence of sedentism and agricultural productivity (e.g., Marcus and Flannery 1996:238), we now understand that institutional, hereditary social inequality also arose in places along the southeastern Atlantic coastline shortly after A.D. 800, several centuries prior to reliance on maize cultivation (Thomas 2008; Worth 1998a,b). Similar trajectories are known among other complex foraging populations, especially those living in coastal environments (Kennett 2005; Yesner 1980).

Although inequality exists in all societies—based typically on gender, age, charisma, and achievement—the hierarchical Mississippian world was characterized by social status ascribed at birth (almost certainly reckoned as genealogical distance from a single noble ancestor), by permanent leadership apart from (and imposed upon) kin-based structures, and the ability to secure the labor of increasing numbers of nonkin for various communal activities. Farmers and complex foragers alike participated in intense status competition and rivalry, formed restricted-access information-sharing groups, recognized kin-group land tenure, understood intragroup variation in frequency/quantity of sharing, and differentially targeted recipients of shared resources.

The institutionalization of social inequity was not necessarily the inevitable outcome of population growth, circumscription, and/or external threat, but rather the result of individual decision making, probably conducted within an "atmosphere of intense competition among ambitious leaders, who had previously possessed no way of bequeathing their achieved power to their offspring" (Marcus and Flannery 1996:240). At first, such leaders probably attributed their extraordinary success to support from the supernatural, and gradually there arose a belief that the best leaders actually *descended* from those supernatural forces. The dominants, a small and privileged chiefly class, probably flaunted a certifiable genealogical relationship to the reigning matrilineages and attempted to monopolize the input from the supernaturals, who exerted life/death power over villagers. Over the generations, the fiction arose that the distinguished ancestors and their immediate elite offspring were qualified to lead—and the more distant relatives were destined to follow. Lesser positions within the dominant elite likely varied with the genealogical distance to the elite leader.

The emerging elite acquired greater status and wealth by manipulating social, economic, and political relationships to their benefit (Earle 1987), by controlling the flow of cultural items that signal status (Flannery 1972), by monopolizing the labor of others (Arnold 1993), and by creating ideologies that justify the inequitable distribution of wealth and power (Earle 1987; Marcus and Flannery 1996). For their part, dominants realized the benefits of controlling and redistributing food resources, extracting their own fitness-related benefit in increasingly disproportionate amounts. The paramounts maintained a large-scale, regional perspective and traveled extensively to conduct war, diplomacy, and ritual, and to participate in complex, rank-enhancing marriage alliances. Mississippian *micos* held important offices in the political and religious hierarchies, with tangible social, political, and economic advantages.

Subordinates in the Mississippian world supported themselves by farming and foraging. They provided virtually all the elite subsistence and luxury goods, as well as the labor necessary to tend the chiefly corn fields and fish weirs, harvest and process the chiefly oysters, hickory nuts, and acorns, build and paddle the chiefly canoes, and wage war against the chiefly enemies. In short, Mississippian commoners supplied the labor, produced the chiefly wealth, and, in the case of the conscripted draft, risked dying in chiefly warfare.[1]

Against this long-term perspective to the entradas, Rodning, Beck, and Moore contrast the Hispanic "materialistic" bent—specifically, the quest for slaves, wealth, food, and Native women—with the Mississippian drive for status and power. Robbie Ethridge and Jeffrey M. Mitchem (this volume) likewise emphasize how Mississippian power relations were negotiated, particularly the interactions and conflicts that tied together the chiefdoms. They also present the extensive evidence for social ranking as reflected in the documentary record. During the entradas, Mississippian warriors continued long-term patterns of chiefly warfare and diplomacy, fighting according to their hierarchical social standing and collecting war trophies that reflect symbolic importance rather than territorial conquest.

Soto and his lieutenants easily read the power relationships within the hierarchical Mississippian societies they encountered. At Chicaza, for instance, there was little doubt that Soto was face-to-face with a high-status Mississippian *mico,* literally borne on a litter by his principals. Similarly, upon arriving at Coosa, Soto encountered another chiefly figure, likewise carried on a litter and wrapped in an ermine robe. As John E. Worth (this volume) emphasizes, the Spanish fully appreciated the importance of decisive actions and working from the top down. Readily recognizing the lines of authority and decision making, the Spanish could draw to a large degree upon previous colonial experiences in Peru and elsewhere. Soto took the Coosa chief captive, along with his sister, the bearers, and various supplies (Ethridge and Mitchem, this volume). After moving into eastern Tennessee, Soto's force recognized that because several towns were already under Coosa's hegemony, they could readily negotiate a web of tribute relationships based on the preexisting Mississippian hierarchical relationships.

The route of the sixteenth-century entradas across the American Southeast was heavily conditioned by the sociopolitical structure of Indigenous groups living there. Worth emphasizes the degree to which Spanish colonial efforts were significantly constrained by the sociopolitical organization of the Mississippian people already living there. As Ethridge and Mitchem (this volume) emphasize, when the Soto expedition hit the margins of the Mississippian world, they turned back, seeking out the chiefly interactions that would translate into food, supplies, and plunder.

Mississippian Trajectories and Transformations in the Deep Interior

Historical and archaeological evidence from across the American Southeast has long pointed to a significant sixteenth-century demographic collapse of Indigenous populations, long attributed to introduced infectious diseases (Dobyns 1983; Hudson et al. 1989; Ramenofsky 1987). But the demographic effects and extent of disease episodes across the Southeast is currently under debate. Dale L. Hutchinson (this volume) calls into question previous models that suggest 90 percent depopulation across the American Southeast, citing the total lack of archaeological and bioarchaeological evidence for catastrophic population loss during the initial century of Spanish contact in the Southeast (see also Charles Ewen, this volume). While conceding that the Native population did indeed collapse, Hutchinson argues that demographic shift did not happen in a century, but rather over the course of three hundred to four hundred years, probably a slow demographic drain of the population through serial disease episodes and slave raiding throughout the seventeenth and early eighteenth centuries. Ethridge and Mitchem (this volume) suggest a possible mechanism for this process. They emphasize the vast differences across the "Mississippian shatter zone" (Ethridge 2006) between the Southeastern Indians of the sixteenth century and those of the eighteenth century. Major interior chiefdoms collapsed creating a "new geopolitical landscape." Although acknowledging the role of introduced infectious disease, Ethridge and Mitchem emphasize the importance of early military losses to Soto, a conquering army that exposed the Mississippian chiefdoms to an intense mode of combat never before experienced. And they were never the same afterward. Unlike Indigenous warfare conducted over the centuries, Soto's strategies—the prolonged stay and the wholesale ransacking of Native communities for food—created local starvation and political unrest.

These Mississippian chiefdoms were no strangers to internal political stresses, but the Soto expedition cut a swath through the entire Mississippian world, transmitting "colonial shockwaves" that destabilized many chiefdoms and laid bare the inadequacy of Native polities to resist the new Hispanic threat (Ethridge and Mitchem, this volume). After arriving at Casqui, for instance, Soto recognized that he was being courted as the Mississippian paramount sought Spanish military support against Pacaha, a longtime rival. Such top-down negotiations became critical in establishing alliances and enforcing tributary obligations. Soto became adept in Mississippian-style power politics—sometimes attempting to negotiate between the two chiefdoms—but

Ethridge and Mitchem think it likely that his mere presence may have inadvertently led to the destruction of several chiefdoms. Beyond the role of infectious disease, Soto upset the balance of power by creating a crisis of confidence in long-standing Mississippian political hierarchies and by empowering lesser *micos* to draw upon the Soto influence and military might in fighting old battles against rival chiefdoms.

Two distinctive footprints showed up—one in the interior, the other along the Atlantic coastline and Apalachee (in what became La Florida). After the entradas of Soto, Luna y Arellano, and Pardo, many chiefdoms of the deep interior were spared direct or sustained contact with Europeans for more than 130 years because, with only rare exceptions, soldiers and friars stuck pretty close to the established mission provinces along the coast of Spanish Florida (Ethridge and Mitchem, this volume; Worth, this volume).

During the Mississippian collapse in the Southeastern interior, Indigenous survivors clung to some of their ancient ways and devised some new social strategies for coping. European demography was shifting as well. Dennis Blanton (this volume) evaluates the impact of paleoclimatic issues during this interval; Ethridge and Mitchem stress the importance of slaving raids to the interior, emphasizing that interior relations were "not transforming" and arguing that European interactions beyond Spain were required to do this. Increasingly linked into the capitalist economy, they still resorted to ancient methods of diplomacy and warfare, although Ethridge notes the degree to which Mississippian *micos* went from divine gods to "savvy mortals."

Mississippian Trajectories and Transformations in La Florida

Beyond demographics, the economics of the Pueblo world also parallel Spanish Florida during the seventeenth century. The interior South, as noted, is in collapse by the late seventeenth century, with the survivors starting to restructure from chiefdoms into the coalescent societies. But whereas the colonial policies of La Florida hindered any market enterprises (in both the Southeast and Spanish Florida), imperialist strategies of the English, French, and Dutch led to the introduction of a market economy through the Indian slave trade within the interior Southeast (Ethridge and Mitchem, this volume).

As Worth (this volume) emphasizes, "lacking the profit motive to encourage private settlement and local economic development within a colonial context, the territory of Spanish Florida was effectively relegated to a marginal role within the broader Spanish empire." In stark contrast to the Southeastern interior, by the mid-seventeenth century Spanish Florida had morphed into a multiethnic colonial society based on unique political and economic relations between the Mississippian and Hispanic worlds—one of those novel, hybrid forms of culture emphasized in the "postcolonial critique" that challenges traditional colonialist epistemologies that question the colonial and imperial representations of the "other" being colonized (e.g., Liebmann 2008a:2; Lightfoot 2005:17).

In 1565, Pedro Menéndez de Avilés established St. Augustine as a strategic Spanish foothold to quell the rising fear of French settlement in the very same region and to safeguard the Fleet of the Indies through the Bahama channel as the treasure-laden ships sailed back to Spain. Its strategic significance ultimately ensured a relatively stable source of royal funding, but it also required that Spanish colonists in La Florida rely heavily on local Native American populations to buffer against interruptions in external supply lines. The unreliability of the royal *situado* left the seventeenth-century citizenry of St. Augustine "in the precarious position of having too many poor military families and not enough colonial farmers"; as a poorly supplied garrison-town, St. Augustine quickly developed the reputation of a "wretched frontier town to which few colonists would relocate willingly" (Worth 2002:54–55).

This is why the Spaniards were forced to rely heavily on the human and natural riches of La Florida. Borderlands historians have long emphasized the unique Hispanic agenda: the Spanish colonial enterprise sought out not unoccupied land for immigrants but rather local Native groups from which to create (from scratch) new multiethnic communities. To be sure, military and political forces backed up this strategy, but the basic idea was to foster communities that were more Native than Spanish (Bannon 1964; Weber 1992:7–11). Worth (this volume) likewise stresses the impact of the "New Laws of the Indies," promulgated by the Spanish Crown in 1542. Mathers (this volume) stresses the widespread importance of the New Laws and New Ordinances—not only for New Spain, but elsewhere as well. His comparative data suggest that these pieces of legislation had a significant impact on the size, composition, and conduct of later sixteenth-century entradas. Because both slavery and abusive treatment of Indigenous people had been explicitly banned, Menéndez de Avilés was constrained to ensuring good treatment for Indigenous peoples, acting with explicit permission from all Native leaders. Ethnohistoric and archaeological evidence clearly demonstrates the degree to which the sixteenth- and seventeenth-century Indigenous chiefdoms of La Florida were subjected to global issues of climate change, epidemic disease, warfare, and food shortages.

By the same token, Europeans living in Spanish Florida became active participants in the local political dynamics, bolstering and reinforcing the political power of traditional Indian leaders. Hereditary chiefs retained considerable internal autonomy over secular matters and ruled using traditional lines of authority (Weber 1992:439). "While the Christian Indians in the Southeast played an important part in supporting the Spanish friars, soldiers, and settlers, they did so with comparatively little change in their own material culture and political organization" (Bushnell 1994:28).

By pledging allegiance and obedience to Spanish officials, Indigenous Timucua, Mocama, and Guale chiefs annexed a powerful military ally in the Spanish garrison at St. Augustine. The seventeenth-century economy of Spanish Florida evolved into an exchange network through which Native populations channeled their surplus food (primarily maize) and labor into colonial St. Augustine (Bushnell 1994:15). These paramounts not only generated a new market for their agricultural surplus but also gained access to new tools and technologies to improve their yield. Readily able to convert their surpluses into symbolically important Spanish goods such as cloth, tools, and beads, the caciques positioned themselves to receive tribute from both the Spaniards and their own people. In this way, the paramount chiefs of La Florida continued the Mississippian tradition of employing ostentatious displays of wealth and status items to reinforce their hereditary status. "It seems no surprise that most aboriginal chiefs struggled to gain entry into the mission system, and remained there for so long" (Worth 1998:126–214; see also Worth 2002:58).

Analysis of food remains from Spanish towns and Franciscan missions highlights the dynamic negotiation between Natives and immigrants that resulted in new, hybrid subsistence patterns. The coastal Guale, for instance, supplied foods to Spaniards in great quantities, augmenting and expanding the Spanish menu to look more like traditional, pre-Contact Mississippian diets. In fact, the residents of Mission Santa Catalina de Guale (on St. Catherines Island) likely enjoyed a much higher standard of living than either Franciscan friars dining in the Convento de San Francisco in St. Augustine or Spanish citizens living elsewhere in the town (Blair et al. 2009; Reitz et al. 2010; Thomas 1988, 2010).

In both Spanish Florida and the American Southwest, the Franciscan friars served as the face-to-face primary agents of directed social change, but the two mission systems were vastly different. Bushnell (1994:28) argues that the mission in Spanish Florida "was no theocracy"; rather, she continues, "It was a fully functioning Native town governed by an interlocking set of hereditary and elected native leaders." Because Franciscan missionaries had authority only over religious matters, they functioned as religious practitioners answerable to chiefly authority, just as Indigenous Mississippian religious specialists had done before the arrival of the Spanish:

> In converting to Christianity and accepting resident Franciscan friars within their local jurisdiction, chiefs gained not only the largesse of the Catholic church and the Spanish crown, but also a resident cultural broker and advocate to act on their behalf with respect to the Spanish military government. All things being equal, the establishment of a tributary labor arrangement with the governor of St. Augustine must have seemed a small price to pay in return for the anticipated benefits of assimilation through missionization." (Worth 2002:57)

In his classic *The Martyrs of Florida* (1937, originally published in 1617), Franciscan Luis Gerónimo de Oré vividly recounted a chilling tale of the deadly Guale uprising in 1597, during which five Franciscan friars were martyred. Although Gerónimo de Oré was not in La Florida when the uprising occurred, his account of this bloody Indigenous revolt against Spanish rule has survived as the authoritative voice describing the 1597 uprising. Borderlands historiography has long been unanimous in reading this event as a violent Indigenous revolt against

Spanish rule—as basically an unsuccessful Southeastern rehearsal of the Pueblo Revolt staged eighty years later. Virtually all modern treatments of the 1597 unpleasantness emphasize both Franciscan interference in Guale affairs and missionary opposition to the practice of polygamy. This historiography singles out a Guale Indian named Don Juan as the principal leader against the Spaniards, so much so that in several recent accounts of the episode, it is simply referred to as "Juanillo's revolt" (e.g., Gannon 1965; Hoffman 2001; Lanning 1935).

Based on extensive new documentary research, Francis and Kole (2011) believe the Guale uprising of 1597 was not an Indigenous rebellion against Spanish authority at all. Instead, they argue, the root cause of unrest reflects the underlying tensions and conflicts between competing Indigenous chiefdoms (see also Thomas 2010), and they highlight the serious limitations and sometimes tenuous footing of Spanish rule in Florida and highlight the importance of Indian allies to Spain's Florida ambitions.

In effect, St. Augustine had transformed into another powerful Mississippian chiefdom, both competing and allied with existing Guale, Mocama, and Timucua chiefdoms (Thomas 2010; Worth 1998). To maintain hegemony during the late sixteenth century, the paramount Guale chief had become dependent not only upon alliances and tribute relationships from lesser Guale polities but also upon support from the Spanish government. The violence of 1597 underscores the extent to which Native people struggled to adapt, resist, and conform to the challenges of Spanish colonial rule. Even within the span of a few years, these brittle alliances seem to have been repeatedly forged, broken, and reestablished.

Although the 1597 uprising is the best known, several other rebellions are documented in Spanish Florida: in Guale, 1645 and the early 1680s; in Apalachee and Timucua, 1565; in Apalachee, 1647; in Apalachicola, 1675 and 1681. In the previous historiography, each of these uprisings has been interpreted (like the Pueblo Revolt of 1680) as a Native resistance attempting to throw off Spanish unwarranted authority (e.g., Bushnell 1990:481; Matter 1975; Weber 1992:133). In light of more recent research (Francis and Kole 2011; Worth 1998, 2002, this volume), it seems likely that reexamination of the documentary evidence will disclose that most (if not all) of these rebellions reflect warfare between competing Mississippian-style chiefdoms, vying for power, access, alliance, and tribute obligations from Spanish St. Augustine. To be sure, there was likely considerable "coercion and involuntary constraints on the freedom of action exercised by individuals and leaders living within the mission provinces of Spanish Florida" (Worth, this volume), but this had been the reality for subordinates living in the Mississippian world for centuries before the Spanish entradas. In La Florida, both colonists and Indigenous people were locked into a social, economic, and political hierarchy that bore considerably more similarity to Mississippian-style chiefdoms than Spanish military outposts in the rest of the New World.

For a while, Franciscan missions survived (even prospered) in La Florida because they reinforced long-standing traditions of chiefly power over land and labor. As Worth (2002:55) puts it, "Florida was not so much an independent Spanish outpost interacting with neighboring and autonomous Indian societies . . . but was instead a broader community of interdependent Spanish and Indian populations woven into a functioning, though inherently flawed, colonial system." By the late seventeenth century, "there were too many chiefs and nobles, and not enough subordinate Indians to support their existence. . . . In clinging to their traditional power by birthright, the mission chiefs ultimately ensured the persistence of a dysfunctional sociopolitical system that would not survive the trauma of the colonial era" (Worth, this volume).

This Spanish colonial–Mississippian hybrid continued to provide the external support necessary to maintain the authority of hereditary chiefs, clinging to time-worn vestiges of traditional rank and privilege "even in the face of near-total demographic collapse, accompanied by English-sponsored raiding . . . [that] forced the retreat of all surviving mission communities to St. Augustine chiefly matrilineages persisted. . . . Ultimately, the Spanish colonial strategy served to preserve these ancient social systems in a way unparalleled by other forms of European interaction" (Worth 2002:58–59).

Encountering the Pueblo World

As with Hudson's groundbreaking research on the Soto swath through the Mississippian world, a paradigm shift likewise conditions our understanding of sixteenth-century entradas into the American Southwest. Building upon three decades of documentary research, Richard Flint and Shirley Cushing Flint (this volume) conclude that the long-entrenched conventional wisdom regarding the Vázquez de Coronado entrada is "badly distorted . . . in fact, it is grossly inaccurate on every count." This is decidedly not "a small army of Spanish knights in clanking armor dispatched by the king of Spain to look for gold" (Flint 2005:204); in fact, if this entrada demonstrated only a "faintly military complexion," Flint and Flint have opened the door to fresh interpretations of the nature of Hispanic–Native interactions across the American Southwest.[2]

Hispanic Hierarchies?

We now understand that the Vázquez de Coronado expedition was a "miscellaneous, ad hoc group assembled principally for the purpose of taking economic control of a presumably large and prosperous Indigenous polity known as Cíbola" (Flint and Flint, this volume). Funded by civilian investors for the principal purpose of obtaining Indian tribute, the expedition was disbanded when the American Southwest failed to live up to expectations.[3]

In effect, Vázquez de Coronado imported a rather curious brand of sociopolitical hierarchy into the American Southwest—yet another of those novel, hybrid forms emphasized in the "postcolonial critique" (as mentioned above). This entrada "grew by accretion" as it progressed northward during the fall of 1539. Annexing individuals and constituent units, the expedition was "only nominally under the leadership of Francisco Vázquez de Coronado . . . a polyglot of languages, traditions, motives, and practices" (Flint and Flint, this volume).[4]

At the apex of the entrada hierarchy were four hundred free Europeans—many with civilian occupations and professions, who doubtless fit into the typical Hispanic social hierarchy. Toward the bottom of the social ladder was the roughly equal number of mostly African slaves and servants, plus an unknown number of women and children.

Unlike the Soto entrada, the Hispanic hierarchical framework of the Vázquez de Coronado expedition was enhanced by the inclusion of many hundreds (likely thousands) of *indios amigos* that filled the intermediate social ranks. In documents prepared by Spaniards, *indios amigos* are virtually invisible (Flint 2009:66–67), but new evidence indicates that nearly three-quarters of the expedition members were Native contingents recruited from a variety of (sometimes antagonistic) tribes in Michoacán, Jalisco, Nayarit, Sinaloa, and Sonora. These *indios amigos* remained largely autonomous groups, retaining their own leadership power structures and acting quite independently, sometimes even departing the expedition when it suited them (Flint 2009).

These Indian allies were attracted by outright cash payments from the viceroy and his representatives, bestowal of honors, reductions in *encomienda* obligations, promise of socioeconomic betterment, and perhaps the right to keep prisoners.[5] Social advancement in the valley of Mexico had long been tied to performing deeds of war, and potential allies were eager to participate in the venture northward to Tierra Nueva de Cíbola. Since pre-Conquest times, status in central Mesoamerica had been tied to capture of high-ranking prisoners of war, which became nearly impossible within territories administered by the Spanish colonial administration (Flint 2009:72). To several central Mexican Indigenous communities, this was not an opportunity to be missed.

So far, the documentary evidence is mute about the possibility of trade between the Indian allies and the people of Tierra Nueva. Likewise, the testimony does not determine conclusively whether or not the *indios amigos* continued their pre-Conquest practice of capture and sacrifice of high-status war prisoners during the Vázquez de Coronado entrada. Flint and Flint suggest that despite their unpredictability, the *indios amigos* were most likely the primary combatants—following their own traditions of combat, sometimes ritualized and formalized performances.

Although the occasional *amigo* leader might have been equipped with Spanish weapons as explicit material confirmation of their high status (Flint 2009:67), the overwhelming majority of the *indios amigos* were armed with their own weapons, including atlatls, bows and arrows, slings, thrusting spears, obsidian-edged swords, clubs, shields, wood and bone helmets, and quilted cotton body armor. Mathers (this volume) argues that *indios amigos* warriors likely wore menacing costumes and performed theatrical ("shock and awe") displays of weaponry and horsemanship designed to bring Native communities quickly to peace. This is not, of course, to minimize the actual violence (including mutilations and burnings at the stake) that characterized the Vázquez de Coronado entrada.

Mathers also contrasts this evidence with the nature of pre-Columbian warfare among the Pueblos, which differed markedly from the extraordinary material and institutional investments both among the *indios amigos* and within the Mississippian world. Nowhere in the American Southwest do we see the sustained conflict, the symbol-laden, status-graded approach to warfare, the widespread procurement and display of body parts as trophies, and complex webs of intra- and interregional tribute relations. These differences raise some pivotal issues regarding the nature of Pueblo conceptions of power, politics, hierarchy, and complexity (explored below).

If the Vázquez de Coronado expedition was only nominally a fighting force, it was essentially—in the marvelous phraseology of Flint (2008:2)—"an imperial town seeking a site for itself." And the Pueblo Southwest was a very curious place indeed for this oddly stratified and ad hoc community to attempt to establish roots.

Pueblo Hierarchies, Trajectories, and Transformations

As Juan de Oñate y Salazar equipped his 1598 entrada into New Mexico, he packed with him the lingering Cíbola myth—the "grandiose expectations" that the American Southwest was rich in mineral wealth, tribute, populations, and agricultural surpluses (Wilcox 2009:130). Not long after their arrival, Oñate y Salazar's colonists discovered their error, and paid a heavy price in mutiny and desertion. After Viceroy Montesclaros penned a letter to King Phillip to "inform your majesty that this conquest is becoming a fairy tale," Oñate y Salazar was recalled to Mexico City, where he was stripped of his commission (Wilcox 2009:129–134).[6]

In the transition from entrada to permanent colonization, as elsewhere in the New World, the Spanish crafted ways (some legal, some not so much) to extract tribute and exploit the Native Pueblo population. The *encomienda* (in which trustees held a specific number of Natives in trust) and the *repartimiento de indios* (which distributed Native men to work on a rotating basis for the public good) were the favored "legal" institutions. Some Spaniards also turned to the patently illegal practice of taking Indian slaves—rarely among mission Indians (their labor was exploited in other ways), rather seizing "pagans" beyond the expanding rim of Christendom (Weber 1992:124–129; see also Brooks 2002).

As the Spanish would learn in painful detail, the Pueblo and Mississippian worlds differed in many ways and each would require individually crafted colonial strategies of conquest. One difference was demographic. Taking note of evidence suggesting a sixteenth-century population collapse across the American Southeast, Ann F. Ramenofsky and Jeremy Kulisheck (this volume) recognize a very different pattern in the northern Southwest. Both contemporary Spanish accounts and the archaeological record reveal a clear-cut pattern of relative continuity and stability in the numbers of villages from the fourteenth through early seventeenth centuries throughout the northern Southwest (see also Kulisheck 2010). They emphasize key differences defining the nature of depopulation in the Pueblo and Mississippian worlds: the remote Southwestern geography, the "uneven" distribution of Pueblo people across that landscape, relatively infrequent encounters between Hispanic and Indigenous populations, and the small size of expeditionary forces (with the Vázquez de Coronado expedition being the exception, but only partly so). Ramenofsky and Kulisheck conclude that the "sum total, singly or in combination, inadvertently shielded Native peoples from the onslaught of European conquest, resulting in demographic stability in the sixteenth century."

In light of such demographic stability and continuity, initial prospects for successful missionization in the Southwest must have seemed bright. As David Weber (1994:4) put it, "For Franciscans, who insisted that Indians live like Spaniards and tried to congregate them into towns if they did not, the apartment-dwelling Pueblos seemed a godsend." The Spanish called these apparently permanent towns—and the people who lived there—*los pueblos*, to distinguish them from the more mobile Apache and Navajos.[7]

To be sure, the Spanish that entered the Rio Grande valley encountered fully clothed Indigenous people living in large village complexes and farming nearby fields. The newcomers were encouraged, simply assuming that these *pueblos* were home to year-round political polities and as a result, excellent candidates for a village-based *encomienda* system that would funnel labor and resources into the Spanish colonial economy.

But early Hispanic perceptions conflict with archaeological evidence from the Upper Middle Rio Grande valley. Richard C. Chapman (this volume) believes that these Classic Period sites reflect a considerably more fluid settlement strategy characterized by an annual cycle of seasonal dispersal and aggregation, with households frequently relocating among villages (see also Lekson 1990; Ramenofsky et al. 2009). Drawing an analogy to Tewa household organization, Chapman stresses the importance of complex household elders in decision making, with the overarching social entities (such as sodalities and moieties) more flexibly integrated across the fluid village structure. If Pueblo socioeconomic organization was indeed characterized by annual seasonal dispersal and aggregation during the entrada period, this posed a problem for Franciscans seeking full-time sedentary populations, preferably under the control of a single political leader.

> The reality may have been that the actual individuals treating with the European expeditionaries and their allies might well have . . . had no specific political power over other social units at the village. . . . Whereas the Spanish interpreted reluctance of the village inhabitants to provide them with food as disrespectful, given the seasonal nature of aggregating stores at the villages, there may not in fact have been any surplus to offer, at least during some times of year. (Chapman, this volume)

Spanish narratives also reflect a growing frustration with the presumed village leaders, who promised to provision and shelter colonial settlers and treat the Franciscan friars fairly. But time after time, the Pueblos "voted with their feet," treating the Hispanic interlopers as merely another environmental issue to be confronted in traditional fashion (by relocating to another village location within the region; Chapman, this volume). As quoted by Flint and Flint (2005), the Pueblos "were not familiar with his Majesty, nor did they wish to be his subjects."

This concern also recalls Juan de Oñate y Salazar's classic complaint about decision making within Pueblo society: "In government they are free, for although they have petty captains, they obey them badly and in very few things" (quoted in Bolton 1908; see also McGuire and Saitta 1996:203). In effect, Oñate y Salazar defined a dilemma that would bedevil top-down Hispanic colonists for centuries: Who, exactly, are the Pueblo leaders? Who, exactly, makes the decisions? Who, exactly, has the power to negotiate commitments? Where, exactly, is the leadership hierarchy?

The same issue has also intrigued generations of anthropologists and students of Pueblo culture. Elsie Clews Parsons (1933:77) spoke of not one but "many bosses" at Zuni. Ruth Benedict's classic *Patterns of Culture* (1934) identified the "egalitarian ethos" for Pueblo societies, an iconic Apollonian ideal that Lekson (2008:56) terms "the Benedict Fallacy . . . the assumption that Pueblo societies were always egalitarian, prayful, peaceful, contemplative, and so forth." Fred Eggan (1964:182) characterized the Hopi as an "egalitarian" culture that "never developed a political society." For generations, anthropologists tended to follow suit, viewing the pueblos as "egalitarian societies," lacking formal hierarchies beyond sex and age, organized by cross-cutting ties (sodalities) embedded within the larger social structure.

> Authority is phrased in ritual rather than in secular terms and is not concentrated in any single position. There is no central authority for the Hopi as a whole. . . . Within each major village there is a hereditary group of priests or chiefs but the order of this hierarchy varies from village to village, and they have a minimum of secular authority. (Eggan 1950:506)

Others see social power (including supernatural power) rather differently, questioning how these beliefs impact the conception of politics and its relationship to wealth and labor flow in Pueblo society.[8] Parsons (1933:53), for instance, viewed Pueblo society in terms of theocracy and hierarchy, with "incipient social classes." Particularly since the 1980s, the Southwestern literature has been dominated by debates over the nature of hierarchy and social stratification among ethnohistorical and Ancestral Pueblo communities—especially as expressed in inequalities in wealth and power (e.g., Brandt 1994) and differential access to esoteric knowledge and ceremonial objects (e.g., McGuire and Saitta 1996). These conversations continue today because, as Lekson has recently put it, "hierarchy in the Southwest actually matters" (2008:185).

"To the extent that the Pueblos are governed at all," cautions John Ware (2002:94), "they are governed by hierarchies of priests—members of secret sodalities who exercise authority over the ritual, and in many communities, the mundane aspects of everyday life." Whiteley (1988) suggests that, at least among the Hopi, society (sodality) chiefs had a considerably more important role in political life that conventional pueblo ethnographies allow—they were not subservient assistants to village chiefs, but were independent participants with the groups of decision makers, with village chiefs being merely "first among equals."[9] He concludes:

> Hopi *is* a hierarchical society. But the terms of its hierarchy are constituted within a particular cultural cast that is ineffectively accommodated by Western formalist models . . . the Hopi are clearly as engaged in "political" action and social inequality as "we" are. Why the contradictions, then . . . "Egalitarian,"? "Hierarchical?," "Tribal"? The problem . . . lies not with Hopi society, but with theoretical premises that . . . underlie basic Western notions of human action [as] a cultural datum, not a guarantee of self-evident truth. (Whiteley 1998:82, 103)[10]

The picture becomes vastly more intriguing when moving back in the Pueblo past. Many archaeologists today believe that the ancient Chacoan Southwest was characterized by politically complex, hierarchical power structures that involved considerable social inequity, heritable leadership, and complex tribute networks. Barbara Mills (2004) discusses the "establishment and defeat" of political hierarchies among prestate societies (including Chaco), and Stephen Lekson (2008:330–331) postulates that after the Chaco sphere fell apart, Pueblo people deliberately rejected the hierarchical governance that had once ruled the ancient Southwest (see also the papers in Adams and Duff 2004; Spielmann 1998).

In other words, archaeological evidence suggests that two or three centuries prior to Spanish entradas into the Southwest, the post-Chaco Pueblo world had already deliberately rejected its own heritage of hierarchy and stratification. Such an interpretation, then, indicates that the post–A.D. 1300 migrations involved a "devolution" from a politically complex Chaco power structure into more corporate "syncretic" forms that characterize historic and modern pueblos.[11]

The point here is simple: If the nature of Pueblo decision making and embedded sociopolitics has confounded generations of academics, one can only imagine the confusion and frustration experienced by Vázquez de Coronado, Oñate y Salazar, and their colonial cronies as they attempted to negotiate and administer top-down tribute and labor requirements among the Pueblos. Such deep divisions and intercultural tensions foreshadowed up to seven decades of colonial conflict as the Franciscans erected *conventos* and churches at many of the larger pueblos. Preucel et al. (2002:88) define the Revolt era (1623–1696) as "a period of considerable social and political experimentation as different leaders sought to define and control systems of representation by means of a broad-based cultural revitalization movement." A number of investigators have recently explored the tensions and conflicts that characterized the seventeenth-century Franciscan missions among the Pueblos and led directly to the Pueblo Revolt of 1680 (e.g., Liebmann 2008a; Liebmann and Preucel 2007; Preucel 2002; Weber 1999). Individual *encomenderos* often abused their rights and neglected their responsibilities. Discussing the degree of religious and economic oppressions, Preucel (2002:4) also suggests that both household-to-household variability and longer-term responses to drought and depopulation may have "heightened the effects" of the *encomienda* upon the Pueblos (see also Gutiérrez 1991:105). As Carla R. Van West, Thomas C. Windes, Frances Levine, Henri D. Grissino-Mayer, and Matthew W. Salzer discuss (this volume), the Pueblo Revolt of 1680 transpired at a time following two decades "of unimaginable hardship" including a devastating freeze that summer leading to crop failures, epidemic disease, and depopulation. The Pueblo Revolt became "one of those rare moments in more than three hundred years of colonial rule in the Americas that Spaniards suffered a thorough defeat by natives whom they had long subjected" (Weber 1999:8).

Some Concluding Comparisons

The chapters in this volume underscore both similarities and vast differences that characterized the entrada period in the American Southeast and Southwest. Three very different long-term cultural and historical trajectories emerged.

Shortly after the entradas, the deepest interior Southeast became, in Ethridge's (2006) felicitous phrase, the "Mississippian shatter zone." The Soto expedition established beyond all doubt that the Mississippian world contained neither readily available sources of gold or silver nor any other form of intrinsic wealth. To be sure, although these Native polities hardly rivaled the powerful Native empires of the Peruvian Inca or the Aztec in the valley of Mexico, the Mississippian world was heavily hierarchical, and the Spaniards knew how to address a hierarchy. The entradas of Soto, Luna y Arellano, and Pardo not only created a significant demographic impact due to infectious disease, but their mere presence undermined long-standing Mississippian hereditary *micos* and empowered lesser leaders to foster temporary Hispanic alliances against their traditional enemies, further destabilizing the interior. Slaving raids by Spanish rivals thrust the nonmission Indigenous survivors into the capitalist system. Between the sixteenth and seventeenth centuries, the Mississippian chiefdoms of the deep colonial frontier eventually transformed themselves into "new social forms more appropriate for the world in which they found themselves" (Worth 2002:59).

The interior Southeast differed vastly from La Florida, where strategic concerns fostered the founding of colonial St. Augustine, from which soldiers and friars found ready access to still-powerful hereditary chiefs. The Spanish colonial system reinforced internal chiefly power by providing a tributary exchange system in which access to Indigenous land and labor was channeled through hereditary chiefs. So empowered, traditional Mississippian leaders mobilized agricultural surpluses, land, and labor—all commodities under their chiefly control—thus assuring military backing and continuing the long-term traditional practices of ostentatious public display. In effect, St. Augustine became a colonial paramount chiefdom, using support from the Spanish Crown in exchange with chiefly matrilineages of destabilized chiefdoms. Similarly, as Worth (this volume) writes:

> Indigenous Florida chiefdoms became *de facto* members of a Spanish paramountcy in which Native American labor and staple foods supported the Spanish administrative center in exchange for Spanish

> luxury goods and military protection . . . a sort of *Pax Hispanum*, in which a diversity of local Native American societies were assimilated into a far-flung, multiethnic colonial society centered at the Spanish port city of St. Augustine.

This hybrid Spanish–Native society survived throughout much of the seventeenth century, until internal political and economic difficulties coupled with catastrophic population loss brought down the entire colonial polity and lead directly to the (first) withdrawal of the Spanish from Florida.

Still another colonial outcome played out in the Pueblo world. As Vázquez de Coronado and his "imperial town seeking a site for itself" (Flint 2008:2) made its way across Tierra Nueva, the Spanish colonial leadership had difficulty understanding the nature of Indigenous power and politics, hierarchy, and complexity. Not only did Pueblo concepts differ vastly from those of Mississippian people, the Pueblos were also quite different from the *indios amigos*, who comprised nearly three-quarters of the Vázquez de Coronado expedition. The Franciscans who followed initially believed the Pueblos to be a "godsend" (Weber 1999:4) because they were sedentary farmers. But the mission and accompanying *encomienda* quickly encountered serious problems with the embedded nature of Pueblo decision making and the diffuse ritualized power balances involved. In fact, archaeological evidence strongly suggests that the Pueblo world deliberately rejected the hierarchical and stratified society of its Chacoan past in favor of the more diffuse, embedded decision-making strategies that characterize historic and modern pueblos.

The era of the entradas triggered a demographic collapse that cost hundreds of thousands (perhaps millions) of Indigenous lives. But the events and processes differed greatly between the Mississippian and Pueblo worlds. The sixteenth and seventeenth century was a time of monumental environmental stress, but the climates and stresses differed greatly between the American Southeast and Southwest.

In Spanish colonial Florida, embattled paramount chiefs engaged in bloody conflict with one another, struggling to enter and remain in the Franciscan mission system. Forced conversions and Native resistance to the missions of the colonial Southwest fostered revolution aimed at driving the Spanish away forever. Dozens of Franciscan friars were martyred in the Mississippian and Pueblo worlds, but they perished for very different reasons.

Such was the complexity and diversity that manifest across the Spanish Borderlands during the era of the entradas.

Acknowledgments

I sincerely thank Clay Mathers and Charles Haecker for pulling together both the initial session at the Society for American Archaeology meetings (in Atlanta) and particularly the focused follow-up seminar organized by Clay, Charlie, and Jeffrey M. Mitchem, held at the Amerind Foundation (Dragoon). I also thank John Ware for his interest and guidance in making the seminar such a warming and stimulating experience. I gratefully acknowledge the assistance of Linda Cordell, Robbie Ethridge, Michael Francis, Lorann S. A. Pendleton, Ann Ramenofsky, Diana Rosenthal, and Peter Whiteley in preparing this chapter.

15

History, Prehistory, and the Contact Experience

Charles R. Ewen

The Contact Period, or when different cultures meet and interact, is arguably one of the most interesting to anthropologically oriented archaeologists. Is the encounter hostile or conciliatory? Does one culture change or are both affected? If they change, what aspects of their culture do they retain and what do they discard? In the southern United States, the area Herbert Bolton (1921) called the Spanish Borderlands, this involves the meeting of European (primarily Spanish) cultures with the Indigenous inhabitants (see Foster 1960; Spicer 1962). The degree and direction of change that was brought about by the encounter has been scrutinized by archaeologists for decades. Yet, as this volume shows, there is still much to be learned.

There are many obstacles facing the Contact Period scholar. There is the lack of documents, as well as the inherent bias in those documents that do exist. On the material side, there is the paucity of archaeological sites and the bias of the archaeologists interpreting those sites. To make the most of the skimpy and often ephemeral data on this period, a multidisciplinary approach is mandated and cherished concepts must be reexamined. This means moving beyond the dogmatic beliefs about the Contact Period (mostly gleaned from the documentary record) and surveying the material record for new insights.

One of the most commonly held views of the Encounter is that of the conquering microbe. That is, Europeans brought with them devastating diseases for which the Native inhabitants had no immunity. This resulted in an immediate, tragic, and tremendous population loss. The following quotes by respected scholars document this belief:

> The most spectacular period of mortality among the American Indians occurred during the first hundred years of contact with the Euro-

> peans and Africans. Almost all of the contemporary historians of the early settlements, from Bartolomé de las Casas to William Bradford of Plymouth Plantation, were awed by the ravages of epidemic disease among the native populations of America. (Crosby 1972:37–38)
>
> From before the beginning of European colonization on the continent until the twentieth century, more Indians had died every year than were born, and for a simple reason. Colonists brought with them Old World pathogens that escaped from their original hosts to invade new territory. Because the native population lacked immunity to viruses and germs that evolved in the Old World, Indians succumbed in large numbers to ailments that scarcely afflicted the immune colonists. (Dobyns 1983:8)
>
> Precontact societies were changed, and most quite radically so, by a century of lethal epidemics introduced from 1493 on that so devastatingly reduced their numbers—at least by two-thirds; the latest researches suggest *perhaps by as much as 95 percent*—that no aspect of life remained untouched. (Sale 1990:304)

These are bold statements, and have been the basis of our understanding of the Contact Period for over a generation.

Even as I was preparing this chapter, I attended a lecture by a noted historian on my campus regarding the Native inhabitants of eastern North Carolina. She led off her talk with the assertion that it was "a well-known fact" that disease had decimated the local Native population in North Carolina even before the English could establish a foothold on the coast. This is the accepted wisdom of today, but is it accurate? On what data is this assertion based? Evidence in the ground, or oft-repeated interpretations of past explorer accounts? What else might we be missing as we follow along the well-worn ruts of past scholarship? This volume addresses this very question, and provides some surprising answers.

The Symposium

The primary goal of the seminar convened at the SAA meetings in Atlanta in 2009 was a better understanding of the interactions between sixteenth-century Native and European communities in what is now the Southwestern and Southeastern United States. The organizers wanted to explore the many factors that affected this contact, including social, economic, political, military, environmental, and demographic influences. The contributors to the seminar focused on how these factors varied between the Southeastern and Southwestern United States and influenced the Contact experience in both regions. The aim was to better understand the processes of societal change that resulted from the interaction between the Spanish explorers, priests, and settlers and the Native communities on the southern borderlands of North America. Evaluating the transformations (what the organizers termed the *morphogenesis*) of the European and Native communities was the focus of the participant discussions.

The organizers paired participants to address similar thematic issues in both geographic areas, so that their comparisons could really assess the importance of the social and natural environmental impacts on the invading Spaniards as well as the Indigenous cultures of the sixteenth-century Southwest and Southeast. It provided an opportunity for scholars in both regions to discuss their research, on a professional level in a formal, and later informal, setting. This provided the impetus and venue for them to share their ideas, discuss their sites, and even identify artifacts. It began collaborative relationships that will extend far beyond the publication of this volume.

The result of all this enforced interaction is a volume that truly synthesizes the state of the research, pushes the boundaries of the interpretation of the existing data, and suggests areas for productively mining new data. I know it's my job as discussant to say these things, but this volume genuinely does what Clay Mathers, Charlie Haecker, and Jeff Mitchem set out to do with the original symposium.

The organization of the original seminar and this book centers around four major variables that the organizers saw as affecting the successes and failures of the early Spanish efforts to explore and exploit North America, as well as their impacts on the Native inhabitants. The climate they encountered, the timing and spread of diseases they introduced, the political organization and reorganization of the Native polities, and the conflict that occurred before, during, and after the Encounter were all variables that influenced and shaped the consequences of contact.

The participants in this endeavor brought their expertise and differing perspectives to the areas they were charged to explore. The result was a lively and well-attended discussion at the 2009 SAA meetings (standing room only!). This same cadre of scholars, with some substitutions, continued the dialog at the Amerind Center at Dragoon, Arizona, with the result of the intensive interactions being this volume.

Synopsis: Southeast vs. Southwest

In these days of near-instant communication with potentially everyone in the world, it seems remarkable that scholars pursuing similar research topics in different areas of the same country might be unaware of each other's work. And yet, this is not an uncommon occurrence. Thus, an important accomplishment of the symposium that led to this book was the assembling of scholars from both the Southeastern and Southwestern United States. In these times of regional and topical specialization in archaeology, few people have had the opportunity to undertake extensive research in both theaters. And whereas many of us had read each other's work, scholars at most conferences, even national ones, tend to congregate with others from their own academic neighborhood. This leads to academic inbreeding and stagnation of innovative thought. Fortunately, the academic dyad experiment had the desired effect of beginning a dialog that soon involved the entire group. Concepts some Southeasterners had taken for granted were revelations to our colleagues in the Southwest, and vice versa. Techniques for fieldwork vary as widely as the terrain and after a fieldtrip to the Dos Cabezas Mountains, I have a new appreciation for the stamina of our Southwestern brethren.

The tone of the volume is immediately apparent in the opening chapters. Richard and Shirley Flint and Robbie Ethridge were excellent choices to summarize the baseline data and suggest where the research should continue. Both challenge, not only the traditional historical interpretations, but indeed, even the way in which those interpretations were derived.

The Flints decry the old romantic paradigm that recalled a noble and adventurous past in the old Southwest. The arrival of an anthropological approach, in the guise of Adolph Bandelier, Edward Spicer, and others, dialed back the drama and laid the groundwork for a multidisciplinary approach espousing multiple perspectives on the past. One of the key breaks with past historical interpretation is their reinterpretation of the nature of Vázquez de Coronado's army. Not the disciplined Knights of Spain, but rather a ragtag collection of diverse mercenary groups sharing a common goal, El Dorado.

Robbie Ethridge agrees that a more expansive view of the past is needed. She feels that most historians have shied away from the Contact Period due to the lack of available documentation. Apparently, historians need their papers as much as archaeologists need their potsherds. However, it is imperative that we historicize prehistory if we are ever to understand that period. While this is not a new idea (see Fish 1978), it has not been fully embraced by our historian colleagues. Ethridge encourages archaeologists and historians alike to use the Contact Period and the direct historic approach to challenge the accepted wisdom of the past on such matters as disease and the fragility of chiefly polities. The fall of the Mississippian chiefdoms and their coalescence into the historic Indian "tribes" of the Southeast is not well understood, but it is a growing area of scholarship today (Ethridge and Shuck-Hall 2009). Perhaps such overlooked factors as the role of commercial aboriginal slaving by both the Natives and the Europeans in the destabilization of the region might well be considered in future research.

Disease

As mentioned at the beginning of my comments, disease has always been considered the *Deus ex machina* that explains virtually all change to Native populations resulting from contact with the invading Europeans. "Not so fast!" caution the next pair of symposium participants.

Ramenofsky and Kulisheck accept the common perception that decimation by disease was a reality in the Southeast, but they counter that it was much less in the Southwest. To the contrary, they assert that, for the Pueblos, the sixteenth century was a period of relative demographic stability. The arrival of the Spanish resulted in severe short-term disruptions and localized abandonments. Significant population changes, however, including decline, did not occur until the early or mid-seventeenth century. They attribute this delay to the dispersed settlement pattern and rugged terrain that characterizes the Southwest, claiming this blunted the effect of disease on the Native population. It was only later, when the Spaniards consolidated the Native population, that disease began to take its toll.

Hutchinson takes issue with the assumption that the demographic collapse in the Southeast was immediate and widespread after contact. He examines the direct and indirect evidence and comes to the conclusion that there was no pandemic during the sixteenth century. Instead, the collapse happened over the course of three centuries. In fact, he asserts that most demographers agree that the Native population nadir was actually reached in the latter half of the nineteenth century. He invokes a multiple-effects model to explain that many factors, of which disease was but one, adversely impacted the Native population. It is no coincidence that many of these other factors form the basis for discussion by the other contributors to this volume.

Climate

Dennis Blanton readily accepts the challenge to consider other factors in interpreting the impacts on the Contact experience. In a fresh spin on cultural ecology, he reemphasizes the need to consider the influence of the environment on past human behavior. As I mentioned earlier, this is not a new idea, but we do have a lot of new environmental data available, of which archaeologists need to make better use. La Niña, El Niño, and volcanoes are having huge impacts on the current climate—droughts, floods, warming, and cooling. Being good Uniformitarianists since the mid-nineteenth century, why would we think it was any different in the past?

Dendrochronology indicates that there were droughts as early as the sixteenth century, but within a hundred years the colonists had developed adaptive strategies that allowed them to cope. The Indigenous population had long-standing coping strategies for the natural environment, but it was the changing cultural environment that was their ultimate undoing. Blanton argues that disease became a factor, but only after the population had coalesced in response to other social and environmental pressures.

Van West et al. apply these same ideas to understanding the successes and failures of the various Spanish entradas in the Southwest. By charting the changes in the precipitation and temperature during the sixteenth and seventeenth centuries, they are essentially able to generate a predictive model of Spanish colonization for the region. It is this ability to draw upon disparate data and apply them to specific research questions that demonstrates the value of the archaeologist. Few other disciplines so readily seek other disciplines' data to further their own research.

Political Organization

If the disease and environmental paradigms are challenged, then what are the implications for the interpretation of the past sociopolitical organization? They are many and equally surprising.

The invading Spaniards, and, later, historians and archaeologists alike, have long assumed that the large pueblos in the Southwest were occupied year-round. Chapman, invoking the data generated by decades of CRM archaeology, asserts that this is probably an incorrect oversimplification. The discovery of dozens of small summer extraction camps reveals that, since at least A.D. 1300, these large settlements were occupied only in the colder months. The population dispersed in the summer to take advantage of seasonal resources. The flexible leadership and kinship system allowed rapid relocation of populations to more favorable areas. It was also this existing flexibility that allowed the ancient Puebloan peoples to largely avoid direct conflict with the Spaniards, a strategy that frustrated the Spanish entradas and preserved the local polities well into the Historic Period.

Freed from the monocausal confines of a catastrophic disease model, researchers in the Southeast are looking for additional reasons to explain the social upheaval in the region after Spanish contact. That the arrival of the Spaniards spelled the end of Native hegemony in the Southeast is not disputed. However, Ethridge and Mitchem point out that the polities in the region were not homogeneous, and that their responses to the arrival of Europeans varied with their size and complexity. The impact of the first encounter with Soto was, indeed, severe, but the Indigenous societies of the interior would have recovered had not the aftershocks of introduced disease and increased Indian slave raiding not further destabilized them during the ensuing centuries.

Other authors have commented on the brutality of the conquistadors in the sixteenth-century Southeast (see Ramenofsky and Kulisheck, this volume), but Worth notes that after the initial attempts by the Spaniards to overwhelm the Indians militarily all met with failure, their strategy changed to a more accommodating approach. The "New Laws of the Indies" promulgated in 1542 ultimately led to the Franciscan mission system that came to depend upon the local populations to provide food and labor to support Spanish efforts to protect the coast from other European invasion. This led to a *Pax Hispanum* that lasted over a century. Ironically, it was this switch that probably caused the most harm to the Native inhabitants, as the reduction of the scattered villages to surrounding Spanish settlements introduced diseases and accompanying social upheaval that by the eighteenth century caused the Native demographic collapse.

Conflict

A later, seventeenth-century *Pax Hispanum* aside, the pre-Contact period, on both sides of the Atlantic, was characterized by conflict. So both Spaniard and Native American already had a military strategy in place at the beginning of the sixteenth century. Mathers (this volume) describes the Native response to initial Spanish aggression as ranging from "creative compliance, negotiation, and passive resistance to open conflict, guerilla warfare, and large-scale, sustained campaigns of armed confrontation." Much of their response depended upon the constitution of the Spanish entrada, which usually consisted primarily of *indios amigos* (mercenaries). Comparative data from across the Americas suggests that overwhelming force was brought to bear in many early entradas, that the composition of early sixteenth-century expeditions was consistently over 95 percent Natives, that the use of such force was certainly problematic in many ways (e.g., facilitating success in conflicts, but creating provisioning problems and lasting antipathy), and that the New Laws/New Ordinances fundamentally affected both the conduct and composition of entradas throughout the Spanish Empire. As Chapman (this volume) has already noted, the flexibility of the Puebloan communities allowed them to maintain their social and spatial integrity well into the seventeenth century.

Rodning et al. have found similarities and differences from the Southwest with Native–European conflict in the Southeast. They point out that Spanish aggression almost invariably failed in the long term due to the logistical difficulties inherent in garrisoning a New World empire. Alliances and gift giving worked better, at least until the gifts ran out. The most important point they make is that the root cause for Native conflict lay not in the acquisition of the gifts, but in the status they conferred. Prestige was gained by fighting one's enemy. This proved unsustainable as, ultimately, "Spanish contact . . . created cycles of conflict and other conditions from which those chiefdoms could not recover in traditional forms, leading to the coalescence of the confederacies and tribal societies present in the Southeast during the eras of French and English exploration and settlement in the 1600s and 1700s" (Rodning et al., this volume).

The Tyranny of the Written Record

So what new have we learned in this volume? More than I originally expected, or at least we have learned how little we actually know about the Contact Period. Much of what I consider the problem with research into the Contact Period can be chalked up to an overreliance on the documentary evidence. Or to put a historical archaeological spin on Wobst's (1978) cautionary article on the use of ethnographic literature, we suffer from "the tyranny of the documentary record." As archaeologists, we should probably know better. There are many ways that the historical accounts can get it wrong: omission of seemingly unimportant events, misinterpretation of what is being observed, and blatant prevarication to cover one's incompetence. Still, the lure of an eyewitness accounting of an event about which we so desperately want to know is irresistible. But resist we must, or at least we must be skeptical.

Going Beyond the Written Record

There are many other avenues of research that bear further investigation. The role of Indian slavery has been largely overlooked in the Colonial Period and has been positively ignored in the Contact and Prehistoric Periods. If this trade were as active at Contact as it was in the early

Historic Period, how does this affect our interpretation of the Encounter? Could this activity have contributed to sociopolitical instability and collapse of some Mississippian chiefdoms? Does adding the Europeans as ready customers take this activity to a higher and unsustainable level? Merely asking these questions directs us to reexamine both the historical and archaeological records with new eyes.

Archaeology, especially historical archaeology, is in the position to challenge the old assumptions gleaned from the documentary record. An example is the case of the Pandemic Theory, where there is virtually no direct material evidence of the virulent epidemics that earlier scholars claim decimated the Native populations at Contact. Yes, it was a factor, but could not other factors, such as drought, conflict, and political instability also account for the changes in settlement pattern and technology noted in the archaeological record? And yet, many scholars become indignant when the primacy of the role of disease at Contact is challenged.

With so little evidence outside of the sparse and often ambiguous documentary record, why are we so quick to play the disease card? I believe it is because this single agency appears to be a satisfying explanation that accounts for all change and lets everyone off the hook. The descendants of the Native inhabitants can claim that their weak resistance was due to a weapon for which they had no defense. What could they do? The European descendants can equally claim that the introduction of the diseases was unintentional. So no one suffers any blame. It is an explanation we can all shake our heads sadly about.

However, this latest version of the "Black Legend" does a disservice to past Spaniard and Indian alike. As archaeological and renewed historical investigations into the Contact Period are revealing, the past, like the present, is a complex web of social and natural interrelationships. No group had exclusive claim on noble or ignoble behavior. Some individuals connived to profit from the misfortunes of their fellow man, while others fought to protect them. The New World was a stage upon which a very human drama played itself out. Thinking of the players as anything other than completely human biases our interpretation of their actions.

Appendix A: Annual Values and Equivalent Z-Scores for the MRG Basin and San Francisco Peaks Chronologies

Middle Rio Grande Tree-Ring Values			San Francisco Peaks Tree-Ring Values (selected yrs from much longer chronology)			
Year AD	Reconstructed June PDSI Values	*Z*-Score	Year AD	Mean Max Annual Temp F	*Z*-Score	Frost Ring?
1500	−1.54	−0.84	1500	59.28	−0.11	
1501	−1.64	−0.90	1501	59.73	0.39	
1502	−0.77	−0.42	1502	58.76	−0.69	
1503	−0.97	−0.53	1503	59.10	−0.31	
1504	0.08	0.04	1504	59.06	−0.36	
1505	0.55	0.30	1505	59.04	−0.38	
1506	−3.15	−1.72	1506	59.51	0.14	
1507	2.74	1.50	1507	58.99	−0.44	
1508	2.23	1.22	1508	59.26	−0.14	
1509	1.09	0.60	1509	59.50	0.13	
1510	−0.24	−0.13	1510	59.17	−0.24	
1511	3.88	2.12	1511	59.17	−0.24	
1512	1.43	0.78	1512	58.51	−0.97	
1513	0.79	0.43	1513	58.71	−0.75	
1514	0.29	0.16	1514	58.54	−0.94	
1515	0.74	0.40	1515	58.36	−1.14	
1516	−2.64	−1.44	1516	58.71	−0.75	
1517	−2.85	−1.56	1517	57.74	−1.83	

(continued)

Middle Rio Grande Tree-Ring Values			San Francisco Peaks Tree-Ring Values (selected yrs from much longer chronology)			
Year AD	Reconstructed June PDSI Values	*Z*-Score	Year AD	Mean Max Annual Temp F	*Z*-Score	Frost Ring?
1518	0.31	0.17	1518	57.85	−1.71	
1519	0.00	0.00	1519	57.80	−1.76	
1520	1.30	0.71	1520	57.27	−2.35	
1521	1.26	0.69	1521	58.03	−1.50	
1522	−2.04	−1.11	1522	58.43	−1.06	
1523	−3.14	−1.72	1523	58.99	−0.44	
1524	−3.18	−1.74	1524	58.86	−0.58	
1525	−0.62	−0.34	1525	58.86	−0.58	
1526	1.54	0.84	1526	59.13	−0.28	
1527	0.21	0.11	1527	58.83	−0.61	
1528	−0.91	−0.50	1528	59.37	−0.01	
1529	1.62	0.89	1529	60.57	1.32	
1530	1.81	0.99	1530	60.38	1.11	
1531	0.12	0.07	1531	61.89	2.79	
1532	−1.50	−0.82	1532	61.63	2.50	
1533	−0.32	−0.17	1533	60.39	1.12	
1534	1.34	0.73	1534	60.52	1.27	
1535	1.77	0.97	1535	59.24	−0.16	
1536	2.26	1.23	1536	59.43	0.05	
1537	2.10	1.15	1537	59.07	−0.35	
1538	−1.73	−0.95	1538	60.48	1.22	
1539	1.83	1.00	1539	60.26	0.98	

Middle Rio Grande Tree-Ring Values			San Francisco Peaks Tree-Ring Values (selected yrs from much longer chronology)			
Year AD	Reconstructed June PDSI Values	*Z*-Score	Year AD	Mean Max Annual Temp F	*Z*-Score	Frost Ring?
1540	3.04	1.66	1540	59.90	0.58	
1541	0.66	0.36	1541	59.55	0.19	
1542	−1.80	−0.98	1542	59.57	0.21	
1543	0.84	0.46	1543	60.15	0.85	
1544	0.14	0.08	1544	60.80	1.58	FR
1545	−1.50	−0.82	1545	59.86	0.53	
1546	−1.58	−0.86	1546	59.49	0.12	
1547	−1.26	−0.69	1547	60.21	0.92	
1548	−0.35	−0.19	1548	59.65	0.30	
1549	−0.45	−0.25	1549	59.94	0.62	
1550	1.79	0.98	1550	59.09	−0.33	
1551	−1.31	−0.72	1551	59.18	−0.23	
1552	−0.32	−0.17	1552	59.27	−0.12	
1553	3.86	2.11	1553	59.18	−0.23	
1554	2.82	1.54	1554	58.74	−0.71	
1555	5.56	3.04	1555	59.26	−0.14	
1556	5.05	2.76	1556	58.63	−0.84	
1557	0.73	0.40	1557	58.64	−0.83	
1558	−1.41	−0.77	1558	58.77	−0.68	
1559	−0.21	−0.11	1559	59.54	0.18	
1560	−1.86	−1.02	1560	59.44	0.06	
1561	−1.89	−1.03	1561	59.46	0.09	
1562	−1.38	−0.75	1562	60.62	1.38	

(continued)

Middle Rio Grande Tree-Ring Values			San Francisco Peaks Tree-Ring Values (selected yrs from much longer chronology)			
Year AD	Reconstructed June PDSI Values	*Z*-Score	Year AD	Mean Max Annual Temp F	*Z*-Score	Frost Ring?
1563	−1.83	−1.00	1563	60.30	1.02	
1564	0.82	0.45	1564	59.21	−0.19	
1565	−0.08	−0.04	1565	58.71	−0.75	
1566	−0.69	−0.38	1566	58.54	−0.94	
1567	−1.32	−0.72	1567	58.90	−0.54	
1568	0.64	0.35	1568	58.95	−0.48	
1569	0.94	0.51	1569	59.44	0.06	FR
1570	1.33	0.73	1570	58.64	−0.83	
1571	−2.71	−1.48	1571	59.51	0.14	
1572	0.32	0.17	1572	59.01	−0.41	
1573	−3.00	−1.64	1573	59.45	0.08	
1574	−0.69	−0.38	1574	59.16	−0.25	
1575	−2.03	−1.11	1575	60.01	0.70	
1576	−2.68	−1.46	1576	58.94	−0.49	
1577	−0.58	−0.32	1577	58.40	−1.09	
1578	0.78	0.43	1578	58.53	−0.95	
1579	−3.81	−2.08	1579	58.60	−0.87	
1580	−2.04	−1.11	1580	59.69	0.34	
1581	−2.56	−1.40	1581	59.49	0.12	
1582	−1.85	−1.01	1582	59.05	−0.37	
1583	−4.10	−2.24	1583	58.74	−0.71	
1584	−3.08	−1.68	1584	59.18	−0.23	

Middle Rio Grande Tree-Ring Values			San Francisco Peaks Tree-Ring Values (selected yrs from much longer chronology)			
Year AD	Reconstructed June PDSI Values	*Z*-Score	Year AD	Mean Max Annual Temp F	*Z*-Score	Frost Ring?
1585	−4.59	−2.51	1585	59.62	0.26	
1586	−1.10	−0.60	1586	59.92	0.60	
1587	−1.91	−1.04	1587	60.48	1.22	
1588	0.30	0.16	1588	60.22	0.93	
1589	−2.20	−1.20	1589	60.28	1.00	
1590	−2.07	−1.13	1590	60.40	1.13	
1591	0.55	0.30	1591	60.63	1.39	
1592	−1.59	−0.87	1592	60.44	1.18	
1593	−3.69	−2.02	1593	60.24	0.95	
1594	1.70	0.93	1594	59.55	0.19	
1595	0.51	0.28	1595	59.52	0.15	FR
1596	0.00	0.00	1596	59.73	0.39	
1597	0.90	0.49	1597	59.97	0.65	
1598	−1.20	−0.66	1598	59.13	−0.28	
1599	−0.78	−0.43	1599	58.30	−1.20	
1600	−1.38	−0.75	1600	58.78	−0.67	
1601	−3.74	−2.04	1601	58.48	−1.00	
1602	−0.20	−0.11	1602	59.29	−0.10	
1603	0.37	0.20	1603	58.92	−0.51	
1604	0.01	0.01	1604	58.52	−0.96	
1605	−0.49	−0.27	1605	57.94	−1.61	
1606	−0.91	−0.50	1606	58.82	−0.63	

(continued)

Middle Rio Grande Tree-Ring Values			San Francisco Peaks Tree-Ring Values (selected yrs from much longer chronology)			
Year AD	Reconstructed June PDSI Values	*Z*-Score	Year AD	Mean Max Annual Temp F	*Z*-Score	Frost Ring?
1607	−1.03	−0.56	1607	59.23	−0.17	
1608	0.50	0.27	1608	58.46	−1.03	
1609	0.50	0.27	1609	58.17	−1.35	
1610	2.18	1.19	1610	58.54	−0.94	
1611	1.43	0.78	1611	59.17	−0.24	
1612	2.53	1.38	1612	59.04	−0.38	
1613	0.35	0.19	1613	60.22	0.93	
1614	−1.92	−1.05	1614	59.44	0.06	
1615	−0.02	−0.01	1615	59.57	0.21	FRew
1616	0.18	0.10	1616	59.23	−0.17	
1617	−0.12	−0.07	1617	58.74	−0.71	
1618	2.44	1.33	1618	58.71	−0.75	
1619	−0.30	−0.16	1619	59.65	0.30	
1620	2.52	1.38	1620	58.65	−0.81	
1621	2.06	1.13	1621	59.13	−0.28	
1622	0.56	0.31	1622	58.98	−0.45	
1623	−0.42	−0.23	1623	58.49	−0.99	
1624	−2.81	−1.54	1624	59.27	−0.12	
1625	−2.32	−1.27	1625	59.22	−0.18	FRew
1626	−0.59	−0.32	1626	59.44	0.06	
1627	2.29	1.25	1627	60.20	0.91	

Middle Rio Grande Tree-Ring Values			San Francisco Peaks Tree-Ring Values (selected yrs from much longer chronology)			
Year AD	Reconstructed June PDSI Values	*Z*-Score	Year AD	Mean Max Annual Temp F	*Z*-Score	Frost Ring?
1628	−1.41	−0.77	1628	60.64	1.40	
1629	2.86	1.56	1629	60.13	0.83	
1630	2.39	1.31	1630	59.64	0.29	
1631	−0.80	−0.44	1631	59.79	0.45	
1632	−1.04	−0.57	1632	59.26	−0.14	
1633	1.87	1.02	1633	59.95	0.63	
1634	4.30	2.35	1634	59.56	0.20	
1635	1.79	0.98	1635	59.13	−0.28	
1636	1.72	0.94	1636	59.00	−0.43	
1637	4.97	2.72	1637	58.94	−0.49	
1638	1.08	0.59	1638	58.34	−1.16	
1639	2.36	1.29	1639	58.54	−0.94	
1640	3.72	2.03	1640	58.46	−1.03	FR+
1641	1.94	1.06	1641	57.97	−1.57	
1642	0.30	0.16	1642	57.53	−2.06	
1643	0.86	0.47	1643	56.96	−2.70	
1644	1.47	0.80	1644	57.18	−2.45	
1645	−1.11	−0.61	1645	57.24	−2.38	
1646	2.37	1.30	1646	56.43	−3.29	
1647	0.99	0.54	1647	57.14	−2.50	
1648	−2.53	−1.38	1648	57.74	−1.83	
1649	2.03	1.11	1649	57.79	−1.77	

(continued)

Middle Rio Grande Tree-Ring Values			San Francisco Peaks Tree-Ring Values (selected yrs from much longer chronology)			
Year AD	Reconstructed June PDSI Values	*Z*-Score	Year AD	Mean Max Annual Temp F	*Z*-Score	Frost Ring?
1650	0.79	0.43	1650	58.31	−1.19	
1651	3.06	1.67	1651	57.75	−1.82	FR
1652	1.56	0.85	1652	58.01	−1.53	
1653	1.33	0.73	1653	58.65	−0.81	
1654	−1.95	−1.07	1654	59.46	0.09	
1655	1.90	1.04	1655	60.07	0.77	
1656	0.38	0.21	1656	59.82	0.49	
1657	−1.33	−0.73	1657	60.18	0.89	
1658	−0.19	−0.10	1658	59.92	0.60	
1659	−1.54	−0.84	1659	59.63	0.28	
1660	0.73	0.40	1660	60.08	0.78	
1661	0.94	0.51	1661	59.01	−0.41	
1662	0.01	0.01	1662	58.89	−0.55	
1663	0.00	0.00	1663	59.65	0.30	
1664	−1.41	−0.77	1664	58.83	−0.61	
1665	0.46	0.25	1665	59.11	−0.30	
1666	−1.93	−1.05	1666	58.58	−0.89	
1667	−1.32	−0.72	1667	58.76	−0.69	
1668	−3.17	−1.73	1668	58.39	−1.10	
1669	−1.37	−0.75	1669	58.12	−1.40	
1670	−2.12	−1.16	1670	58.51	−0.97	
1671	−0.58	−0.32	1671	58.18	−1.34	

Middle Rio Grande Tree-Ring Values			San Francisco Peaks Tree-Ring Values (selected yrs from much longer chronology)			
Year AD	Reconstructed June PDSI Values	*Z*-Score	Year AD	Mean Max Annual Temp F	*Z*-Score	Frost Ring?
1672	−2.09	−1.14	1672	58.57	−0.90	
1673	−0.92	−0.50	1673	58.52	−0.96	
1674	−1.25	−0.68	1674	59.14	−0.27	
1675	1.15	0.63	1675	58.94	−0.49	
1676	−1.18	−0.64	1676	58.48	−1.00	
1677	0.12	0.07	1677	58.84	−0.60	
1678	−1.18	−0.64	1678	58.58	−0.89	
1679	0.72	0.39	1679	57.93	−1.62	
1680	1.50	0.82	1680	56.93	−2.73	FR+
1681	0.05	0.03	1681	58.84	−0.60	
1682	0.88	0.48	1682	58.53	−0.95	
1683	0.18	0.10	1683	59.02	−0.40	
1684	−1.78	−0.97	1684	59.31	−0.08	
1685	−3.68	−2.01	1685	59.59	0.23	
1686	2.31	1.26	1686	59.30	−0.09	
1687	−0.19	−0.10	1687	58.74	−0.71	
1688	0.25	0.14	1688	59.91	0.59	
1689	2.54	1.39	1689	60.67	1.43	
1690	0.51	0.28	1690	60.19	0.90	
1691	−1.05	−0.57	1691	60.47	1.21	
1692	3.32	1.81	1692	60.39	1.12	
1693	2.51	1.37	1693	61.40	2.25	

(continued)

Middle Rio Grande Tree-Ring Values			San Francisco Peaks Tree-Ring Values (selected yrs from much longer chronology)			
Year AD	Reconstructed June PDSI Values	*Z*-Score	Year AD	Mean Max Annual Temp F	*Z*-Score	Frost Ring?
1694	−0.35	−0.19	1694	61.59	2.46	
1695	−0.53	−0.29	1695	60.33	1.05	
1696	−2.41	−1.32	1696	60.24	0.95	
1697	0.96	0.52	1697	60.24	0.95	
1698	0.05	0.03	1698	59.70	0.35	
1699	2.37	1.30	1699	59.34	−0.05	
1700	−0.62	−0.34	1700	59.28	−0.11	

Key
FR: Presence of a frost ring in the San Francisco Peaks chronology; FR+: Presence of a frost ring in more than one high-elevation tree-ring chronologies (i.e., frosts widely experienced); FRew: Presence of frost ring in the earlywood of the that year's annual growth.

Notes

Chapter 1. Entradas in Context

1. The utility of these characterizations may be enhanced in the future with greater precision about the meaning of specific terms and further clarification regarding their context of use. Like other early entradas, the Vázquez de Coronado expedition was regularly involved in armed conflict with Indigenous communities, often leading to significant loss of life. Leaving aside the large number of Native warriors recruited for this expedition, to characterize the Vázquez de Coronado entrada as having a "faintly military complexion" may express more about its *predeparture* characteristics and perhaps aspirations than its actual conduct in Tierra Nueva. The martial nature of encounters between the Vázquez de Coronado entrada and Pueblo communities in the Southwest, first at Zuni and then in Tiguex, suggest that any ambiguity about the military character of the expedition at its outset rapidly disappeared by the winter of 1540–1541 with the onset of activities described by one contemporary eyewitness, Diego López, as a "war that was waged . . . without mercy" (Flint 2002:395).

2. The extent to which the expedition was an "ad hoc" assembly can also be challenged in a number of respects. The choice of principals (captains) for this expedition was certainly not so, since a significant number had been in positions of authority during the earlier entradas of Nuño Beltrán de Guzmán—a close friend and associate of Viceroy Antonio de Mendoza (one of the primary sponsors of the Vázquez de Coronado entrada). In addition, it is unlikely that the entrada's Native auxiliaries were chosen at random, since there is clear evidence that Spaniards of the period distinguished social classes within different regional groupings of auxiliaries, with some selected specifically as warriors and others recruited as *tamemes* (burden bearers). Also, like other entradas throughout the sixteenth century, it is highly likely that many European members of the Vázquez de Coronado expedition were selected from a set of close relations and loyal colleagues—a practice adopted by other commanders and sponsors in organizing early Spanish, French, and English expeditions, from *conquista* campaigns in Mexico and Peru to the settlement efforts at Santa Elena, Fort Caroline, and Jamestown. Finally, while entrada participants clearly had a personal, and often financial, stake in the success of such ventures, it is clear that the Spanish Crown and its viceroys did also. The latter were often instrumental in vetting, selecting, and promoting entrada leaders, overseeing expedition planning, monitoring postdeparture correspondence with expedition leaders, and in some cases supplying additional support and provisions for expeditions in the field. Apart from their administrative approval for entradas and the potential impact of

expeditions on their careers/reputations, a number of viceroys had direct financial interests in the outcome of these ventures, again suggesting that not all aspects of entrada planning, logistics, and recruitment were ad hoc affairs.

It is important to recognize too that the notion of "taking economic control" of Cíbola or any other prosperous, inhabited territory in the Americas was not a process of peaceful negotiation or diplomacy, but of violent struggle. Spanish-led campaigns in Hispaniola, the valley of Mexico, Cuba, Colombia, Panama, Nicaragua, Peru, Honduras, Guatemala, Yucatan, and Nueva Galicia—all prior to the Vázquez de Coronado expedition—demonstrated the cost of entradas in lives and resources, and the necessity of military action to secure land, labor, and other valued commodities. Entradas that ignored the required scale and persistent necessity of armed force did so at significant peril to individual expedition members and to the success of the enterprise as a whole. With knowledge of these historical precedents and an experience of regular Native conflict and rebellions in their immediate neighborhood (Nueva Galicia) in the decade or so preceding the Vázquez de Coronado entrada, members of this expedition would have recognized the necessity for a significant armed force. That need was accentuated by their plan to explore territories known to be inhabited by hostile Native groups. Furthermore, the expedition's travels placed them sufficiently far from their original point of departure to make reinforcement impractical when trouble occurred. The emphasis on a large number of Native auxiliaries, and at a personal level, on the military equipment for each of the 288 men listed on the expedition's muster roll, therefore, does not come as a surprise.

3. In discussing the conduct of early entradas in Nueva Vizcaya in the 1550s, for example, Meachem (1968:58) indicates:

> Francisco de Ibarra, nephew of Diego de Ibarra, Velasco's son-in-law, was put in charge of the enterprise. When he entered upon his arduous duties as a conquistador, Francisco was a mere stripling of about sixteen years of age. The appointment of mere boys to such responsible positions was not uncommon in those days; the most essential qualifications were birth and wealth.

Equally, Simmons (1991:37), describing the early career of Juan de Oñate y Salazar in the same area of New Spain during the 1570s, states:

> By order of the viceroy every citizen of Zacatecas was obligated to arm himself with harquebus or crossbow and go on forays against the fearsome Chichimecas whenever he received a summons to duty. As in the days of the Moorish crusades, it was a case of every Spaniard a soldier. Cristóbal de Oñate and Juan de Tolosa often assumed command of these punitive expeditions. In later years Juan de Oñate would claim that he accompanied his father on such occasions, "from the time he was able to bear arms." So, precisely how old was he when he first faced the Chichimecas? His friend Pérez de Villagrá with a flowery pen wrote that Juan was a mere boy of ten, undoubtedly an exaggeration. But Spanish youths were in the habit of going to war at a tender age, not uncommonly in their beginning teens, hence it is safe to conclude that Juan got a very early start as an apprentice fighter . . .

Although not exclusively an enterprise for young men, sixteenth-century entradas in Tierra Nueva and elsewhere often involved a significant number of younger individuals with the energy and stamina required to survive the rigors of such campaigns—not unlike the present. The notion of formal military training for these and other participants in sixteenth-century expeditions also needs to be examined carefully, since most of the institutions that offered such training were either being established (in Iberia) at the time of the Vázquez de Coronado entrada, or came into existence after the expedition returned to Mexico in 1542.

4. But since European armies of the sixteenth century were only gradually becoming professionalized by formal schooling, academies, training, and instruction manuals, the Flints' characterization of the Vázquez de Coronado expedition (Flint and Flint, this volume) could apply equally to the wide range of armed forces confronting one another in western, southern, and eastern Europe during the same period. Leaving aside the issue of the number of extant biographies for expedition members, it is important to be clear about what defines *formal military training* in the sixteenth-century Americas and Europe, how many individuals were likely to have received it, and how precisely we can determine the military career of any one expedition member. Furthermore, in reviewing the battlefield conduct of entrada leaders with some of the most significant military experience, notably Hernán Cortés and Hernando de Soto, there are certainly cases in their careers that parallel the experience and injuries of Vázquez de Coronado at Hawikku. Cortés suffered serious wounds during the siege of Tenochtitlán, and Soto so repeatedly exposed himself to personal injury in battle that it became a hallmark of his career. In these and other cases of entrada-related combat, leading in battle was often both literal and figurative. It was expected by others and—as in the Crusades and *Reconquista*—was recognized frequently by both commanders and their subordinates as a badge of honor rather than foolhardy bravado or a sign of inexperience.

Chapter 4. Contact Era Studies and the Southeastern Indians

1. Parts of this essay were previously published in the coauthored introduction to *Light on the Path: The Anthropology and History of the Southeastern Indians*, (University of Alabama Press, 2006).

2. This is not to say that all anthropologists ignored history. In 1950 the British anthropologist E. E. Evans-Pritchard and American anthropologist Melville Herskovitz both advocated a historical perspective. For a more comprehensive summary of Southeastern Indian ethnohistory, see Usner 1998:4–7.

Chapter 5. The Role of Climate in Early Spanish–Native American Interactions in the US Southwest

1. A Growing Degree Day (GDD) unit is a measure of heat needed to bring modern crop varieties to maturity. Agronomists generally use a base of 50°F (10°C)

for corn and 60°F (15.6°C) for cotton. These estimates are published on the Western Regional Climate Center website, *www.wricc@dri.edu*, for each weather station in their database. This website provides the following description of this measure:

> Growing Degree Day units are computed as the difference between the daily average temperature and the base temperature (Daily Av. Temp. – Base Temp.). One unit is accumulated for each degree Fahrenheit the average temperature is above the base temperature. Negative numbers are discarded. Example: If the day's high temperature was 95 and the low temperature was 51, the base 60 heating degree day units is ((95 + 51) / 2) – 60 = 13. This is done for each day of the month and summed. *Corn Growing Degree Day* units have the limitations that the maximum daily temperatures greater than 86°F are set to 86°F and minimums less than 50°F are set to 50°F.

2. Grissino-Mayer et al. (2002) developed their MRGB chronology from a sample of long-lived and climate-sensitive conifer trees (Douglas-fir, ponderosa pine, limber pine, and southwestern white pine) growing in the Sandia Mountains, the Magdalena Mountains, and El Malpais National Monument. In addition, Grissino-Mayer et al. (2002) were able to extend their chronology backward in time from ring data recorded from remnant subfossil wood (Douglas-fir and ponderosa pine) preserved on the lava flows of El Malpais National Monument. The resulting MRGB chronology was based on 239 measured tree-ring series with an average length of over 450 years. The collections in the Sandia Mountains were made at five sites within the spruce-fir zone (above 2,800 m AMSL). Collections in the Magdalena Mountains were made at three sites in the spruce-fir zone (above 3,000 m ASML). Collections in El Malpais National Monument were made at two sites on pahoehoe lava, one near Bandera Crater and the other near Cerro Rendija. These long-lived conifer species include Douglas-fir (*Pseudotsuga menziesii* [Mirb.] Franco); Ponderosa pine (*Pinus ponderosa* Douglas ex C. Lawson), limber pine (*Pinus flexilis* James), and southwestern white pine (*Pinus strobiformus* Engelm).

3. Salzer (2000) updated an existing bristlecone chronology (*Pinus aristata* Engelm) from the San Francisco Peaks north of Flagstaff, Arizona. The SFP chronology is exceptional for several reasons. First, it is one of the two longest continuous tree-ring chronologies based on a single species in the US Southwest (2,660 years from 663 B.C. to A.D. 1997). The other long chronology is associated with Mammoth Creek, Utah, extending back into the 700s B.C. Second, it is remarkable for its strong sample depth through time (234 series representing 130 trees with 89,478 annual rings). Third, the chronology is one of only a few high-elevation chronologies in the US Southwest, and it was created from bristlecone pines growing at the extreme upper timberline (3,536 m AMSL). Fourth, the SFP chronology is the only high-elevation chronology in the US Southwest that has been demonstrated statistically to be a proxy of mean maximum annual temperature. Fifth, the chronology was examined for the presence of "frost rings," which are annual growth rings damaged by exposure to prolonged subfreezing tempera-

tures during the growing season of the tree. Documentation of when these damaging frosts occurred may be used to infer when crops growing at lower elevations may have been adversely impacted by detrimental frosts during their own growing season. Finally, because trends rather than absolute values in temperature are shared over large geographic areas, the SFP chronology can serve as a model for other localities in the northern US Southwest that tend to experience similar climate.

4. The Palmer Drought Severity Index (PDSI) is a temporally sensitive measure of soil moisture. It was designed as an index of meteorological drought, defined as a "period of prolonged and abnormal moisture deficiency" (Palmer 1965:1). Its creator, Wayne Palmer, a meteorologist working for the US Weather Bureau, developed a quantitative method for calculating moisture-departure values that could be compared through time and across space. Palmer (1965:28, Table 11) created a classification scheme to interpret the PDSI values that resulted from his calculations. Positive values represented normal and wetter-than-normal conditions; negative values represented dry to drought conditions. Eleven interpretive categories were created: Near Normal (−0.49 to +0.49), Incipient (Wet or Drought, ±0.50 to 0.99), Slight (Wet or Drought, ±1.00 to 1.99), Moderate (Wet or Drought, ±2.00 to 2.99), Unusual (Wet or Drought, ±3.00 to 3.99), Extreme (Wet or Drought, ≤4.00 and ≤−4.00). Dendroclimatologists often reconstruct PDSI values because they (1) are a measure that integrates the cumulative effects of both precipitation and temperature in a single value that can be interpreted over time for a given area and (2) can be used to compare effects among differing areas.

5. A *Z*-score is a standardized standard-deviation unit that has a long-term mean of zero and a standard deviation of 1.0. This score was derived by calculating the series mean and standard deviation for each original series (Grissino-Mayer et al.'s MRGB PDSI series for A.D. 622–1992 and Salzer's SFP temperature series for 663 B.C. to A.D. 1997) and then subtracting the series mean from each annual value and dividing the result by the standard deviation of the overall series.

6. Salzer (2000) reconstructed a long-term average annual mean maximum temperature for his San Francisco Peaks bristlecone pine chronology as 59.38°F (15.21°C) for an upper-elevation tree-ring collection site at approximately 11,600 ft (3,536 m) AMSL. Using the Environmental Lapse Rate (ELR) of 0.65°C per 100 meters to estimate temperature in the lower, arable settings of the MRGB, we calculate that the long-term average is equivalent to 28.29°C (82.92°F) for an elevation of 1,524 m (5,000 ft) AMSL. For the year A.D. 1680, Salzer reconstructed an average annual mean maximum temperature of 56.93°F (13.85°C), equivalent to 2.73 standard deviations (*Z*-scores) below the long-term mean value at 3,536 m AMSL. Using the ELR, we estimate that the average annual mean maximum temperature at 1,524 m AMSL would be equivalent to 26.93°C (80.47°F).

7. One of the most positive aspects of the colonization of the US Southwest by Europeans was the introduction of cool- and cold-tolerant crops and livestock from the Old World. Some of these crops, especially cereal crops, expanded the area that could be successfully farmed with Indigenous crops (e.g., corn, common beans, squash) alone, and certainly supplemented aboriginal diet once established. According to Dunmire (2004), varieties of wheat, melons, and watermelons were introduced to what is now New Mexico in the 1500s. By 1680, the list of introduced cultigens expanded to include barley, oats, grapes, artichoke, cabbage, lettuce, beets, carrots, garlic, onion, radish, turnip, cucumber, broad beans, garbanzo beans, lentils, peas, apricot, cherry, nectarine, peach, plum, apple, quince, and the garden herbs of coriander, cumin, and anise. The successful introduction of cool-tolerant wheat was particularly important.

Chapter 7. Regarding Sixteenth-Century Native Population Change in the Northern Southwest

1. Figure 7.1 identifies the geographic regions we use throughout the chapter. These areas are taken from Barrett (2002) and are not necessarily isomorphic with linguistic units.

Chapter 10. The Interior South at the Time of Spanish Exploration

1. Hudson (1997) reconstructs the geopolitical landscape of the Mississippian South at the time Soto came through the region. We refer readers to this work for a good understanding of the Mississippian world at the time of contact.

2. Hudson and his colleagues place Talisi at the Kymulga phase sites east of the Coosa River in present-day Talladega County, Alabama. Recent investigations, however, conclude that Talisi is most likely represented by a large cluster of sites on the lower Tallapoosa River (see DePratter et al. 1985:120; Jenkins 2009:220; Waselkov et al. 2009:229–239).

Chapter 12. Contest and Violence on the Northern Borderlands Frontier

1. The notable exception being the 1959–1962 excavations by Florence Hawley Ellis at San Gabriel—the location of Juan de Oñate y Salazar's colonial capital at Ohkay Owingeh Pueblo in the Upper Rio Grande valley of northern New Mexico from 1598 to 1610 (Ellis 1987, 1989).

2. While Álvar Núñez Cabeza de Vaca and his three colleagues entered the Southwestern United States in the period 1528 to 1536, their presence in the area was due more to accident (being shipwreck survivors of the Pánfilo de Narvaez expedition) and captivity than a desire to explore the area. The earliest entrada-

related activity in the Southwest—that is, that of Esteban the Moor, Marcos de Niza, and Melchoir Díaz/Juan de Zaldívar—constituted scouting or reconnaissance parties in advance of the larger Vázquez de Coronado entrada that was to follow shortly afterward.

Chapter 13. Conflict, Violence, and Warfare in La Florida

1. Leaders of Spanish entradas in the Southeast were veterans of colonial activity elsewhere. Ponce de León participated in exploration of Hispaniola and Puerto Rico and conquests of local Taino groups on those islands. Ayllón was a landowner and planter on Hispaniola before undertaking his 1521 and 1526 expeditions to La Florida. Narváez was sent by the governor of Cuba to arrest Hernán Cortés in Mexico after Cortés had ignored orders from the governor. Soto participated in the Francisco Pizarro campaign in Peru and in so doing he met the Inca leader Atahualpa. Luna y Arellano participated in the Vázquez de Coronado expedition and helped to suppress a rebellion in Oaxaca before sailing for La Florida. By contrast, Pardo had only just arrived in La Florida from Spain before Pedro Menéndez de Avilés dispatched him on his expeditions inland.

2. Not every burned structure and settlement reflects warfare. Mississippian structures and settlements sometimes burned down accidentally or were burned down intentionally when they were abandoned. During the sixteenth century, Native groups sometimes abandoned and burned settlements in advance of the arrival of Spanish entradas. On the other hand, warfare probably accounts for some burned structures and settlements, as at sites associated with the Powers phase in southeastern Missouri (Pauketat 2004:158; Price 1978) and the Orendorf site in Illinois (Harn 1978; Pauketat 2004:156).

3. Soto's first winter encampment at the abandoned Apalachee settlement of Anhaica has been identified at the Martin site, in modern Tallahassee, Florida (Ewen 1990; Ewen and Hann 1998). Soto's second winter encampment at Chicaza has not been located, but it is probably located in the vicinity of Tupelo, Mississippi (Ethridge 2010:31; Hudson 1997:261, 262–270, 475–476).

4. While in South Carolina in 1540, Soto likewise took the "Lady of Cofitachequi" hostage, although her kidnapping did not lead directly to any attacks (Hudson 1997:172–184). While visiting the province of Coosa in 1540, Soto took many Native people captive, and he kept the chief of Coosa and his sister hostage during his march south from Coosa toward the town of Itaba and the province of Ulibahali (Hudson 1997:217–221; King 1999, 2003).

5. Mallios (2006) demonstrates that Spanish and English violations of Native American rules and expectations related to gifting and reciprocity led to attacks on colonists in coastal North Carolina and Tidewater Virginia in the late 1500s

and early 1600s. Gallivan (2003, 2007) and others have demonstrated relationships between gifting, trade, diplomacy, and power relations within and between Algonkian villages and English groups in the Chesapeake region.

6. Pardo established three forts in North Carolina, one in eastern Tennessee, and two in South Carolina. Pardo's primary outpost was Fort San Juan, which is the only one of Pardo's forts whose location has been identified archaeologically, through our investigations at the Berry site, in the upper Catawba valley in western North Carolina (Beck 1997; Beck and Moore 2002; Beck et al. 2006, 2011; Moore 2002).

Chapter 14. Honor and Hierarchies

1. Why should a majority submit to the wishes of those who seek to subordinate and exploit (Arnold 2001; Boone 1992)? Assuming rationale and self-interest in behavior, one expects that interest-based individuals would chose to live in such large groups only when net payoff for doing so exceeds the rewards of living in smaller, more dispersed groups. The biogeographic and ecological specifics condition both the costs of relocating and the benefits of remaining with the natal group, defining an endurance threshold after which subordinates are likely to bud off into new settlements. Because subordinates have built the council houses and granaries, farmed the fields, collected and rendered the hickory nut and acorn oil, built and maintained the fish weirs, and cultivated the oyster beds, they enjoy the consumption of more food over longer periods of time, despite the "rake-off" by dominants (Bird and O'Connell 2006:169). Add to this the cost of relocating and the lack of unoccupied territories and even the self-interested, disadvantaged subordinate individuals might benefit from such heritable inequality (Arnold 2001).

2. Mathers and Mitchem (this volume; personal communication, 2010), however, question some aspects of the Flints' proposal, in particular:

> Whether this characterization is intended to apply to the expedition's intentions prior to departure, or to the actual pursuit of its activities during the course of this entrada. Whether the notion of a "faintly military complexion" applies to either aspect of this expedition, it is difficult to imagine how the largest entrada to enter the Southwest in the sixteenth century, and the inclusion of perhaps two thousand Native allies within it, constitutes a minor military component. Even if all Native auxiliaries were not intended to engage in direct combat, the large numbers of allies included in this entrada suggest that they represented a significant fighting force, as they had in previous entradas elsewhere.

3. Mathers and Mitchem (this volume) also question the extent to which the expedition was an "ad hoc" assembly, arguing that the choice of entrada commanders, captains, allies, and other participants may have involved more purposeful decisions and planning.

4. Mathers and Mitchem (this volume, personal communication 2011) also challenge the notion of "economic control without sustained coercive force—especially on the Northern frontiers of New Spain." They suggest instead that "in

most cases, both intimidation and lethal violence were required" and that "in the Middle Rio Grande and in the Chichimec Arc, economic control was achieved not by short-term battles or limited conflict but by periods of sustained and systematic warfare lasting years and decades, respectively." Furthermore, they emphasize that "economic control in Northern New Spain, in whatever sense it was achieved ultimately, required substantial investments (time, resources, and personnel), as well as considerable violence."

5. *Indios amigos* did not disappear entirely in the post-entrada Southwest. A settlement of Tlaxcaltecans from central Mexico, for instance, were living in Santa Fe's Barrio de Analco (around the San Miguel chapel) when the Pueblo Revolt broke out (Wilcox 2009:153; see also Simmons 1964).

6. The irony, of course, is that (unlike the Southeast) there was metal wealth (in the form of silver) in New Mexico. As Ramenofsky et al. (2008) emphasize, because Juan de Oñate y Salazar was a mining engineer, he knew exactly what he had discovered, and metal production did in fact take hold in the New Mexico colony.

7. The terminology is important here. As Flint (2009:78) points out, "Spanish society of the era was thoroughly hierarchical. Persons had their ranks and stations, but so did political and social entities. When speaking of settlements, that hierarchy was never out of mind." The term *ciudad* was reserved for only the largest, most important settlements (literally, this term had to be designated by the king). Elsewhere in Spanish-controlled territory, terms like *villa*, *lugar*, and *aldea* (hamlet) were applied. Significantly, the term *pueblo*, while used less precisely, meant "a place of minor importance."

8. Whereas all modern Pueblos distinguish between ritual elites and commoners, between the ceremonially rich and the ceremonially poor (Brandt 1994; Levy 1992), considerable variability existed. Ware (2002:94) emphasizes the variability among ethnohistoric pueblo groups. Among western Pueblos (such as the Hopi) ceremonies were owned by matrilineal descent groups, with the principal lineage of the controlling descent group caring for the ceremonial paraphernalia and providing the head priest for a fraternal sodality. In eastern (Rio Grande) pueblos, sodalities emerged as central village political organizations that function independent of kinship control and enjoy considerable influence beyond ritual life of their communities; in the eastern Keresan pueblos, political, economic, and ceremonial authority vested exclusively in a priestly hierarchy controlled by the principal medicine-clown sodalities.

9. Whiteley (1988) challenged the assumptions of clan corporateness and equality in matters economic that underwrite the egalitarian model. The economic, social, and ceremonial relations that structure Puebloan society—specifically relating to landholding, inheritance, and participation in ritual—are more open to modification and negotiation by agents than either an egalitarian or stratified model permits. Hopi clans have differential access to ceremonies and social duties, and significant inequality existed within clans and between family/

lineage segments. Levy (1992) found a contradiction in early twentieth-century Hopi between an ideology of cooperation and integration, opposed to a stratified system of land control—as reflected in differential access according to membership in powerful, ranked clans, suggesting a social organization that is neither egalitarian nor stratified.

10. Whiteley (2004:152) has cogently summarized the evidence this way: "Chaco clearly involved centralization, tribute, and hierarchy—a vertical mode of integrating a social structure. The modern Pueblos are principally kinship-based systems of social integration: descent groups with cross-cutting sodality ties among the Western Pueblos, and bilateral families overlain by ceremonial moieties with alternating leadership among the Tanoans, with Eggan's famous (1950) Keresan bridge in between."

11. Ware (2002) has explored the development and variability of sodalities in the post-Chaco/post-Migration Pueblo world.

References Cited

Achúe Zapata, José Enrique

2011 Some News about Don Garci López de Cárdenas: A Native of Madrid in the Canyon of the Colorado. In *The Latest Word from 1540: People, Places, and Portrayals of the Coronado Expedition*, edited by Richard Flint and Shirley Cushing Flint, pp. 39–72. University of New Mexico Press, Albuquerque.

Acuna-Soto, Rodolfo, David W. Stahle, Malcolm K. Cleaveland, and Matthew D. Therell

2002 Megadrought and Megadeath in 16th-Century Mexico. *Emerging Infectious Diseases* 8(4):360–362.

Adams, E. Charles, and Andrew I. Duff

2004 Settlement Clusters and the Pueblo IV Period. In *The Protohistoric Pueblo World, A.D. 1275–1600,* edited by E. Charles Adams and Andrew I. Duff, pp. 4–16. University of Arizona Press, Tucson.

Adams, E. Charles, and Andrew I. Duff (editors)

2004 *The Protohistoric Pueblo World, A.D. 1275–1600.* University of Arizona Press, Tucson.

Adams, Karen R., Cathryn M. Meegan, Scott G. Ortman, R. Emerson Howell, Lindsay C. Werth, Deborah A. Muenchrath, Michael K. O'Neill, and Candice A. C. Gardner

2006 *Maís (Maize of American Indigenous Societies) Southwest: Ear Descriptions and Traits that Distinguish 27 Morphologically Distinct Groups of 123 Historic USDA Maize (Zea mays L.spp mays], Accessions and Data Relevant to Archaeological Subsistence Models. Report to the James S. McDonnell Foundation Grant #21002035.* Electronic Document, http://farmingtonsc.nmsu.edu/documents/maissouthwestcopyrightedmanuscript1.pdf, accessed January 31, 2010.

Adler, Michael A., Todd Van Pool, and Robert D. Leonard

1996 Ancestral Pueblo Population Aggregation and Abandonment in the North American Southwest. *Journal of World Prehistory* 10(3):375–438.

Adorno, Rolena, and Patrick Charles Pautz (editors)

1999 *Álvar Núñez Cabeza de Vaca: His Account, His Life, and the Expedition of Pánfilo de Narváez.* Volume 1. University of Nebraska Press, Lincoln.

Agoyo, Herman

2002 Holy War. In *Archaeologies of the Pueblo Revolt: Identity, Meaning, and Renewal in the Pueblo World,* edited by Robert W. Preucel, pp. xi–xiv. University of New Mexico Press, Albuquerque.

Alchon, Susan Austin
2003 *A Pest in the Land: New World Epidemics in a Global Perspective.* University of New Mexico Press, Albuquerque.
Allan, Robert J.
2000 ENSO and Climate Variability in the Past 150 Years. In *El Niño and the Southern Oscillation, Multiscale Variability and Global and Regional Impacts*, edited by Henry F. Diaz and V. Markgraf, pp. 3–56. Cambridge University Press, Cambridge.
Allison, Marvin J., D. Mendoza, and A. Pezzia
1973 Documentation of a Case of Tuberculosis in Precolumbian America. *American Review of Respiratory Disease* 107:985–991.
Altman, Ida
2007 Conquest, Coercion, and Collaboration: Indian Allies and the Campaigns in Nueva Galicia. In *Indian Conquistadors: Indigenous Allies in the Conquest of Mesoamerica*, edited by Laura E. Matthew and Michel R. Oudijk, pp. 145–174. University of Oklahoma Press, Norman.
2010 *The War for Mexico's West: Indians and Spaniards in New Galicia, 1524–1550.* University of New Mexico Press, Albuquerque.
Altman, Ida, Sarah Cline, and Juan Javier Pescador
2003 *The Early History of Greater Mexico.* Prentice Hall, Upper Saddle River, New Jersey.
Anderson, Arthur J. O., and Charles E. Dibble
1978 *The War of Conquest: How It Was Waged Here in Mexico. The Aztecs' Own Story as Given to Fr. Bernardino de Sahagún.* University of Utah Press, Salt Lake City.
Anderson, David G.
1994 *The Savannah River Chiefdoms: Political Change in the Late Prehistoric Southeast.* University of Alabama Press, Tuscaloosa.
Anderson, David G., David W. Stahle, and Malcolm R. Cleaveland
1995 Paleoclimate and the Potential Food Reserves of Mississippian Societies: A Case Study from the Savannah River Valley. *American Antiquity* 60:258–286.
Anschuetz, Kurt F.
1998 Not Waiting for the Rain: Integrated Systems of Water Management by Pre-Columbian Pueblo Farmers in North-Central New Mexico. Unpublished PhD Dissertation, Department of Anthropology, University of Michigan, Ann Arbor.
Archivo General de Indias (AGI), Sevilla, Spain
1537 AGI, Patronato, 184, R.27, Carta de don Antonio de Mendoza al Rey, México.
1546 AGI, Justicia, 270, Pieza 4, Visita al alcalde que fue Gerónimo de Medina, Ciudad de México.
1559 AGI, México, 97, R.1, Méritos y servicios, Tristán de Luna y Arellano

Archivo General de la Nación (AGN), Mexico City.

1550 AGN, Mercedes, Vol. 3, exp. 48bis, fols. 22v – 24r, List of payments of ayuda to 95 persons who participated in the armada to Perú.

Arnold, J. Barto III, and Robert Weddle

1978 *The Nautical Archaeology of Padre Island: The Spanish Shipwrecks of 1554*. Academic Press, New York.

Arnold, Jeanne E.

1993 Labor and the Rise of Complex Hunter-gatherers. *Journal of Anthropological Archaeology* 12:75–119.

2001 *The Origins of a Pacific Coast Chiefdom: The Chumash of the Channel Islands*. University of Utah Press, Salt Lake City.

Arnold, Thomas

2001 *The Renaissance at War*. Cassell and Company, London.

Atkinson, James R.

1987 The De Soto Expedition through Northeast Mississippi in 1540–1541. *Mississippi Archaeology* 22(1):61–73.

2004 *Splendid Land, Splendid People: The Chickasaw Indians to Removal*. University of Alabama Press, Tuscaloosa.

Avellaneda, Ignacio

1997 Hernando de Soto and His Florida Fantasy. In *The Hernando de Soto Expedition: History, Historiography, and "Discovery" in the Southeast*, edited by Patricia Galloway, pp. 207–218. University of Nebraska Press, Lincoln.

Axtell, James

1982 *The European and the Indian: Essays in the Ethnohistory of Colonial North America*. Oxford University Press, New York.

Baker, Brenda J., and Lisa Kealhofer

1996 *Bioarchaeology of Native American Adaptation in the Spanish Borderlands*. University Press of Florida, Gainesville.

Baker, Stephen G.

1974 Cofitachique: Fair Province of Carolina. Unpublished MA Thesis, Department of History, University of South Carolina, Columbia.

Bandelier, Adolph F.

1888 *History of the Colonization and Missions of Sonora, Chihuahua, New Mexico and Arizona to the Year 1700*. Vatican Library, Bandelier Collection—Manuscripts, Vat. Lat. 14112–14116, Rome.

1890 Hemenway Southwestern Archaeological Expedition: Contributions to the History of the Southwestern Portion of the United States. Carried on Mainly in the Years from 1880 to 1885, Part 1. *Papers of the Archaeological Institute of America, American Series 5*. John Wilson and Son, Cambridge, Massachusetts.

1892 Hemenway Southwestern Archaeological Expedition 1, An Outline of the Documentary History of the Zuni Tribe. *Journal of American Ethnology and Archaeology* 3(4):1–115.

Bannon, John Francis (editor)

1964 *Bolton and the Spanish Borderlands.* University of Oklahoma Press, Norman.

1970 *The Spanish Borderlands Frontier, 1513–1821.* Holt, Rinehart and Winston, New York.

1974 *The Spanish Borderlands Frontier, 1513–1821.* University of New Mexico Press, Albuquerque.

Barcia Carballido y Zúñiga, Andrés González de

1951 *Barcia's Chronological History of the Continent of Florida.* Translated by Anthony Kerrigan. University of Florida Press, Gainesville.

Barnes, Jay

1995 *North Carolina's Hurricane History.* University of North Carolina Press, Chapel Hill.

1998 *Florida's Hurricane History.* University of North Carolina Press, Chapel Hill.

Barrett, Elinore M.

2002 *Conquest and Catastrophe: Changing Rio Grande Pueblo Settlement Patterns in the Sixteenth and Seventeenth Centuries.* University of New Mexico Press, Albuquerque.

Beck, Robin A., Jr.

1997 From Joara to Chiaha: Spanish Exploration of the Appalachian Summit Area, 1540–1568. *Southeastern Archaeology* 16:162–169.

2003 Consolidation and Hierarchy: Chiefdom Variability in the Mississippian Southeast. *American Antiquity* 68(4):641–664.

2006 Persuasive Politics and Domination at Cahokia and Moundville. In *Leadership and Polity in Mississippian Society*, edited by Brian M. Butler and Paul D. Welch, pp. 19–42. Southern Illinois University, Center for Archaeological Investigations Occasional Paper No. 33, Carbondale.

2009 Catawba Coalescence and the Shattering of the Carolina Piedmont, 1540–1675. In *Mapping the Mississippian Shatter Zone: The Colonial Indian Slave Trade and Regional Instability in the American South*, edited by Robbie Ethridge and Sheri M. Shuck-Hall, pp. 115–141. University of Nebraska Press, Lincoln.

Beck, Robin A., Jr., and David G. Moore

2002 The Burke Phase: A Mississippian Frontier in the North Carolina Foothills. *Southeastern Archaeology* 21:192–205.

Beck, Robin A., Jr., David G. Moore, and Christopher B. Rodning

2006 Identifying Fort San Juan: A Sixteenth-Century Spanish Occupation at the Berry Site, North Carolina. *Southeastern Archaeology* 25:65–77.

2011 Resisting Resistance: Juan Pardo and the Shrinking of Spanish *La Florida*, 1566–1568. In *Enduring Conquests: Rethinking the Archaeology of Resistance to Spanish Colonialism in the Americas*, edited by Matthew

Liebmann and Melissa S. Murphy, pp. 19–39. School for Advanced Research Press, Santa Fe, New Mexico.

Benedict, Ruth
1934 *Patterns of Culture*. Houghton and Mifflin, Boston.

Berkhofer, Robert F., Jr.
1971 The Political Context of a New Indian History. *Pacific Historical Review* 40:357–382.

Biella, Jan V.
1979 Changing Residential Patterns among the Anasazi, A.D. 750–1525. In *Archeological Investigations in Cochiti Reservoir, New Mexico Volume 4: Adaptive Change in the Northern Rio Grande Valley*, edited by Jan V. Biella and Richard C. Chapman, pp 103–144. OCA/UNM Report No. 101-127B. Office of Contract Archeology, University of New Mexico, Albuquerque.

Biella, Jan V., and Richard C. Chapman
1977a Survey of Cochiti Reservoir: Presentation of Data. In *Archeological Investigations in Cochiti Reservoir, New Mexico, Volume 1: A Survey of Regional Variability*, edited by Richard C. Chapman and Jan V. Biella, pp. 201–294. OCA/UNM Report No. 101-82. Office of Contract Archaeology, University of New Mexico, Albuquerque.

Biella, Jan V., and Richard C. Chapman (editors)
1977b *Archeological Investigations in Cochiti Reservoir, New Mexico, Volume 1: A Survey of Regional Variability*. OCA/UNM Report No. 101-82. Office of Contract Archeology, University of New Mexico, Albuquerque.
1979 *Archeological Investigations in Cochiti Reservoir, New Mexico Volume 4: Adaptive Change in the Northern Rio Grande Valley*. OCA/UNM Report No. 101-127B. Office of Contract Archeology, University of New Mexico, Albuquerque.

Billeck, William
2009 Traces of Coronado: Spanish Glass Beads in the Southwest and the Plains. Poster presented at the 74th Annual Meeting of the Society for American Archaeology, Atlanta.

Bird, Douglas W., and James F. O'Connell
2006 Behavioral Ecology and Archaeology. *Journal of Archaeological Research* 14:143–188.

Blair, Elliot H., Lorann S. A. Pendleton, and Peter Francis
2009 *The Beads of St. Catherines Island*. Anthropological Papers Vol. 89, American Museum of Natural History, New York.

Blakely, Robert L. (editor)
1988 *The King Site: Continuity and Contact in Sixteenth-Century Georgia*. University of Georgia Press, Athens.

Blakeslee, Donald J., Richard Flint, and Jack T. Hughes

1997 Una Barranca Grande: Recent Archaeological Evidence and a Discussion of Its Place in the Coronado Route. In *The Coronado Expedition to Tierra Nueva: The 1540–1542 Route Across the Southwest*, edited by Richard Flint and Shirley Cushing Flint, pp. 370–383. University of Colorado Press, Niwot.

Blanton, Dennis B.

2000 Drought as a Factor in the Jamestown Colony, 1606–1612. *Historical Archaeology* 34(4):74–81.

2004 The Climate Factor in Late Prehistoric and Post-Contact Human Affairs. In *Indian and European Contact in Context: The Mid-Atlantic Region*, edited by Dennis B. Blanton and Julia A. King, pp. 6–21. University Press of Florida, Gainesville.

Blanton, Dennis, and Frankie Snow

2009 Early Sixteenth-Century Spanish Activity on the Lower Ocmulgee River: New Findings and New Questions. Paper Presented at the 66th Annual Meeting of the Southeastern Archaeological Conference, Mobile, Alabama.

Blanton, Dennis B., and David Hurst Thomas

2008 Paleoclimates and Human Responses along the Central Georgia Coast: A Tree-Ring Perspective. In *Native American Landscapes of St. Catherines Island, Georgia: 2. The Data*, edited by David Hurst Thomas, pp. 799–806. Anthropological Papers No. 88. American Museum of Natural History, New York.

Blitz, John H.

1993 *Ancient Chiefdoms of the Tombigbee*. University of Alabama Press, Tuscaloosa.

1999 Mississippian Chiefdoms and the Fission-Fusion Process. *American Antiquity* 64:577–592.

Bolton, Herbert E.

1908 *Spanish Explorations in the Southwest, 1542–1706*. Barnes and Noble, New York.

1921 *The Spanish Borderlands: A Chronicle of Old Florida and the Southwest*. Yale University Press, New Haven.

1925 *The Debatable Land: A Sketch of the Anglo-Spanish Contest for the Georgia Country*. University of California, Berkeley.

1949 *Coronado, Knight of Pueblos and Plains*. Whittlesey House, New York, and University of New Mexico Press, Albuquerque.

Boone, James L.

1992 Competition, Conflict, and Development of Social Hierarchies. In *Evolutionary Ecology and Human Behavior*, edited by Eric Alden Smith and Bruce Winterhalder, pp. 301–338. Aldine de Gruyter, Hawthorne.

Bowne, Eric E.
2005 *The Westo Indians: Slave Traders of the Early Colonial South.* University of Alabama Press, Tuscaloosa.

Bradley, Raymond S., and Philip D. Jones
1995 Records of Explosive Volcanic Eruptions over the Last 500 Years. In *Climate Since A.D. 1500*, edited by Raymond S. Bradley and Phillip D. Jones, pp. 606–622. Routledge, London.

Brain, Jeffrey
1978 Review of *The Southeastern Indians* by Charles M. Hudson. *American Antiquity* 43(2):310–313.

Brain, Jeffrey, Alan Toth, and Antonio Rodríguez-Buckingham
1974 Ethnohistoric Archaeology and the De Soto Entrada into the Lower Mississippi Valley. *The Conference on Historic Site Archaeology Papers* 7:232–289.

Brandt, Elizabeth
1994 Egalitarianism, Hierarchy, and Centralization in the Pueblos. In *The Ancient Southwestern Community*, edited by W. H. Wills and Robert D. Leonard, pp. 9–23. University of New Mexico, Albuquerque.

Brasher, Nugent
2009 The Red House Camp and the Captain General: The 2009 Report on the Coronado Expedition Campsite of Chichilticale. *New Mexico Historical Review* 84:1–64.

Bratten, John R.
2009 Mesoamerican Component of the Emanuel Point Ships: Obsidian, Ceramics, and Projectile Points. *Florida Anthropologist* 62(3–4):109–114.

Braun, M., D. C. Cook, and S. Pfeiffer
1998 DNA from *Mycobacterium tuberculosis* Complex Identified in North American, Pre-Columbian Human Skeletal Remains. *Journal of Archaeological Science* 25:271–277.

Braund, Kathryn E. Holland
1993 *Deerskins and Duffels: The Creek Indian Trade with Anglo-America, 1685–1815.* University of Nebraska Press, Lincoln.

Brewer, David M., and Elizabeth A. Horvath
2004 *In Search of Lost Frenchmen: Report on the 1990 and 1995 Archeological Investigations at the Oyster Bay Site (CANA-73, 8VO3128), Canaveral National Seashore, Volusia County, Florida.* Southeast Archeological Center, Tallahassee.

Briffa, K. R., P. D. Jones, F. H. Schweingruber, and T. J. Osborn
1998 Influence of Volcanic Eruptions on Northern Hemisphere Summer Temperature Over the Past 600 Years. *Nature* 393:450–455.

Brigden, Susan
2000 *New Worlds, Lost Worlds: The Rule of the Tudors, 1485–1603.* Viking, New York.

Brooks, James F.
2002 *Cousins and Captives: Slavery, Kinship, and Community in the Southwest Borderlands.* University of North Carolina Press, Chapel Hill.

Brosch, R., S. V. Gordon, M. Marmiesse, P. Brodin, C. Buchrieser, K. Eiglmeier, T. Gutierrez, G. Hewinson, K. Kremer, L. M. Parsons, A. S. Pym, S. Samper, D. van Soolingen, and S. T. Cole
2002 A New Evolutionary Scenario for the *Mycobacterium tuberculosis* Complex. *Proceedings of the National Academy of Sciences* 99:3684–3689.

Brose, David S., C. Wesley Cowan, and Robert C. Mainfort, Jr. (editors)
2001 *Societies in Eclipse: Archaeology of the Eastern Woodlands Indians, A.D. 1400–1700.* Smithsonian Institution Press, Washington, D.C.

Burnett, Barbara A., and Katherine A. Murray
1993 Death, Drought, and de Soto: The Bioarchaeology of Depopulation. In *The Expedition of Hernando de Soto West of the Mississippi, 1541–1543,* edited by Gloria A. Young and Michael P. Hoffman, pp. 227–236. University of Arkansas Press, Fayetteville.

Bushnell, Amy Turner
1990 The Sacramental Imperative: Catholic Ritual and Indian Sedentism in the Provinces of Florida. In *Columbian Consequences, Vol. 2: Archaeological and Historical Perspectives on the Spanish Borderlands East,* edited by David Hurst Thomas, pp. 475–490. Smithsonian Institution Press, Washington, D.C.
1994 *Situado and Sabana: Spain's Support System for the Presidio and Mission Provinces of Florida.* Anthropological Papers No. 74. American Museum of Natural History, New York.

Calloway, Colin G.
1988 *New Directions in American Indian History.* University of Oklahoma Press, Norman.

Camden, William
1630 *The history of the most renowned and victorious Princess Elizabeth, late Queen of England; containing all the most important and remarkable passages of state, both at home and abroad (so far as they were linked with English affairs) during her long and prosperous reign.* N. Okes, London.

Card, Jeb, and Laura Matthew
2009 Indigenous Mesoamerican Conquerors in Central America. Paper presented at the 74th Annual Meeting of the Society for American Archaeology, Atlanta.

Carmack, Robert M., and Silvia Salgado González
2006 A World-Systems Perspective on the Archaeology and Ethnohistory of the Mesoamerican/Lower Central American Border. *Ancient Mesoamerica* 17:219–299.

Carroll, Patrick J.
2001 *Blacks in Colonial Veracruz: Race, Ethnicity, and Regional Development.* 2nd ed. University of Texas Press, Austin.

Carson, James Taylor
1999 *Searching for the Bright Path: The Mississippi Choctaws from Prehistory to Removal.* University of Nebraska Press, Lincoln.

Chacon, Richard J., and Rubén G. Mendoza (editors)
2007a *Latin American Indigenous Warfare and Ritual Violence.* University of Arizona Press, Tucson.
2007b *North American Indigenous Warfare and Ritual Violence.* University of Arizona Press, Tucson.

Chaliand, Gérard
2005 *Mirrors of a Disaster: The Spanish Military Conquest of America.* Transaction Publishers, New Brunswick, New Jersey.

Chamberlain, Robert S.
1948 *The Conquest and Colonization of Yucatan, 1517–1550.* Publication 582. Carnegie Institution of Washington, Washington, D.C.
1953 *The Conquest and Colonization of Honduras, 1502–1550.* Publication 598. Carnegie Institution of Washington, Washington, D.C.

Chapman, Richard C., and Jan V. Biella (editors)
1977 *Archeological Investigations in Cochiti Reservoir, New Mexico Volume 2: Excavation and Analysis, 1975 Season.* OCA/UNM Report No. 101-82. Office of Contract Archeology, University of New Mexico, Albuquerque.

Chapman, Richard C., and J. Robert Estes
2004 *An Assessment of Cultural Resources within a Proposed High School Site on the West Mesa of Albuquerque, Bernalillo County, New Mexico.* OCA/UNM Report No. 185-864. Office of Contract Archeology, University of New Mexico, Albuquerque.

Chapman, Richard C. and Ronald L. Stauber
2009 Rock Alignments, Isolated Sherds, and Classic Period Settlement Dynamics: A Review of Evidence for Prehistoric Agricultural Use of Albuquerque's West Mesa. Paper presented at the New Mexico Archeological Council Fall 2009 Conference, Albuquerque.

Chipman, Donald E.
1967 *Nuño de Gúzman and the Province of Panuco in New Spain 1518–1533.* Spain in the West Volume 10. Arthur H. Clark, Glendale.
1992 *Spanish Texas, 1519–1821.* University of Texas Press, Austin.

Chuchiak, John F. IV
2007 Forgotten Allies: The Origins and Roles of Native Mesoamerican Auxiliaries and Indios Conquistadores in the Conquest of Yucatan, 1526–1550. In *Indian Conquistadors: Indigenous Allies in the Conquest of*

Mesoamerica, edited by Laura E. Matthew and Michel R. Oudijk, pp. 175–225. University of Oklahoma Press, Norman.

Clayton, Lawrence A., Vernon J. Knight, Jr., and Edward C. Moore (editors)
1993 *The De Soto Chronicles: The Expedition of Hernando de Soto to North America in 1539–1543*. 2 vols. University of Alabama, Tuscaloosa.

Cleaveland, Malcolm K.
2000 A 963-Year Reconstruction of Summer (JJA) Streamflow in the White River, Arkansas, USA, from Tree-Rings. *The Holocene* 10:33–41.

Clune, John. J., and Margo S. Stringfield
2009 *Historic Pensacola*. University Press of Florida, Gainesville.

Cobb, Charles C.
2003a Mississippian Chiefdoms: How Complex? *Annual Review of Anthropology* 32:63–84.
2005 Archaeology and the "Savage Slot": Displacement and Emplacement in the Premodern World. *American Anthropologist* 107(4):563–574.

Cobb, Charles C. (editor)
2003b *Stone Tool Traditions in the Contact Era*. University of Alabama Press, Tuscaloosa.

Cobb, Charles R., and Eric Drake
2008 The Colour of Time: Head Pots and Temporal Convergences. *Cambridge Archaeological Journal* 18:85–93.

Cobb, Charles R., and Bretton Giles
2009 War is Shell: The Ideology and Embodiment of Mississippian Conflict. In *Warfare in Cultural Context: Practice, Agency, and the Archaeology of Violence,* edited by Axel E. Nielsen and William H. Walker, pp. 56–83. University of Arizona Press, Tucson.

Connelly, John C.
1979 Hopi Social Organization. In *Southwest*, edited by Alfonso Ortiz, pp. 539–553. *Handbook of North American Indians*. Vol. 9. William C. Sturtevant, General Editor, Smithsonian Institution, Washington, D.C.

Cook, Edward R., R. D. D'Arrigo, and M. E. Mann
2002 A Well-Verified, Multi-Proxy Reconstruction of the Winter North Atlantic Oscillation Index Since AD 1400. *Journal of Climate* 15:1754–1764.

Cook, E. R., and P. J. Krusic
2004 *The North American Drought Atlas*. Lamont-Doherty Earth Observatory and the National Science Foundation, New York. Electronic document, http://iridl.ldeo.columbia.edu/SOURCES/.LDEO/.TRL/.NADA2004/.pdsi-atlas.html, accessed December 11, 2009.

Cook, Edward R., U. Lall, C. Woodhouse, and D. M. Meko
2008 *North American Summer PDSI Reconstructions, Version 2a*. IGBP PAGES/World Data Center for Paleoclimatology Data Contribution Series # 2008-046. NOAA/NGDC Paleoclimatology Program, Boul-

der, Colorado. Electronic document, http://www.ncdc.noaa.gov/paleo/pdsi.html, accessed December 5, 2009.

Cook, Edward R., D. M. Meko, D. W. Stahle, and M. K. Cleaveland

1999 Drought Reconstructions for the Continental United States. *Journal of Climate* 12:1145–1162.

Cook, Edward R., Richard Seager, Mark A. Cane, and David W. Stahle

2007 North American Drought: Reconstructions, Causes, and Consequences. *Earth-Science Reviews* 81:93–134.

Cook, Edward R., Richard Seager, Richard R. Heim, Jr., Russel S. Vose, Celine Herweijer, and Connie Woodhouse

2009 Megadroughts in North America: Placing IPCC Projections of Hydroclimatic Change in a Long-term Paleoclimatic Context. *Journal of Quaternary Science* 25:48–61.

Cook, Edward R., C. A. Woodhouse, C. M. Eakin, D. M. Meko, and D. W. Stahle

2004 Long-Term Aridity Changes in the Western United States. *Science* 306:1015–1018.

Cook, Gregory C.

2009 Current Excavation on Emanuel Point II and Preliminary Comparisons with the First Emanuel Point Shipwreck. *Florida Anthropologist* 62(3–4):93–99.

Cook, Noble David

1998 *Born to Die: Disease and New World Conquest, 1492–1650*. Cambridge University Press, Cambridge.

Cook, Noble David, and W. George Lovell (editors)

1992 *Secret Judgments of God: Native Peoples and Old World Disease in Colonial Spanish America*. University of Oklahoma Press, Norman.

Cooper, Thomas

1578 *Thesaurus linguae Romanae & Britannicae*. H. Denham, London.

Cordell, Linda S. (editor)

1980 *Tijeras Canyon: Analyses of the Past*. University of New Mexico Press, Albuquerque.

Cordero, Robin M.

2007 *A Window into Landscape Use of the West Mesa: An Archeological Survey of 90 Acres at the Entrance to the Northern Geologic Window*. OCA/UNM Report No. 185-915. Office of Contract Archeology, University of New Mexico, Albuquerque.

2008 *LA 134645: Excavations at an Agricultural Production Site on Albuquerque's West Mesa, Bernalillo County, New Mexico*. OCA/UNM Report No. 185-926B. Office of Contract Archeology, University of New Mexico, Albuquerque.

Corkran, David

1962 *The Cherokee Frontier: Conflict and Survival, 1740–1762*. University of Oklahoma Press, Norman.

1967 *The Creek Frontier, 1540–1783*. University of Oklahoma Press, Norman.

Cotterill, Robert S.

1954 *The Southern Indians: The Story of the Civilized Tribes Before Removal*. University of Oklahoma Press, Norman.

Crane, Verner

1929 *The Southern Frontier, 1670–1732*. University of Michigan Press, Ann Arbor.

Creamer, Winifred

1993 *The Architecture of Arroyo Hondo Pueblo, New Mexico*. School of American Research Press, Santa Fe.

Crosby, Alfred W.

1972 *The Columbian Exchange: Biological and Cultural Consequences of 1492*. Greenwood Publishing, Westport.

1986 *Ecological Imperialism*. Cambridge University Press, Cambridge.

Crowley, Thomas J.

2000 Causes of Climate Change Over the Past 1000 Years. *Science* 289:270–276.

Cushing, Frank H.

1896 Outlines of Zuni Creation Myths. In *Thirteenth Annual Report of the Bureau of American Ethnology for the Years 1891–1892*, pp. 321–447. Smithsonian Institution, Washington, D.C.

Damp, Jonathan E.

2005 *The Battle of Hawikku, Archaeological Investigations of the Zuni-Coronado Encounter at Hawikku, the Ensuing Battle, and the Aftermath during the Summer of 1540*. Zuni Cultural Resources Enterprise Report 884, Research Series 13. Submitted to the American Battlefield Protection Program, Grant Agreement No. GA-2255-02-008, and the National Park Service Cost-Share Program, Project No. P7481 03 2003. Copies available from Zuni Cultural Resources Enterprise, Zuni.

D'Arrigo, Rosanne D., and Gordon C. Jacoby

1991 1000-Year Record of Winter Precipitation from Northwestern New Mexico, USA: A Reconstruction from Tree-rings and its Relation to El Niño and the Southern Oscillation. *The Holocene* 1:95–101.

Davidson, Robert I.

2001 *Indian River: A History of the Ais Indians in Spanish Florida*. Ais Indian Project, West Palm Beach.

Davis, W. W. H.

1869 *The Spanish Conquest of New Mexico*. Doylestown, Pennsylvania.

Day, A. Grove

1940 *Coronado's Quest: The Discovery of the Southwestern States*. University of California Press, Berkeley.

Deagan, Kathleen A.

1983 *Spanish St. Augustine: The Archaeology of a Colonial Creole Community.* Academic Press, New York.

1985 Spanish-Indian Interaction in Sixteenth-Century Florida. In *Cultures in Contact: The European Impact on Native Cultural Institutions in Eastern North America, A.D. 1000–1800*, edited by William W. Fitzhugh, pp. 281–317. Smithsonian Institution Press, Washington, D.C.

1998 Transculturation and Spanish American Ethnogenesis: The Archaeological Legacy of the Quincentenary. In *Studies in Culture Contact: Interaction, Culture Change, and Archaeology,* edited by James G. Cusick, pp. 23–43. Occasional Paper No. 25, Center for Archaeological Investigations, Southern Illinois University, Carbondale.

2008 *Historical Archaeology at the Fountain of Youth Park, St. Augustine, Florida.* Miscellaneous Project Reports in Archaeology, no. 59. Florida Museum of Natural History, Gainesville.

Deagan, Kathleen, and José María Cruxent

2002 *Columbus's Outpost among the Taínos: Spain and America at La Isabella, 1493–1498.* Yale University Press, New Haven.

Dean, Jeffrey S.

1988 A Model of Anasazi Behavioral Adaptation. In *The Anasazi in a Changing Environment*, edited by George J. Gumerman, pp. 119–167. Cambridge University Press, Cambridge.

1996 Demography, Environment, and Subsistence Stress. In *Evolving Complexity and Environmental Risk in the Prehistoric Southwest,* edited by Joseph A. Tainter and Bonnie Bagley Tainter, pp. 25–56. Santa Fe Institute Studies in the Sciences of Complexity, Proceedings Volume 24. Addison-Wesley, Reading.

2000 Complexity Theory and Sociocultural Change in the American Southwest. In *The Way the Wind Blows: Climate, History, and Human Action*, edited by Roderick J. McIntosh, Joseph A. Tainter, and Susan K. McIntosh, pp. 89–118. Columbia University Press, New York.

Debo, Angie

1934 *The Rise and Fall of the Choctaw Republic.* University of Oklahoma Press, Norman.

1941 *The Road to Disappearance: A History of the Creek Confederacy.* University of Oklahoma Press, Norman.

deMenocal, Peter B.

2001 Cultural Responses to Climate Change during the Late Holocene. *Science* 292:667–673.

DePratter, Chester B.

1983 Late Prehistoric and Early Historic Chiefdoms in the Southeastern United States. Unpublished PhD dissertation, Department of Anthropology, University of Georgia, Athens.

1994 The Chiefdom of Cofitachequi. In *The Forgotten Centuries: Indians and Europeans in the American South, 1521–1704*, edited by Charles Hudson and Carmen Chaves Tesser, pp. 197–226. University of Georgia Press, Athens.

DePratter, Chester, Charles Hudson, and Marvin T. Smith

1985 The Hernando de Soto Expedition: From Chiaha to Mabila. In *Alabama and the Borderlands: From Prehistory to Statehood*, edited by R. Reid Badger and Lawrence A. Clayton, pp. 108–127. University of Alabama Press, Tuscaloosa.

DePratter, Chester B., and Marvin T. Smith

1980 Sixteenth-Century European Trade in the Southeastern United States: Evidence from the Juan Pardo Expeditions (1566–1568). In *Spanish Colonial Frontier Research*, edited and compiled by Henry F. Dobyns, pp. 67–77. Spanish Borderlands Research 1, Center for Anthropological Studies, University of New Mexico, Albuquerque.

Dettinger, Michael D., Daniel R. Cayan, Gregory J. McCabe, and Jose A. Marengo

2000 Multiscale Streamflow Variability Associated with *El Niño*/Southern Oscillation. In *El Niño and the Southern Oscillation, Multiscale Variability and Global and Regional Impacts*, edited by Henry F. Diaz and V. Markgraf, pp. 113–148. Cambridge University Press, Cambridge.

Diamond, Jared

1999 *Guns, Germs, and Steel: The Fates of Human Societies.* W. W. Norton, New York.

Dobyns, Henry F.

1983 *Their Number Become Thinned: Native American Population Dynamics in Eastern North America.* University of Tennessee Press, Knoxville.

1992 Native American Trade Centers as Contagious Disease Foci. In *Disease and Demography in the Americas*, edited by D. H. Ubelaker and J. W. Verano, pp. 215–222. Smithsonian Institution Press, Washington, D.C.

1993 Disease Transfer at Contact. *Annual Reviews of Anthropology* 22: 273–291.

2002 Puebloan Historic Demographic Trends. *Ethnohistory* 49(1):171–204.

Dongoske, Kurt, and Larry Zimmerman

2010 Working Together on Race and Racialism in American Archaeology. *The SAA Archaeological Record* 10(3):3–4.

Doolittle, William E.

2000 *Cultivated Landscapes of Native North America.* Oxford University Press, Oxford.

Doolittle, William E., and Jonathan B. Mabry

2006 Environmental Mosaics, Agricultural Diversity, and the Evolutionary Adoption of Maize in the American Southwest. In *Histories of Maize*, edited by John E. Staller, Robert H. Tykot, and Bruce F. Benz, pp. 109–121. Academic Press/Elsevier, New York.

Drancourt, M., G. Aboudharam, M. Signoli, O. Dutour, and D. Raoult

1998 Detection of 400-Year-Old *Yersinia pestis* DNA in Human Dental Pulp: An Approach to the Diagnosis of Ancient Septicemia. *Proceedings of the National Academy of Science* 95:12637–12640.

Duff, Andrew I.

2002 *Western Pueblo Identities: Regional Interaction, Migration, and Transformation*. University of Arizona Press, Tucson.

Duncan, David Ewing

1995 *Hernando de Soto: A Savage Quest in the Americas*. Crown Publishers, New York.

Dunmire, William W.

2004 *Gardens of New Spain: How Mediterranean Plants and Food Changed America*. University of Texas Press, Austin.

Dunnell, Robert C.

1991 Methodological Impacts of Catastrophic Depopulation on American Archaeology and Ethnology. In *Columbian Consequences, Volume 3: The Spanish Borderlands in Pan-American Perspective*, edited by David Hurst Thomas, pp. 561–580. Smithsonian Institution Press, Washington, D.C.

Durkee, J. D., J. D. Frye, C. M. Fuhrmann, M. C. Lacke, H. G. Jeong, and T. L. Mote

2007 Effects of the North Atlantic Oscillation on Precipitation-Type Frequency and Distribution in the Eastern United States. *Theoretical and Applied Climatology* 94(1–2):51–65.

Dye, David H.

1990 Warfare in the Sixteenth-Century Southeast: The de Soto Expedition in the Interior. In *Columbian Consequences, Volume 2: Archaeological and Historical Perspectives on the Spanish Borderlands East*, edited by David Hurst Thomas, pp. 211–222. Smithsonian Institution Press, Washington, D.C.

1993 Reconstruction of the de Soto Expedition Route in Arkansas: The Mississippi Alluvial Plain. In *The Expedition of Hernando de Soto West of the Mississippi, 1541–1543*, edited by Gloria A. Young and Michael P. Hoffman, pp. 36–57. University of Arkansas Press, Fayetteville.

1994 The Art of War in the Sixteenth-Century Central Mississippi Valley. In *Perspectives on the Southeast: Linguistics, Archaeology, and Ethnohistory*, edited by Patricia B. Kwachka, pp. 44–60. Southern Anthropological Society Proceedings No. 27, University of Georgia Press, Athens.

1995 Feasting with the Enemy: Mississippian Warfare and Prestige-Goods Circulation. In *Native American Interactions: Multiscalar Analyses and*

Interpretations in the Eastern Woodlands, edited by Michael S. Nassaney and Kenneth E. Sassaman, pp. 289–316. University of Tennessee Press, Knoxville.

2002 Warfare in the Protohistoric Southeast, 1500–1700. In *Between Contacts and Colonies: Archaeological Perspectives on the Protohistoric Southeast*, edited by Cameron B. Wesson and Mark A. Rees, pp. 126–141. University of Alabama Press, Tuscaloosa.

2004 Art, Ritual, and Chiefly Warfare in the Mississippian World. In *Hero, Hawk, and Open Hand: Ancient Indian Art of the Midwest and Southeast*, edited by Richard F. Townsend, pp. 191–205. Yale University Press, New Haven, Connecticut.

2007 Ritual, Medicine, and the War Trophy Iconographic Theme in the Mississippian Southeast. In *Ancient Objects and Sacred Realms: Interpretations of Mississippian Iconography*, edited by F. Kent Reilly III, pp. 152–173. University of Texas Press, Austin.

2009 *War Paths, Peace Paths: An Archaeology of Cooperation and Conflict in Native Eastern North America*. AltaMira Press, Walnut Creek, California.

Earle, Timothy K.

1987 Chiefdoms in Archaeological and Ethnohistoric Perspective. *Annual Review of Anthropology* 16:279–308.

Ebright, Malcolm, and Rick Hendricks

2006 *The Witches of Abiquiu: The Governor, the Priest, the Genízaro Indians, and the Devil*. University of New Mexico Press, Albuquerque.

Echo-Hawk, Roger

2000 Ancient History in the New World: Integrating Oral Traditions and the Archaeological Record in Deep Time. *American Antiquity* 65:267–290.

Eddy, John A.

1981 Climate and the Role of the Sun. In *Climate and History: Studies in Interdisciplinary History*, edited by Robert I. Rotberg and Theodore K. Rabb, pp.145–167. Princeton University Press, Princeton.

Eggan, Frederick

1950 *Social Organization of the Western Pueblos*. University of Chicago Press, Chicago.

1964 Alliance and Descent in a Western Pueblo Society. In *Process and Pattern in Culture*, edited by Robert A. Manners, pp. 175–184. University of Chicago Press, Chicago.

Ellis, Florence H.

1951 Patterns of Aggression and the War Cult in Southwestern Pueblos. *Southwestern Journal of Anthropology* 7:177–201.

1987 The Long Lost "City" of San Gabriel del Yungue, Second Oldest European Settlement in the United States. In *When Cultures Meet: Remembering San Gabriel del Yungue Oweenge*, pp. 10–38. Sunstone Press, Santa Fe.

1989 *San Gabriel del Yungue as Seen by an Archaeologist.* Sunstone Press, Santa Fe.

Eltis, David

1995 *The Military Revolution in Sixteenth-Century Europe.* I.B. Tauris Publishers, New York.

Elvas, Gentleman of

1993 True Relation of the Hardships Suffered by Governor Hernando de Soto and Certain Portuguese Gentlemen during the Discovery of the Province of Florida. In *The De Soto Chronicles: The Expedition of Hernando de Soto to North America in 1539–1543,* Vol. I, edited by Lawrence A. Clayton, Vernon J. Knight, Jr., and Edward C. Moore, pp. 25–219. University of Alabama Press, Tuscaloosa.

Espinosa, José M.

1988 *The Pueblo Revolt of 1696 and the Franciscan Missions of New Mexico.* University of New Mexico Press, Albuquerque.

Ethridge, Robbie

2003 *Creek Country: The Creek Indians and Their World.* University of North Carolina Press, Chapel Hill.

2006 Creating the Shatter Zone: The Indian Slave Trader and the Collapse of the Mississippian World. In *Light on the Path: The Anthropology and History of the Southeastern Indians,* edited by Thomas J. Pluckhahn and Robbie Ethridge, pp. 207–218. University of Alabama Press, Tuscaloosa.

2009a Introduction: Mapping the Mississippian Shatter Zone. In *Mapping the Mississippian Shatter Zone: The Colonial Indian Slave Trade and Regional Instability in the American South,* edited by Robbie Ethridge and Sheri M. Shuck-Hall, pp. 1–62. University of Nebraska Press, Lincoln.

2009b Afterword: Some Thoughts on Further Work. In *Mapping the Mississippian Shatter Zone: The Colonial Indian Slave Trade and Regional Instability in the American South,* edited by Robbie Ethridge and Sheri M. Shuck-Hall, pp. 418–424. University of Nebraska Press, Lincoln.

2010 *From Chicaza to Chickasaw: The European Invasion and the Transformation of the Mississippian World, 1540–1715.* University of North Carolina Press, Chapel Hill.

Ethridge, Robbie, and Charles Hudson

1998 The Early Historic Transformation of the Southeastern Indians. In *Cultural Diversity in the US South: Anthropological Contributions to a Region in Transition,* edited by Patricia D. Beaver and Carole E. Hill, pp. 34–50. Proceedings of the Southern Anthropological Society No. 31, University of Georgia Press, Athens.

Ethridge, Robbie, and Charles Hudson (editors)

2002 *The Transformation of the Southeastern Indians, 1540–1760*. The University Presses of Mississippi, Jackson.

Ethridge, Robbie, Kathyrn E. Holland Braund, Lawrence A. Clayton, George E. Lankford, and Michael D. Murphy

2009 A Comparative Analysis of the De Soto Accounts on the Route to, and Events at, Mabila. In *The Search for Mabila: The Decisive Battle between Hernando de Soto and Chief Tascalusa*, Edited by Vernon James Knight, Jr., pp. 153–181. University of Alabama Press, Tuscaloosa.

Ethridge, Robbie, and Sheri M. Shuck-Hall (editors)

2009 *Mapping the Mississippian Shatter Zone: The Colonial Indian Slave Trade and Regional Instability in the American South*. University of Nebraska Press, Lincoln.

Ewen, Charles

1990 Soldier of Fortune: Hernando de Soto in the Territory of the Apalachee, 1539–1540. In *Columbian Consequences, Volume 2: Archaeological and Historical Perspectives on the Spanish Borderlands East*, edited by David Hurst Thomas, pp. 83–91. Smithsonian Institution Press, Washington, D.C.

1996 Continuity and Change: De Soto and the Apalachee. *Historical Archaeology* 30(2):41–53.

Ewen, Charles R., and John H. Hann

1998 *Hernando de Soto among the Apalachee: The Archaeology of the First Winter Encampment*. University Press of Florida, Gainesville.

Fagan, Brian M.

2001 *The Little Ice Age: How Climate Made History, 1300–1850*. Basic Books, New York.

Feng, S., R. J. Ogleby, C. M. Rowe, D. B. Looper, and Q. Hu

2008 Atlantic and Pacific SST Influences on Medieval Drought in North America Simulated by the Community Atmospheric Model. *Journal of Geophysical Research* 113:D11101, doi:10.1029/2007JD009347. Electronic document, http://www.agu.org/pubs/crossref/2008/2007JD009347.shtml, accessed August 11, 2009.

Ferguson, R. Brian, and Neil L. Whitehead (editors)

1992 *War in the Tribal Zone: Expanding States and Indigenous Warfare*. School of American Research Advanced Seminar Series, School of American Research Press, Santa Fe.

Ferguson, Thomas J.

2002 Dowa Yalanne: The Architecture of Zuni Resistance and Social Change during the Pueblo Revolt. In *Archaeologies of the Pueblo Revolt: Identity, Meaning, and Renewal in the Pueblo World*, edited by Robert W. Preucel, pp. 33–44. University of New Mexico Press, Albuquerque.

Ferguson, Thomas J., and E. Richard Hart
1985 *A Zuni Atlas*. University of Oklahoma Press, Norman.

Fernández de Oviedo, Gonzalo
2006 *Writing from the Edge of the World: The Memoirs of Darién, 1514–1527*. Translated by G. F. Dille. University of Alabama Press, Tuscaloosa.

Fewkes, Jesse W.
1891 Reconnaissance of Ruins in or Near the Zuni Reservation. *Journal of American Ethnology and Archaeology* 1(3):93–133.

Fiorato, V., A. Boylston, and Chrisopher Knüsel
2000 *Blood Red Roses: The Archaeology of a Mass Grave from the Battle of Towton, A.D. 1461*. Oxbow Books, Oxford.

Fish, Carl R.
1978 Relation of Archaeology and History. In *Historical Archaeology: A Guide to Substantive and Theoretical Contributions*, edited by Robert L. Schuyler, pp. 11–15. Baywood Publishing Company, Farmingdale, New York.

Fitts, Mary Elizabeth, and Charles L. Heath
2009 "Indians Refusing to Carry Burdens": Understanding the Success of Catawba Political, Military, and Settlement Strategies in Colonial Carolina. In *Mapping the Mississippian Shatter Zone: The Colonial Indian Slave Trade and Regional Instability in the American South*, edited by Robbie Ethridge and Sheri M. Shuck-Hall, pp. 142–161. University of Nebraska Press, Lincoln.

Fitzhugh, William W. (editor)
1985 *Cultures in Contact: The European Impact on Native Cultural Institutions in Eastern North America, A.D. 1000–1800*. Smithsonian Institution Press, Washington, D.C.

Fixico, Donald (editor)
1997 *Rethinking American Indian History*. University of New Mexico Press, Albuquerque.

Flannery, Kent V.
1972 The Cultural Evolution of Civilizations. *Annual Review of Ecology and Systematics* 3:399–426.

Flint, Richard
1992 The Pattern of Coronado Expedition Material Culture: A Thesis. Unpublished MA Thesis, Department of Behavioral Sciences, New Mexico Highlands University, Las Vegas.
1997 *Armas de la Tierra*: The Mexican Indian Component of Coronado Expedition Material Culture. In *The Coronado Expedition to Tierra Nueva: The 1540–1542 Route Across the Southwest*, edited by Richard Flint and Shirley Cushing Flint, pp. 57–70. University of Colorado Press, Niwot.

2002 *Great Cruelties Have Been Reported. The 1544 Investigation of the Coronado Expedition*. Southern Methodist University Press, Dallas.

2003 What's Missing from this Picture? The *Alarde*, or Muster Roll, of the Coronado Expedition. In *The Coronado Expedition from the Distance of 460 Years*, edited by Richard Flint and Shirley Cushing Flint, pp. 57–80. University of New Mexico Press, Albuquerque.

2005 What They Never Told You about the Coronado Expedition. *Kiva* 71:203–217.

2008 *No Settlement, No Conquest: A History of the Coronado Entrada*. University of New Mexico Press, Albuquerque.

2009 Without Them, Nothing Was Possible: The Coronado Expedition's Indian Allies. *New Mexico Historical Review* 84(1):65–118.

Flint, Richard, and Shirley Cushing Flint

2011 Guido de Lavezariis: The Life of a Financier of the Coronado and Villalobos Expeditions. *New Mexico Historical Review* 86(1):1–19.

Flint, Richard, and Shirley Cushing Flint (editors)

2003 *The Coronado Expedition from the Distance of 460 Years*. University of New Mexico Press, Albuquerque.

Flint, Richard, and Shirley Cushing Flint (editors and translators)

2005 *Documents of the Coronado Expedition, 1539–1542. "They Were Not Familiar with His Majesty, nor Did They Wish to Be His Subjects."* Southern Methodist University Press, Dallas.

Flint, Shirley Cushing

2002 Putting Faces on the Coronado Expedition, Part 1. Paper presented at the 50th Anniversary of the Coronado National Memorial, Hereford.

Ford, Richard I.

2009 Maatu'in on the Move. Paper presented at the New Mexico Archaeological Council 2009 Fall Conference, November 14, 2009.

Foreman, Grant

1932 *Indian Removal: The Emigration of the Five Civilized Tribes of Indians*. University of Oklahoma, Norman.

Foster, George

1960 *Culture and Conquest*. Quadrangle Books, Chicago.

Fowles, Severin M.

2004 Tewa versus Tiwa: Northern Rio Grande Settlement Patterns and Social History, A.D. 1275 to 1540. In *The Protohistoric Pueblo World, A.D. 1275–1600*, edited by E. Charles Adams and Andrew I. Duff, pp. 17–25. University of Arizona Press, Tucson.

Francis, J. Michael, and Kathleen M. Kole

2011 *Murder and Martyrdom in Spanish Florida: Don Juan and the Guale Uprising of 1597*. Anthropological Papers No.95, American Museum of Natural History, New York.

Fraser, Walter J., Jr.
2006 *Lowcountry Hurricanes: Three Centuries of Storms at Sea and Ashore.* University of Georgia Press, Athens.

Fritts, Harold C.
1976 *Tree Rings and Climate.* Academic Press, New York.

Fritts, Harold C., David G. Smith, and Marvin A. Stokes
1965 The Biological Model for Paleoclimatic Interpretation of Mesa Verde Tree-Ring Series. *American Antiquity* 31:101–121.

Fritz, Curtis L., David T. Dennis, Margaret A. Tipple, Grant L. Campbell, Charles R. McCance, and Duane J. Gubler
1996 Surveillance for Pneumonic Plague in the United States during an International Emergency: A Model for Control of Imported Infectious Diseases. *Emerging Infectious Diseases* 2:30–36.

Gallay, Alan
2003 *The Indian Slave Trade: The Rise of the English Empire in the American South, 1670–1717.* Yale University Press, New Haven.
2006 Beachheads into Empires, Villages into Confederacies: Atlantic World Trade and the Transformation of the American South. Paper presented at Transformations: The Atlantic World in the Late Seventeenth Century, Harvard University, Cambridge.

Gallivan, Martin D.
2003 *James River Chiefdoms: The Rise of Social Inequality in the Chesapeake.* University of Nebraska Press, Lincoln.
2007 Powhatan's Werowocomoco: Constructing Place, Polity, and Personhood in the Chesapeake, C.E. 1200–C.E. 1609. *American Anthropologist* 109:85–100.

Galloway, Patricia K.
1991 The Archaeology of the Ethnohistoric Narrative. In *Columbian Consequences, Volume 3: The Spanish Borderlands in Pan-American Perspective,* edited by David Hurst Thomas, pp. 453–470. Smithsonian Institution Press, Washington, D.C.
1993 Ethnohistory. In *The Development of Southeastern Archaeology,* edited by Jay Johnson, pp. 78–108. University of Alabama Press, Tuscaloosa.
1995 *Choctaw Genesis 1500–1700.* University of Nebraska Press, Lincoln.
1997a Conjoncture and Longue Durée: History, Anthropology, and the Hernando de Soto Expedition. In *The Hernando de Soto Expedition: History, Historiography, and "Discovery" in the Southeast,* edited by Patricia Galloway, pp. 283–294. University of Nebraska Press, Lincoln.
1997b The Incestuous Soto Narratives. In *The Hernando de Soto Expedition: History, Historiography, and "Discovery" in the Southeast,* edited by Patricia Galloway, pp. 11–44. University of Nebraska, Lincoln.
2006 *Practicing Ethnohistory: Mining Archives, Hearing Testimony, Constructing Narrative.* University of Nebraska, Lincoln.

Galloway, Patricia (editor)

1997c *The Hernando de Soto Expedition: History, Historiography, and "Discovery" in the Southeast.* University of Nebraska Press, Lincoln.

Gannon, Michael V.

1965 *The Cross in the Sand: The Early Catholic Church in Florida, 1513–1870.* University of Florida Press, Gainesville.

Garcilaso de la Vega

1993 La Florida. In *The De Soto Chronicles: The Expedition of Hernando de Soto to North America in 1539–1543,* Vol. 2, edited by Lawrence A. Clayton, Vernon J. Knight, Jr., and Edward C. Moore, translated by James Robertson, pp. 25–559. University of Alabama Press, Tuscaloosa.

Gaspar, David B., and Darlene C. Hine (editors)

1996 *More than Chattel: Black Women and Slavery in the Americas.* Indiana University Press, Bloomington.

Gergis, J. L., and A. M. Fowler

2006 How Unusual Was Late 20th-Century *El Niño*-Southern Oscillation (ENSO)? Assessing Evidence from Tree-Ring, Coral, Ice-Core, and Documentary Paleoarchives, A.D. 1525–2002. *Advances in Geosciences* 6:173–179.

Gerhard, Peter

1978 A Black Conquistador in Mexico. *Hispanic American Historical Review* 58(3):451–459.

1982 *The North Frontier of New Spain.* Revised ed. University of Oklahoma Press, Norman.

Gerónimo de Oré, Luis

1937 *The Martyrs of Florida (1513–1616).* Translated by Maynard Geiger. Franciscan Studies 18. Joseph W. Wagner, New York.

Gerow, Peggy A., and William H. Doleman

2002 *Across the Caja Del Rio Plateau: Hunters and Farmers in the Northern Rio Grande; A Class III Inventory of the NMARNG Camel Tracks Training Site, Santa Fe County, New Mexico.* OCA/UNM Report No. 185-688. Office of Contract Archeology, University of New Mexico, Albuquerque.

Gerow, Peggy A., and Patrick Hogan (editors)

2005 *Across the Caja Del Rio Plateau III: Hunters and Farmers in the Northern Rio Grande; Archeological Investigations at 10 Sites in the NMARNG Camel Tracks Training Area, Santa Fe County, New Mexico.* OCA/UNM Report No. 185-845. Office of Contract Archeology, University of New Mexico, Albuquerque.

Gerow, Peggy A., and Alexander Kurota

2004 *Across the Caja Del Rio Plateau II: Hunters and Farmers in the Northern Rio Grande; Archeological Investigations at 15 Sites in the NMARNG Camel Tracks Training Area, Santa Fe County, New Mexico.* OCA/

UNM Report No. 185-790. Office of Contract Archeology, University of New Mexico, Albuquerque.

Gibson, Charles

1952 *Tlaxcala in the Sixteenth Century*. Yale University Press, New Haven.

Gottfried, Robert S.

1983 *The Black Death: Natural and Human Disaster in Medieval Europe*. Free Press, New York.

Granberry, Julian

1993 *A Grammar and Dictionary of the Timucua Language*. University of Alabama Press, Tuscaloosa.

Gregg, Charles T.

1978 *Plague!: The Shocking Story of a Dread Disease in America Today*. Charles Scribner's Sons, New York.

Grissino-Mayer, Henri D.

1995 The Climate and Fire History of El Malpais National Monument, New Mexico. Unpublished PhD Dissertation, Department of Geosciences, University of Arizona, Tucson.

1996 A 2,129-Year Reconstruction of Precipitation for Northwestern New Mexico, USA. In *Tree Rings, Environment, and Humanity*, edited by Jeffrey S. Dean, David M. Meko, and Thomas W. Swetnam, pp. 191–204. Department of Geosciences, University of Arizona, Tucson.

Grissino-Mayer, Henri D., Christopher H. Baisan, Kiyomi A. Morino, and Thomas W. Swetnam

2002 *Multi-Century Trends in Past Climate for the Middle Rio Grande Basin, A.D. 622–1992*. Final Report Submitted to the USDA Forest Service, Rocky Mountain Research Station, Albuquerque, Laboratory of Tree-Ring Research Report 2000/6, Laboratory of Tree-Ring Research, University of Arizona, Tucson.

Gutiérrez, Ramón A.

1991 *When Jesus Came, the Corn Mothers Went Away: Marriage, Sexuality, and Power in New Mexico, 1500–1846*. Stanford University Press, Stanford.

Hackett, Charles Wilson (editor and translator)

1923–1937 *Historical Documents Relating to New Mexico, Nueva Vizcaya, and Approaches Thereto, to 1773*. 3 vols, collected by Adolph F. A. Bandelier and Fanny R. Bandelier. Carnegie Institution of Washington, Washington, D.C.

Hackett, Charles W., and Charmion C. Shelby (translators)

1942 *Revolt of the Pueblo Indians of New Mexico and Otermin's Attempted Reconquest, 1680–1682*. University of New Mexico Press, Albuquerque.

Hahn, Steven

2004a *The Invention of the Creek Nation*. University of Nebraska Press, Lincoln.

2004b New Paths Beaten: Verner Crane's The Southern Frontier, 1670–1732. In *The Southern Frontier*, by Verner Crane, pp. xv–vii. University of Alabama, Tuscaloosa.

Hakluyt, Richard

1969 [1589–1600] *The Principal Navigations, Voyages, Traffiques and Discoveries of the English Nation. Made by Sea or Over-land to the Remote and Farthest Distant Quarters of the Earth at Any Time Within the Compasse of these 1600 Yeeres. Made to the South and South-east Quarters of the World, and the Voyages Undertaken for the Finding of a Northwest Passage, with the Directions, Letters, Privileges, Discourses and Observations Incident to the Same. Seventh Volume.* Bishop and Ralph Newberie, London. 1969 facsimile ed., Volume IX, Augustus M. Kelley Publishers, New York.

Hall, Bert S.

1997 *Weapons and Warfare in Renaissance Europe: Gunpowder, Technology, and Tactics.* Johns Hopkins University Press, Baltimore.

Hall, Joseph M.

2009 *Zamumo's Gift: Indian-European Exchange in the Colonial Southeast, 1400–1735.* University of Pennsylvania Press, Philadelphia.

Hally, David J.

1979 *Archaeological Investigation of the Little Egypt Site (9Mu102), Murray County, Georgia, 1969 Season.* Laboratory of Archaeology Series Report No. 18, University of Georgia, Athens.

1980 *Archaeological Investigation of the Little Egypt Site (9Mu102), Murray County, Georgia, 1970–72 Seasons.* Laboratory of Archaeology, University of Georgia, Athems. Submitted to Heritage Conservation and Recreation Service, US Department of the Interior, Contract Nos. 14-10-9-900-390, 1910P21041, 9911T000411, and C5546. Copies available from Laboratory of Archaeology, University of Georgia, Athens.

1993 The Territorial Size of Mississippian Chiefdoms. In *Archaeology of Eastern North America: Papers in Honor of Stephen Williams,* edited by James B. Stoltman, pp. 143–168. Archeological Report No. 25, Mississippi Department of Archives and History, Jackson.

1994 The Chiefdom of Coosa. In *The Forgotten Centuries: Indians and Europeans in the American South, 1521–1704,* edited by Charles Hudson and Carmen Chaves Tesser, pp. 227–253. University of Georgia Press, Athens.

1996 Platform Mound Construction and the Instability of Mississippian Chiefdoms. In *Political Structure and Change in the Prehistoric Southeastern United States,* edited by John F. Scarry, pp. 92–127. University Press of Florida, Gainesville.

2006 The Nature of Mississippian Regional Systems. In *Light on the Path: The Anthropology and History of the Southeastern Indians,* edited by

Thomas H. Pluckhahn and Robbie Ethridge, pp. 26–42. University of Alabama Press, Tuscaloosa.

2008 *King: The Social Archaeology of a Late Mississippian Town in Northwestern Georgia*. University of Alabama Press, Tuscaloosa.

Hally, David J., Marvin T. Smith, and James B. Langford, Jr.

1990 The Archaeological Reality of de Soto's Coosa. In *Columbian Consequences, Vol. 2: Archaeological and Historical Perspectives on the Spanish Borderlands East*, edited by David Hurst Thomas, pp. 121–138. Smithsonian Institution Press, Washington, D.C.

Hammond, George P., and Agapito Rey (editors and translators)

1940 *Narratives of the Coronado Expedition, 1540–1542*. University of New Mexico Press, Albuquerque.

1953 *Don Juan de Oñate: Colonizer of New Mexico, 1595–1628*. 2 vols. Coronado Cuarto Centennial Publications II. University of New Mexico Press, Albuquerque.

1966 *The Rediscovery of New Mexico 1580–1594: The Explorations of Chamuscado, Espejo, Castaño de Sosa, Morlete, and Leyva de Bonilla and Humaña*. Coronado Cuarto Centennial Publications, 1540–1940, Vol. III. University of New Mexico Press, Albuquerque.

1967 *Expedition into New Mexico Made by Antonio de Espejo 1582–1583 as Revealed in the Journal of Diego Pérez de Luxán, A Member of the Party*. Reprinted Arno Press, New York. Originally published 1929, Quivira Society Publications, Volume I, The Quivira Society, Los Angeles.

Hann, John H.

1986 Translation of Governor Rebolledo's 1657 Visitation of Three Florida Provinces and Related Documents. *Florida Archaeology* 2:81–145.

1988 *Apalachee: The Land between the Rivers*. University Presses of Florida, Gainesville.

1991 *Missions to the Calusa*. University Presses of Florida, Gainesville.

1993a The Mayaca and Jororo and Missions to Them. In *The Spanish Missions of La Florida*, edited by Bonnie G. McEwan, pp. 111–140. University Press of Florida, Gainesville.

1993b Visitations and Revolts in Florida, 1656–1695. *Florida Archaeology* 7.

1994 The Apalachee of the Historic Era. In *The Forgotten Centuries: Indians and Europeans in the American South, 1521–1704*, edited by Charles M. Hudson and Carmen Chaves Tesser, pp. 327–354. University of Georgia Press, Athens.

1996 *A History of the Timucua Indians and Missions*. University Press of Florida, Gainesville.

2003 *Indians of Central and South Florida, 1513–1763*. University Press of Florida, Gainesville.

2006 *The Native American World beyond Apalachee: West Florida and the Chattahoochee Valley*. University Press of Florida, Gainesville.

Hann, John H., and Bonnie G. McEwan

1998 *The Apalachee Indians and Mission San Luis.* University Press of Florida, Gainesville.

Harn, Alan D.

1978 Mississippian Settlement Patterns in the Central Illinois River Valley. In *Mississippian Settlement Patterns,* edited by Bruce D. Smith, pp. 233–268. Academic Press, New York.

Hassig, Ross

1988 *Aztec Warfare: Imperial Expansion and Political Control.* University of Oklahoma Press, Norman.

2006 *Mexico and the Spanish Conquest.* 2nd ed. University of Oklahoma Press, Norman.

Hays, J. N.

1998 *The Burdens of Disease: Epidemics and Human Response in Western History.* Rutgers University Press, New Brunswick, New Jersey.

Hernández de Biedma, Luys

1993 Relation of the Island of Florida. In *The De Soto Chronicles: The Expedition of Hernando de Soto to North America in 1539–1543,* Vol. 1, edited by Lawrence A. Clayton, Vernon J. Knight, Jr., and Edward C. Moore, pp. 221–246. Translated by John E. Worth. University of Alabama Press, Tuscaloosa.

Hill, J. Brett, Jeffery J. Clark, William H. Doelle, and Patrick D. Lyons

2004 Prehistoric Demography in the Southwest: Migration, Coalescence, and Hohokam Population Decline. *American Antiquity* 69(4):689–716.

Himmerlich y Valencia, Robert

1998 The 1536 Siege of Cuzco: An Analysis of Inca and Spanish Warfare. *Colonial Latin American Historical Review* 7(4):387–418.

Hodge, Frederick W.

1918 Excavations at the Zuni Pueblo of Hawikuh in 1917. *Art and Archaeology* 7(9):367–379.

1937 *History of Hawikuh, New Mexico: One of the So-Called Cities of Cibola.* Frederick W. Hodge Anniversary Publication 1. Southwest Museum. Ward Ritchie Press, Los Angeles.

Hodge, Frederick W., George P. Hammond, and Agapito Rey

1945 *Fray Alonso de Benavides' Memorial of 1634.* University of New Mexico Press, Albuquerque.

Hoffman, Paul E.

1980 A New Voyage of North American Discovery: Pedro de Salazar's Visit to the "Island of Giants." *Florida Historical Quarterly* 58(4):415–426.

1990 *A New Andalucia and a Way to the Orient: The American Southeast during the Sixteenth Century.* Louisiana State University Press, Baton Rouge.

1992 Lucas Vázquez de Ayllón. In *Columbus and the Land of Ayllón: The Exploration and Settlement of the Southeast*, edited by Jeannine Cook, pp. 27–49. Lower Altamaha Historical Society, Darien, Georgia.

1994a Lucas Vázquez de Ayllón's Discovery and Colony. In *The Forgotten Centuries: Indians and Europeans in the American South, 1521–1704*, edited by Charles Hudson and Carmen Chaves Tesser, pp. 36–49. University of Georgia Press, Athens.

1994b Narváez and Cabeza de Vaca in Florida. In *The Forgotten Centuries: Indians and Europeans in the American South, 1521–1704*, edited by Charles Hudson and Carmen Chaves Tesser, pp. 50–73. University of Georgia Press, Athens.

2001 *Florida's Frontiers*. Indiana University Press, Bloomington.

2004 *A New Andalucia and a Way to the Orient: The American Southeast during the Sixteenth Century*. Louisiana State University Press, Baton Rouge.

Hogue, S. Homes, and Evan Peacock

1995 Environmental and Osteological Analysis at the South Farm Site (22OK534), a Mississippian Farmstead in Oktibbeha County, Mississippi. *Southeastern Archaeology* 14(1):31–45.

Hordes, Stanley M.

1989 The Historical Context of LA 54147. In *A Sixteenth-Century Spanish Campsite in the Tiguex Province*, edited by Bradley J. Vierra, pp. 207–221. Laboratory of Anthropology Note No. 475. Research Section, Museum of New Mexico, Santa Fe.

Horsman, Reginald

1979 Recent Trends and New Directions in Native American History. In *The American West: New Perspectives, New Dimensions*, edited by Jerome O. Steffen, pp. 124–151. University of Oklahoma Press, Norman.

Hudson, Charles M., Jr.

1974 The Historical Approach in Anthropology. In *Handbook of Social and Cultural Anthropology*, edited by John J. Honigmann, pp. 111–141. Rand McNally College Publishing Company, New York.

1976 *The Southeastern Indians*. University of Tennessee Press, Knoxville.

1990 *The Juan Pardo Expeditions: Exploration of the Carolinas and Tennessee, 1566–1568*. Smithsonian Institution Press, Washington, D.C.

1993 Research on the Early Southeast: Retrospective and Prospective. Presidential Address, American Society of Ethnohistory Annual Meeting, Bloomington, IN.

1994 The Hernando de Soto Expedition, 1539–1543. In *The Forgotten Centuries: Indians and Europeans in the American South, 1521–1704*, edited by Charles Hudson and Carmen C. Tesser, pp. 74–103. University of Georgia Press, Athens.

1997 *Knights of Spain, Warriors of the Sun: Hernando de Soto and the South's Ancient Chiefdoms.* University of Georgia Press, Athens.

2002 Introduction. In *The Transformation of the Southeastern Indians, 1540–1760,* edited by Robbie Ethridge and Charles Hudson, pp. xi–xix. University Press of Mississippi, Jackson.

2005 *The Juan Pardo Expeditions: Explorations of the Carolinas and Tennessee, 1566–1568.* University of Alabama Press, Tuscaloosa.

Hudson, Charles, Robin A. Beck, Jr., Chester B. DePratter, Robbie Ethridge, and John E. Worth

2008 On Interpreting Cofitachequi. *Ethnohistory* 55(3):465–490.

Hudson, Charles, Marvin T. Smith, and Chester B. DePratter

1990 The Hernando de Soto Expedition: From Mabila to the Mississippi River. In *Towns and Temples along the Mississippi,* edited by David H. Dye and Cheryl Anne Cox, pp. 181–207. University of Alabama Press, Tuscaloosa.

Hudson, Charles, Marvin T. Smith, Chester B. DePratter, and Emilia Kelley

1989 The Tristán de Luna Expedition, 1559–1561. *Southeastern Archaeology* 8(1):31–45.

1991 The Tristan de Luna Expedition, 1559–1561. In *First Encounters: Spanish Explorations in the Caribbean and the United States, 1492–1570,* edited by Jerald T. Milanich and Susan Milbrath, pp. 119–134. University of Florida Press, Gainesville.

Hudson, Charles, Marvin Smith, David Hally, Richard Polhemus, and Chester DePratter

1985 Coosa: A Chiefdom in the Sixteenth-Century Southeastern United States. *American Antiquity* 50(4):723–737.

Hudson, Charles, and Carmen Chaves Tesser (editors)

1994 *The Forgotten Centuries: Indians and Europeans in the American South, 1521–1704.* University of Georgia Press, Athens.

Hughes, Malcolm, K., and P. M. Brown

1992 Drought Frequency in Central California since 101 B.C. Recorded in Giant Sequoia Tree Rings. *Climatic Dynamics* 6:161–167.

Hutchinson, Dale L.

1990 Postcontact Biocultural Change: Mortuary Site Evidence. In *Columbian Consequences, Volume 2: Archaeological and Historical Perspectives on the Spanish Borderlands East,* edited by David Hurst Thomas, pp. 61–70. Smithsonian Institution Press, Washington, D.C.

2006 *Tatham Mound and the Bioarchaeology of Spanish Contact: Disease and Depopulation in Gulf Coast Florida.* University Press of Florida, Gainesville.

Hutchinson, Dale L., and Lorraine V. Aragon

2002 Collective Burials and Community Memories: Interpreting the Placement of the Dead in the Southeastern and Mid-Atlantic United States with Reference to Ethnographic Cases from Indonesia. In *The Space and Place of Death*, edited by Helaine Silverman and David B. Small, pp. 27–54. Archeological Papers of the American Anthropological Association No. 11, Washington, D.C.

Hutchinson, Dale L., and Clark S. Larsen

1988 Determination of Stress Episode Duration from Linear Enamel Hypoplasias: A Case Study from St. Catherines Island, Georgia. *Human Biology* 601:93–110.

1990 Stress and Lifeway Change on the Georgia Coast: The Evidence from Enamel Hypoplasia. In *The Archaeology of Mission Santa Catalina de Guale: Biocultural Interpretations of a Population in Transition*, edited by C. S. Larsen, pp. 50–65. Anthropological Papers of the American Museum of Natural History No. 2, American Museum of Natural History, New York.

2001 Enamel Hypoplasia and Stress in North Florida. In *Bioarchaeology of Spanish Florida: The Impact of Colonialism*, edited by Clark Spencer Larsen, pp. 181–206. University Press of Florida, Gainesville.

Hutchinson, Dale L., Clark S. Larsen, Lynette Norr, and Margaret J. Schoeninger

2000 Agricultural Melodies and Alternative Harmonies in Florida and Georgia. In *Bioarchaeological Studies of Life in the Age of Agriculture: A View from the Southeast*, edited by P. M. Lambert, pp. 96–115. University of Alabama Press, Tuscaloosa.

Hutchinson, Dale L., Clark S. Larsen, Margaret J. Schoeninger, and Lynette Norr

1998 Regional Variation in the Pattern of Maize Adoption and Use in Florida and Georgia. *American Antiquity* 63(3):397–416.

Hutchinson, Dale L., and Jeffrey M. Mitchem

2001 Correlates of Contact: Epidemic Disease in Archaeological Context. *Historical Archaeology* 35(2):58–72.

Alva Ixtlilxochitl, Fernando de

1969 *Ally of Cortes. Account 13: Of the Coming of the Spaniards and the Beginning of Evangelical Law.* Douglas K. Ballentine (translator). Texas Western Press, El Paso.

Jackson, Jason Baird

2003 *Yuchi Ceremonial Life*. University of Nebraska Press, Lincoln.

Jenkins, Ned

2009 Tracing the Origins of the Early Creeks, 1050–1700 C.E. In *Mapping the Mississippian Shatter Zone: The Colonial Indian Slave Trade and Regional Instability in the American South*, edited by Robbie Ethridge and Sheri M. Shuck-Hall, pp. 188–249. University of Nebraska Press, Lincoln.

Jeter, Marvin D.

2002 From Prehistory through Protohistory to Ethnohistory in and Near the Northern Lower Mississippi Valley. In *The Transformation of the*

Southeastern Indians, 1540–1760, edited by Robbie Ethridge and Charles Hudson, pp. 177–224. University Press of Mississippi, Jackson.

Johnson, Jay K.

1992 Conclusion. In *The Development of Southeastern Archaeology*, edited by Jay K. Johnson, pp. 207–213. University of Alabama Press, Tuscaloosa.

1997 From Chiefdom to Tribe in Northeast Mississippi: The Soto Expedition as a Window on a Culture in Transition. In *The Hernando de Soto Expedition: History, Historiography, and "Discovery" in the Southeast*, edited by Patricia Galloway, pp. 295–312. University of Nebraska Press, Lincoln.

2000 The Chickasaws. In *Indians of the Greater Southeast: Historical Archaeology and Ethnohistory*, edited by Bonnie G. McEwan, pp. 85–121. University Press of Florida, Gainesville.

Johnson, Jay K., and John T. Sparks

1986 Protohistoric Settlement Patterns in Northeastern Mississippi. In *The Protohistoric Period in the Mid-South: 1500–1700,* edited by David H. Dye and Ronald C. Brister, pp. 64–82. Archaeological Report No. 18. Mississippi Department of Archives and History, Jackson.

Jones, Grant D.

1978 The Ethnohistory of the Guale Coast through 1684. In *The Anthropology of St. Catherines Island 1. Natural and Cultural History*, edited by David Hurst Thomas, Grant D. Jones, Roger S. Durham, and Clark Spencer Larsen, pp. 178–210. Anthropological Papers Vol. 55, Part 2. American Museum of Natural History, New York.

Kamen, Henry

2002 *Spain's Road to Empire: The Making of a World Power, 1492–1763*. Penguin, London.

2008 *Imaging Spain: Historical Myth and National Identity*. Yale University Press, New Haven.

Kanter, John

2004 *Ancient Puebloan Southwest*. Cambridge University Press, Cambridge.

Karlen, Arno

1995 *Man and Microbes: Disease and Plagues in History and Modern Times*. G. P. Putnam's Sons, New York.

Kelton, Paul

2007 *Epidemics and Enslavement: Biological Catastrophe in the Native Southeast, 1492–1715*. University of Nebraska Press, Lincoln.

Kennedy, Tom R., and Dan Simplicio

2009 First Contact at Hawikku (Zuni): The Day the World Stopped. In *Telling New Mexico: A New History,* edited by Marta Weigle, pp. 63–71. Museum of New Mexico Press, Santa Fe.

Kennett, Douglas J.

2005 *The Island Chumash: Behavioral Ecology of a Maritime Society*. University of California Press, Berkeley.

Kessell, John L.

2002 *Spain in the Southwest: A Narrative History of Colonial New Mexico, Arizona, Texas, and California*. University of Oklahoma Press, Norman.

2011 A Long Time Coming: The Seventeenth-Century Pueblo-Spanish War. *New Mexico Historical Review* 86(2):141–156.

Kessell, John L., Rick Hendricks, and Meredith Dodge (editors)

1998 *Blood on the Boulders: The Journals of Don Diego de Vargas, New Mexico, 1694–97*. University of New Mexico Press, Albuquerque.

Kidd, Kenneth E.

1953 The Excavation and Historical Identification of a Huron Ossuary. *American Antiquity* 18:359–379.

King, Adam

1999 De Soto's Itaba and the Nature of Sixteenth-Century Paramount Chiefdoms. *Southeastern Archaeology* 18:110–123.

2003 *Etowah: The Political History of a Chiefdom Capital*. University of Alabama Press, Tuscaloosa.

Kludt, Trevor

2005 *Archaeological Survey of the Santa Fe Canyon Ranch, Santa Fe County, New Mexico*. OCA/UNM Report No. 185-868. Office of Contract Archeology, University of New Mexico, Albuquerque.

Knight, Vernon J., Jr.

1986 The Institutional Organization of Mississippian Religion. *American Antiquity* 51:675–687.

Knight, Vernon J., Jr. (editor)

2009 *The Search for Mabila: The Decisive Battle between Hernando de Soto and Chief Tascalusa*. University of Alabama Press, Tuscaloosa.

Knight, Vernon James, Jr., and Vincas P. Steponaitis (editors)

2007 *Archaeology of the Moundville Chiefdom*. Reprinted. University of Alabama Press, Tuscaloosa. Originally published 1998, Smithsonian Institution Press, Washington, D.C.

Kohler, Timothy A., Sarah Herr, and Matthew J. Root

2004 The Rise and Fall of the Towns on the Pajarito Plateau (A.D. 1375–1600). In *The Archaeology of Bandelier National Monument: Village Formation on the Pajarito Plateau, New Mexico*, edited by Timothy A. Kohler, pp. 215–264. University of New Mexico Press, Albuquerque.

Kolman, Connie J., A. Centurion-Lara, S. A. Lukehart, Douglas W. Owsley, and Noreen Tuross

1999 Identification of *Treponema pallidum* Subspecies pallidum in a 200-Year-Old Skeletal Specimen. *The Journal of Infectious Diseases* 180:2060–2063.

Krech, Shepard, III

1991 The State of Ethnohistory. *Annual Review of Anthropology* 20:345–375.

Kroeber, Alfred L.

1917 *Zuñi Kin and Clan*. Anthropological Papers Vol. 18:39–205. American Museum of Natural History, New York.

Kulisheck, Jeremy R.

2003 Pueblo Population Movements, Abandonment and Settlement Change in Sixteenth and Seventeenth Century New Mexico. *Kiva* 69(1):30–54.

2005 The Archaeology of Pueblo Population Change on the Jemez Plateau, A.D. 1200 to 1700: The Effects of Spanish Contact and Conquest. Unpublished PhD Dissertation, Department of Anthropology, Southern Methodist University, Dallas. University International Microfilms, Ann Arbor.

2010 "Like Butterflies on a Mounting Board:" Pueblo Mobility and Demography before 1825. In *Across a Great Divide: Continuity and Change in Native North American Societies*, edited by Laura L. Scheiber and Mark D. Mitchell, pp. 174–191. University of British Columbia Press, Toronto.

Kunitz, Stephen J.

1994 *Disease and Social Diversity: The European Impact on the Health of Non-Europeans*. Oxford University Press, Oxford.

Kurota, Alexander

2006a *Class III Cultural Resources Inventory of 435 Acres in Pueblo Blanco Country, Galisteo Basin, New Mexico*. OCA/UNM Report No. 185-880. Office of Contract Archeology, University of New Mexico, Albuquerque.

2006b *The Volcano Vista High School Site: Excavations at LA 134636 on the West Mesa of Albuquerque, Bernalillo County, New Mexico*. OCA/UNM Report No. 185-871. Office of Contract Archeology, University of New Mexico, Albuquerque.

Kurota, Alexander and Patrick Hogan

2009 *Cultural Resources Survey of 207 Acres for the UNM Rio Rancho Campus, Sandoval County, New Mexico*. OCA/UNM Report No. 185-991. Office of Contract Archeology, University of New Mexico, Albuquerque.

Ladd, Edmund J.

1997 Zuni on the Day the Men in Metal Arrived. In *The Coronado Expedition to Tierra Nueva: The 1540–1542 Route Across the Southwest*, edited by Richard Flint and Shirley Cushing Flint, pp. 225–233. University of Colorado Press, Niwot.

Lambert, Patricia M.

2002 The Archaeology of War: A North American Perspective. *Journal of Archaeological Research* 10:207–241.

Lane, Kris

1998 *Pillaging the Empire: Piracy in the Americas, 1500–1750.* M. E. Sharpe, Armonk, New York.

Lanning, John Tate

1935 *The Spanish Missions of Georgia.* University of North Carolina Press, Chapel Hill.

Lapham, Heather

2005 *Hunting for Hides: Deerskins, Status, and Cultural Change in the Protohistoric Appalachians.* University of Alabama Press, Tuscaloosa.

Larsen, Clark Spencer

1993 On the Frontier of Contact: Mission Bioarchaeology in *La Florida.* In *The Spanish Missions of La Florida,* edited by Bonnie G. McEwan, pp. 322–356. University Press of Florida, Gainesville.

Larsen, Clark Spencer (editor)

2001 *Bioarchaeology of Spanish Florida: The Impact of Colonialism.* University Press of Florida, Gainesville.

Larsen, Clark S., Mark C. Griffin, Dale L. Hutchinson, Vivian E. Noble, Lynette Norr, Robert F. Pastor, Christopher B. Ruff, Katherine F. Russell, Margaret J. Schoeninger, Michael Schultz, Scott W. Simpson, and Mark F. Teaford

2001 Frontiers of Contact: Bioarchaeology of Spanish Florida. *Journal of World Prehistory* 15:69–123.

Larson, Lewis H., Jr.

1972 Functional Considerations of Warfare in the Southeast during the Mississippian Period. *American Antiquity* 37(3):383–392.

Lawson, Edward W.

1946 *The Discovery of Florida and Its Discoverer Juan Ponce de León.* Edward W. Lawson, St. Augustine, Florida.

Lekson, Stephen H.

1990 Sedentism and Aggregation in Anasazi Archaeology. In *Perspectives on Southwestern Prehistory,* edited by Paul R. Minnis and Charles L. Redman, pp. 333–340. Westview Press, Boulder.

2008 *A History of the Ancient Southwest.* SAR Press, Santa Fe.

Levy, Janet E., J. Alan May, and David G. Moore

1990 From Ysa to Joara: Cultural Diversity in the Catawba Valley from the Fourteenth to the Sixteenth Century. In *Columbian Consequences, Volume 2: Archaeological and Historical Perspectives on the Spanish Borderlands East,* edited by David Hurst Thomas, pp. 153–168. Smithsonian Institution Press, Washington, D.C.

Levy, Jerrold E.

1992 *Orayvi Revisited: Social Stratification in an "Egalitarian" Society.* SAR Press, Santa Fe.

LeBlanc, Steven A.

2001 Warfare and Aggregation in the El Morro Valley, New Mexico. In *Deadly Landscapes: Case Studies in Prehistoric Southwestern Warfare*, edited by Glen E. Rice and Steven A. LeBlanc, pp. 19–49. University of Utah Press, Salt Lake City.

Le Page du Pratz, A. S.

1972 *The History of Louisiana or of the Western Parts of Virginia and Carolina.* Originally published in 1774. Claitor's Publishing Division, Baton Rouge.

Lewis, Clifford M., and Albert J. Loomie

1953 *The Spanish Jesuit Mission in Virginia, 1570–1572*. University of North Carolina Press, Chapel Hill.

Liebmann, Matthew J.

2008a Introduction: The Intersections of Archaeology and Post-Colonial Studies. In *Archaeology and the Postcolonial Critique*, edited by Matthew J. Liebmann and Uzma Z. Rizvi, pp. 1–20. AltaMira Press, Lanham, Maryland.

2008b The Innovative Materiality of Revitalization Movements: Lessons from the Pueblo Revolt of 1680. *American Anthropologist* 110:360–372.

2010a The Best of Times, the Worst of Times: Pueblo Resistance and Accommodation during the Spanish Reconquista of New Mexico. In *Enduring Conquests: Rethinking the Archaeology of Resistance to Spanish Colonialism in the Americas*, edited by Matthew J. Liebmann and Melissa S. Murphy, pp. 199–221. School for Advanced Research Press, Santa Fe.

2010b The Battle of Astialakwa: Conflict Archaeology of the Spanish Reconquest in Northern New Mexico. *The SAA Archaeological Record* 10(4):40–42.

Liebmann, Matthew, Thomas J. Ferguson, and Robert W. Preucel

2005 Pueblo Settlement, Architecture, and Social Change in the Pueblo Revolt Era, A.D. 1680 to 1696. *Journal of Field Archaeology* 30:45–60.

Liebmann, Matthew J., and Robert W. Preucel

2007 The Archaeology of the Pueblo Revolt and the Formation of the Modern Pueblo World. *Kiva* 73(2):195–217.

Liebmann, Matthew, and Christopher Toya

2010 Foreword. In *Pecos Pueblo Revisited: The Biological and Social Context*, edited by Michèlle E. Morgan, pp. xi–xii. Papers of the Peabody Museum of Archaeology and Ethnology, No. 85. Harvard University, Cambridge.

Lightfoot, Kent G.

1995 Culture Contact Studies: Redefining the Relationship between Prehistoric and Historical Archaeology. *American Antiquity* 60:199–217.

2005 *Indians, Missionaries, and Merchants: The Legacy of Colonial Encounters on the California Frontiers*. University of California Press, Berkeley.

Limerick, Patricia Nelson

1987 *The Legacy of Conquest: The Unbroken Past of the American West.* W. W. Norton, New York.

Little, Keith J.

2008 European Artifact Chronology and Impacts of Spanish Contact in the Sixteenth-Century Coosa Valley. Unpublished PhD dissertation, Department of Anthropology, University of Alabama, Tuscaloosa.

Little, Keith J., and Caleb Curren

1990 Conquest Archaeology of Alabama. In *Columbian Consequences, Volume 2: Archaeological and Historical Perspectives on the Spanish Borderlands East*, edited by David Hurst Thomas, pp. 169–195. Smithsonian Institution Press, Washington, D.C.

Livingood, Patrick C.

2008 Recent Discussions in Late Prehistoric Southern Archaeology. *Native South* 1:1–26.

López Portillo y Weber, José

1939 *La rebelión de la Nueva Galicia.* Instituto Panamericano de Geografia e Historia. Publicación No. 37, Antigua Imprenta de E. Murguía, Tacubaya, D. F.

Loren, Diana DiPaolo

2008 *In Contact: Bodies and Spaces in the Sixteenth- and Seventeenth-Century Eastern Woodlands.* AltaMira Press, New York.

Lowery, Woodbury

1911 *The Spanish Settlements within the Present Limits of the United States, 1513–1561.* G. P. Putnam's Sons, New York.

Ludlum, David M.

1963 *Early American Hurricanes, 1492–1870.* American Meteorological Society, Boston.

Luer, George M.

1994 A Third Ceremonial Tablet from the Goodnow Mound, Highlands County, Florida; With Notes on Some Peninsular Tribes and Other Tablets. *Florida Anthropologist* 47(2):180–188.

Lycett, Mark T.

1995 Archaeological Implications of European Contact: Demography, Settlement, and Land Settlement, and Land Use in the Middle Rio Grande Valley, New Mexico. Unpublished PhD Dissertation, Department of Anthropology, University of New Mexico, Albuquerque.

Lyon, Eugene

1967 More Light on the Indians of the Ais Coast. Research Paper. P. K. Yonge Library of Florida History, University of Florida, Gainesville.

1976 *The Enterprise of Florida: Pedro Menéndez de Avilés and the Spanish Conquest of 1565–1568.* University Press of Florida, Gainesville.

1990 The Enterprise of Florida. In *Columbian Consequences, Volume 2: Archaeological and Historical Perspectives on the Spanish Borderlands East*, edited by David Hurst Thomas, pp. 281–296. Smithsonian Institution Press, Washington, D.C.

1995 Memorial of Pedro Menéndez' Ships Lost in the Florida Conquest. In *Pedro Menéndez de Avilés*, edited by Eugene Lyon, pp. 211–213. Spanish Borderlands Sourcebooks, Garland, New York.

2009 Florida Outreach. Paper presented at the 74th Annual Meeting of the Society for American Archaeology, April 22–26, Atlanta, Georgia.

MacNutt, Francis A.

1977 *Fernando Cortés, His Five Letters of Relation to the Emperor Charles V. 1519–1526*. Vol. 1. Rio Grande Press, Glorieta.

MacQuarrie, Kim

2007 *The Last Days of the Incas*. Simon and Schuster, New York.

Mallios, Seth

2006 *The Deadly Politics of Giving: Exchange and Violence at Ajacán, Roanoke, and Jamestown*. University of Alabama Press, Tuscaloosa.

Mann, Charles C.

2002 1491. *Atlantic Monthly*, March, 41–53.

Mann, Michael E.

2001a Climate during the Past Millennium. *Weather* 56:91–101.

2001b Large-Scale Temperature Patterns in Past Centuries: Implications for North American Climate Change. *Human and Ecological Risk Assessment* 7:1247–1254.

2001c Medieval Climatic Optimum. In *Encyclopedia of Global Environmental Change*, edited by M. C. MacCracken and J. S. Perry, pp. 514–516. John Wiley and Sons, London.

2001d Little Ice Age. In *Encyclopedia of Global Environmental Change*, edited by M. C. MacCracken and J. S. Perry, pp. 504–509. John Wiley and Sons, London.

Mann, Michael E., Raymond S. Bradley, and Malcolm K. Hughes

1998 Global-scale Temperature Patterns and Climate Forcing Over the Past Six Centuries. *Nature* 392:779–787.

Mann, Michael E., E. P. Gille, R. S. Bradley, M. K. Hughes, J. T. Overpeck, F. T. Keimig, and W. S. Gross

2000 *Global Temperature Patterns in Past Centuries: An Interactive IGBP Pages/World Data Center for Paleoclimatology Contribution, Series #2000-075*. NOAA/National Climate Data Center Paleoclimatology Program, Boulder, Colorado. Electronic document, http://www.ncdc.noaa.gov/paleo/ei/eidata/volcanic.dat, accessed August 9, 2009.

Marcus, Joyce, and Kent V. Flannery
1996 *Zapotec Civilization: How Urban Society Evolved in Mexico's Oaxaca Valley.* Thames and Hudson, London.

Marquardt, William H.
1987 The Calusa: Social Formation in Protohistoric South Florida. In *Power Relations and State Formation,* edited by Thomas C. Patterson and Christine W. Gailey, pp. 98–116. Archeology Section, American Anthropological Association, Washington, D.C.

Marr, J. S., and J. B. Kiracofe
2000 Was the Huey Cocoliztli a Haemorrhagic Fever? *Medical History* 44:341–362.

Marrinan, Rochelle A., John F. Scarry, and Rhonda L. Majors
1990 Prelude to de Soto: The Expedition of Pánfilo de Narváez. In *Columbian Consequences, Volume 2: Archaeological and Historical Perspectives on the Spanish Borderlands East,* edited by David Hurst Thomas, pp. 71–82. Smithsonian Institution Press, Washington, D.C.

Marshall, Michael P.
1987 *Qualacu: Archeological Investigation of a Piro Pueblo.* US Fish and Wildlife Service and University of New Mexico Office of Contract Archeology, Albuquerque.

Martin, Debra L., and David W. Frayer (editors)
1997 *Troubled Times: Violence and Warfare in the Past.* Gordon and Breach, Amsterdam.

Martin, Joel W.
1994 Southeastern Indians and the English Trade in Skins and Slaves. In *The Forgotten Centuries: Indians and Europeans in the American South, 1521–1704,* edited by Charles M. Hudson and Carmen Chaves Tesser, pp. 304–324. University of Georgia Press, Athens.

Martín, Luis
1983 *Daughters of the Conquistadores: Women of the Viceroyalty of Peru.* Southern Methodist University, Dallas.

Marx, Robert, and Jenifer Marx
1994 *New World Shipwrecks, 1492–1825: A Comprehensive Guide.* Ram Publishing, Dallas.

Mathers, Clay
2011 Tangled Threads, Loose Ends, and Knotty Problems: The Place of Moho in Tiguex Archaeology, Geography, and History. In *The Latest Word from 1540: People, Places, and Portrayals of the Coronado Expedition,* edited by Richard Flint and Shirley Cushing Flint, pp. 367–397. University of New Mexico Press, Albuquerque.
2013 Borderlands Violence in Sixteenth-Century New Spain: Morphogenesis and Reformation on the Frontiers of Empire. In *Building Transnational*

Archaeologies, edited by Elisa Villapando Canchola and Randall McGuire, in press. University of Arizona Press and the Arizona State Museum, Tucson.

Mathers, Clay, and Charles Haecker

2009 *Social and Spatial Modeling of Historic-Period Expeditions at El Morro National Monument, New Mexico.* Report Prepared for El Morro National Monument, NM. Submitted to the National Park Service, Heritage Partnerships Program, Santa Fe, NM. Manuscript on file at El Morro National Monument, Ramah.

2011 Between Cíbola and Tiguex: A Vázquez de Coronado Presence at the El Morro National Monument, New Mexico. In *The Latest Word from 1540: People, Places, and Portrayals of the Coronado Expedition,* edited by Richard Flint and Shirley Cushing Flint, pp. 286–307. University of New Mexico Press, Albuquerque.

Mathers, Clay, Charles Haecker, James W. Kendrick, and Steve Baumann

2010 Before the Signatures: Evidence of the Vázquez de Coronado Expedition at El Morro National Monument, West-Central New Mexico. *CRM: The Journal of Heritage Stewardship* 7(1):68–73.

Mathers, Clay, Charles Haecker, and Dan Simplicio

2009 Kechiba:wa: A New Vázquez de Coronado Site in West-Central New Mexico. *CRM: The Journal of Heritage Stewardship* 6(2):67–72.

Mathers, Clay, Phillip Leckman, and Nahide Aydin

2008 "Non-Ground Breaking" Research at the Edge of Empire: Geophysical and Geospatial Approaches to Sixteenth-Century Interaction in Tiguex Province (New Mexico). Paper presented at the 41st Annual Conference on Historical and Underwater Archaeology, Albuquerque.

Mathers, Clay, Matthew Schmader, Richard Flint, Shirley Cushing Flint, Phillip Leckman, Charles Haecker, and Christopher Adams

2007 *Piedras Marcadas: Proposed Research Plan.* Statistical Research, Inc., City of Albuquerque, and the National Park Service, Heritage Partnerships Program. Submitted to the New Mexico Cultural Properties Review Committee. Copies available from the New Mexico Department of Cultural Affairs, Historic Preservation Division, Santa Fe.

Mathers, Clay, Dan Simplicio, and Tom Kennedy

2011 "Everywhere They Told Us He Had Been There": Evidence of the Vázquez de Coronado Entrada at the Ancestral Zuni Pueblo of Kechiba:wa, New Mexico. In *The Latest Word from 1540: People, Places, and Portrayals of the Coronado Expedition*, edited by Richard Flint and Shirley Cushing Flint, pp. 262–285. University of New Mexico Press, Albuquerque.

Matter, Robert A.

1975 Missions in Defense of Spanish Florida. *Florida Historical Quarterly* 54:18–38.

Matthew, Laura E.
2007 Whose Conquest?: Nahua, Zapoteca, and Mexica Allies in the Conquest of Central America. In *Indian Conquistadors: Indigenous Allies in the Conquest of Mesoamerica*, edited by Laura E. Matthew and Michel R. Oudijk, pp. 102–126. University of Oklahoma Press, Norman.

Matthew, Laura E., and Michel R. Oudijk (editors)
2007 *Indian Conquistadors: Indigenous Allies in the Conquest of Mesoamerica*. University of Oklahoma Press, Norman.

McAlister, Lyle N.
1984 *Spain and Portugal in the New World, 1492–1700*. University of Minnesota Press, Minneapolis.

McCabe, Gregory J., and Robert A. Muller
2002 Effects of ENSO on Weather-type Frequencies and Properties at New Orleans, Louisiana, USA. *Climate Research* 20:95–105.

McEwan, Bonnie G.
1991 The Archaeology of Women in the Spanish New World. *Historical Archaeology* 25(4):33–41.

McEwan, Bonnie G. (editor)
1993 *The Spanish Missions of La Florida*. University Press of Florida, Gainesville.
2000 *Indians of the Greater Southeast: Historical Archaeology and Ethnohistory*. University Press of Florida, Gainesville.

McGuire, Randall H., and Dean J. Saitta
1996 Although They Have Petty Captains, They Obey Them Badly: The Dialectics of Prehistoric Western Pueblo Social Organization. *American Antiquity* 61(2):197–216.

McIntosh, Roderick J., Joseph A. Tainter, and Susan Keech McIntosh
2000 Climate, History, and Human Action. In *The Way the Wind Blows: Climate, History, and Human Action*, edited by Roderick J. McIntosh, Joseph A. Tainter, and Susan K. McIntosh, pp. 1–42. Columbia University Press, New York.

Meachem, J. Lloyd
1968 *Francisco de Ibarra and Nueva Vizcaya*. Reprinted. Greenwood Press, New York. Originally published 1927 Duke University Press, Durham.

Meade, Melinda S., and Robert J. Earickson
2000 *Medical Geography*, 2nd ed. Guilford Press, New York.

Mera, H. P.
1940 *Population Changes in the Rio Grande Glaze-Paint Area*. Laboratory of Anthropology Technical Series Bulletin 11 Santa Fe.

Mijares Ramírez, Ivonne (editor)
1997 Miguel Núñez, vecino y Bautista Personel, mercader, vecino, se obligaron de mancomún a pagar a Tomás Blaque, mercader, vecino, 165 pesos de oro común que les prestó, Ciudad de México, 23 de Octubre 1564.

In *Catálogo, Resumen e Índices de Protocolos del Archivo General de Notarías de la Ciudad de México, 1554–1581, Gaspar Calderón y Antonio Alonso, escribanos.* Instituto de Investigaciones Históricas, México.

Milanich, Jerald T.

1990 The European Entrada into La Florida: An Overview. In *Columbian Consequences, Volume 2: Archaeological and Historical Perspectives on the Spanish Borderlands East*, edited by David Hurst Thomas, pp. 3–29. Smithsonian Institution Press, Washington, D.C.

1994 Franciscan Missions and Native Peoples in Spanish Florida. In *The Forgotten Centuries: Indians and Europeans in the American South, 1521–1704*, edited by Charles Hudson and Carmen Chaves Tesser, pp. 276–303. University of Georgia Press, Athens.

1995 *Florida Indians and the Invasion from Europe.* University Press of Florida, Gainesville.

1996 *The Timucua.* Blackwell, Oxford.

1998 *Florida's Indians from Ancient Times to the Present.* University Press of Florida, Gainesville.

1999 *Laboring in the Fields of the Lord: Spanish Missions and Southeastern Indians.* University Press of Florida, Gainesville.

Milanich, Jerald T., and Charles Hudson

1993 *Hernando de Soto and the Indians of Florida.* University of Press of Florida, Gainesville.

Milanich, Jerald T., and Susan Milbrath (editors)

1989 *First Encounters: Spanish Explorations in the Caribbean and the United States, 1492–1570.* University Press of Florida, Gainesville.

Milanich, Jerald T., and Samuel Proctor (editors)

1994 *Tacachale: Essays on the Indians of Florida and Southeastern Georgia during the Historic Period.* University Presses of Florida, Gainesville.

Milanich, Jerald T., and William C. Sturtevant (editors)

1972 *Francisco Pareja's 1613 Confesionario.* Translated by Emilio F. Moran. Florida Department of State, Tallahassee.

Mills, Barbara

2004 The Establishment and Defeat of Hierarchy: Inalienable Possessions and the History of Collective Prestige Structures in the Pueblo Southwest. *American Anthropologist* 106(2):238–251.

Milner, George R.

1999 Warfare in Prehistoric and Early Historic Eastern North America. *Journal of Archaeological Research* 7:105–151.

Milner, George R., and George Chaplin

2010 Eastern North American Population at ca. A.D. 1500. *American Antiquity* 75(4):707–726.

Mindeleff, Victor

1891 *A Study of Pueblo Architecture in Tusayan and Cibola*. Eighth Annual Report of the Bureau of Ethnology to the Secretary of the Smithsonian Institution 1886–87. United States Government Printing Office, Washington D.C.

Mitchem, Jeffrey M.

1989 Redefining Safety Harbor: Late Prehistoric/Protohistoric Archaeology in West Peninsular Florida. Unpublished PhD Dissertation, Department of Anthropology, University of Florida, Gainesville.

1990 Initial Spanish-Indian Contact in West Peninsular Florida: The Archaeological Evidence. In *Columbian Consequences, Volume 2: Archaeological and Historical Perspectives on the Spanish Borderlands East*, edited by David Hurst Thomas, pp. 49–59. Smithsonian Institution Press, Washington, D.C.

1996a Investigations of the Possible Remains of de Soto's Cross at Parkin. *The Arkansas Archeologist* 35:87–95.

1996b Mississippian Research at Parkin Archaeological State Park. In *Proceedings of the 14th Mid-South Archaeological Conference*, edited by Richard Walling, Camille Wharey, and Camille Stanley, pp. 25–39. Special Publication No. 1, Panamerican Consultants, Memphis, Tennessee.

Montané Martí, Julio César

2002 *Francisco Vázquez Coronado: Sueño y Decepción*. El Colegio de Jalisco, Zapopan, Jalisco.

Moore, David G.

2002 *Catawba Valley Mississippian: Ceramics, Chronology, and Catawba Indians*. University of Alabama Press, Tuscaloosa.

Moorhead, Max L.

1975 *The Presidio: Bastion of the Spanish Borderlands*. University of Oklahoma Press, Norman.

1995 *New Mexico's Royal Road: Trade and Travel on the Chihuahua Trail*. University of Oklahoma, Norman.

Morgan, David

1996 Historic Period Chickasaw Indians: Chronology and Settlement Patterns. *Mississippi Archaeology* 31(1):1–39.

Morse, Dan F., and Phyllis A. Morse

1990 The Spanish Exploration of Arkansas. In *Columbian Consequences, Vol. 2: Archaeological and Historical Perspectives on the Spanish Borderlands East*, edited by David Hurst Thomas, pp. 197–210. Smithsonian Institution Press, Washington, D.C.

Morse, Phyllis A.

1981 *Parkin: The 1978–1979 Archeological Investigations of a Cross County, Arkansas Site*. Research Series Vol. 13. Arkansas Archeological Survey, Fayetteville.

Nassaney, Michael S., and Eric S. Johnson

2000 The Contributions of Material Objects to Ethnohistory in Native North America. In *Interpretations of Native North American Life: Material Contributions to Ethnohistory*, edited by Michael S. Nassaney and Eric S. Johnson, pp. 1–30. University Press of Florida, Gainesville.

Nelson, Ben A., Timothy A. Kohler, and Keith W. Kintigh

1994 Demographic Alternatives: Consequences for Current Models of Southwestern Prehistory. In *Understanding Complexity in the Prehistoric Southwest*, edited by George J. Gumerman and Murray Gell-Mann, pp. 113–146. Addison-Wesley, Reading.

Núñez Cabeza de Vaca, Álvar

1989 *Naufragios*. Juan Francisco Maura, editor. Ediciones Cátedra, Madrid.

O'Brien, Greg

2002 *Choctaws in a Revolutionary Age, 1750–1830*. University of Nebraska Press, Lincoln.

O'Callaghan, Joseph F.

2003 *Reconquest and Crusade in Medieval Spain*. University of Pennsylvania Press, Philadelphia.

Ortlieb, Luc

2000 The Documented Historical Record of *El Niño* Events in Peru: An Update of the Quinn Record (Sixteenth through Nineteenth Centuries). In *El Niño and the Southern Oscillation: Multiscale Variability and Global and Regional Impacts*, edited by Henry F. Diaz and V. Markgraf, pp. 207–296. Cambridge University Press, Cambridge.

Oudjik, Michel R., and Matthew Restall

2007 Mesoamerican Conquistadors in the Sixteenth Century. In *Indian Conquistadors: Indigenous Allies in the Conquest of Mesoamerica*, edited by Laura E. Matthew and Michel R. Oudijk, pp. 28–63. University of Oklahoma Press, Norman.

Palkovich, Ann M.

1985 Historic Populations of the Eastern Pueblos: 1540–1910. *Journal of Anthropological Research* 41(3):401–426.

Palmer, Wayne C.

1965 *Meteorological Drought*. Research Paper No. 45. US Department of Commerce, Office of Climatology, US Weather Bureau, Washington, D.C.

Parker, Geoffrey

1998 *The Grand Strategy of Phillip II*. Yale University Press, New Haven.

Parsons, Elsie C.

1918 War God Shrines of the Laguna and Zuni. *American Anthropologist* 20(4):381–405.

1933 *Hopi and Zuni Ceremonialism*. Memoirs No. 39. American Anthropological Association, Menasha, Wisconsin.

Pauketat, Timothy
2004 *Ancient Cahokia and the Mississippians.* Cambridge University Press, Cambridge.
2007 *Chiefdoms and Other Archaeological Delusions.* AltaMira Press, Lanham, Maryland.

Pauketat, Timothy (editor)
2001 *The Archaeology of Traditions: Agency and History Before and After Columbus.* University Press of Florida, Gainesville.

Peacock, Evan
1995 Test Excavations at an Upland Mississippian Site in Oktibbeha County, Mississippi. *Mississippi Archaeology* 30(2):1–20.

Peacock, Evan, and S. Homes Hogue
2005 A New Series of Absolute Dates from Lyon's Bluff (22OK520), East-Central Mississippi. *Southeastern Archaeology* 24(1):46–58.

Perdue, Theda
2004 *Cherokee Women: Gender and Culture Change, 1700–1835.* University of Nebraska Press, Lincoln.

Perttula, Timothy K.
1992 The "Caddo Nation": Archaeological and Ethnohistoric Perspectives. University of Texas Press, Austin.
2002 Social Changes among the Caddo Indians in the 16th and 17th Centuries. In *Transformation of the Southeastern Indians, 1540–1760,* edited by Robbie Ethridge and Charles Hudson, pp. 249–270. University Press of Mississippi, Jackson.

Plog, Stephen
1997 *Ancient Peoples of the American Southwest.* Ancient Peoples and Places Series, Thames and Hudson, New York.

Pluckhahn, Thomas J.
2003 *Kolomoki: Settlement, Ceremony, and Status in the Deep South,* A.D. *350 to 750.* University of Alabama Press, Tuscaloosa.

Pluckhahn, Thomas J., Robbie Ethridge, Jerald Milanich, and Marvin T. Smith
2006 Introduction. In *Light on the Path: The Anthropology and History of the Southeastern Indians,* edited by Thomas J. Pluckhahn and Robbie Ethridge, pp. 1–25. University of Alabama Press, Tuscaloosa.

Pluckhahn, Thomas J., and Robbie Ethridge (editors)
2006 *Light on the Path: The Anthropology and History of the Southeastern Indians.* University of Alabama Press, Tuscaloosa.

Pocock, H. R. S.
1967 *The Conquest of Chile.* Stein and Day, New York.

Pohl, John, and Charles M. Robinson III
2005 *Aztecs and Conquistadores: The Spanish Invasion and the Collapse of the Aztec Empire.* Osprey, New York.

Poore, Richard Z., Milan J. Pavich, and Henri D. Grissino-Mayer

2005 Record of the Southwest Monsoon from Gulf of Mexico Sediment Cores. *Geology* 33(3):209–212.

Post, John D.

1977 *The Last Great Subsistence Crisis in the Western World.* Johns Hopkins University Press, Baltimore.

Powell, Phillip W.

1952 *Soldiers, Indians, and Silver: The Northward Advance of New Spain, 1550–1600.* University of California Press, Berkeley.

1977 *Mexico's Miguel Caldera: The Taming of America's First Frontier.* University of Arizona Press, Tucson.

Powers, Karen V.

2005 *Women in the Crucible of Conquest: The Gendered Genesis of Spanish American Society, 1500–1600.* University of New Mexico Press, Albuquerque.

Prescott, William H.

1900a *Mexico and the Life of the Conqueror Fernando Cortés.* Vol. 1. Peter Fenelon Collier and Son, New York.

1900b *Peru.* Vol. 2. Peter Fenelon Collier and Son, New York.

Preston, Douglas

1992 *Cities of Gold: A Journey Across the American Southwest in Pursuit of Coronado.* Simon & Schuster, New York.

Preucel, Robert W.

2002 Writing the Pueblo Revolt. In *Archaeologies of the Pueblo Revolt: Identity, Meaning, and Renewal in the Pueblo World,* edited by Robert W. Preucel, pp. 1–15. University of New Mexico Press, Albuquerque.

Preucel, Robert W. (editor)

2002 *Archaeologies of the Pueblo Revolt: Identity, Meaning, and Renewal in the Pueblo World.* University of New Mexico Press, Albuquerque.

Preucel, Robert W., Loa P. Traxler, and Michael V. Wilcox

2002 "Now the God of the Spaniards is Dead": Ethnogenesis and Community Formation in the Aftermath of the Pueblo Revolt of 1680. In *Traditions, Transitions, and Technologies: Themes in Southwestern Archaeology,* edited by Sarah H. Schlanger, pp. 71–93. University of Colorado Press, Boulder.

Price, James E.

1978 The Settlement Pattern of the Powers Phase. In *Mississippian Settlement Patterns,* edited by Bruce D. Smith, pp. 201–231. Academic Press, New York.

Priestley, Herbert Ingram (translator and editor)

1928 *The Luna Papers, Documents Relating to the Expedition of Don Tristán de Luna y Arellano for the Conquest of Florida in 1559–1561.* 2 vols. Florida State Historical Society, Deland.

Prudden, T. M.
1903 The Prehistoric Ruins of the San Juan Watershed in Utah, Arizona, Colorado, and New Mexico. *American Anthropologist* 5:224–288.

Quinn, William H.
1992 A Study of Southern Oscillation-Related Climate Activity for A.D. 622–1900 Incorporating Nile River Flood Data. In *El Niño: Historic and Paleoclimatic Aspects of the Southern Oscillation*, edited by Henry F. Diaz and Vera Markgraf, pp. 119–149. Cambridge University Press, New York.
1993 The Large-Scale ENSO Event, the El Niño, and Other Important Features. *Bulletin de l'Institut Français d'Estudies Andines* 22(1):363–374.

Quinn, W. H., and V. T. Neal
1995 The Historical Record of *El Niño* Events. In *Climate Since A.D. 1500*, edited by Raymond S. Bradley and Phillip D. Jones, pp. 623–648. Routledge, London.

Rafferty, Janet
2003 Prehistoric Settlement Patterning on the Mississippi Black Prairie. In *Blackland Prairies of the Gulf Coastal Plain: Nature, Culture, and Sustainability*, edited by Evan Peacock and Tim Schauwecker, pp. 167–193. University of Alabama Press, Tuscaloosa.

Ramenofsky, Ann F.
1987 *Vectors of Death: The Archaeology of European Contact*. University of New Mexico Press, Albuquerque.
1990 Loss of Innocence: Explanations of Differential Persistence in the Sixteenth-Century Southeast. In *Columbian Consequences, Volume 2: Archaeological and Historical Perspectives on the Spanish Borderlands East*, edited by David Hurst Thomas, pp. 31–48. Smithsonian Institution Press, Washington, D.C.
1996 The Problem of Introduced Infectious Diseases in New Mexico: A.D. 1540–1680. *Journal of Anthropological Research* 52(2):161–184.

Ramenofsky, Ann F., Michael K. Church, and Jeremy Kulisheck
2011 Investigating Differential Persistence of Pueblo Populations: A Landscape Approach. In *Contemporary Archaeologies of the Southwest*, edited by William H. Walker and Kathryn R. Venzor, pp. 261–289. University Press of Colorado, Boulder.

Ramenofsky, Ann F., and James K. Feathers
2002 Documents, Ceramics, Tree Rings, Dates and Luminescence: Estimating Final Native Abandonment of the Lower Rio Chama. *Journal of Anthropological Research* 58(1):121–159.

Ramenofsky, Ann F., and Patricia Galloway
1997 Disease and the Soto Entrada. In *The Hernando De Soto Expedition: History, Historiography, and "Discovery" in the Southeast*, edited by Patricia Galloway, pp. 259–279. University of Nebraska Press, Lincoln.

Ramenofsky, Ann F., Fraser D. Neiman, and Christopher D. Pierce

2009 Measuring Time, Population, and Residential Mobility from the Surface at San Marcos Pueblo, North-Central New Mexico. *American Antiquity* 74(3):505–530.

Ramenofsky, Ann F., C. David Vaughan, and Michael N. Spilde

2008 Seventeenth-Century Metal Production at San Marcos Pueblo, North-Central New Mexico. *Historical Archaeology* 42(4):105–131.

Ramenofsky, Ann F., Alicia K. Wilbur, and Anne C. Stone

2003 Native American Disease History: Past, Present and Future Directions. *World Archaeology* 35:241–257.

Rangel, Rodrigo

1993 Account of the Northern Conquest and Discovery of Hernando de Soto. In *The De Soto Chronicles: The Expedition of Hernando de Soto to North America in 1539–1543*, Vol. 1, edited by Lawrence A. Clayton, Vernon James Knight, Jr., and Edward C. Moore, pp. 247–306. Translated by John E. Worth. University of Alabama Press, Tuscaloosa.

Rausch, Jane M.

1984 *A Tropical Plains Frontier: The Llanos of Colombia 1531–1831*. University of New Mexico Press, Albuquerque.

Reff, Daniel

1991 *Disease, Depopulation, and Culture Change in Northwestern New Spain, 1518–1764*. University of Oklahoma Press, Norman.

Regnier, Amanda R.

2006a A Stylistic Analysis of Burial Urns from the Protohistoric Period in Central Alabama. *Southeastern Archaeology* 25(1):121–134.

2006b An Examination of the Social Composition of Late Mississippian Towns in the Alabama River Valley through Ceramic Styles. Unpublished PhD dissertation, Department of Anthropology, University of Alabama, Tuscaloosa.

2009 What Indian Pottery of Sixteenth-Century Central Alabama Looks Like and Why It Matters. In *The Search for Mabila: The Decisive Battle between Hernando de Soto and Chief Tascalusa*, edited by Vernon James Knight, Jr., pp. 83–93. University of Alabama Press, Tuscaloosa.

Reinhartz, Dennis

1998 Legado: The Information of the Entradas Portrayed through the Early Nineteenth Century. In *The Mapping of the Entradas into the Greater Southwest*, edited by Dennis Reinhartz and Gerald D. Saxon, pp. 132–151. University of Oklahoma, Norman.

Reitz, Elizabeth J., Barnet Pavao-Zuckerman, Daniel C. Weinand, and Gwyneth A. Duncan

2010 *Mission and Pueblo Santa Catalina de Guale, St. Catherines Island, Georgia (USA): A Comparative Zooarchaeological Analysis*. Anthropological Papers No. 91. American Museum of Natural History, New York.

Renfrew, Colin

1980 The Great Tradition versus the Great Divide: Archaeology as Anthropology? *American Journal of Archaeology* 84:287–298.

Restall, Matthew

2003 *Seven Myths of the Spanish Conquest.* Oxford University Press, Oxford.

Restall, Matthew (editor)

2005 *Beyond Black and Red: African-Native Relations in Colonial Latin America.* University of New Mexico Press, Albuquerque.

Restall, Matthew, and Florine Asselbergs

2007 *Invading Guatemala: Spanish, Nahua and Maya Accounts of the Conquest Wars.* Pennsylvania State University Press, University Park.

Restall, Matthew, and Felipe Fernández-Armesto

2012 *The Conquistadors: A Very Short Introduction.* Oxford University Press, New York.

Reston, James, Jr.

2009 *Defenders of the Faith: Charles V, Suleyman the Magnificent, and the Battle for Europe, 1520–1536.* Penguin Press, New York.

Rice, Glen E., and Steven A. LeBlanc (editors)

2001 *Deadly Landscapes: Case Studies in Prehistoric Southwestern Warfare.* University of Utah Press, Salt Lake City.

Richey, J. N., R. Z. Poore, B. P. Flower, and T. M. Quinn

2007 1400 Yr Multiproxy Record of Climate Variability from the Northern Gulf of Mexico. *Geology* 35(5):423–426.

Riley, Carroll L.

1995 *Rio del Norte: People of the Upper Rio Grande from Earliest Times to the Pueblo Revolt.* University of Utah Press, Salt Lake City.

Roberts, Frank. H. H.

1932 *The Village of the Great Kivas on the Zuñi Reservation, New Mexico.* Smithsonian Institution, Bureau of Ethnology Bulletin 111. Smithsonian Institution, Washington, D.C.

Robertson, A., J. Overpeck, D. Rind, E. Mosely-Thompson, G. Zielinski, J. Lean, D. Koch, J. Penner, I. Tegan, and R. Healy

2001 Hypothesized Climate Forcing Time Series for the Last 500 Years. *Journal of Geophysical Research* 106:14783–14803.

Robertson, James Alexander (translator and editor)

1995 The Account by a Gentleman from Elvas. In *The De Soto Chronicles: The Expedition of Hernando de Soto to North America in 1539–1543,* Vol. I, edited by Lawrence A. Clayton, Vernon J. Knight, Jr., and Edward C. Moore, pp. 19–170. University of Alabama Press, Tuscaloosa.

Rodack, Madeleine Turrell

1988 Adolph Bandelier's History of the Borderlands. *Journal of the Southwest* 30:33–46.

1997 Cíbola, from Fray Marcos to Coronado. In *The Coronado Expedition to Tierra Nueva: The 1540–1542 Route Across the Southwest*, edited by Richard Flint and Shirley Cushing Flint, pp. 102–115. University of Colorado Press, Niwot.

Rogers, J. Daniel, and Samuel M. Wilson

1993 *Ethnohistory and Archaeology: Approaches to Post-Contact Change in the Americas*. Plenum Press, New York.

Ropelewski, C. F., and M. S. Halpert

1986 North American Precipitation and Temperature Patterns Associated with the *El Niño*-Southern Oscillation (ENSO). *Monthly Weather Review* 115:1606–1626.

Ruiz, Alfonso

2001 Plague in the Americas. *Emerging Infectious Diseases* 7, Supplement 3:539–540.

Sale, Kirkpatrick

1990 *The Conquest of Paradise: Christopher Columbus and the Columbian Legacy*. Plume, New York.

Salo, W. L., A. C. Aufderheide, J. Buikstra, and T. A. Holcomb

1994 Identification of *Mycobacterium tuberculosis* DNA in a Pre-Columbian Peruvian Mummy. *Proceedings of the National Academy of Sciences* 91:2091–2094.

Salzer, Matthew W.

2000a Dendrochronology in the San Francisco Peaks Region of Northern Arizona, USA. Unpublished PhD dissertation, Department of Geosciences, University of Arizona, Tucson.

2000b Temperature Variability and the Northern Anasazi: Possible Implications for Regional Abandonment. *Kiva* 65:295–318.

Salzer, Matthew W., and Kurt F. Kipfmueller

2005 Reconstructed Temperature and Precipitation on a Millennial Timescale from Tree-Rings in the Southern Colorado Plateau, USA. *Climatic Change* 70:465–487.

Sánchez-Crispin, Alvaro

1994 The Territorial Organization of Metallic Mining in New Spain. In *In Quest of Mineral Wealth: Aboriginal and Colonial Mining and Metallurgy in Spanish America*, edited by Alan K. Craig and Robert C. West, Geoscience and Man Vol. 33, pp. 155–170. Department of Geography and Anthropology, Louisana State University, Baton Rouge.

Sánchez, Joseph P.

1992 Pueblo Indian Warfare in the Spanish Colonial Period A.D. 1540–1680. In *Current Research on the Late Prehistory and Early History of New Mexico,* edited by Bradley J. Vierra, pp. 93–99. Special Publication No. 1, New Mexico Archaeological Council, Albuquerque.

Sando, Joe S., and Herman Agoyo (editors)
2005 *Po'pay: Leader of the First American Revolution.* Clear Light Publishing, Santa Fe.

Sandrik, Al, and Chris Landsea
2003 Chronological Listing of Tropical Cyclones Affecting North Florida and Coastal Georgia, 1565–1899. *NOAA Technical Memorandum NWS SR-224.* National Oceanic and Atmospheric Administration, Southern Region, Fort Worth, Texas.

Santa Cruz, Alonso de
1923 *Crónica del Emperador Carlos V, Tomo IV.* A. Blázquez y Delgado-Aguilera and R. Beltrán y Rózpide, editors. Patronato de Huérfanos de Intendencia é Intervención Militares, Madrid.

Saunders, Rebecca
2000 The Guale Indians of the Lower Atlantic Coast: Change and Continuity. In *Indians of the Greater Southeast: Historical Archaeology and Ethnohistory,* edited by Bonnie G. McEwan, pp. 26–56. University Press of Florida, Gainesville.
2002 Seasonality, Sedentism, Subsistence, and Disease in the Protohistoric: Archaeological versus Ethnohistoric Data along the Lower Atlantic Coast. In *Between Contacts and Colonies: Archaeological Perspectives on the Protohistoric Southeast,* edited by Cameron B. Wesson and Mark A. Rees, pp. 32–48. University of Alabama Press, Tuscaloosa.

Saunt, Claudio
1999 *A New Order of Things: Property, Power, and the Transformation of the Creek Indians, 1733–1816.* Cambridge University Press, Cambridge.

Scarry, John F.
1990 Beyond Apalachee Province: Assessing the Evidence for Early European-Indian Contact in Northwest Florida. In *Columbian Consequences, Volume 2: Archaeological and Historical Perspectives on the Spanish Borderlands East,* edited by David Hurst Thomas, pp. 93–105. Smithsonian Institution Press, Washington, D.C.

Schaafsma, Polly
2000 *Warriors, Shield, and Star: Imagery and Ideology in Pueblo Warfare.* Western Edge Press, Santa Fe.

Scholes, Frances V.
1930 The Supply Service of the New Mexico Missions in the Seventeenth Century, Part 2: 1631–1664. *New Mexico Historical Review* 5(2):186–210.

Schroeder, Albert H.
1992 Protohistoric Pueblo Demographic Change. In *Current Research on the Late Prehistory and Early History of New Mexico,* edited by Bradley J. Vierra, pp. 29–36. Special Publication 1, New Mexico Archaeological Council, Albuquerque.

Schroeder, Albert H., and Dan S. Matson

1965 *A Colony on the Move: Gaspar Castaño de Sosa's Journal, 1590–1591.* School of American Research, Santa Fe.

Schroeder, Susan

2007 Introduction: The Genre of Conquest Studies. In *Indian Conquistadors: Indigenous Allies in the Conquest of Mesoamerica,* edited by Laura E. Matthew and Michel R. Oudijk, pp. 5–27. University of Oklahoma Press, Norman.

Schroeder, Susan, Stephanie Wood, and Robert Haskett (editors)

1997 *Indian Women of Early Mexico.* University of Oklahoma Press, Norman.

Seager, Richard, Alexandrina Tzanova, and Jennifer Nakamura

2009 Drought in the Southeastern United States: Causes, Variability over the Last Millennium, and the Potential for Future Hydroclimatic Change. *Journal of Climate* 22:5021–5045.

Sheldon, Craig T., Jr.

2001 Introduction. In *The Southern and Central Alabama Expeditions of Clarence Bloomfield Moore,* edited by Craig T. Sheldon, Jr., pp. 1–114. University of Alabama Press, Tuscaloosa.

2009 The Present State of Archaeological Survey and Site File Data for the Alabama River and Adjacent Regions. In *The Search for Mabila: The Decisive Battle between Hernando de Soto and Chief Tascalusa,* edited by Vernon James Knight, Jr., pp. 107–128. University of Alabama Press, Tuscaloosa.

Shindell, Drew T., Gavin A. Schmidt, Michael E. Mann, David Rind, and Anne Waple

2001 Solar Forcing of Regional Climate Change during the Maunder Minimum. *Science* 294:2149–2152.

Shoemaker, Nancy (editor)

2001 *Clearing a Path: Theoretical Approaches to the Past in Native American Studies.* Routledge, London.

Siebert L., and T. Simkin

2002 *Volcanoes of the World: An Illustrated Catalog of Holocene Volcanoes and Their Eruptions.* Global Volcanism Program Digital Information Series GVP-3, Smithsonian Institution, Washington, D.C. Electronic document, http://www.volcano.si.edu/world/, accessed August 3, 2009.

Silva, Shanaka L. de, and Gregory A. Zielinski

1998 Global Influence of the A.D. 1600 Eruption of Huaynaputina, Peru. *Nature* 393:455–456.

Simmons, Marc

1964 Tlascalans in the Spanish Borderlands. *New Mexico Historical Review* 39(2):101–110.

1991 *The Last Conquistador, Juan de Oñate and the Settling of the Far Southwest.* University of Oklahoma Press, Norman.

Simplicio, Dan
2009 Zuni Conversations about Social and Cultural Adaptation to the Influence of Spanish Entradas. Paper presented at the 74th Annual Meeting of the Society for American Archaeology, Atlanta.

Simpson, James H.
1872 Coronado's March in Search of the "Seven Cities of Cibola" and Discussion of their Probable Location. In *Annual Report of the Board of Regents of the Smithsonian Institution for 1869*, pp. 309–340. Smithsonian Institution, Washington, D.C.

Simpson, Lesley B.
1982 *The Encomienda in New Spain: The Beginning of Spanish New Mexico.* University of California Press, Berkeley.

Skowronek, Russell K.
1989 A New Europe in the New World: Hierarchy, Continuity and Change in the Spanish Sixteenth-Century Colonization of Hispaniola and Florida. Unpublished PhD dissertation, Department of Anthropology, Michigan State University, East Lansing.
1998 The Spanish Phillippines: Archaeological Perspectives on Colonial Economics and Society. *International Journal of Historical Archaeology* 2(1):45–71.
2009 On the Fringes of New Spain: The Northern Borderlands and the Pacific. In *International Handbook of Historical Archaeology*, Part 2, edited by Teresita Majewski and David Gaimster, pp. 471–505. Springer, New York.

Sluiter, Engel
1985 *The Florida Situado: Quantifying the First Eighty Years, 1571–1651.* Research Publications of the P. K. Yonge Library of Florida History, No. 1. University of Florida, Gainesville.

Smith, Bruce D.
1985 The Archaeology of the Southeastern United States: From Dalton to DeSoto, 10,500–500 *B.P.* *Advances in World Archaeology* 5:1–88.

Smith, Claire, and H. Martin Wobst (editors)
2005 *Indigenous Archaeologies: Decolonizing Theory and Practice.* Routledge Press, New York.

Smith, Fay J., John I. Kessell, and Francis J. Fox
1966 *Father Kino in Arizona.* Arizona Historical Society, Tucson.

Smith, Linda Tuhiwai
1999 *Decolonizing Methodologies: Research and Indigenous Peoples.* Zed Books, New York.

Smith, Marvin T.
1976 The Route of De Soto through Tennessee, Georgia, and Alabama: The Evidence from Material Culture. *Early Georgia* 4:27–48.

1987 *Archaeology of Aboriginal Culture Change in the Interior Southeast: Depopulation during the Early Historic Period.* University Press of Florida, Gainesville.

2000 *Coosa: The Rise and Fall of a Southeastern Mississippian Chiefdom.* University Press of Florida, Gainesville.

Smith, Marvin T., and David J. Hally

1992 Chiefly Behavior: Evidence from Sixteenth-Century Spanish Accounts. In *Lords of the Southeast: Social Inequality and the Native Elites of Southeastern North America*, edited by Alex W. Barker and Timothy R. Pauketat, pp. 99–109. Archeological Papers 3, American Anthropological Association, Washington, D.C.

Smith, Marvin T., David J. Hally, and John E. Worth

2008 Sixteenth-Century European Artifact Dispersion in the Southeast. Paper presented at the 65th Annual Meeting of the Southeastern Archaeological Conference, Charlotte, North Carolina.

Smith, Watson, Richard B. Woodbury, and Nathalie F. S. Woodbury

1966 *The Excavation of Hawikuh by Frederick Webb Hodge. Report of the Hendricks-Hodge Expedition 1917–1923.* Contributions from the Museum of the American Indian, Heye Foundation, Vol. 20. Museum of the American Indian, Heye Foundation, New York.

Snow, David H. (assembler and editor)

1976 Archeological Excavations at Pueblo del Encierro, LA 70, Cochiti Dam Salvage Project, Cochiti, New Mexico. Final Report: 1964–1965 Field Seasons. Museum of New Mexico Laboratory of Anthropology Notes No. 78, Santa Fe.

Snyder, Christina

2010 *Slavery in Indian Country: The Changing Face of Captivity in Early America.* Harvard University Press, Cambridge, Massachusetts.

Solís de Merás, Gonzalo

1964 *Pedro Menéndez de Avilés: Memorial.* Translated by Jeannette Thurber Connor. University of Florida Press, Gainesville.

Sorset, Scott

2009 Preliminary Ceramic Analysis of the Emanuel Point II Ship. *Florida Anthropologist* 62(3–4):115–119.

South, Stanley A.

1988 Santa Elena: Threshold of Conquest. In *The Recovery of Meaning: Historical Archaeology in the Eastern United States*, edited by Mark P. Leone and Parker B. Potter, Jr., pp. 27–71. Smithsonian Institution Press, Washington, D.C.

South, Stanley A., Russell K. Skowronek, and Richard E. Johnson

1988 *Spanish Artifacts from Santa Elena.* Anthropological Studies 7, Occasional Papers of the South Carolina Institute of Archaeology and Anthropology, University of South Carolina, Columbia.

Spanish Crown

1514 Capitulation with Juan Ponce de León, October 27, 1514. Archivo General de Indias, Indiferente General 419, Libro 5, ff. 293r–295r.

1523 Capitulation with Lucas Vázquez de Ayllón, June 12, 1523. Archivo General de Indias, Indiferente General 415, Libro 1, ff. 36r–41r.

1526 Cédula to Pánfilo de Narváez, December 11, 1526. Archivo General de Indias, Indiferente General 415, Libro 1, ff. 98v–105v.

1537 Asiento with Hernando de Soto, April 20, 1537. Archivo General de Indias, Indiferente General 415, Libro 1, ff. 41r–45r.

Spicer, Edward H.

1962 *Cycles of Conquest: The Impact of Spain, Mexico, and the United States on the Indians of the Southwest, 1533–1960*. University of Arizona Press, Tucson.

Spielmann, Katherine A. (editor)

1998 *Migration and Reorganization: The Pueblo IV Period in the American Southwest*. Anthropological Research Papers No. 51, Arizona State University, Tempe.

Spielmann, Katherine A., Tiffany Clark, Diane Hawkey, Katharine Rainey, and Suzanne K. Fish

2009 ". . . Being Weary, They Had Rebelled": Pueblo Subsistence and Labor under Spanish Colonization. *Journal of Anthropological Archaeology* 28(1):102–125.

Stahle, David W.

2006 *Tree Ring Data Set, Altamaha River USA; 31N,81W.* NOAA Paleoclimatology website. Electronic document, http://hurricane.ncdc.noaa.gov/pls/paleo/ftpsearch.treering, accessed January 12, 2007.

Stahle, David W., and Malcolm K. Cleaveland

1992 Reconstruction and Analysis of Spring Rainfall over the Southeastern U.S. for the Past 1000 Years. *Bulletin of the American Meteorological Society* 73:1947–1961.

Stahle, David W., Malcolm K. Cleaveland, Dennis B. Blanton, Matthew D. Therrell, and D. A. Gay

1985 A 450-Year Drought Reconstruction for Arkansas, United States. *Nature* 316:530–532.

Stahle, David W., Malcolm K. Cleaveland, and J. G. Hehr

1988 North Carolina Climate Changes Reconstructed from Tree Rings: A.D. 372 to 1985. *Science* 240:1517–1519.

1998 The Lost Colony and Jamestown Droughts. *Science* 280:564–567.

Stahle, David W., Edward R. Cook, Malcolm K. Cleaveland, Matthew D. Therrell, David M. Meko, Henri D. Grissino-Mayer, Emma Watson, and Brian Luckman

2000 Tree Ring Data Document 16th-Century Megadrought over North America. EOS, *Transactions of the American Geophysical Union* 81:121–125.

Stannard, David E.

1992 *American Holocaust: The Conquest of the New World.* Oxford University Press, Oxford.

Steinen, Karl

1992 Ambushes, Raids, and Palisades: Mississippian Warfare in the Interior Southeast. *Southeastern Archaeology* 11:132–139.

Steponaitis, Vincas P.

1978 Location Theory and Complex Chiefdoms: A Mississippian Example. In *Mississippian Settlement Patterns,* edited by Bruce Smith, pp. 417–453. Academic Press, New York.

1986 Prehistoric Archaeology in the Southeastern United States, 1970–1985. *Annual Review of Anthropology* 15:363–404.

Steponaitis, Vincas P., and Vernon J. Knight, Jr.

2004 Moundville Art in Historical and Social Context. In *Hero, Hawk, and Open Hand: American Indian Art of the Ancient Midwest and South,* edited by Richard F. Townsend and Robert V. Sharp, pp. 166–181. Yale University Press, New Haven.

Stevenson, Matilda C.

1887 The Religious Life of the Zuni Child. In *Fifth Annual Report of the Bureau of American Ethnology for the Years 1883–1884,* pp. 533–555. Smithsonian Institution, Washington, D.C.

Stojanowski, Christopher

2004 Population History of Native Groups in Pre- and Post-Contact Spanish Florida. *American Journal of Physical Anthropology* 123(4):316–332.

2005 *Biocultural Histories in La Florida: A Bioarchaeologial Perspective.* University of Alabama Press, Tuscaloosa.

Stokes, Marvin A., and Terah L. Smiley

1996 *An Introduction to Tree-Ring Dating.* University of Arizona Press, Tucson.

Suina, Joseph

2002 The Persistence of the Corn Mothers. In *Archaeologies of the Pueblo Revolt: Identity, Meaning, and Renewal in the Pueblo World,* edited by Robert W. Preucel, pp. 212–216. University of New Mexico Press, Albuquerque.

Swadesh, Frances L.

1974 *Los Prímeros Pobladores: Hispanic Americans of the Ute Frontier.* University of Notre Dame Press, Notre Dame.

Swanton, John R.

1985 *Final Report of the United States De Soto Expedition Commission.* Reprinted. Smithsonian Institution Press, Washington, D.C. Originally published 1939, 76th Congress, 1st Session, Document 71, Government Printing Office, Washington, D.C.

Tallet, Frank
1992 *War and Society in Early-Modern Europe 1495–1715*. Routledge, London.
Taylor, Colin F.
2001 *Native American Weapons*. University of Oklahoma Press, Norman.
Taylor, F. L.
2006 *The Art of War in Italy 1494–1529*. The Scholar's Bookshelf, Cranbury, New Jersey.
Ternaux-Compans, Henri
1838 *Voyages, Relations et Memoires Originaux pour Servir a l'Histoire de la Découverte de l'Amérique*. Vol. 9. Arthur Bertrand, Libraire-Éditeur, Paris.
Thomas, David Hurst
1988 Saints and Soldiers at Santa Catalina: Hispanic Designs for Colonial America. In *The Recovery of Meaning: Historical Archaeology in the Eastern United States*, edited by Mark P. Leone and Parker B. Potter, Jr., pp. 73–140. Smithsonian Institution Press, Washington, D.C.
2010 Indian Agency in Spanish Florida: Some New Findings from Mission Santa Catalina de Guale. *Journal of Global Initiatives* 5(1):99–112.
Thomas, David Hurst (editor)
1989–1991 *Columbian Consequences*. 3 vols. Smithsonian Institution Press, Washington, D.C.
2008 *Native American Landscapes of St. Catherines Island, Georgia*. 3 vols. Anthropological Papers No. 88. American Museum of Natural History, New York.
Thornton, Russell
1987 *American Indian Holocaust and Survival: A Population History Since 1492*. University of Oklahoma Press, Norman.
Thornton, Russell (editor)
1998 *Studying Native America: Problems and Prospects*. University of Wisconsin Press, Madison.
Thrower, Robert
2009 Southeastern Indian Perspectives on Sixteenth-Century Spanish Entradas. Paper presented at the 74th Annual Meeting of the Society for American Archaeology, Atlanta.
Thwaites, Rueben Gold
1896–1901 *The Jesuit Relations and Allied Documents: Travels and Explorations of the Jesuit Missionaries in New France 1610–1791*. 73 Volumes. McGill-Queen's University Press, Montreal.
Titiev, Mischa
1944 *Old Oraibi: A Study of the Hopi Indians of Third Mesa*. Papers of the Peabody Museum of American Archaeology and Ethnology 22(1). Harvard University, Cambridge.

Toll, Mollie S.

1992 Patterns of Plant Use from the Late Prehistoric to Spanish Contact in the Rio Grande Valley. In *Current Research on the Late Prehistoric and Early Historic of New Mexico*, edited by Bradley J. Vierra, pp. 51–54. Special Publication 1, New Mexico Archaeological Council, Albuquerque.

Townsend, Camilla

2006 *Malintzin's Choices: An Indian Woman in the Conquest of Mexico*. University of New Mexico Press, Albuquerque.

Trigger, Bruce

1982 Ethnohistory: Problems and Prospects. *Ethnohistory* 29(1):1–19.

1984 Archaeology at the Crossroads: What's New? *Annual Review of Anthropology* 13:275–300.

Trouillot, Michel-Rolph

1991 Anthropology and the Savage Slot: The Poetics and Politics of Otherness. In *Recapturing Anthropology: Working in the Present*, edited by Richard G. Fox, pp. 17–44. School of American Research, Santa Fe.

Tu Tiempo.net

2009 Electonic document, http://www.tutiempo.net/en/Climate/Burgos_Villafria/80750.htm, accessed December 11, 2009.

Tyler, S. Lyman

1980 *Spanish Laws Concerning Discoveries, Pacifications, and Settlements among the Indians: With an Introduction and the First English Translation of the New Ordinances of Philip II, July 1573, and of Book IV of the Recopilación de leyes de los reinos de las Indias, Relating to these Subjects*. American West Center, University of Utah, Salt Lake City.

Ubelaker, Douglas H.

1988 North American Indian Population Size, A.D. 1500–1985. *American Journal of Physical Anthropology* 77:289–294.

Udall, Stewart L.

1987 *To the Inland Empire: Coronado and Our Spanish Legacy*. Doubleday, Garden City, New York.

Upham, Steadman

1982 *Polities and Power: An Economic and Political History of the Western Pueblo*. Academic Press, New York.

1986 Smallpox and Climate in the American Southwest. *American Anthropologist* 88(1):115–127.

1992 Population and Spanish Contact in the Southwest. In *Disease and Demography in the Americas*, edited by Douglas H. Ubelaker and John W. Verano, pp. 223–236. Smithsonian Institution Press, Washington, D.C.

Usner, Daniel, Jr.

1992 *Indians, Settlers, and Slaves in a Frontier Exchange Economy: The Lower Mississippi Valley before 1783*. University of North Carolina Press, Chapel Hill.

1998 *American Indians in the Lower Mississippi Valley: Social and Economic Histories*. University of Nebraska Press, Lincoln.

Van Buren, Mary

2009 The Archaeological Study of Spanish Colonialism in the Americas. *Journal of Archaeological Research* 18(2):151–201.

Vargas Machuca, Bernardo

2008 *The Indian Militia and Description of the Indies*. Edited by Kris Lane. Translated by Timothy F. Johnson. Duke University Press, Durham and London.

Vansina, Jan

1985 *Oral Tradition as History*. University of Wisconsin Press, Madison.

Vierra, Bradley J. (editor)

1989 *A Sixteenth-Century Spanish Campsite in the Tiguex Province*. Laboratory of Anthropology Note 475. Museum of New Mexico, Santa Fe.

Vinson, Ben III, and Matthew Restall

2005 Black Soldiers, Native Soldiers: Meanings of Military Service in the Spanish American Colonies. In *Beyond Black and Red: African-Native Relations in Colonial Latin America*, edited by Matthew Restall, pp. 15–52. University of New Mexico Press, Albuquerque.

Wagner, Henry R.

1966 *Spanish Voyages to the Northwest Coast of America in the Sixteenth Century*. Reprinted. N. Israel, Amsterdam. Originally published 1929, Special Publication No. 4, California Historical Society, San Francisco.

1967 *The Life and Writings of Bartolomé de las Casas*. University of New Mexico Press, Albuquerque.

Ware, John A.

2002 Descent Group and Sodality: Alternative Pueblo Social Histories. In *Traditions, Transitions, and Technologies: Themes in Southwestern Archaeology*, edited by Sarah H. Schlanger, pp. 94–112. University of Colorado Press, Boulder.

Waselkov, Gregory A.

1989 Seventeenth-Century Trade in the Colonial Southeast. *Southeastern Archaeology* 8:117–133.

2001 Historical Archaeology with Sails Set and Tacking into the Wind. *Historical Archaeology* 35(2):20–22.

Waselkov, Gregory A., Linda Derry, and Ned J. Jenkins

2009 The Archaeology of Mabila's Cultural Landscape. In *The Search for Mabila: The Decisive Battle between Hernando de Soto and Chief Tascalusa*, edited by Vernon James Knight, Jr., pp. 227–244. University of Alabama Press, Tuscaloosa.

Weber, David J.

1990 Blood of Martyrs, Blood of Indians: Toward a More Balanced View of Spanish Missions in Seventeenth-Century North America. In *Columbian*

Consequences, Volume 2: Archaeological and Historical Perspectives on the Spanish Borderlands East, edited by David Hurst Thomas, pp. 429–448. Smithsonian Institution Press, Washington, D.C.

1992 *The Spanish Frontier in North America*. Yale University Press, New Haven.

Weber, David J. (editor)

1999 *What Caused the Pueblo Revolt of 1680?* Bedford/St. Martins, Boston.

Weddle, Robert S.

1985 *Spanish Sea: The Gulf of Mexico in North American Discovery, 1500–1685*. Texas A&M University Press, College Station.

Wesson, Cameron B.

1999 Chiefly Power and Food Storage in Southeastern North America. *World Archaeology* 31(1):145–164.

2008 *Households and Hegemony: Early Creek Prestige Goods, Symbolic Capital, and Social Power*. University of Nebraska Press, Lincoln.

Wesson, Cameron B., and Mark A. Rees

2002 Protohistory and Archaeology: An Overview. In *Between Contacts and Colonies: Archaeological Perspectives on the Protohistoric Southeast*, edited by Cameron B. Wesson and Mark A. Rees, pp. 1–11. University of Alabama Press, Tuscaloosa.

Wesson, Cameron B., and Mark A. Rees (editors)

2002 *Between Contacts and Colonies: Archaeological Perspectives on the Protohistoric Southeast*. University of Alabama Press, Tuscaloosa.

Wheeler, Ryan J.

2000 *Treasure of the Calusa, the Johnson/Willcox Collection from Mound Key, Florida*. Rose Printing, Tallahassee.

White, Leslie

1935 *The Pueblo of Santo Domingo, New Mexico*. Memoirs of the American Anthropological Association 43. American Anthropological Association, Menasha.

Whiteley, Peter M.

1988 *Deliberate Acts: Changing Hopi Culture through the Oraibi Split*. University of Arizona Press, Tucson.

1998 *Rethinking Hopi Ethnography*. Smithsonian Institution Press, Washington, D.C.

2002 Archaeology and Oral Tradition—The Scientific Importance of Dialogue. *American Antiquity* 67(3):405–415.

2004 Social Formations in the Pueblo IV Southwest: An Ethnological View. In *The Protohistoric Pueblo World, A.D. 1275–1600*, edited by E. Charles Adams and Andrew I. Duff, pp. 144–156. University of Arizona Press, Tucson.

Widmer, Randolph J.

1988 *The Evolution of the Calusa*. University of Alabama Press, Tuscaloosa.

Wiget, Andrew O.
1982 Truth and the Hopi: An Historiographic Study of Documented Oral Tradition Concerning the Coming of the Spanish. *Ethnohistory* 29(3):181–199.

Wilcox, David R., and Jonathan Haas
1994 The Scream of the Butterfly: Competition and Conflict in the Prehistoric Southwest. In *Themes in Southwest Prehistory*, edited by George J. Gumerman, pp. 211–238. School of American Research, Santa Fe.

Wilcox, Michael V.
2009 *The Pueblo Revolt and the Mythology of Conquest: An Indigenous Archaeology of Contact*. University of California Press, Berkeley.

Wilson, Samuel M.
1993 Structure and History: Combing Archaeology and Ethnohistory in the Contact Period Caribbean. In *Ethnohistory and Archaeology: Approaches to Post-Contact Change in the Americas*, edited by J. Daniel Rogers and Samuel M. Wilson, pp. 19–30. Plenum Press, New York.

Winship, George Parker
1896 The Coronado Expedition, 1540–1542. In *Fourteenth Annual Report of the United States Bureau of Ethnology*, Part I, pp. 329–613. Smithsonian Institution, Washington, D.C.

Wobst, H. Martin
1978 The Archaeo-Ethnology of Hunter-Gatherers or The Tyranny of the Ethnographic Record in Archaeology. *American Antiquity* 43(2):303–309.

Wolf, Eric R.
1990 *Europe and the People Without History*. University of California Press, Berkeley.

Wood, Peter H., Gregory A. Waselkov, and M. Thomas Hatley (editors)
1989 *Powhatan's Mantle: Indians in the Colonial Southeast*. University of Nebraska Press, Lincoln.

Woodhouse, C. A., and J. T. Overpeck
1998 2000 Years of Drought Variability in the Central United States. *Bulletin of the American Meteorological Society* 79:2693–2714.

Worman, Frederick Scott
2009 Down by the River: Recent Geoarchaeological Investigations at Alameda Pueblo (LA 421). Paper presented at the New Mexico Archeological Council Fall Conference entitled, "The Middle and Northern Rio Grande," Albuquerque.

Worth, John E.
1994 Late Spanish Military Expeditions in the Interior Southeast, 1597–1628. In *The Forgotten Centuries: Indians and Europeans in the American South, 1521–1704*, edited by Charles Hudson and Carmen Chaves Tesser, pp. 104–122. University of Georgia Press, Athens.

1995 *The Struggle for the Georgia Coast: An Eighteenth Century Retrospective on Guale and Mocama*. Anthropological Papers of the American Museum of Natural History No. 75. American Museum of Natural History, New York.

1998a *The Timucuan Chiefdoms of Spanish Florida, Vol. 1: Assimilation*. University Press of Florida, Gainesville.

1998b *The Timucuan Chiefdoms of Spanish Florida, Vol. 2: Resistance and Destruction*. University Press of Florida, Gainesville.

1999 Coastal Chiefdoms and the Question of Agriculture: An Ethnohistorical Overview. Paper presented at the 56th Annual Meeting of the Southeastern Archaeological Conference, Pensacola.

2002 Spanish Missions and the Persistence of Chiefly Power. In *The Transformation of the Southeastern Indians, 1540–1760*, edited by Robbie Ethridge and Charles Hudson, pp. 39–64. University Press of Mississippi, Jackson.

2005 Pineland during the Spanish Period. Manuscript on file, Division of Anthropology and Archaeology, University of West Florida, Pensacola.

2007 *The Struggle for the Georgia Coast: An Eighteenth-Century Spanish Retrospective on Guale and Mocama*. Reprinted. University of Alabama Press, Tuscaloosa. Originally published 1995, Anthropological Papers No. 75, American Museum of Natural History, New York.

2009a Discovering Florida: First-Contact Narratives from Florida's Lower Gulf Coast. Manuscript on file, Division of Anthropology and Archaeology, University of West Florida, Pensacola.

2009b Documenting Tristán de Luna's Fleet, and the Storm that Destroyed It. *Florida Anthropologist* 62(3–4):83–92.

2009c Razing Florida: The Indian Slave Trade and the Devastation of Spanish Florida, 1659–1715. In *Mapping the Mississippian Shatter Zone: The Colonial Indian Slave Trade and Regional Instability in the American South*, edited by Robbie Ethridge and Sheri M. Shuck-Hall, pp. 295–311. University of Nebraska Press, Lincoln.

Worth, John E. (translator and editor)

1995a Relation of the Island of Florida. In *The De Soto Chronicles: The Expedition of Hernando de Soto to North America in 1539–1543*, Vol. I, edited by Lawrence A. Clayton, Vernon J. Knight, Jr., and Edward C. Moore, pp. 221–246. University of Alabama Press, Tuscaloosa.

1995b Account of the Northern Conquest and Discovery of Hernando de Soto. In *The De Soto Chronicles: The Expedition of Hernando de Soto to North America in 1539–1543*, Vol. I, edited by Lawrence A. Clayton, Vernon J. Knight, Jr., and Edward C. Moore, pp. 247–306. University of Alabama Press, Tuscaloosa.

Wozniak, Frank E.
1987 *Irrigation in the Rio Grande, New Mexico: A Study of the Development of Irrigation Systems Before 1945*. Report Prepared for the New Mexico Historic Preservation Division, Santa Fe, and Bureau of Reclamation, Southwest Regional Office, Amarillo.

Wray, Charles F., Martha L. Sempowski, and Lorraine P. Saunders
1991 *The Adams and Culbertson Sites*. Rochester Museum and Science Center Research Records No. 19, Rochester, New York.

Wrong, G. W. (editor)
1939 *The Long Journey to the Country of the Hurons by Gabriel Sagard*. The Champlain Society, Toronto.

Yesner, David R.
1980 Maritime Hunter-gatherer Ecology and Prehistory. *Current Anthropology* 21(6):727–750.

Zimmerman, Larry J., Thomas Emerson, P. Willey, M. Swegle, John B. Gregg, P. Gregg, E. White, C. Smith, T. Haberman, and M. P. Bumsted
1981 The Crow Creek Massacre: A Preliminary Report. Submitted to the Army Corps of Engineers, Omaha District, Omaha, Nebraska. Purchase No. DACW45-78-C0018.

About the Contributors

ROBIN A. BECK, JR., is an Assistant Professor of Anthropology and an Assistant Curator at the University of Michigan Museum of Anthropology. His interests include the archaeology of late prehistoric societies and the Contact period in the US Southeast, and architecture in the ancient Andes. He has written about Native American chiefdoms and Spanish expeditions in the US Southeast, the effects of early European contact on Native American societies, and archaeological theory about events and social transformations.

DENNIS B. BLANTON served as Curator, Native American Archaeology at Fernbank Museum of Natural History in Atlanta from 2005 to 2011; he now resides in Costa Rica. His research interests include sixteenth- and seventeenth-century Indian–Spanish interaction in the Southeast and broader questions concerning the role of climate and weather in human affairs. Earlier work in the Middle Atlantic region, including at Jamestown, focused on similar topics.

RICHARD C. CHAPMAN has been Director of the Office of Contract Archeology at the University of New Mexico since 2000, having served in research, project director, and assistant director capacities for the office since 1984. Chapman has forty-five years experience in cultural resource survey, excavation, and analysis throughout New Mexico and adjacent states, and holds a Research Associate Professor appointment with the UNM Anthropology Department. His research interests include prehistoric lithic artifact analysis, regional-scale settlement dynamics, and processes of social and economic change undergone by prehistoric and early historical cultural groups. He has taught courses in Southwestern Archaeology and Cultural Resource Management, and has supervised, directed, and published dozens of cultural resource project reports concerning the prehistory and early history of Middle Rio Grande valley of New Mexico.

CINDY K. DONGOSKE AND KURT E. DONGOSKE are both archaeologists with broad experience in the Four Corners region and the Northern Southwest. They have a particular interest in anthropological and archaeological collaboration with Native communities and have written extensively about the development of Indigenous archaeologies. Cindy and Kurt have worked for a number of years with the Hopi and Zuni communities, and are currently working on a range of cultural resource management and research projects with their Zuni colleagues.

ROBBIE ETHRIDGE is a Professor of Anthropology at the University of Mississippi. In addition to writing several articles and book chapters on the ethnohistory of the Southeastern Indians, she is the author of *Creek Country: The Creek Indians and Their World* (2003), coeditor, along with Charles Hudson, of *The Transformation of the Southeastern Indians, 1540–1760* (2002), and coeditor with Thomas J. Pluckhahn of *Light on the Path: The Anthropology and History of the Southeastern Indians* (2006). Her latest co-edited volume is *Mapping the Mississippian Shatter Zone: The Colonial Indian Slave Trade and Regional Instability in the American South* (2009), coedited with Sherri Shuck-Hall, and her latest monograph is *From Chicaza to Chickasaw: The European Invasion and the Transformation of the Mississippian World, 1540–1715* (2010).

CHARLES R. EWEN is a Professor of Anthropology and the director of the Phelps Archaeology Laboratory at East Carolina University. His research interests focus on the Contact and Early Colonial Periods of the Southeastern United States and Caribbean. His publications on Spanish Colonialism include *From Spaniard to Creole* (1991) and, with John Hann, *Hernando de Soto among the Apalachee: The Archaeology of the First Winter Encampment* (1998). Recently he coedited *X Marks the Spot: The Archaeology of Piracy* (2006) with Russ Skowronek.

RICHARD FLINT AND SHIRLEY CUSHING FLINT are independent historians whose major research has been, for thirty years, on the Vázquez de Coronado expedition, its motivations, context, and aftermath. Both together and separately, they have published many articles and five books about the expedition. Three more books are in the works, including *A Most Splendid Company: Members of the Coronado Expedition,* which is the result of four years of concerted research in many archives in Mexico and Spain. The Flints live in New Mexico. They are Research Associate Professors in the Latin American and Iberian Institute at the University of New Mexico, and Research Associates in History at the Center for Desert Archaeology in Tucson.

HENRI D. GRISSINO-MAYER is a Professor of Geography in the Department of Geography at the University of Tennessee, where he directs the university's Laboratory of Tree-Ring Science. He specializes in dendrochronology, primarily using techniques in the tree-ring sciences to reconstruct past climate from tree species throughout the United States. He also specializes in the use of tree-ring data to reconstruct the history of wildfires and to better understand the disturbance regimes of western and eastern forests. His teaching interests include dendrochronology, natural hazards, quantitative methods, climate change, and biogeography.

CHARLES M. HAECKER is the staff archaeologist for the National Park Service (NPS) Intermountain Region-Heritage Partnerships Program, and is based in Santa Fe, New Mexico. Charles received his Master's degree in Anthropology from Eastern New Mexico University in 1976, and has developed a specialization in historical archaeology. In his position with NPS, Charles develops partnerships with federal and state agencies, Native American tribes, communities, and private citizens toward protecting those places holding national significance in our nation's history. As an associate of the NPS-American Battlefield Protection Program, he works with other archaeologists in the investigation of historic battlefields, forts, and military encampments.

DALE L. HUTCHINSON is a Professor and Interim Chair of the Department of Anthropology, Fellow of the Institute of Arts and Humanities, and Research Associate of the Research Laboratories of Archaeology, all at the University of North Carolina, Chapel Hill. His research interests include skeletal biology, human health and disease, and forensic anthropology. He has been studying the changing disease ecology and health changes for Native populations of the Americas for nearly three decades.

JEREMY KULISHECK is the Forest Archaeologist and Heritage Program Manager for the Cibola National Forest and Grasslands. He received a PhD in anthropology from Southern Methodist University in 2005. Kulisheck has recently published several articles on colonial-era demographic changes among the Pueblo of the northern Southwest. His most recent publication is "'Like Butterflies on a Mounting Board': Pueblo Mobility and Demography before 1825," in *Across a Great Divide: Continuity and Change in Native North American Societies, A.D. 1400–1900*, edited by Mark D. Mitchell and Laura L. Scheiber, and published in 2010 by University of Arizona Press. The paper is from a 2007 Amerind Seminar.

FRANCES LEVINE is the Director of the Palace of the Governors, New Mexico History Museum in Santa Fe, New Mexico. She received her BA in Anthropology from the University of Colorado, Boulder, and a MA and PhD in Anthropology from Southern Methodist University, Dallas. Her interests are in the colonial archaeology, history, and ethnohistory of the American Southwest.

CLAY MATHERS is an archaeologist and is Executive Director of the Coronado Institute in Albuquerque, New Mexico, a nonprofit corporation dedicated to an understanding of Old and New World interactions in the Southwestern United States and Southern Plains between the sixteenth and eighteenth centuries. He has a BA in Anthropology from the University of Pennsylvania, an MPhil in GIS and Remote Sensing from the University of Cambridge (UK), a PhD in Spanish prehistory from the University of Sheffield (UK), and is a Research Associate at the Maxwell Museum of Anthropology, University of New Mexico. Together with colleagues, he has identified, investigated, and published several new Vázquez de Coronado sites in New Mexico. His primary research interests lie in geospatial predictive modeling, colonialism, social identity, conflict, and technological change.

JEFFREY M. MITCHEM is an Associate Archeologist with the Arkansas Archeological Survey and a Research Associate Professor at the University of Arkansas. He directs research at Parkin Archeological State Park in Arkansas. His research interests include the archaeology of Mississippian cultures of the Southeastern United States and evidence of early Spanish explorations. He has expertise in sixteenth-century Spanish material culture, especially beads, armor, and weaponry. He has conducted archaeological research in several southeastern states, Idaho, and Jordan.

DAVID G. MOORE is an archaeologist at Warren Wilson College in Asheville, North Carolina, with interests in the archaeology of Catawba and Cherokee settlements and societies. He has conducted archaeological investigations at sites in western North Carolina dating to many periods of prehistory, and to the Contact and post-Contact periods. His dissertation research in the Catawba valley set the stage for current investigations at Berry and other sites.

ANN F. RAMENOFSKY is Professor Emerita of the Department of Anthropology, University of New Mexico. Her archaeological research during the past twenty-five years spans the Spanish Borderlands, including the Lower Mississippi and Rio Grande valleys, with particular emphasis on the protohistoric period. Her research interests include landscape and settlement evidence of Native American demographic change, infectious disease introduction and evolution, and technology transfer, especially the beginnings of metallurgical production in the Southwest.

CHRISTOPHER B. RODNING is an Associate Professor in the Department of Anthropology at Tulane University. His interests include archaeology in the US Southeast, Native American responses to European contact, and the built environment of Cherokee towns before and after European contact. With David G. Moore and Robin A. Beck, Jr., he is co-director of the Exploring Joara Project, focused on the archaeology of Native societies and Spanish entradas in western North Carolina.

MATTHEW W. SALZER is a Research Associate at The University of Arizona's Laboratory of Tree-Ring Research. His interdisciplinary research focuses on environmental and cultural change primarily in the Southwest and the Great Basin, USA. He has developed climatically sensitive multimillennial bristlecone pine ring-width chronologies for this purpose and authored several papers on these subjects in scientific journals, including in *The Proceedings of the US National Academy of Sciences.*

DAVID HURST THOMAS has served since 1972 as Curator of Anthropology at the American Museum of Natural History (New York). A specialist in Native American archaeology, he holds four degrees from the University of California, Davis (PhD, 1971) and a Doctor of Science (*honoris causa*) from The University of the South (conferred 1995). He has taught at Columbia University, New York University, University of California (Davis), University of Florida, University of Nevada, the City College of New York, and lectured in more than forty countries. Thomas has written thirty books, edited ninety additional volumes, and written more than one hundred scientific papers. His most recent book is the award-winning *Skull Wars: Kennewick Man, Archaeology, and the Battle for Native American Identity.* In 1989, Thomas was appointed as a Founding Trustee of the National Museum of the American Indian (Smithsonian Institution) and elected as a member of the National Academy of Sciences.

CARLA R. VAN WEST is Director of Historic Preservation Programs at the SRI Foundation, Rio Ranch, New Mexico, a nonprofit organization created to improve the practice of historic preservation through education, training, and research. She received her anthropology degrees from Elmira College (BA), University of Arizona (MA), and Washington State University (PhD). Her enduring interests include paleoenvironmental reconstruction, socionatural interactions, and the archaeology of the US Southwest.

THOMAS C. WINDES is a retired US National Park Service archaeologist with thirty-seven years of fieldwork in and around Chaco Canyon, northwestern New Mexico, with many publications relating to the Puebloan occupation there. Currently he is an adjunct in the Anthropology Department of the University of New Mexico, Albuquerque (where he received an MA in 1965). He is also a volunteer with the National Park Service and runs his own tiny contracting business, Dusty Resources. His interests include Puebloan settlement in the Four Corners region, Chacoan road systems and greathouses, the intervisibility of Puebloan communication systems, early Hispanic settlement in the Taos, Middle Rio Grande valley, and the Upper Pecos River valley areas, chronometric refinement of historic and Puebloan architecture, and the use of structural wood in both historic and prehistoric contexts.

JOHN E. WORTH is an Associate Professor of Anthropology at the University of West Florida. He received his PhD in 1992 from the University of Florida. Specializing in ethnohistory and archaeology, his research focuses on the impact of European exploration and colonization in the Southeastern United States, including cultural adaptation, transformation, and creolization by members of Indigenous and immigrant societies under a range of differing political and economic circumstances.

Index

Italic numbers indicate tables or figures

AMERIND STUDIES IN ANTHROPOLOGY

SERIES EDITOR **JOHN WARE**

Trincheras Sites in Time, Space, and Society
Edited by Suzanne K. Fish, Paul R. Fish, and M. Elisa Villalpando

Collaborating at the Trowel's Edge: Teaching and Learning in Indigenous Archaeology
Edited by Stephen W. Silliman

Warfare in Cultural Context: Practice, Agency, and the Archaeology of Violence
Edited by Axel E. Nielsen and William H. Walker

Across a Great Divide: Continuity and Change in Native North American Societies, 1400–1900
Edited by Laura L. Scheiber and Mark D. Mitchell

Leaving Mesa Verde: Peril and Change in the Thirteenth-Century Southwest
Edited by Timothy A. Kohler, Mark D. Varien, and Aaron M. Wright

Becoming Villagers: Comparing Early Village Societies
Edited by Matthew S. Bandy and Jake R. Fox

Hunter-Gatherer Archaeology as Historical Process
Edited by Kenneth E. Sassaman and Donald H. Holly, Jr.

Religious Transformation in the Late Pre-Hispanic Pueblo World
Edited by Donna M. Glowacki and Scott Van Keuren

Crow-Omaha: New Light on a Classic Problem of Kinship Analysis
Edited by Thomas R. Trautmann and Peter M. Whiteley

Native and Spanish New Worlds: Sixteenth-Century Entradas in the American Southwest and Southeast
Edited by Clay Mathers, Jeffrey M. Mitchem, and Charles M. Haecker